International Review of
RESEARCH IN
MENTAL RETARDATION

VOLUME 14

Consulting Editors

International Review of
RESEARCH IN
MENTAL RETARDATION

EDITED BY

NORMAN R. ELLIS

DEPARTMENT OF PSYCHOLOGY
UNIVERSITY OF ALABAMA
UNIVERSITY, ALABAMA

NORMAN W. BRAY

UNIVERSITY OF ALABAMA
AT BIRMINGHAM
BIRMINGHAM, ALABAMA

VOLUME 14

1986

ACADEMIC PRESS, INC.
Harcourt Brace Jovanovich, Publishers

Orlando   San Diego   New York   Austin
Boston   London   Sydney   Tokyo   Toronto

PLG 3/36
36B

ACADEMIC PRESS, INC.
Orlando, Florida 32887

United Kingdom Edition published by
ACADEMIC PRESS INC. (LONDON) LTD.
24–28 Oval Road, London NW1 7DX

LIBRARY OF CONGRESS CATALOG CARD NUMBER: 65-28627

ISBN 0–12–366214–1 (alk. paper)

PRINTED IN THE UNITED STATES OF AMERICA

86 87 88 89   9 8 7 6 5 4 3 2 1

Contents

Preface ix

Intrinsic Motivation and Behavior Effectiveness in Retarded Persons

H. Carl Haywood and Harvey N. Switzky

I. Individual Differences Variables in Mental Retardation Research 2
II. A Research Program on Intrinsic Motivation and Behavior Effectiveness in Retarded and Nonretarded Persons 8
III. Special Applications to Mental Retardation 29
IV. Related Work by Others 35
V. Summary 39
References 40

The Rehearsal Deficit Hypothesis

Norman W. Bray and Lisa A. Turner

I. Introduction 47
II. The Research on Rehearsal Strategies 53
III. Conclusions and Implications 64
References 68

Molar Variability and the Mentally Retarded

Stuart A. Smith and Paul S. Siegel

I. Theories of Molar Response Variability 74
II. Response Variability and the Mentally Retarded 82
III. Disinhibition 90
IV. Disinhibition and the Mentally Retarded 92
V. Summary 97
References 98

Computer-Assisted Instruction for the Mentally Retarded

Frances A. Conners, David R. Caruso, and Douglas K. Detterman

I. Introduction 105
II. Trends and Findings in CAI 106
III. A Lesson from One-to-One Tutoring 112
IV. CAI for Mentally Retarded Persons 115
References 129

Procedures and Parameters of Errorless Discrimination Training with Developmentally Impaired Individuals

Giulio E. Lancioni and Paul M. Smeets

I. Introduction 135
II. Applications of Errorless Discrimination Training Procedures 138
III. Basic Parameters of Errorless Discrimination Training 147
IV. Conclusion 158
References 160

Reading Acquisition and Remediation in the Mentally Retarded

Nirbhay N. Singh and Judy Singh

I. Introduction 165
II. The Reading Process 167
III. Word Recognition 170
IV. Comprehension 180
V. Remediation of Oral Reading Errors 184
VI. Conclusions and Future Perspectives 189
References 192

Families with a Mentally Retarded Child

Bernard Farber and Louis Rowitz

I. Introduction 201
II. The Clinical Model 202
III. Labeling–Dramaturgical Model 210
IV. Family Organization Model 213
V. Conclusions 220
References 221

Social Competence and Employment of Retarded Persons

Charles L. Salzberg, Marilyn Likins, E. Kathryn McConaughy,
and Benjamin Lignugaris/Kraft

I. Introduction 225
II. Social–Vocational Competence 227
III. Survey Research 229
IV. Observational Research 241
V. Conclusions and Suggestions for Future Research 249
   References 253

Toward a Taxonomy of Home Environments

Sharon Landesman

I. Introduction 259
II. Definitions 260
III. Why Classify Environments? 262
IV. Existing Classification Schemes 269
V. A Conceptual Framework for Studying and Classifying Home Environments 272
VI. Summary 286
   References 287

Behavioral Treatment of the Sexually Deviant Behavior of Mentally Retarded Individuals

R. M. Foxx, R. G. Bittle, D. R. Bechtel, and J. R. Livesay

I. Introduction 291
II. Behaviors Treated 292
III. Evaluation 305
IV. Conclusions and Recommendations 313
   References 315

Behavioral Approaches to Toilet Training for Retarded Persons

S. Bettison

I. Introduction 319
II. The Nature and Development of Bladder and Bowel Control 320
III. Acquisition of Toileting Skills with Training 322
IV. Conclusions and New Directions for Research 345
   References 347

Index 351

Preface

In the past volumes of this series an attempt has been made to present the highest quality research findings and theory relating to understanding behavior and cognition in intellectually handicapped persons. The present volume continues in this tradition. While research involving mentally retarded persons has never enjoyed great popularity in the scientific community, the efforts of a small group of dedicated investigators have resulted in a sophisticated base of data and theory. Many of these investigators would describe their work as "basic" science, the main thrust being directed to problems such as learning, memory, problem solving, information processing, and perception. Their purpose is to gain a better understanding of the consequences of damage to the brain resulting from disease, injury, or inheritance. A key product is new knowledge about behavioral/cognitive phenomena in normal persons and individual differences in particular. Some researchers focus on applied issues, those that affect the daily life and well being of retarded persons. These have to do with living environments, education and training, treatment of severe behavior disorders, and the like. Both approaches are useful and, indeed, it is often difficult to categorize research in this way.

The present volume, like those of the past, reports research and theory on fundamental aspects of cognition and behavior as well as those that deal with the daily management, care, and training of retarded persons. Haywood and Switzky address basic issues in motivation and personality charactersitics of retarded persons. While focusing primarily on their own work at Peabody College, they provide an overview of research on motivation and personality characteristics from the social learning theory perspective. They report reliable measures of motivational orientation that relate to other significant aspects of functioning. This area has been an arid plain in the past with little more than contradictions and fickle variables. The work of Haywood and Switzky seems to reflect genuine progress in this difficult but important area.

One of the more important findings in the field has been the demonstration that retarded persons do not use cognitive strategies in a normal fashion. Their memories are poorly organized, they do not fully use mnemonics, and they do not rehearse to-be-remembered information adequately. Bray and Turner provide a much needed review of the research pertaining to the last. Among the important points they make is that rehearsal is not an all-or-none phenomenon, occurring in normal persons but not in the mentally retarded. They show that rehearsal occurs to some extent in most of the retarded persons studied and that many who rehearse minimally can, under certain conditions, rehearse in an effective manner. Their review should serve to clarify some confusion and misunderstanding in this area.

Psychologists have traditionally viewed the discrimination learning paradigm as an important model for studying learning in general. Lancioni and Smeets follow in this tradition. They are concerned with procedures that facilitate rate of learning.

Smith and Siegel address a ubiquitous problem in investigations of retarded behavior. Retarded persons are more variable in responding than nonretarded persons. This is reflected in both intra- and intersubject variability. Too often in the past researchers have viewed this only as a nuisance in data analysis. While Smith and Siegel conclude that the data base is inadequate for understanding this phenomenon, they make clear that this is an important issue, deserving study in its own right.

Farber and Rowitz review research relating to the families of severely and profoundly retarded persons. They attempt to define the impact of the child on the family, the means families use to continue community ties, and the extent to which family stress may affect the family–community relationships. The philosophical ancestry of their approach lies in Farber's classic studies of the family of retarded persons published in the 1960s. In a somewhat related chapter, Landesman attempts to develop a taxonomy of home environments. This is an important issue. Without some objective measures of the quality and richness of home environments, we will not be able to establish the extent to which this variable(s) influences the behavior and development of the child.

Singh and Singh review the various approaches to teaching the retarded to read. Their conclusion is optimistic and should serve as a catalyst for future study of this area. Conners and associates are also interested in teaching academic skills to retarded persons. Computers may well result in advances never realized with the "learning machines" of 20 years ago. The approach of Conners and colleagues, focusing more on understanding the cognitive capacities of the learner than did the teaching machine approach, may be necessary for progress.

Salzberg and associates review research on the employment of retarded persons, and their conclusions leave little doubt that social competence is one of the key determinants in the employment success of these persons. The person with high social skills typically proves to be a dependable worker and their job tenure differs little from that of nonhandicapped persons.

Foxx and colleagues provide a straightforward discussion of the emotionally laden issue of sexual deviancy in the retarded. Society, including behavioral scientists, have tended to ignore this important aspect of some retarded persons' behavior. In fact, this area has developed little beyond sex education programs. Perhaps this paper will stimulate much needed research in this area.

Bettison describes a number of approaches to toilet training severely and profoundly retarded persons. She also adds a number of modifications to existing procedures which are based on her own extensive research on this issue.

Are we gaining a better understanding of the behavior and cognitive process in retarded persons? We think so and the chapters in this volume reflect that. But not everyone seems to agree. For example, Smith and Siegel conclude their chapter with the statement ''And the failure to tie constructs into a meaningful theoretical package must lead us to the humbling conclusion that we know little about response variability and not a great deal about mental retardation itself.'' While it seems apparent that the particular issue they address has had little systematic study, this is not true for all problem areas. Nevertheless, their complaints are disquieting and should not be dismissed out of hand.

NORMAN R. ELLIS
NORMAN W. BRAY

Editor's note: Dr. Norman W. Bray will assume full editorial responsibility for the series beginning with Volume 15. Twenty years of this is long enough! I want to thank the many authors for their patience and tolerance over the years. I hope this series has been, and will continue to be, of help to behavioral scientists in this field.

NORMAN R. ELLIS

Intrinsic Motivation and Behavior Effectiveness in Retarded Persons

H. CARL HAYWOOD

DEPARTMENT OF PSYCHOLOGY AND HUMAN DEVELOPMENT
VANDERBILT UNIVERSITY
NASHVILLE, TENNESSEE 37203

HARVEY N. SWITZKY

DEPARTMENT OF LEARNING AND DEVELOPMENT
NORTHERN ILLINOIS UNIVERSITY
DEKALB, ILLINOIS 60115

Individual differences in behavior, particularly in personality and motivational characteristics, tend to be somewhat like the weather: psychologists do a lot of talking about them, but hardly anyone does anything about them, especially in the field of research on mental retardation. In spite of this general neglect (in favor of an implicit assumption that mentally retarded persons are, on the whole, more like each other than different), there have been persistent efforts to explain part of the variance in the behavior and behavior effectiveness of retarded persons in terms of individual differences in personality characteristics and motivational states. The major function of this chapter is to examine the relationships between one set of individual differences characteristics, referred to as "task-intrinsic motivation," and the behavior effectiveness of mentally retarded persons within the context of a historical view of research on personality variables and mental retardation. Within this general orientation we review here primarily a single program of research, instigated around 1963 and carried out mainly by Haywood and his students and colleagues at Peabody College/Vanderbilt University, and by Switzky.

1

I. INDIVIDUAL DIFFERENCES VARIABLES IN MENTAL RETARDATION RESEARCH

Even though many of our historic theories of personality have been developed from observations of persons who were considered to be abnormal (e.g., neurotic or psychotic; Lindzey, Hall, & Manoscvitz, 1973), few such general theories have come from, or even reflected to a small degree, observation of mentally retarded persons. Even the research that has been reported specifically focused on personality and mental retardation has been done under the aegis of theoretical systems derived primarily from observation of the behavior of nonretarded persons. In some cases these conceptual approaches have been revised and extended in ingenious ways in order to incorporate and explain phenomena observed in retarded persons. Several such systematic approaches have been quite productive of thought and research.

The notion that personality (a major reflector of individual differences) might be different in retarded and nonretarded persons is not a new one (e.g., Cromwell, 1963; Heber, 1964; Zigler & Balla, 1982). Hirsch (1959) has argued that the psychological principles that govern the behavior of retarded persons have fewer and less adequate environmental (ego) supports in relation to their limited ability to function independently. Haywood (1981) has reflected this interaction of person characteristics and environmental characteristics in the notion of differential social vulnerability. It is, then, quite possible that Zigler's (1969) general view that retarded persons follow the same developmental sequence and qualities as do nonretarded persons, but more slowly and to a less highly developed endpoint, may be true and that we could still explain differences in behavior effectiveness as the interactive product of an invariant sequence/quality of cognitive development and a differential system of learned personality and motivational characteristics.

Some major historic attempts to conceptualize the behavior of retarded persons in personality and motivational terms have been (1) *the rigidity hypothesis* (Kounin, 1941a,b, 1948; Lewin, 1935; Stevenson, 1961; Zigler, 1961, 1962), (2) *self-concept theory* (Jahoda, 1958; Rogers, 1947; Snygg & Combs, 1949), (3) *the frustration–aggression hypothesis* (Angelino & Shedd, 1956; Dollard, Doob, Miller, Mowrer, & Sears, 1939; Portnoy & Stacey, 1954), (4) *social learning theory* (Cromwell, 1963; Rotter, 1954), (5) *concepts of effectance motivation* (Harter, 1978, 1983; Harter & Zigler, 1974; Zigler & Balla, 1982), and (6) *the concept of intrinsic motivation* (Haywood, 1964, 1971; Haywood & Burke, 1977; Herzberg, 1966; Herzberg, Mausner, & Snyderman, 1959).

A. The Rigidity Hypothesis

One of the most fruitful, and certainly one of the earliest, personality constructs in the field of mental retardation has been the "dynamic theory of feeblemindedness'' of Kurt Lewin (1936). The central concept in this theory was rigidity. Retarded persons were seen as having fewer regions in their ''skill structure'' than nonretarded persons and less permeability of the regional boundaries of their ''life space.'' The repeated failure that was thought to be encountered by retarded children in the process of growing up was held to lead to a rigid behavioral lifestyle. This formulation led to a series of studies on concept switching (in general, retarded persons appear to be less inclined to abandon unproductive ideas or unsuccessful strategies in favor of potentially more productive ones than are nonretarded persons—although the literature is not clear on whether this is an effect of retardation itself or of institutionalization). This research led in turn to the formulation of systematic concepts dealing with differential histories of social interaction in retarded and nonretarded children, particularly with respect to socioculturally disadvantaged circumstances of child rearing that were thought to be frequently associated with the diagnosis of ''cultural–familial retardation.''

Goldstein (1943) distinguished between primary rigidity (''an abnormality of the *Einstellung* mechanism, most frequently observed in lesions of the basal ganglia'') and secondary rigidity (''due to a primary defect of the higher mental processes occurring in cortical damage and cortical malformations, such as feeblemindedness''). He associated secondary rigidity with an impairment of abstract thinking.

Failing to find reliable differences in rigid behavior between retarded and nonretarded persons who were matched on mental age, Stevenson and Zigler (1957) proposed a motivational hypothesis as an explanation of the differences in rigidity reported in previous research. They proposed that institutionalized retarded persons may be more motivated to interact with an experimenter (or any adult) and to comply with instructions than would nonretarded persons or even noninstitutionalized retarded persons. In other words, a strong motive in institutionalized retarded persons is to instigate and maintain interpersonal interaction, and that motive is said to arise from the chronic deprivation of interpersonal interaction that, at least at that time, characterized institutional life. Studying performance in a simple persistence task, Zigler, Hodgden, and Stevenson (1958) found that their retarded subjects persisted in the task longer under conditions of social support than under nonsupport conditions, a difference that was not found in their nonretarded subjects. Further, the retarded subjects were more persistent than were the nonretarded subjects in both conditions. The notion that differences in rigidity between retarded and nonretarded persons may be due to greater social deprivation in the lives of retarded persons was supported by Gewirtz and Baer (1958a,b). Zigler found support for the notion that the degree of social deprivation within a sample of cultural–familial retarded persons covaries with responsiveness to social reinforcement expressed as persistence in a simple task. The ideas of responsiveness to social reinforcement and interpersonal distance stimulated a considerable and productive string of empirical studies and eventually lent substantial support to the idea that apparent performance deficiencies in retarded persons may be attributable in some measure to developmental differences in motivation rather than to inherent deficits in performance potential.

B. Self-Concept

Research on self-concept as a personality dimension was stimulated by the systematic formulations of Carl Rogers (1947) and his successors in the field of mental health. (Jahoda, 1958; Snygg & Combs, 1949). This work has been extended to the field of mental retardation with varying degrees of success. Ringness (1961) found that retarded children tend to overestimate their own success more than do average or intellectually superior children. His mentally retarded children rated themselves less favorably than did those in the superior group but not less favorably than did those in the average group. The self-concept, measured as expectancy of success, of mentally retarded children was found to be less realistic in terms of actual achievement than that of nonretarded children. Further, self-ratings of mentally retarded children were found to be less reliable than those for average or intellectually superior children. While there have been subsequent studies of the self-concept of mentally retarded children, these have often been of inadequate design and have yielded results that have not been especially helpful to research in this field. Even though it would seem obvious on the surface that one's evaluation of his own characteristics should exert considerable influence on the efficiency with which one learns and performs, research in the area has been and continues to be seriously inhibited by the unavailability of reliable research instruments for the measurement of self-concept, especially with mentally retarded persons.

C. The Frustration–Aggression Hypothesis

The classical frustration–aggression hypothesis of Dollard *et al.* (1939) has also given rise to a series of investigations with retarded persons. The original authors were somewhat ambiguous with respect to the relationship between the frustration–aggression hypothesis and mental retardation, holding alternatively that low intelligence should lead to greater frustration on the one hand, and on the other hand, that lower conditioned expectancies of success among mentally retarded persons might in fact lead to lower levels of frustration than would be found in nonretarded persons. The latter prediction would seem to fall short in light of the Ringness (1961) work showing that expectancy of success in mentally retarded persons is not significantly less than in persons of average intelligence and is typically unrealistic relative to actual performance. Thus, the "conditioned expectancy" appears not to take place. As often happens, research in this area was considerably facilitated by the appearance of a psychometric research instrument with satisfactory measurement characteristics, in this case the Rosenzweig Picture Frustration Study (Rosenzweig, 1945), a technique for measuring the extent to which one's reaction to frustration is intropunitive, extrapunitive, or impunitive. Angelino and Shedd (1956) gave this instrument to 102 mentally retarded children in public schools. They found that the developmental progression of reaction to frustration, from extrapunitive to intropunitive with increasing chronological age, was the same for retarded children as for nonretarded children, but typical shifts were about 2 years later for the retarded children. In addition, 12- and 13-year-old retarded children were more intropunitive than were those in Rosenzweig's nonretarded normative group. Portnoy and Stacy (1954) found some evidence that retarded children may be less "ego defensive" than nonretarded children matched with them on chronological age. This area of research yielded some interesting differences in developmental progressions in a potentially important dimension of personality, but these differences in personality development had not been systematically related to the important variables of learning, task persistence, or general behavior effectiveness until an experimental offspring, Amsel's (1958, 1962) notion of frustrative nonreward, came on the scene. Amsel held that nonreinforced responses produce frustration reactions that could energize responses occurring after the nonrewarded responses, thus accounting for the partial reinforcement extinction effect as well as resistance to extinction in general. This notion stimulated a significant series of studies with mentally retarded persons in the 1960s (Libb, 1972; Lobb, Moffitt, & Gamlin, 1966; Ryan & Watson, 1968; Spradlin, 1962; Viney, Clarke, & Lord, 1973). These studies in general demonstrated in moderately and severely retarded persons that nonreinforced responses did produce frustration effects, i.e., increases in response rates following the nonrewarded responses, and that there was greater resistance to extinction in retarded persons than in their nonretarded matches. Little further research that can be related to the frustration–aggression hypothesis has been produced in recent years.

D. Social Learning Theory

Rotter's (1954) development of social learning theory gave rise to a long and productive series of studies of individual differences in the behavior of mentally retarded persons. Much of that work took place under the direction of Rue Cromwell (1963) between about 1955 and 1965, with only scattered studies appearing in the mental retardation research literature since that time (although the concept continues to be studied and expanded in research on nonretarded persons). The principal constructs derived from social learning theory as it has been applied to the behavior of retarded persons were "locus of control" and "success-striving versus failure-avoiding" motivation. Locus of control refers to the extent to which persons believe that their own behavior can be instrumental in determining what happens to them, as opposed to the extent to which they believe that what happens to them is either random or under the control of external persons or forces. In general, retarded children and adults are typically found to be more characterized by external locus of control than are nonretarded persons and to focus their efforts more on avoidance of failure than on striving for success. Internal locus of control appears to develop as a joint function of mental age and chronological age. While the predictive efficiency of the locus-of-control concept has been inconsistent and scattered (McConnell, 1965), the locus-of-control scale has continued to yield some contribution to the prediction of learning and achievement (Butterfield & Weaver, 1969). In general, internal locus of control is positively related to task persistence and learning efficiency and makes a statistically significant contribution to factors that describe the structure of personality and motivation in both retarded and nonretarded persons, but the magnitude of these relationships is relatively modest. In recent years improved methods of measuring these variables have appeared, and that fact might result in a renewal of interest in research in mental retardation within the social learning theory framework.

A rather close, and more recent, relative of social learning theory is "attribution theory" (Weiner, 1974, 1976; Weiner, Frieze, Kukla, Reed, Rest, & Rosenbaum, 1972; Weiner & Sierad, 1975). According to this concept, performance in various tasks is influenced by the extent to which persons, including mentally retarded persons, attribute their success or failure to causal elements, e.g., their own ability, their effort, the difficulty of the tasks, or chance/luck. Horai and Guarnaccia (1975) gave a coding task under success and failure experimental conditions to educable mentally retarded adults and interviewed them with an exhaustive forced-choice procedure to determine their attributions of their success or failure. They found that these participants tended significantly to attribute their success to their own ability, but not to attribute their failure to their inability. Failure was attributed to their inadequate effort more than success was attributed to their adequate effort. Neither success nor failure was attributed significantly to variations in task difficulty. Bad luck was invoked more often to explain failure than was good luck to explain success. Thus, this concept, developed in work with nonretarded persons, was shown to be reliably measurable and useful in exploring the motivational systems of mentally retarded persons. Attribution theory is also a close relative of concepts of task-intrinsic motivation, since one's notion of the source of rewards that follow behavior should be expected to influence the incentive value of different kinds of rewards, hence their effectiveness in accelerating or decelerating that (antecedent) behavior in subsequent encounters.

Since mentally retarded persons encounter failure relatively more often than do nonretarded persons (on the same tasks), the effect of success or failure upon performance in subsequent tasks is an especially important relationship in the study of mental retardation. In another study on attribution theory with retarded persons, Hoffman and Weiner (1978) used a coding task to give success and failure experiences to severely mentally retarded adults. Using only three causal attributions (ability, effort, and task difficulty), these authors found that the effect of success feedback upon subsequent performance depends on type of causal attribution for the outcome, that "retarded persons respond to attributions in a manner reasonably similar to nonretarded adults" (1978, p. 452), and that the learning and performance of retarded persons "can be facilitated if adaptive attributions are combined with outcome information, typically high ability attributions for success are combined with outcome information, typically high ability attributions for success and lack of effort ascriptions given failure" (Hoffman & Weiner, 1978, p. 452). What is missing in this interesting literature is work on the possibility of cross-task, relatively enduring attribution tendencies that might characterize persons in the manner of personality traits.

E. Effectance Motivation

White's (1959) formulation of effectance or mastery motivation has had considerable influence on our understanding of such behavior as exploration, curiosity, mastery, and play in both retarded and nonretarded persons (see, e.g., Harter & Zigler, 1974; Haywood & Burke, 1977; Switzky & Rotatori, 1981; Switzky, Ludwig, & Haywood, 1979; Switzky, Haywood, & Isett, 1974; Tzuriel & Haywood, 1984) and in the view that using one's own cognitive resources to the fullest is intrinsically gratifying and motivating (Harter, 1978; Haywood & Wachs, 1981; Switzky & Haywood, 1984; Zigler & Balla, 1982). Zigler and his students and associates (Zigler & Balla, 1981, 1982) have conceptualized the motivational problems of retarded persons as due in part to deficient effectance motivation and lack of concern for the intrinsic motivation that inheres in being correct regardless of whether or not an external agent dispenses the reinforcer for such correctness. This deficiency in effectance motivation leads to overreliance on clues from the external environment to help guide behavioral performance (i.e., outerdirectedness), with a concomitant increase in extrinsically motivated behavior. Harter and colleagues (Harter, 1983; Harter & Pike, 1984; Silon & Harter, 1985) have recently developed a program of developmental research in which White's (1959) theories of effectance and mastery motivation have been refined, detailed, and operationalized. The influence of these current theoretical formulations based on effectance motivation on the behavior and performance of both retarded and nonretarded persons and their relationship to our conceptions of task-intrinsic motivation are investigated more fully in Section IV.

F.   Task-Intrinsic Motivation

Task-intrinsic motivation refers to differential tendencies of persons either to seek their principal satisfactions from factors inherent in tasks, such as challenge, creativity, responsibility, learning, psychological excitement, or task-related aesthetic considerations, or on the other hand simply to try to avoid dissatisfaction by concentrating their attention on, and responding to incentives characterized by, task-extrinsic variables such as ease, comfort, safety, security, practicality, and material gain. The derivation of this set of notions is given in some detail in the next section. While everyone is assumed to have some of both kinds of motivation, i.e., to respond to both kinds of incentives in different situations, the trait variable refers to the relative balance within persons of the two kinds of motives—the number of different situations in which given persons are disposed to seek and respond to these different kinds of incentives. It is likely that nobody is "purely" intrinsically [Herzberg & Hamlin (1961, 1963) referred to "the starving artist working happily away in his freezing garret" as a rare example of "pure" intrinsic motivation] or extrinsically motivated. In the remainder of this chapter, we refer to persons who have high intrinsic motivation scores on tests of motivational orientation as intrinsically motivated (IM) persons and to those who have low intrinsic motivation scores as extrinsically motivated (EM) to reflect the relative balance of these kinds of motives in the incentive choices of these persons. This characterization is also an artifact of our methods of measurement, which force total dependence of the IM and EM scores by permitting only one or the other choice for each item in the tests.

II.   A RESEARCH PROGRAM ON INTRINSIC MOTIVATION AND BEHAVIOR EFFECTIVENESS IN RETARDED AND NONRETARDED PERSONS

From the early days of experimental psychology until well into the testing movement, motivation was studied by manipulating need conditions of the subjects, often by deprivation (Woodworth, 1918), or by indexing the vigor and persistence of behavior toward some goal or away from noxious stimuli (Brown, 1942, 1948; N. E. Miller, 1944), often as a function of need states created and maintained by deprivation. Movement of the motivational inference inside the organism got a major boost from the work of Janet Taylor (Spence), in which she inferred variations in drive from individual differences in manifest anxiety, measured by human subjects' responses to selected MMPI items (the Manifest Anxiety Scale; Taylor, 1951). The huge volume of psychological studies done with the Manifest Anxiety Scale helped to create acceptance of the notion that disposition to display specific motivational states across situations might be a relatively stable personality characteristic or trait. Our work on individual differences in task-intrinsic motivation follows in this tradition.

In our terms of reference, intrinsic motivation refers to the disposition to find one's rewards in tasks themselves; that is, to behave, work, learn, solve problems, seek and assimilate new experience, persist in tasks, and process information for the sheer psychological satisfaction of doing these things rather than for the opportunity to secure task-extrinsic rewards. Hunt (1963) has referred to "motivation inherent in information processing and action," and that is much of what we mean by intrinsic motivation (see, e.g., Haywood & Burke, 1977). It is, first of all, an incentive system. As such, persons may vary from situation to situation in the extent to which they seek or respond to task-intrinsic or task-extrinsic incentives. Haywood (1971) has argued that the disposition to respond to or seek such incentives characterizes persons across situations, is measurable, is relatively stable within persons across both time and situations, and is correlated with important performance and cognitive variables. To the extent that those conditions are true, the variable of motivational orientation (orientation toward task-intrinsic versus task-extrinsic incentives) constitutes a personality trait.

Our concept of intrinsic motivation was derived directly from the two-factor theory of work motivation formulated by Herzberg (Herzberg, 1966; Herzberg *et al.,* 1959). Herzberg *et al.* (1959), looking for sources of job satisfaction and dissatisfaction in industrial workers, asked workers to think of times when they had been quite satisfied with their jobs and times when they had been so dissatisfied that they had had thoughts of changing jobs, and then to identify the variables to which they attributed their satisfaction or dissatisfaction. In characterizing periods of dissatisfaction the workers listed such variables as low pay, poor, unhealthy, hazardous, or uncomfortable working conditions (i.e., the *context* in which the job was performed), and lack of security—all conditions extrinsic to the job itself. In characterizing periods of positive job satisfaction, instead of referring to the opposite poles of the dissatisfying task-extrinsic conditions, the workers listed such task-intrinsic variables as the sheer psychological satisfaction of doing a task, opportunities to learn new things, and opportunities to exercise creativity, take responsibility, or experience aesthetic aspects of the job. Herzberg conceived of these variables not as lying on a single bipolar dimension but as constituting two nonoverlapping dimensions that could vary simultaneously. Subsequent research revealed the power of the "motivator" (i.e., task-intrinsic in our terms) variables in improving job satisfaction and job performance in a variety of industrial settings. A significant relationship to mental health was demonstrated by Hamlin and Nemo (1962), who found that "improved" schizophrenic patients gave reasons for vocational or activity choices that were more indicative of task-intrinsic motivation than were the reasons for choice given by "unimproved" schizophrenic patients, while both patient groups gave more task-extrinsic reasons for their choices than did their nonpsychiatric subjects. In other words, intrinsic motivation as they measured it appeared to be positively correlated with mental health and negatively correlated with mental illness.

These notions, suggesting the possibility of a trait variable associated with some part of the variance in behavior effectiveness, appeared to hold significant promise for understanding individual differences in the learning and performance of mentally retarded persons in particular and to offer some interesting possibilities for applied work with retarded persons. First, there was the now-familiar unexplained variance in prediction of learning effectiveness, especially school achievement, from intelligence test scores. The usual correlation between IQs derived from the best individually administered intelligence tests and the most reliable standard tests of school achievement, separated by 1 to 2 years, is about +.70. This correlation leaves about one-half of the variance in the criterion, school achievement, not associated with the predictor, intelligence. To think of all of that as error variance would be correct only in the most formal statistical sense. The joint unreliability of the predictor and criterion tests would not leave so much variance unexplained. Less than perfect validity of both intelligence tests and achievement tests would contribute another slice of error variance. Differential experience between predictor and criterion tests would similarly contribute some error variance. When all of these sources of ''error'' in prediction are estimated, one is still left with less than perfect prediction. A quite reasonable inference is that individual differences in performance (in this case, learning) are produced by more than one antecedent variable, i.e., that intelligence alone does not wholly explain individual differences in performance, because intelligence is not the only determinant. Given the strong place of motivational concepts in classical learning theory, e.g., those of Thorndike (1932), Hull (1951), and Skinner (1953), it seemed reasonable to expect that the combination of intelligence and motivational variables would be associated with a larger portion of the variance in learning than would intelligence alone. Thus, the need to understand the imperfect prediction of learning differences from differences in intelligence was a prime stimulus for this program of research.

A second set of questions addressed in much of our research has been what we have come to refer to (Haywood, 1981; Haywood, Meyers, & Switzky, 1982; Switzky & Haywood, 1984) as the ''MA deficit.'' This term refers to the observation that, when retarded and younger nonretarded persons are matched on mental age (MA), the retarded persons still perform less well on a wide variety of tasks than do the equal-MA nonretarded persons (see, e.g., Blue, 1963; Girardeau, 1959; Johnson & Blake, 1960; Lipman, 1963; Stevenson & Zigler, 1958; Zigler, 1966, 1969, 1973; Zigler & Balla, 1981, 1982; Zigler et al., 1958). If individual differences in performance within a tightly restricted IQ range could be associated with a ''nonintellective'' variable, such an MA deficit would be more explicable.

Finally, the revolution in services to mentally retarded persons that has taken place since 1965 has resulted in the need for many more retarded persons to function relatively independently in society than had previously been the case. Suggestions had begun to appear (Edgerton, 1967; Edgerton & Bercovici, 1976; Edgerton, Bollinger, & Herr, 1984) that unsuccessful community adjustment of formerly institutionalized retarded persons was frequently associated with inability to engage in self-regulatory behavior rather than with lack of vocational or social skills necessary for such adjustment. Self-instigation, self-maintenance, and self-direction of the activities of daily living are more necessary when one is in a relatively unrestricted environment than when one is in an institutional setting, and such ability appears to be relatively deficient in retarded persons. The possibility of a trait variable that might be associated with individual differences in self-regulatory behavior, especially if that trait were seen as alterable over time, offered a strong reason for pursuing the study of intrinsic motivation in retarded persons.

Research on Five Important Questions

There are at least five important questions that should be asked of proponents of any supposed trait variable. These are:

1. Are there reliable individual differences in the expression of the trait?
2. How is the trait thought to develop; e.g., by genetic determination and maturational "unfolding" or by cumulative experience?
3. Are there important developmental and behavioral correlates of individual differences in this trait?
4. Do individual differences in the trait interact with other organismic variables and/or with environmental conditions in systematic ways?
5. Is the expression of the trait modifiable, and if so, how?

We believe that we and others have accumulated evidence that leads us to answer each of these five questions in such a way as to suggest that it is both conceptually and empirically worthwhile to regard task-intrinsic motivation as a personality trait variable and to examine the association between individual differences in intrinsic motivation and behavior effectiveness.

1. MEASUREMENT OF INDIVIDUAL DIFFERENCES

The situational assessment of intrinsic motivation can be accomplished merely by observing people's behavior in different situations under task-intrinsic and task-extrinsic incentive conditions. That is essentially what was done, indirectly, by Herzberg et al. (1959) in their studies of the association of different incentives with job satisfaction or dissatisfaction. If one wishes instead to determine the tendency of persons to be motivated by task-intrinsic versus task-extrinsic incentives across situations (i.e., to examine person characteristics rather than situation characteristics), an "inventory" approach is more appropriate. Hamlin and Nemo (1962) reported the first such scale. Theirs was a free-response questionnaire in which subjects were asked for each item to choose between two possible vocations or activities (e.g., "Would you rather be a bus driver or an airplane pilot?"). Following each choice, the subjects were merely asked why that choice appealed to them. Their responses (reasons for choice) were recorded verbatim and later scored by "manifest content analysis." Following the Herzberg concepts, reasons that suggested psychological engagement with tasks and satisfaction inherent in them, e.g., challenge, responsibility, learning, excitement from the activity itself, or aesthetic aspects of the task, were scored as "motivator" (intrinsically motivated) reasons. Reasons that suggested nontask factors, e.g., salary, comfort, ease, safety, security, practicality, or status, were scored as "hygiene" (extrinsically motivated) reasons. They reported delayed-parallel-form reliability coefficients with this free-response scale of +.67 for the "motivator" (intrinsic motivation) score and +.65 for the "hygiene" (extrinsic motivation) score. This free-response scale worked well with adults of at least low-average intelligence. This original "Choice Motivator Scale" did not yield the same number of scorable responses for all subjects, since not all reasons for choice could be categorized as indicative of either intrinsic or extrinsic motivation (e.g., the wish to help others, while admirable, appears empirically to be associated with neither category of motivational orientation; see Kahoe, 1966a). Further, this version of the scale was difficult to administer to children or retarded persons, who tended to give unscorable responses or sometimes none at all after choices had been made. Kahoe (1966b) developed a different scale, reflecting vocational choices entirely, based upon a factor analysis of the free-response version. He had found two major factors in the free responses, corresponding to the task-intrinsic and task-extrinsic dimensions predicted by Herzberg, and a third factor that seemed to contain a more-or-less random selection of reasons for choices, neither intrinsic nor extrinsic. Kahoe built into his scale the reasons for job choice that had yielded the highest loadings on the intrinsic and extrinsic factors. He then asked subjects how important each of these considerations would be if they were considering taking a new job, using Likert-type rating scales for each item. His factor structure was replicated in this "strength of motivation" format, but this scale was most appropriate for students and adults. Haywood (1968a,b) devised a multiple-choice version of the Choice Motivator Scale, listing at the top of each page five intrinsic reasons and five extrinsic reasons selected from those that had yielded the highest factor loadings in Kahoe's studies. The remainder of the scale was like the original Choice Motivator Scale, in that each item was a pair of vocations or activities and the subjects' task was to choose between them and then give a reason for the choice, but in this case the reason for choice had to be selected from the list at the top of the page ("Find the reason for choice at the top of the page that comes closest to your reason") and could thus be recorded by letter code. This multiple-choice version assured a standard number of scorable responses and raised the interscorer agreement to 100%.

Even this scale was too sophisticated for use with very young or mentally retarded persons, so Kunca and Haywood (1969) constructed the Picture Motivation Scale specifically for use with persons of low mental age. In that scale, each item is a pair of pictures of people engaged in different activities. The activity is described while the subject looks at the pictures, then the subject chooses between the two activities. The pictures helped to overcome a position response bias in young children and retarded persons in which they tended to choose the second of two named activities. In addition, in this scale, choice is combined with reason for choice (e.g., "Here is a picture of an astronaut going to the moon. Here is a picture of someone watching the astronaut go. Would you rather be an astronaut and do exciting things like go to the moon, or would you rather stay on earth and be sure not to get hurt?"). This version of the scale not only overcame the position response bias but also helped to avoid the tendency of low-MA persons to give reasons that had little apparent relation to the choices they had made. Figure 1 shows a sample of three items from the Picture Motivation Scale.

Using the multiple-choice scale with 10-year-old school children at superior, average, and mildly retarded intellectual levels, Haywood (1968a,b) found that scores were roughly normally distributed, that the retarded children in the studies were able to understand and respond to the items, that there was quite acceptable internal consistency (coefficients generally in the 80s), and that test–retest reliability over a 2-week period was between .79 and .85.

The Picture Motivation Scale similarly yielded a roughly normal distribution (on both total number of intrinsic responses and intrinsic minus extrinsic responses, since these are completely dependent in this version), is useful with subjects down to a mental age of about 3 years and up to adolescence, and yielded acceptable reliability coefficients (Haywood, 1971; Kunca & Haywood, 1969; M. B. Miller, Haywood, & Gimon, 1975). Several studies have shown that the picture scale yields a roughly normal distribution of scores down to about mental age 3 years and that this distribution tends to become skewed (i.e., higher frequencies of intrinsic responses) with increasing chronological and mental age up to middle adolescence (see, e.g., Call, 1968; Haywood, 1966, 1968a,b, 1971; Tahia, 1977). Since the correlation with mental age is less than perfect, one still finds young and mentally retarded children who are relatively more intrinsically than extrinsically motivated.

2. DEVELOPMENT OF INTRINSIC ORIENTATION

Relatively little of an empirical nature is known about the development of a stable intrinsic motivational orientation, but some inferences can be made from the combination of established empirical relationships. First, the CA–MA correlation is well established (see preceding paragraph). Second, intrinsic orienta-

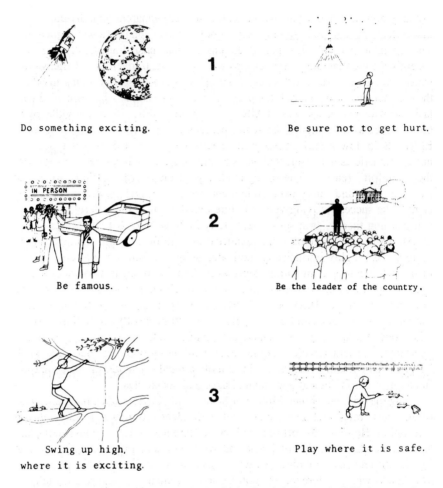

FIG. 1. Sample page from Picture Motivation Scale (Kunca & Haywood, 1969). Items are shown one at a time, with verbal description.

tion appears to be positively correlated with socioeconomic status (SES). Haywood and Miller (reported in Haywood, 1971) gave the Picture Motivation Scale to 1100 primary and elementary school children in Puerto Rico, and from these selected samples of 100 each in the categories of educable mentally retarded (EMR), lower class but not retarded, and middle class not retarded. On 17 of the 20 items these three groups were significantly discriminated according to the proportion of each group who responded to the item in the task-intrinsic direction, with EMR children showing fewest intrinsic responses, lower class children next, and middle class children the most intrinsic responses. Gender effects were virtually nonexistent over the whole scale, but were apparent on individual items that reflected social conditioning (e.g., cook versus captain, flower garden versus vegetable garden). The paired dimension that most dramatically and consistently differentiated the three groups was excitement/adventure/challenge (intrinsic) versus ease/comfort/safety (extrinsic). Across the five items in which these dimensions were paired, the proportion of each sample who responded with task-intrinsic responses was: EMR, 22%; lower SES, 45.4%; middle SES, 65.8%. Across all items in the scale, percentage of intrinsic responding were: EMR, 48.35; lower SES, 59.95; middle SES, 67.25—a striking difference, but not as dramatic as in the selected items contrasting the "adventure" reasons with the "comfort" reasons. The strong tendency for the retarded children to choose ease, comfort, and safety over excitement, adventure, and challenge is reminiscent of the success-striving versus failure-avoiding dichotomy derived from social learning theory. In a subsequent study in New York (M. B. Miller *et al.*, 1975), 13 of the 20 items were identified as significantly discriminating high scorers (i.e., highly intrinsically motivated subjects) from low scorers. Twelve of these thirteen discriminating items were then identified in two widely separated sample: one in Tennessee on a sample of children in preschool education programs (Kunca & Haywood, 1969), the other in the south of France on a sample of immigrant children in special education, mostly from North Africa (Haywood & Paour, 1983). Thus, the picture scale appears to have similar measurement characteristics in quite diverse cultural groups. Further, these studies provided evidence that the intrinsic motivational orientation is an increasing function of chronological age, mental age, and social class.

Using the original Choice Motivator Scale, Call (1968) studied the association of age, sex, race, and social class with individual differences in motivational orientation. He found the oft-reported race differences in IQ, in both lower-class and middle-class samples of black and white children in grades 4, 6, and 8. Similar differences were observed with respect to intrinsic orientation at grade 4. The black–white difference in motivational orientation disappeared totally at grade 6 and at grade 8 for middle-class children, but remained constant over these three age levels in the lower-class samples. The most interesting results were: (1) differences in social class were associated with substantially larger portions of the variance in IQ than were race differences; and (2) when the IQ data were analyzed using intrinsic motivation scores as a covariate, the race difference was significantly reduced but the class difference remained. The data suggested that the combination of developmental events associated with social class and with racial differences produces a differential pattern of intrinsic motivational orientation that is in turn associated with important intellective variables.

Haywood and Burke (1977) reviewed research literature on both intrinsic motivation and early cognitive development, and suggested a three-way transactional relationship among "native" ability, cognitive development, and development of an intrinsic motivational orientation. They suggested that all children, regardless of the native intellectual potential, enter the world with a general motive to explore and gain some mastery over their world, i.e., with both curiosity and competence motives. What happens to those motives is a direct function of the consequences, both direct and social, of their successive attempts to explore and to gain mastery. Beginning with the earliest appearance of the orienting reflex, children's exploratory/mastery behavior meets with relative success or relative failure, and those consequences constitute reinforcing conditions that lead to acceleration or deceleration of such behavior. Parents' responses to exploratory/mastery behavior play a major role in this motivational conditioning, since the reaction of parents helps children to define the outcomes of their behavior as either successful or unsuccessful. Exploratory behavior of relatively incompetent children, meeting often with failure, becomes less and less frequent. One result is that these children, being less and less inclined to expose themselves to novel stimuli, derive less and less information from their (less and less frequent and intense) encounters with their environments, and this smaller store of information about the world gives them less adequate knowledge bases within which to evaluate, understand, and elaborate subsequent new information and fewer exemplars from which to induce generalizations about the structure of the world. This unfortunate effect on cognitive development is accompanied by the beginning of development of the personality trait of task-extrinsic motivation, i.e., the tendency to concentrate one's attention upon non-task (and therefore nonfailure potential) aspects of the environment, to avoid dissatisfaction and failure rather than to seek satisfaction and success. The cognitive and motivational aspects thus develop in a transactional relationship, the developmentally negative aspect of each rendering the developmentally positive aspect of the other more difficult and unlikely of accomplishment. By contrast, relatively competent infants engage similarly in initial attempts to explore and gain mastery; these attempts are met relatively more often by success, exploratory habits are strengthened, the store of relevant knowledge becomes larger as a result of their more frequent and intense exploratory behavior, and they begin to develop a characteristic orientation toward task-intrinsic factors, including a general tendency to seek success and satisfaction through concentrating their attention upon such task-intrinsic aspects as challenge, creativity, increased responsibility, learning, psychological excitement, and task-intrinsic aesthetics. This general tendency is later expressed as a greater frequency of choices of activities in response to task-intrinsic incentives than in response to task-extrinsic incentives. According to this dual conceptualization, the trait variable should be positively correlated with chronological age in intellectually average and above average persons and negatively correlated with chronological age in intellectually subnormal persons, the correlation in each group reflecting the differential experience associated with the respective intelligence level. So far, such an interaction with IQ has not been tested. In fact, to what extent this conceptualization of the development of individual differences in intrinsic motivation is useful has yet to be demonstrated, but if a criterion for personality trait status is that a coherent explanation of the development of individual differences must exist, then the intrinsic motivation concept qualifies.

3. CORRELATES OF THE TRAIT

This is essentially the question of construct validity. A trait has construct validity to the extent that predicted relationships between the trait and other relevant variables can be shown empirically. Demonstrations of construct validity have constituted the heart of the research program that we report here. The principal criteria of construct validity that have been established so far include stimulus seeking and tension induction, exploratory behavior, personality integration, task persistence, learning effectiveness, self regulation, need for reward, school achievement, vigor of work, work aspiration, and cognitive change.

In one of the earliest studies in this series, Haywood and Dobbs (1964), using the original Choice Motivator Scale of Hamlin and Nemo (1962), constituted groups of high school boys who scored at the two extreme ends of the IM distribution, i.e., who were, psychometrically at least, strongly intrinsically motivated or strongly extrinsically motivated. These boys were also given the S-R Inventory of Anxiousness (Endler, Hunt, & Rosenstein, 1962). Boys who scored in the top quartile of the IM distribution were characterized by a tendency to seek tension-inducing situations, especially in verbal interactions ($p < .001$), while those in the top quartile of the EM distribution tended to avoid such tension-inducing situations ($p < .01$). This early indication of a relationship to exploratory behavior was extended by Tzuriel and Haywood (1984), who found that relatively IM children (fifth and tenth grades) explored more when left alone with intellectually challenging materials than did EM children and that the IM children explored more when the conditions of their behavior were left open rather than being imposed on them. This relationship is illustrated in Fig. 2. They concluded that "personality integration and variation seeking appear to characterize relatively IM persons more than relatively EM persons" (Tzuriel & Haywood, 1984, p. 67). Similarly, relating individual differences in motivational orientation to Seeman's (1983) concept of personality integration, Pegg (1970) found correlations of $+.22$ for ninth-grade girls and $+.42$ for ninth-grade boys ($p < .01$). These relationships generally support and extend Hamlin and Nemo's (1962) discovery of higher intrinsic orientation accompanying greater mental health.

Persons who have an intrinsic motivational orientation, even though mentally retarded, appear to work harder, to prefer not to be paid off for their work with task-extrinsic rewards, and to persist in tasks longer than predominantly EM

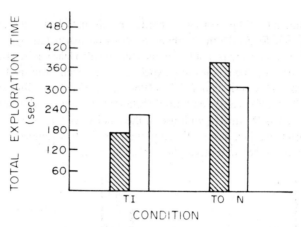

FIG. 2. Total exploration time as a joint function of motivational orientation and task condition. TI, task imposed; TO, task offered; N, neutral; cross-hatching, intrinsic motivation; open, extrinsic motivation. (From Tzuriel & Haywood, 1984.)

persons. In the first of these studies with mentally retarded persons, Haywood and Weaver (1967) used the Choice Motivator Scale (by reading the items to the subjects) to define strongly EM and somewhat IM (i.e., less EM) groups of institutionalized retarded adolescents and adults. While the groups were clearly separated on motivational orientation, the mean IM score of the IM group was considerably less than in samples from other populations, there being a very strong tendency for institutionalized retarded persons to be predominantly extrinsic in motivational orientation. These subjects, in a random-groups design, were given a simple motor task, hole-punching on a teaching-machine answer sheet, over four consecutive 1-minute trials under four different incentive conditions: two money incentives (1¢ and 10¢ per trial: "If you punch a lot of holes you will get 1¢/10¢"), a no-reward control condition ("Punch as many holes as you can"), and a task-incentive condition ("If you punch a lot of holes I'll let you do another task that you might find interesting"). The IM subjects punched more holes under the task incentive than under the money incentive, while EM subjects punched more holes under the money incentive than under the task incentive. The IM subjects worked harder in this task under all incentive conditions except the 10¢ condition. These relationships are shown in Fig. 3. The authors stressed the motivational importance of matching incentive systems to the individual motivational orientations of retarded persons rather than expecting a single incentive system to be equally effective for all persons. This set of relationships, essentially a cross-over interaction between motivational orientation and incentive condition, has been replicated several times, including studies by Switzky and Haywood (1974, 1985a,b) and Haywood and Switzky (1985), studies that will be discussed in a subsequent section on interactive relationships.

If predominantly IM persons work harder, persist in tasks longer, explore more, and appear not to need (and perhaps even to be distracted by) task-extrinsic rewards, then it seems reasonable that they should also learn more effectively than do EM persons. In two studies this expectation has been examined in laboratory learning tasks. Haywood and Wachs (1966) gave a size-discrimination learning task to intellectually average and mildly retarded/borderline adolescents who had been classified as IM or EM with use of the Choice Motivator Scale. Generally, the IM subjects learned more efficiently than did the EM subjects in the same IQ group. The difference in motivational orientation made a larger difference in the

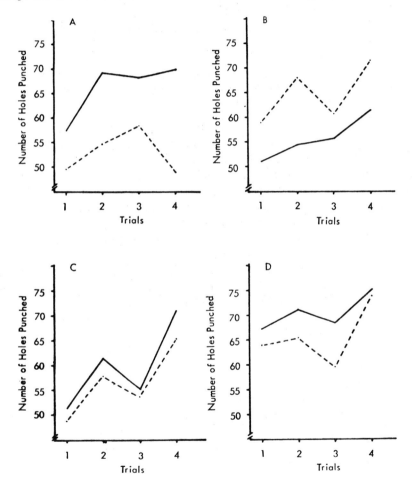

FIG. 3. Hole-punching performance of IM (solid lines) and EM (broken lines) institutionalized retarded persons under task (A), 10¢ (B), 1¢ (C), and control (D) incentive conditions across four trials. (From Haywood & Weaver, 1967.)

low-IQ group, with IM subjects requiring fewer total trials to learn the discrimination, than in the intellectually average group. In the latter group, there was no difference between IM and EM subjects on initial acquisition, but when both groups were required to relearn the problem, i.e., to reach learning criterion again 1 day later, IM subjects relearned in fewer trials than did EM subjects. More EM than IM subjects failed to reach the 90% criterion of learning. The interaction of motivational orientation and ability level is shown in Table I.

This essential superiority of intrinsically oriented persons over extrinsically oriented persons in laboratory learning tasks was supported, but only weakly, by Wachs (1968) in a free-recall verbal learning paradigm. In this latter study, Wachs (1968) gave the multiple-choice version of the Choice Motivator Scale, permitting more than one reason for each choice (thus allowing IM and EM scores to be less than completely dependent), to almost 800 schoolchildren in the fourth, eighth, and twelfth grades, and defined separated groups of predominantly IM, "mixed motivation," and predominantly EM subjects. He then gave these subjects a free-recall verbal learning task, with five trials on 50-word lists. The "learning" curves describing number of words correctly recalled as a function of trials were essentially of the same shape, i.e., negatively accelerated, for all three groups, and tended to diverge over trials, with the groups ordered on trial 5, highest scores to lowest, as IM, mixed motivation, and EM. The IM and

TABLE I

Means and Standard Deviations of Size-
Discrimination Learning Scores (Trials to Criterion)
of High-Intelligence (IQ > 95) and Low-Intelligence
(IQ < 85) Adolescents as a Function
of Motivational Orientation[a]

| | High IQ | | Low IQ | |
Measure	IM	EM	IM	EM
Original acquisiton	44.75	45.10	47.58	59.90
	(33.53)[b]	(36.31)	(34.30)	(42.80)
Relearning	11.30	19.65	19.26	23.97
	(5.46)	(21.93)	(21.38)	(31.18)
Total acquisition[c]	63.32	64.82	70.10	98.10
	(47.80)	(47.25)	(47.23)	(61.55)
Discrimination reversal	26.21	26.94	51.97	32.50
	(34.51)	(36.84)	(55.34)	(36.91)

[a]Data from Haywood & Wachs (1966).

[b]Parenthetical entries are standard deviations.

[c]Total acquisition is the sum of original acquisition and relearning but includes data from subjects who did not learn to criterion.

mixed-group curves were very close together, but both were superior to the learning curve of the EM group. Thus, while all subjects appear to have gotten off to a good start in this recall task, the EM subjects gained relatively less on successive trials than did either of the other two groups. Overall, the relationship of motivational orientation to free-recall learning was much less dramatic than Haywood and Wachs (1966) had found for discrimination learning and must less dramatic than has been found (see below) for school achievement. One possible explanation is that free-recall learning is a relatively more passive task than are other learning paradigms, requiring less personal investment and less effort, thus failing to polarize the motivational groups as sharply as do more demanding tasks. Wachs found some evidence to support the inference that an extrinsic orientation depresses performance in learning tasks rather than that an intrinsic orientation enhances such performance. Not only were the learning curves of his IM and mixed-motivation groups essentially the same while both were superior to that of the EM group, but he also found that the EM score was significantly negatively correlated ($p < .005$) with the number of words recalled on each trial, while the IM score had no significant correlation with that measure.

Sampling a very interesting population in Israel, Tahia (1977) gave the Choice Motivator Scale and several instruments from Feuerstein's Learning Potential Assessment Device (Feuerstein, Rand, & Hoffman, 1979) to 111 bedouin children in grades 6, 7, 8, and 9. First, these children had, on the average, higher IM scores than we had been accustomed to seeing in economically and socially disadvantaged children in the United States, Canada, and Mexico. Second, they showed the usual increase in intrinsic orientation with increasing age. Most significant was the relationship between motivational orientation and performance by these children on several tests of the kind usually associated with the measurement of intelligence. In Feuerstein's procedure, tasks that require cognitive strategies are given without help in order to establish a "baseline" level, then the examiner teaches the cognitive processes and strategies needed to solve the kind of problems represented by the tasks, and finally the children are "posttested" to determine to what extent they have learned the principles and have been able to apply them to new problems that require the same or similar strategies. In this study with bedouin children Tahia found, as usual, substantial individual differences in learning effectiveness, with some children deriving more rapid benefit from teaching than did others. Intrinsically motivated scores were correlated positively and moderately with the children's baseline scores on the cognitive tasks (such as Raven's Progressive Matrices, a stencil design task, and a set of variations on the matrix problems that clearly require analogical thought). Of most particular interest is the finding that, especially among eighth- and ninth-grade children, the correlation between IM score and performance on these tasks was frequently greater in the case of tests given after the special teaching than for those that represented baseline (presumably "typical") performance. That is to say, children who had relatively high intrinsic orientation improved their cognitive performance as a result of teaching more than did similar children who had relatively lower intrinsic orientation. This appears to support the finding of Haywood and Wachs (1966) that IM children relearned a previously learned discrimination task faster than did EM children, leading these authors to conclude that intrinsic motivation is associated with greater ability to derive benefit from learning experiences.

The next link in this inferential chain is that, if learning in relatively simple laboratory tasks and on clinical assessment instruments is in some part a function of individual differences in motivational orientation, this relationship should at least be repeated, and perhaps even amplified, in the more complex learning tasks that children encounter in school. Haywood (1968a,b) gained access to longitudinal developmental data on over 7000 10-year-old children, all of whom had been born in Toronto. These data included birthdate, sex, school placement, IQ, and standardized school achievement test scores for their first three school years. In the first study (Haywood, 1968a), this large group was divided into five-point IQ ranges and then further classified within these narrow IQ ranges according to their deviation scores on the Metropolitan Achievement Tests. The mean and standard deviation of scores in reading, spelling, and arithmetic were calculated for each five-point IQ group for each of the first three school years. Children whose achievement scores were at least one standard deviation above the mean for their IQ range were defined as scholastic overachievers, while those whose achievement scores were at least one standard deviation below the mean for their IQ range were defined as scholastic underachievers. These two selected samples of children were then regrouped into three large ability groups (educable mentally retarded, average, and superior), and given the multiple-choice version of the Choice Motivator Scale. While there was no significant difference in motivational orientation between overachievers and underachievers at the superior IQ level, there was a significant difference at the average level and an even larger difference at the EMR level, indicating that overachievers were on the average more intrinsically oriented than were underachievers. This relationship was confirmed dramatically when the study was turned around and carried out in "natural order." Children were sampled randomly from each of the IQ ranges, given the multiple-choice version of the Choice Motivator Scale, grouped into predominantly IM and predominantly EM subgroups, and then their achievement scores were analyzed as the dependent variable (Haywood, 1968b). This study showed that IM and EM children were not significantly different in school achievement in reading, spelling, or arithmetic in any of the first three school years so long as IQ was in the superior range (IQ > 120), but that motivational orientation made a sizable difference at the average and EMR levels. In all three achievement areas IM children were achieving at a significantly higher level than were EM children, with age, sex, and IQ held constant. In fact, at the EMR level this difference was as large as that usually associated with at least 20 IQ points.

On the average, the IM children in the average-IQ and EMR groups had achievement scores about one full school year higher than those of the EM children in the same IQ group. The achievement of the IM/EMR children was not different from that of the EM/average-IQ children (see Fig. 4). Thus, there was evidence that (1) intrinsic orientation is associated with higher school achievement, independent of the effects of IQ; (2) the effects of individual differences in motivational orientation appear to be greater as IQ is less. These strong associations of intrinsic orientation with school achievement have been replicated and extended by Dobbs (1967) with EMR adolescents using programmed instruction in mathematics, Haywood and Miller (reported in Haywood, 1980) with Puerto Rican students in San Juan, M. B. Miller *et al.* (1975) with Puerto Rican children in New York, Wooldridge (1966) with EMR children, and in unpublished cross-validating research in Chihuahua and Guadalajara, Mexico (by H. C. Haywood and W. G. Lucker) and in Israel (Reuveni, 1975; Tahia, 1977).

Why motivational orientation should have an increasingly large association with learning effectiveness and achievement as IQ is less constitutes an interesting study in itself. One very likely answer is that it is not IQ per se that makes the difference, but task difficulty. That is to say, if the task is held constant and ability is varied, the same task is more difficult for persons with less ability. Kahoe (1966c) tested this notion with university students. He gave his test of motivational orientation to students and then correlated the scores with their grade point averages (GPA). The resulting correlation was not different from zero. He then asked the students to sort their courses into "easy courses" and "hard courses." The correlation between IM scores and GPA for easy courses was again essentially zero, but the correlation between IM score and GPA for hard courses was +.55!

4. INTERACTIVE RELATIONSHIPS

As helpful as the foregoing relationships between motivational orientation and several dependent variables may be, it is nevertheless true that the association is not usually direct. That is to say, motivational orientation often intereacts with other variables to produce differential effects on behavior that depend in part upon values of the interacting variables. One such interacting variable is age. The effect of differences in motivational orientation upon learning, persistence of behavior, or vigor of behavior depends upon the age of the subjects as well as upon their motivational orientation (see, e.g., Call, 1968; Tzuriel & Haywood, 1984; Wachs, 1968). Other important interacting variables that have been studied and on which data are available include the nature of incentives offered, the freedom of the person to select reinforcement conditions, the demands of the task, the feedback available on task performance, the difficulty of the task, relative freedom to do or not to do the task, and such organismic variables as MA, IQ, SES, and gender.

The interaction of motivational orientation with the kinds of incentives offered or available is probably the most conceptually interesting of the interactive relationships. The first of these studies was that of Haywood and Weaver (1967), who found that predominantly IM retarded persons would work harder for the opportunity to do more work than for money rewards (albeit very small money rewards!), while predominantly EM retarded persons worked harder for money rewards than for these "task" incentives. Working with normally developing subjects, Bandura and Perloff (1967) investigated the effects of self-monitored and externally imposed reinforcement systems on the vigor of work, and found no difference. In an extended replication of that study, Switzky and Haywood (1974) essentially replicated the Bandura and Perloff design, but with the addition of the organismic variable of individual differences in motivational orientation. Normally developing children were classified as either predominantly IM or predominantly EM on the basis of their scores on the Picture Motivation Scale (scores in the top or bottom quartiles on intrinsic motivation for IM and EM groups, respectively). They were then given a wheel-cranking task in which it was possible to vary the number of cranks of the wheel required to turn on a light on a column of lights as well as the number of lights that had to be turned on to get a token. Tokens could be exchanged for prizes. In the "self-monitored" condition subjects selected their own schedules, i.e., decided how many cranks were needed to turn on a light and how many lights had to be turned on to earn a token. For each of these subjects there was a yoked subject in the externally imposed condition who had to follow the schedule selected by the self-monitored subject. The first result was that IM subjects worked harder than did EM subjects without respect to condition. Second, there was a cross-over interaction between motivational orientation and the regulation conditions (self-monitored versus externally imposed), with the IM subjects working harder under the self-monitored condition and the EM subjects working harder under the externally imposed condition. Intrinsically motivated subjects not only worked harder, but set leaner schedules in the self-monitored condition than did extrinsically motivated subjects. The interaction of self-monitoring versus externally imposed reinforcement conditions with individual differences in motivational orientation is depicted in Fig. 5. Thus, Bandura and Perloff's (1967) failure to find differential effects of these reinforcement systems appeared to have been attributable to the canceling effects of individual differences in motivational orientation, with very strong differential effects interacting with such individual differences. These effects suggested that persons who are predominantly intrinsically motivated are characterized by a self-regulatory system according to which they are able to determine, choose, and pace their own behavior without direction from or reliance upon external sources and that in fact such external direction interferes with the operation of their self-regulatory systems. This latter inference is supported by work done by social psychologists (see, e.g., Deci, 1971, 1972, 1975; Deci, Nezlek, & Scheinman, 1981) showing generally that, for persons who are

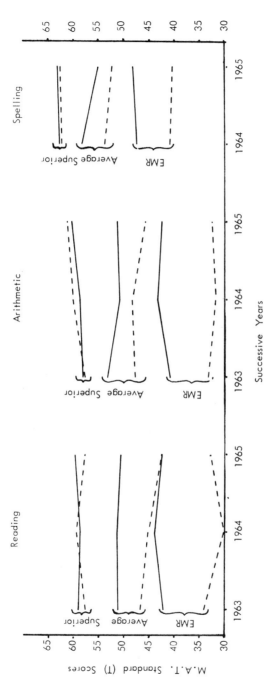

FIG. 4. Metropolitan Achievement Test standard scores over three successive years of IM (solid lines) and EM (broken lines) children at three IQ levels. (From Haywood, 1968b.)

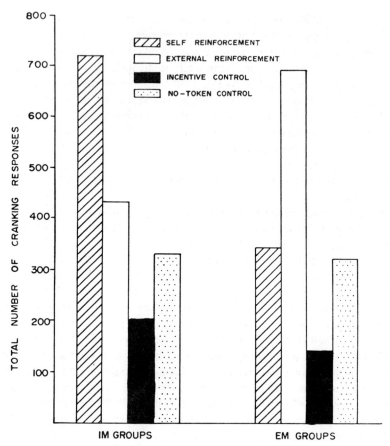

FIG. 5. Number of wheel-cranking responses (an index of "vigor and persistence of behavior") as a function of motivational orientation and reinforcement condition: self-monitored, externally imposed, incentive control, no-token control. (From Switzky & Haywood, 1974.)

already intrinsically motivated, task-extrinsic reward interferes with task-intrinsic motivation. On the other hand, persons who are predominantly extrinsically motivated appear to need external direction and to be less inclined to engage in self-regulated activity for its own sake—indeed, to perform relatively poorly when not given external direction.

5. CAN MOTIVATIONAL ORIENTATION BE DELIBERATELY CHANGED?

If EM persons learn less effectively, derive less satisfaction from task involvement and achievement, work less hard and less persistently, are less positively mentally healthy, and are less able to function productively in conditions that require self-regulation than are IM persons, and if retarded persons are far more likely to be characterized as EM than as IM, it would seem reasonable that part of a treatment strategy for improving the state of retarded persons especially would be simply to make them more intrinsically motivated, i.e., to shift their motivational orientation from EM to IM. In the manner of personality traits, one would expect such changes to come about only slowly and to be reflected more readily in behavioral than in psychometric assessment (since the self-report of trait variables may change even more slowly than the traits themselves do). We do know that changes occur developmentally, so it is reasonable to assume that one could arrange conditions that would hasten and amplify those developmental changes. Nevertheless, little of a systematic nature has been done in pursuit of this question.

In the first study designed to investigate the possibility of change, Haywood and Switzky (1975) arranged a verbal conditioning experiment to determine to what extent it would be possible to shift the verbal expression of intrinsic and extrinsic motivation by contingent reinforcement. The authors also wanted to know to what extent it was reasonable to expect schoolchildren to be able to discriminate task-intrinsic and task-extrinsic motives, assuming that subjects have to be aware of the distinction between the two dimensions in order for verbal conditioning to be effective. Using a Taffel-type task with statements that had been judged to be IM or EM printed on index cards, the authors asked subjects to look at both cares in pairs of cards presented simultaneously and to choose one of the two in each pair to read aloud. Groups of IM and EM subjects had been constituted as usual. Within each of the two motivational groups, subjects were socially reinforced (''Good!'') by the experimenter for statements that were either consistent with or contrary to their own motivational orientation. All conditions produced clear learning curves according to the reinforcement contingencies. Extrinsically motivated subjects learned relatively more effectively, probably because social reinforcement is task extrinsic (consistent with their motivational orientation). It was relatively more difficult to condition the IM subjects to choose EM statements. This study demonstrated that with a classical procedure one can change readily what people say on an intrinsic–extrinsic motivation dimension, but of course showed nothing about the ''actual'' differential response to incentives to these persons.

In three studies motivational orientation has been a criterion variable in the evaluation of programs of cognitive education. Learning to think more effectively and systematically, and thereby experiencing more success in task achievement, should be expected to lead to enhancement of an intrinsic motivational orientation. In all three studies the program of cognitive education was Instrumental Enrichment (Feuerstein, Rand, Hoffman, & Miller, 1980). Subjects in the first study (Beharav, 1978) were ''culturally deprived and low functioning'' adolescents in Israel. They were given the Choice Motivator Scale before and after some 250–400 classroom hours of Instrumental Enrichment spread over two school years. Subjects in the Instrumental Enrichment groups increased in intrinsic motivation scores from pretest to posttest, while the very slight increase for those who got only the regular school program was no more than would be expected on the basis of age alone.

The same program of cognitive education was given to adolescent students in a migrant education program in the American southwest, with scores on the Picture Motivation Scale as one of several criterion measures (study by M. V. Hannel and L. Hannel, reported in Haywood, Arbitman-Smith, Bransford, Delclos, Towery, Hannel, & Hannel, 1982). After one school year there was a significantly greater increase in intrinsic motivation scores for the group who got the cognitive education treatment than for an untreated control group, and a difference that failed to achieve statistical significance ($p < .06$) between the cognitive education group and a "tutored" comparison group (i.e., students who got extra academic help but not of a cognitive-process nature). These gains were extended by the end of the second year of the 2-year program, i.e., the differences held and were significant for both comparisons.

Using a more direct behavioral approach, Delclos and Haywood (also reported in Haywood, Arbitman-Smith, *et al.*, 1982) devised a series of paper-and-pencil mazes of increasing complexity, patterned after the Porteus mazes, and arranged them four to a page with a common goal in the center, accessible from the end point of each maze. Subjects were told that they should enter Maze 1 at the entry point and work through to a final choice point, at which the choice would be to go straight to the common goal and thereby stop work on the mazes or to enter Maze 2. Any maze entered had to be finished, but at the end of Mazes 1, 2, and 3 were similar choice points and the choice of going to the goal and stopping engagement with the task or entering the next maze. In other words, subjects were allowed to choose more mental work as a reward for completing some mental work or to stop work altogether. This task was given to 30 educable mentally retarded and low-functioning adolescents who had been given 0, 10, or 57 classroom hours of Instrumental Enrichment (10 subjects in each group). The number of mazes they chose to enter was a direct increasing function of the number of hours of cognitive education. Further, the amount of time spent on this task was also a function of amount of cognitive education, but this measure was not independent of number of mazes entered. An "efficiency index" was constructed by calculating the number of correct choice-point decisions (i.e., avoiding blind alleys) made per minute of engagement with the task, and on this measure, as well, those with more cognitive education had higher efficiency scores. These results were not repeated later in a larger study that also failed to show intellectual and academic achievement benefits of the program of cognitive education, so this later failure to replicate the motivational effects could be due to failure of the treatment program to produce the primary effect, i.e., enhanced cognitive functioning.

Taken together, these studies suggest rather faintly that it might be possible to shift motivational orientation from predominantly task extrinsic to predominantly task intrinsic and that substantial treatments over significant periods of time will be required to do so. With little of an empirical nature to buttress the suggestion, we suggest that the general method might be to start with individual children using the incentive system that matches their motivational orientation, i.e., task-extrinsic incentives with EM children, fade those as soon as possible, and begin early to substitute task-intrinsic rewards for task-intrinsic behavior. Modeling should also be effective, especially with retarded persons.

III. SPECIAL APPLICATIONS TO MENTAL RETARDATION

The ways in which individual differences in motivational orientation may affect the development and behavior effectiveness of retarded persons have been suggested in the foregoing sections. There are some unique applications that require special attention. We report here just two such applications: (1) work on the "MA deficit," and (2) work on self-regulatory behavior.

A. The MA Deficit

Psychologists have frequently done studies in which a sample of mentally retarded persons would be matched with a sample of younger, nonretarded persons of the same mental age and their performances compared on a variety of learning and performance tasks. If learning and behavior effectiveness were exclusively products of individual differences in intelligence, the performance of these MA-matched persons should be the same. On the contrary, a very frequent finding (Blue, 1963; Lipman, 1963; Stevenson & Zigler, 1958) is that retarded persons do less well than do even these younger MA-matched nonretarded persons. This discrepancy is what we have referred to (Haywood, 1981; Haywood, Meyers, & Switzky, 1982) as the MA deficit. Zigler (1969, 1973) has consistently maintained that at least this difference between performance levels of retarded and nonretarded persons matched on MA, and perhaps more, is attributable to motivational differences.

Call's (1968) data on intelligence, race, social class, and motivational orientation lend some conceptual credence to that notion, in that in his study the race difference in IQ was reduced when motivational orientation was introduced as a covariate. In the Haywood (1968a,b) Toronto studies, age, sex, and IQ were closely controlled, and individual differences in motivational orientation were associated with substantial differences in school achievement, more in the group of mildly retarded children than in groups of intellectually average or superior children. In fact, in the second of these studies (Haywood, 1968b), the school achievement of IM mildly retarded children was very close to (not significantly different from) that of EM children of average intelligence.

The conceptual analysis of Haywood and Burke (1977) suggests that the experience of being retarded makes one more retarded, essentially through the transactional relationship between cognitive development and the development of task-intrinsic motivation (see discussion in Section II,A,2). To the extent that the reciprocal and mutually reinforcing relationship of these domains of development could be interrupted and turned in a positive direction (through guaranteed earned success at exploratory and mastery behavior, modeling of intrinsic motivation, early concentration on development of competence), it is quite possible that at least the MA deficit could be offset. While doing that would not "cure" mental retardation, it would reduce by a manageable magnitude the performance deficit of mildly and moderately retarded persons.

B. Self-Regulation

The ability to regulate one's own behavior rather than being dependent on others for direction is critical to the postinstitutional adjustment and community living of retarded persons (see, e.g., Edgerton, 1967; Edgerton & Bercovici, 1976; Edgerton *et al.*, 1984; Haywood & Newbrough, 1981). Our own conceptual analysis of motivational orientation, in addition to that of Bandura (1978) on self-regulation, suggests that individual differences in motivational orientation may be central to the ability to direct one's behavior independently and to derive satisfaction from doing so.

The complex relationships of individual differences in motivational orientation to self-regulation seemed to be so important that Haywood and Switzky (1985; Switzky & Haywood, 1985a,b) have continued to investigate additional parameters in both mentally retarded and nonretarded persons, adults and children. With respect to retarded persons, these authors have held (Haywood & Switzky, 1985) that (1) self-regulation is extremely important to the ability of retarded persons to adjust to relatively independent living; and (2) the response of retarded persons to expectations of self-regulation or to expectations of external imposition of regulation depends upon individual differences in task-intrinsic motivation. Further, since previous studies had shown that retarded persons are, on the average, less intrinsically motivated than are nonretarded persons, self-regulation might be difficult to produce in retarded persons to the extent that motivational orientation and self-regulatory behavior are related. In addition to the self-regulation relationships, the authors wanted to find out to what extent the incentive-system relationships previously established with normally developing children were transposable to generally lower levels of intrinsic motivation, specifically those lower levels typically found in retarded persons. Working with mildly retarded adults in a community-based facility, they pretested on motivational orientation, selected top (IM) and bottom (EM) quartiles of the distribution of intrinsic motivation scores, and assigned subjects to three conditions: self-regulated reinforcement, externally imposed reinforcement, and no-token control. Subjects in the external-reinforcement condition were matched individually to subjects in the self-regulation condition by sex, age, motivational orientation, and, in a yoked manner, schedule of reinforcement. Those in the control condition were matched for sex, age, and motivational orientation with subjects in the self-regulation condition. All subjects were given a work task consisting of placing a single flat or lock washer into each compartment of an 18-compartment box. Work goals were set by placing a washer in the endmost compartment they intended to reach. Subjects in the self-regulation condition set their own work goals, and, after reaching the work goals, determined the number of tokens they should get for their work. They also determined how long they would work. Tokens were exchanged for prizes at the end of the experimental session. Selections made by the self-regulation subjects were imposed on subjects in the external-reinforcement condition. In the control condition the experimenter set the work goals, subjects worked as long as they wished with no indication of "pay" for their work, and were given a prize at the end.

In this study with retarded adults, IM subjects worked harder (mean of 118 compartments filled) than did EM subjects (mean of 80 compartments filled), without regard to condition. As usual in these studies, the interaction of condition and motivational orientation was of particular interest (in this case it yielded an F ratio of 9.97, df = 2/66, $p < .001$). In both the self-regulation and control conditions IM subjects filled more compartments than did EM subjects, while IM and EM subjects did not differ under the external-reinforcement condition. Intrinsically motivated subjects also filled the compartments under the self-regulation condition than they did under the external-reinforcement condition. Thus, the previously reported effects with normally developing children did appear to transpose to retarded adults with much lower levels of intrinsic motivation. It appears to be true that a higher level of intrinsic motivation is associated with more self-regulatory behavior than is a lower level of intrinsic motivation, and that relationship holds whether the comparison is between very high and moderate IM or between moderate and very low IM. Figure 6 shows the total number of compartments filled by IM and EM retarded adults as a function of differences in self-regulation conditions.

In the next study with mildly retarded adults, Switzky and Haywood (1985a) selected subjects in an analogous manner, i.e., top (IM) and bottom (EM) halves on the Picture Motivation Scale, and gave them a different task, canceling geometric figures in a random sequence of three different figures, according to a cancellation model. The principal experimental conditions were task demands: stringent (instructed to set very high work goals, instructed to work as hard and fast as they could, experimenter modeled a lean schedule of reinforcement),

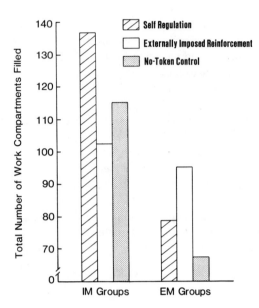

FIG. 6. Work performance of IM and EM mildly retarded adults as a function of regulatory conditions: self regulation, externally imposed reinforcement, no-token control. (From Haywood & Switzky, 1985.)

variable (given choice of high or low work goal, but experimenter modeled a schedule of reinforcement proportional in richness to the work goal chosen, i.e., more tokens for higher goals), or lenient (instructed to set low work goal, experimenter modeled a rich schedule of reinforcement). All subjects were told to perform the task to get tokens that could be exchanged for prizes, the more tokens the better the prize. After reaching their work goals they could pay themselves off with as many tokens from a nearby container as they thought their work had been worth. Dependent variables were (1) number of figures canceled, i.e., total work behavior across trials, (2) average number of figures canceled, i.e., average work behavior across trials (work standard), (3) percent of modeled standard, i.e., goal chosen as a percentage of the goal modeled by the experimenter, (4) schedule of reinforcement, i.e., items of work accomplished divided by number of tokens paid to self, and (5) percent of modeled schedule of reinforcement. Results indicated that both external–environmental conditions (i.e., task demand conditions) and internal–self-characteristics (i.e., motivational orientation) had significant effects on performance. Subjects in the stringent demand condition worked harder, set higher goals, and arranged leaner schedules of reinforcement than did those in the lenient demand condition. Intrinsically motivated subjects also worked harder, set higher goals, and arranged leaner schedules than did extrinsically motivated subjects over all demand conditions. Further, IM subjects chose a higher goal than had been demonstrated to them (in the lenient demand condition, the only reasonable comparison for this variable) and also arranged a leaner schedule of self reinforcement over all demand conditions than had been demonstrated to them, while EM subjects either copied the schedule set by the experimenter or set richer ones. All of these effects were of dramatic magnitude. Differences between IM and EM subjects were most pronounced in the lenient demand condition, suggesting that this individual differences variable will lead to the most divergent performances in situations in which there is least external support and guidance. The data in Fig. 7, percent model standard selected by IM and EM subjects as a function of the three task demand conditions, illustrates again the familiar interaction of individual differences in motivational orientation with external (to the person) variables. The authors concluded that internal self-system characteristics interact with external demand characteristics of the environment to reveal substantial individual differences in patterns of self-reward behavior and, further, that these studies provided data quite consistent with Bandura's (1978) concept of the self system in reciprocal determinism as well as with previous research on motivational orientation.

Switzky and Haywood (1985b) then extended this series of studies to young normally developing children, using the same paradigm. Essentially the same figure-cancellation task as was used in the previous study was given to 32 middle-class children, 16 boys and 16 girls, with a mean age of 4.72 years. As usual, these children had been selected by means of their scores on the Picture Motivation Scale, with one half of the subjects scoring above the median of a standardization sample of comparable children and the other half scoring below

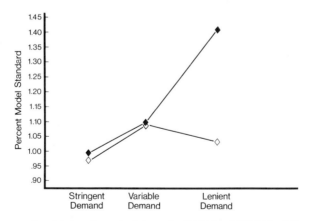

FIG. 7. Percent of modeled work standard chosen by IM (♦) and EM (◇) mildly retarded adults as a function of task demand characteristics: stringent demand, variable demand, lenient demand. (From Switzky & Haywood, 1985a.)

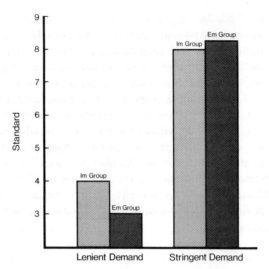

FIG. 8. Work standard chosen by IM and EM preschool children as a function of task demand characteristics: lenient demand or stringent demand. (From Switzky & Haywood, 1985b.)

the median. In this study there were only two task demand conditions: stringent (high goals, lean schedules of reinforcement) and lenient (low goals, rich schedules of reinforcement). Again, both external and internal dimensions influenced performance. Among these young children, the EM subjects actually worked harder and longer than did the IM subjects, supporting the earlier inference that intrinsic motivational orientation is an increasing function of chronological and mental age. Even so, differential performance in the directions expected of adults had begun to appear at 4 years of age. In the lenient demand condition, i.e., the one requiring more self regulation and providing less external support, the IM subjects set higher goals and chose a higher performance standard than was modeled for them by the experimenter. Figure 8 shows both the higher performance level in general of the EM children and the interaction of motivational orientation with task demand condition: the IM children chose a higher performance standard than did the EM children under a lenient demand condition, while the EM children chose a slightly higher performance standard than did the IM children under the stringent demand condition. This demonstrates that, even at this early age, children who have relatively high intrinsic motivation scores diverge in their work performance and the work goals they set for themselves from the performance of their EM peers increasingly as the situation requires or permits more and more self regulation. This early appearance of such differences suggests that the developmental roots occur earlier still, as Haywood and Burke (1977) have suggested.

Taken together, these four studies (Haywood & Switzky, 1985; Switzky &

Haywood, 1974, 1985a,b) suggest that individual differences in motivational orientation are associated with important dimensions of self-regulation, incentive selection, goal setting, work performance, and perhaps most important, satisfaction derived from tasks themselves, both in mentally retarded and in normally developing persons ranging from preschool children to adults.

Bandura's (1977, 1978) model of the self system emphasizes the principle of reciprocal determinism, i.e., a continuous reciprocal interaction among the elements of behavior, internal cognitive processes that can affect perceptions and actions, and the external environment. What we have attempted to do is to specify one of the important "internal cognitive processes" in this formula, i.e., motivational orientation. [While it might seem strange to refer to motivation as a "cognitive process," Haywood and Burke (1977) have discussed the development of individual differences in intrinsic motivation as "a motivational theory of cognition."]

IV. RELATED WORK BY OTHERS

Our conception of motivational orientation as a primary motivational influence on performance in both retarded and nonretarded persons appears to be related to several other current positions relating motivation and performance.

The work that most closely parallels our own is that of Zigler and his colleagues (Zigler & Balla, 1981, 1982), who have conceptualized the performance problems of retarded persons as being due in part to deficient "effectance motivation" (White, 1959) and lack of concern for the intrinsic motivation that inheres in being correct regardless of whether or not an external agent dispenses the reinforcer. Zigler has proposed that the socially depriving life histories of psychosocially retarded children, as well as their cognitive deficiencies and related failure experiences, lead to attenuation of effectance motivation with a concomitant increase in extrinsically motivated behavior and "outerdirectedness." Harter and Zigler (1974) constructed measures of several aspects of effectance motivation including variation seeking, curiosity, mastery for the sake of competence, and preference for challenging tasks. Intellectually average children, noninstitutionalized retarded children, and institutionalized retarded children, all of comparable mental age, were tested. On all components of their effectance motivation measures, the intellectually average children showed more effectance motivation than did the retarded children. Institutionalized retarded children displayed less curiosity than did noninstitutionalized retarded children. Retarded persons appear to be less characterized by intrinsic effectance motives than are children of average intelligence. Other personality variables that have been studied by Zigler and his colleagues (Zigler & Balla, 1982) have included motivation for adult attention and support (i.e., social dependency), wariness of strangers, and expectancy of success. These personality variables have also been used to assess the effectiveness of living settings for mentally retarded persons (Alexander, Huganir, & Zigler, 1985; Zigler, Balla, & Styfco, 1984). Wariness was found to increase with length of institutionalization in the large central institutions, but to decrease in smaller, less institutional settings. In addition, over the 2-year period of the study, expectancy of success of retarded persons from highly deprived backgrounds remain low, while it increased for retarded persons from less socially deprived preinstitutional backgrounds. Personality and motivational variables appear to be quite sensitive to environmental history variables.

Both our own work and that of the Zigler group have shown that internal motivational and personality characteristics as well as cognitive factors can interact with the external demand characteristics of the environment either to compensate for the inadequate learning abilities of psychosocially retarded persons or to intensify their learning deficits.

Harter (1981a,b, 1982a) has recently developed a program of developmental research in which White's (1959) notions of effectance and mastery motivation have been refined, detailed, and operationalized. In White's general model, effectance motivation is associated with such behavior as exploration, curiosity, mastery, play, and one's general attempts to deal competently with the environment. Effectance motivation impels the person toward competent performance, which is satisfied by feelings of efficacy and inherent pleasure.

Harter (1978, 1983) has presented a general framework as a model of effectance motivation that could have implications for the development of extrinsic and intrinsic motivational orientations in mentally retarded persons. According to her concepts, the developmental pathways that lead to an intrinsic orientation consist of positive reinforcement or approval by socialization agents for independent mastery attempts early in children's development. Further, socialization agents may model this approval and not reinforce children for dependency on adults. As a result, children internalize two critical systems: (1) a self-reward system, and (2) a system of standard or mastery goals that diminishes the children's dependency on external social reinforcement. This leads to feelings of competence and feelings of being in control of one's success and failure and increases children's effectance motivation and intrinsic motivation. This increased sense of intrinsic pleasure enhances one's motivation to engage in subsequent mastery behavior. Thus, children's social environments support their inherent need for mastery over the world with the result that their behavior and incentive systems may be characterized as intrinsically motivated.

The developmental pathways that lead to an extrinsic orientation consists of negative outcomes such as lack of reward for or disapproval of independent mastery attempts, modeling of such disapproval, as well as reinforcement for dependency for adults. Children in these circumstances increasingly manifest strong needs for external approval and dependence on externally defined behavioral goals. This leads to feelings of low perceived competence and perceptions that external agents and events are controlling what is happening. These feelings of not being in control of one's successes and failures lead to feelings of anxiety in mastery situations and attenuate the motivation to be engaged in mastery behavior. Thus, such a child's effectance motivation is blocked and reduced, resulting in an extrinsic motivational orientation. Children who have experienced early failure and disapproval by socialization agents become children whose behavior is extrinsically motivated. This latter pattern may be especially characteristic of retarded and otherwise behaviorally incompetent children (e.g., those who are learning disabled or who have sensory handicaps), leading them to display even greater behavioral deficits than would have been predicted on the basis of their initial incompetence: i.e., the MA deficit. This analysis is remarkably similar to that presented by Haywood and Burke (1977) and to the MA-deficit notions discussed by Haywood, Meyers, and Switzky (1982), as well as to ideas discussed by Zigler (1973).

Harter (1983) has developed several self-report instruments to measure components of her model of effectance motivation. The Scale of Intrinsic Versus Extrinsic Orientation in the Classroom (Harter, 1981b) is intended to measure motivational orientation in the classroom in nonretarded children in grades 2–9. The focus of this instrument is on the question as to what extent children's motivation for classroom learning is determined by their intrinsic interest in learning and mastery, curiosity, and preference for challenge and to what degree their motivation for classroom learning is determined by a more extrinsic orientation in which teacher approval and grades are the functional incentives, as well as dependency on the teacher for guidance. Factor analysis resulted in two factors: (1) a motivational factor labeled curiosity/interest, and (2) a cognitive–informational factor labeled independent judgment versus reliance on teacher's judgement.

Different developmental trends were shown for the motivation factor and the cognitive–informational factor. On the motivational factor, children began with a high intrinsic score in the third grade and that shifted systematically to a high extrinsic score by ninth grade. This shift toward extrinsic orientation is difficult to interpret. It might reflect an adaptive reaction of students to the teaching styles of teachers in the upper grades who often use reinforcers and feedback in a controlling fashion (Deci, Nezlek, & Scheinman, 1981; Deci, Schwartz, Scheinman, & Ryan, 1981) that would support an extrinsic orientation.

On the cognitive–informational factor, an opposite linear trend was observed. Third graders had high extrinsic scores, representing dependency on the teacher's judgment and external sources of evaluation, whereas ninth-grade children had high intrinsic scores, representing reliance on their own judgment and self evaluation of success and failure. These trends may represent the internalization of mastery goals of the classroom as well as its performance criteria and the children's knowledge of the rules of the school. The fact that the two factors do not move developmentally in the same direction with respect to motivational orientation is nevertheless puzzling.

Silon and Harter (1985) have used the Scale of Intrinsic Versus Extrinsic Orientation in the Classroom with a sample of 9- to 12-year-old educable mentally retarded children. Factor analysis of the responses of the subjects revealed a two-factor solution similar to the one observed in the sample of nonretarded children: (1) a motivational factor labeled motivation for hard work, and (2) a cognitive–informational factor labeled autonomous judgment. The most salient motivational theme for the retarded sample was wanting to do either difficult or easy school work rather than a more global intrinsic or extrinsic orientation. The retarded children's concern seemed to be more on what one wants to do in the class (hard versus easy work) than on the reasons why one performs in the classroom (curiosity).

Although there are differences in what is being measured by this scale with groups of mentally retarded and nonretarded children, retarded children appear considerably more extrinsically oriented than do nonretarded children on mean subscale scores (Harter, Silon, & Pike, 1981), which is quite consistent with our own findings for 20 years.

Another self-report scale is the Perceived Competence Scale for Children (Harter, 1982b). This scale is an attempt to measure domain-specific feelings of competence and has been used with normally developing children in grades 3–9. Four domains of perceived competence were investigated: (1) cognitive competence, with an emphasis on academic performance, (2) social competence, with an emphasis on peer relationships, (3) physical competence, with an emphasis on sports and outdoor games, and (4) general sense of self-worth. Factor analysis supported the a priori four domains of competence.

Silon and Harter (1985) have attempted to use the Perceived Competence Scale for Children with educable mentally retarded children from 9 to 12 years of age. Factor analyses performed on data from this sample revealed a two-factor solution very similar to the one that had been found by Harter and Pike (1984) in nonretarded children from 4 to 7 years of age. The first factor was labeled general competence and was composed of the cognitive competence and physical competence subscales. The second factor was labeled popularity and was composed of items from the social competence subscale. No general self-worth factor emerged. Mildly retarded children with mental ages less than 8 years appear not to make distinctions about specific competence domains, but rather simply make judgments about one's competence at activities in general, judging people to be competent or not competent, in the manner of younger nonretarded children.

Previous research by Harter and Pike (1984) has shown that self perceptions change developmentally. Children below the age of 8 years do not make judge-ments concerning their worth as persons. They have not yet developed the concept of the self as a global entity that can be evaluated in terms of general worth—or are not yet able to communicate that judgement.

The relevance of the work of Harter and colleagues to our understanding of personality and motivational variables in retarded persons can be summarized as follows. (1) They have presented a general framework and model of development of effectance motivation, as well as intrinsic and extrinsic motivational orientation, which they have attempted to operationalize and measure. (2) They have shown that self-structures change developmentally and are less differential at lower cognitive–developmental levels, specifically at mental ages less than 8 years. Harter's work supports our own conclusion that mentally retarded persons are considerably less intrinsically oriented than are nonretarded persons of the same chronological age. Her work illustrates as well that the self-system conceptions of younger as well as retarded persons may be less domain specific than that of older nonretarded persons and may be applicable to a greater variety of situations and settings supporting in part our more "trait-like" conceptions of motivational orientation. In essence, here is research generated from a rather different conceptual perspective, done independently (indeed, the Harter group seem to be unaware of the Haywood–Switzky work!), that has led to quite similar developmental conclusions to the extent that similar dependent variables have been studied.

V. SUMMARY

Within the context of the history of research on personality and motivational aspects of mental retardation, we have presented an account of one program of research on motivational orientation as a personality trait and have related that to another program of research on similar variables (i.e., the groups of Zigler and colleagues and of Harter) and to a conceptual system regarding the self-system (i.e., the conceptual system of Bandura). Individual differences in motivational orientation have been shown to be reliably measurable down to MA 3 years, to appear in mentally retarded and nonretarded persons, to be correlated with chronological age, mental age, social class, and IQ, and to be associated with effectiveness of laboratory learning and levels of school achievement. There are strong indications that such individual differences are also associated with mental health, work satisfaction, and social adjustment. Behavioral effectiveness is achieved most readily when incentives are matched to individual differences in motivational orientation. Relatively intrinsically motivated persons work harder and longer, choose higher performance goals, and set leaner schedules of reinforcement for themselves than do relatively extrinsically motivated persons.

Retarded persons who are relatively more intrinsically motivated are capable of more self-regulating behavior and may be able to function more effectively in independent living situations than will extrinsically motivated persons of comparable age, sex, and IQ. There are suggestions that motivational orientation may be modifiable with relatively intense, prolonged, and appropriate treatment.

REFERENCES

Alexander, K., Huganir, L. S., & Zigler, E. (1985). Effects of different living settings on the performance of mentally retarded individuals. *American Journal of Mental Deficiency,* **90,** 9–17.

Amsel, A. (1958). The role of frustrative nonreward in continuous reward situations. *Psychological Bulletin,* 55, 102–119.

Amsel, A. (1962). Frustrative nonreward in partial reinforcement and discrimination learning. *Psychological Review,* **69,** 306–328.

Angelino, H., & Shedd, C. L. (1956). A study of the reactions to "frustration" of a group of mentally retarded children as measured by the Rosenzweig Picture Frustration Study. *Psychological Newsletter,* **8,** 49–54.

Bandura, A. (1977). *Social learning theory.* Englewood Cliffs, NJ: Prentice-Hall.

Bandura, A. (1978). The self-system in reciprocal determinism. *American Psychologist,* **33,** 344–358.

Bandura, A., & Perloff, B. (1967). Relative efficacy of self-monitored and externally imposed reinforcement systems. *Journal of Personality and Social Psychology,* **7,** 111–116.

Beharav, Y. (1978). *The impact of cognitive intervention on locus of control.* Unpublished master's thesis, Bowie State College, Bowie, Maryland.

Blue, C. M. (1963). Performance of normal and retarded subjects on a modified paired associates task. *American Journal of Mental Deficiency,* **68,** 228–234.

Brown, J. S. (1942). The generalization of approach responses as a function of stimulus intensity and strength of motivation. *Journal of Comparative and Physiological Psychology,* **33,** 209–226.

Brown, J. S. (1948). Gradients of approach and avoidance responses and their relation to levels of motivation. *Journal of Comparative and Physiological Psychology,* **41,** 450–465.

Butterfield, E., & Weaver, S. J. (1969). *Personality correlates of academic achievement and laboratory learning in elementary school pupils* [Final Report, Project F126, Grant OEG-6-9-008126-0050, 057]. Kansas City: University of Kansas Medical Center.

Call, R. J. (1968). *Motivation-hygiene orientation as a function of socioeconomic status, grade, race and sex.* Unpublished master's thesis, Tennessee State University, Nashville.

Cromwell, R. L. (1963). A social learning approach to mental retardation. In N. R. Ellis (Ed.), *Handbook of mental deficiency.* New York: McGraw-Hill.

Deci, E. L. (1971). Effects of externally mediated rewards on intrinsic motivation. *Journal of Personality and Social Psychology,* **18,** 105–118.

Deci, E. L. (1972). Intrinsic motivation, extrinsic reinforcement and inequity. *Journal of Personality and Social Psychology,* **22,** 113–120.

Deci, E. L. (1975). *Intrinsic motivation.* New York: Plenum.

Deci, E. L., Nezlek, J., & Scheinman, L. (1981). Characteristics of the rewarder and intrinsic motivation of the rewardee. *Journal of Personality and Social Psychology,* **40,** 1–10.

Deci, E. L., Schwartz, A. J., Scheinman, L., & Ryan, R. M. (1981). An instrument to assess adults' orientations toward control versus autonomy with children. *Journal of Educational Psychology*, **73**, 642–650.

Dobbs, V. (1967). *Motivational orientation and programmed instruction achievement gains of educable mentally retarded adolescents.* Unpublished doctoral dissertation, George Peabody College, Nashville, TN.

Dollard, J., Doob, L. W., Miller, N. E., Mowrer, O. H., & Sears, R. R. (1939). *Frustration and aggression.* New Haven, CT: Yale University Press.

Edgerton, R. B. (1967). *The cloak of competence.* Berkeley: University of California Press.

Edgerton, R. B., & Bercovici, S. (1976). The cloak of competence: Years later. *American Journal of Mental Deficiency*, **80**, 485–497.

Edgerton, R. B., Bollinger, M., & Herr, B. (1984). The cloak of competence: After two decades. *American Journal of Mental Deficiency*, **88**, 345–351.

Endler, N. S., Hunt, J. McV., & Rosenstein, A. J. (1962). An S-R inventory of anxiousness. *Psychological Monographs*, **76**, No. 17, 1–33.

Feuerstein, R., Rand, Y., & Hoffman, M. B. (1979). *Dynamic assessment of retarded performers: The Learning Potential Assessment Device.* Baltimore: University Park Press.

Feuerstein, R., Rand, Y., Hoffman, M. B., & Miller, R. (1980). *Instrumental enrichment: An intervention program for cognitive modifiability.* Baltimore: University Park Press.

Gewirtz, J., & Baer, D. (1958a). The effect of a brief social deprivation on behaviors for a social reinforcer. *Journal of Abnormal and Social Psychology*, **56**, 49–56.

Gewirtz, J., & Baer, D. (1958b). Deprivation and satiation of social reinforcers as drive conditions. *Journal of Abnormal and Social Psychology*, **57**, 165–172.

Girardeau, F. L. (1959). The formation of discrimination learning sets in mongoloid and normal children. *Journal of Comparative and Physiological Psychology*, **52**, 566–570.

Goldstein, K. (1943). Concerning rigidity. *Character and Personality*, **11**, 209–226.

Hamlin, R. M., & Nemo, R. S. (1962). Self-actualization in choice scores of improved schizophrenics. *Journal of Clinical Psychology*, **18**, 51–54.

Harter, S. (1978). Effectance motivation reconsidered: Toward a developmental model. *Human Development*, **6**, 34–64.

Harter, S. (1981a). A model of intrinsic motivation in children. In W. A. Collins (Ed.), *Minnesota Symposium on Child Psychology* (Vol. 14). Hillsdale, NJ: Erlbaum.

Harter, S. (1981b). A new self-report scale of intrinsic versus extrinsic orientation in the classroom: Motivational and informational components. *Developmental Psychology*, **17**, 300–312.

Harter, S. (1982a). A developmental perspective on some parameters of self regulation in children. In P. Karoly & F. Kanfer (Eds.), *Self management and behavior change: From theory to practice* (pp. 165–204). Elmsford, NY: Pergamon.

Harter, S. (1982b). The Perceived Competence Scale for Children. *Child Development*, **53**, 87–97.

Harter, S. (1983). Developmental perspectives on the self-system. In E. M. Hetherington (Ed.), *Handbook of child psychology: Socialization, personality and social development* (Vol. 4, pp. 278–386). New York: Wiley.

Harter, S., & Pike, R. (1984). The pictorial scale of perceived competence and social acceptance for young children. *Child Development*, **55**, 1969–1982.

Harter, S., Silon, E., & Pike, R. G. (1981). *Perceived competence, intrinsic versus extrinsic orientation, and anxiety in the educable mentally retarded: A comparison of mainstreaming and self-contained classrooms.* Unpublished manuscript, University of Denver.

Harter, S., & Zigler, E. (1974). The assessment of effectance motivation in normal and retarded children. *Development Psychology*, **10**, 169–180.

Haywood, H. C. (1964, May). *A psychodynamic model with relevance to mental retardation.* Paper presented at the meeting of the American Association on Mental Deficiency, Kansas City, MO.

Haywood, H. C. (1966). *Report of the fourth OAMR visiting professor in mental retardation.* Toronto: Ontario Association for the Mentally Retarded.

Haywood, H. C. (1968a). Motivational orientation of overachieving and underachieving elementary school children. *American Journal of Mental Deficiency, 72,* 662–667.

Haywood, H. C. (1968b). Psychometric motivation and the efficiency of learning and performance in the mentally retarded. In B. W. Richards (Ed.), *Proceedings of the First Congress of the International Association for the Scientific Study of Mental Deficiency* (pp. 276–283). Reigate, England: Michael Jackson.

Haywood, H. C. (1971). Individual differences in motivational orientation: A trait approach. In H. I. Day, D. E. Berlyne, & D. E. Hunt (Eds.), *Intrinsic motivation: A new direction in education.* Toronto: Holt, Rinehart & Winston.

Haywood, H. C. (1980). Motivational influences on learning and performance in disadvantaged youth. In S. Adiel, H. Shalom, & M. Arieli (Eds.), *Fostering deprived youth and residential education* (pp. 69–80). Tel Aviv: Mabat.

Haywood, H. C. (1981). Reducing social vulnerability is the challenge of the eighties (AAMD Presidential Address). *Mental Retardation, 19,* 190–195.

Haywood, H. C., Arbitman-Smith, R., Bransford, J. D., Delclos, V. R., Towery, J., Hannel, M. V., & Hannel, L. (1982, August). Cognitive education with adolescents: Evaluation of Instrumental Enrichment. In A. M. Clarke & A. D. B. Clarke (Chairs), *Psychosocial interventions: Possibilities and constraints.* Symposium conducted at the 6th International Congress of the International Association for the Scientific Study of Mental Deficiency, Toronto.

Haywood, H. C., & Burke, W. P. (1977). Development of individual differences in intrinsic motivation. In I. C. Uzgiris & F. Weizmann (Eds.), *The structuring of experience.* New York: Plenum.

Haywood, H. C., & Dobbs, V. (1964). Motivation and anxiety in high school boys. *Journal of Personality, 32,* 371–379.

Haywood, H. C., Meyers, C. E., & Switzky, H. N. (1982). Mental retardation. In M. R. Rosenzweig & L. W. Porter (Eds.), *Annual Review of Psychology* (Vol. 33). Palo Alto, CA: Annual Reviews.

Haywood, H. C., & Newbrough, J. R. (1981). *Living environments for developmentally retarded persons.* Baltimore: University Park Press.

Haywood, H. C., & Paour, J.-L. (1983). *Sur le développement motivationel chez enfants immigrés.* Unpublished research report, Université de Provence.

Haywood, H. C., & Switzky, H. N. (1975). Use of contingent social reinforcement to change the verbal expression of motivation by children of differing motivational orientation. *Perceptual and Motor Skills, 40,* 547–561.

Haywood, H. C., & Switzky, H. N. (1985). Work response of mildly mentally retarded adults to self versus external regulation as a function of motivational orientation. *American Journal of Mental Deficiency, 90,* 151–159.

Haywood, H. C., & Wachs, T. D. (1966). Size discrimination learning as a function of motivation-hygiene orientation in adolescents. *Journal of Educational Psychology, 57,* 279–286.

Haywood, H. C., & Wachs, T. D. (1981). Intelligence, cognition, and individual differences. In M. J. Begab, H. C. Haywood, & H. Garber (Eds.), *Psychosocial influences in retarded performance. Vol. 1: Issues and theories in development.* Baltimore: University Park Press.

Haywood, H. C., & Weaver, S. J. (1967). Differential effects of motivational orientation and incentive conditions on motor performance in institutionalized retardates. *American Journal of Mental Deficiency, 72,* 459–467.

Heber, R. (1964). Personality. In H. A. Stevens & R. Heber (Eds.), *Mental retardation: A review of research* (pp. 143–174). Chicago: University of Chicago Press.

Herzberg, F. (1966). *Work and the nature of man.* Cleveland: World.

Herzberg, F., & Hamlin, R. M. (1961). A motivation-hygiene concept of mental health. *Mental Hygiene, 45,* 394–401.

Herzberg, F., & Hamlin, R. M. (1963). The motivation-hygiene concept and psychotherapy. *Mental Hygiene, 47,* 384–397.

Herzberg, F., Mausner, B., & Synderman, B. B. (1959). *The motivation to work.* New York: Wiley.

Hirsch, E. A. (1959). The adaptive significance of commonly described behavior of the mentally retarded. *American Journal of Mental Deficiency, 63,* 639–646.

Hoffman, J., & Weiner, B. (1978). Effects of attributions for success and failure on the performance of retarded adults. *American Journal of Mental Deficiency, 82,* 449–452.

Horai, J., & Guarnaccia, V. J. (1975). Performance and attributions to ability, effort, task, and luck of retarded adults after success or failure feedback. *American Journal of Mental Deficiency, 79,* 690–694.

Hull, C. L. (1951). *Essentials of behavior.* New York: Appleton-Century-Crofts.

Hunt, J. McV. (1963). Motivation inherent in information processing and action. In O. J. Harvey (Eds.), *Motivation and social interaction: Cognitive determinants.* New York: Ronald.

Jahoda, M. (1958). *Current concepts of mental health.* New York: Basic Books.

Johnson, G. O., & Blake, K. A. (1960). Learning performance of retarded and normal children. *Syracuse University Special Education and Rehabilitation Monographs,* No. 5.

Kahoe, R. D. (1966a). A factor-analytic study of motivation-hygiene variables. *Peabody Papers in Human Development, 4*(3).

Kahoe, R. D. (1966b). Motivation-hygiene aspects of vocational indecision and college achievement. *Personnel Guidance Journal, 44,* 1030–1036.

Kahoe, R. D. (1966c). *Development of an objective factorial motivation-hygiene inventory.* Unpublished doctoral dissertation, George Peabody College, Nashville, TN.

Kounin, J. (1941a). Experimental studies of rigidity: I. The measurement of rigidity in normal and feebleminded persons. *Character and Personality, 9,* 251–273.

Kounin, J. (1941b). Experimental studies of rigidity: II. The explanatory power of the concept of rigidity as applied to feeblemindedness. *Character and Personality, 9,* 273–282.

Kounin, J. (1948). The meaning of rigidity: A reply to Heinz Werner. *Psychological Review, 55,* 157–166.

Kunca, D. F., & Haywood, N. P. (1969). The measurement of motivational orientation in low mental age subjects. *Peabody Papers in Human Development, 7*(Whole No. 2).

Lewin, K. (1935). *A dynamic theory of personality: Selected papers* (A. K. Adams & K. E. Zener, Trans). New York: McGraw-Hill.

Lewin, K. (1936). *A dynamic theory of personality.* New York: McGraw-Hill.

Libb, W. J. (1972). Stimuli previously associated with reinforcement: reinforcing or frustrating to the mentally retarded. *Journal of Experimental Child Psychology, 14,* 1–10.

Lindzey, G., Hall, C. S., & Manoscvitz, M. (1973). *Theories of personality* (2nd ed.). New York: McGraw-Hill.

Lipman, R. S. (1963). Learning: verbal, perceptual–motor, and classical conditioning. In N. R. Ellis (Ed.), *Handbook of mental deficiency.* New York; McGraw-Hill.

Lobb, H., Moffitt, A., & Gamlin, P. (1966). Frustration and adaptation in relation to discrimination learning ability of mentally defective children. *American Journal of Mental Deficiency, 76,* 256–265.

McConnell, T. R. (1965). *Locus of control, examiner presence, and source and type of reinforce-*

ment as factors in visual discrimination learning with mental retardates. Unpublished doctoral dissertation, George Peabody College, Nashville, TN.

Miller, M. B., Haywood, H. C., & Gimon, A. T. (1975). Motivational orientation of Puerto Rican children in Puerto Rico and the U.S. mainland. In G. Marin (Ed.), *Proceedings of the 15th Interamerican Congress of Psychology.* Bogota: Sociedad Interamericana de Psicología.

Miller, N. E. (1944). Experimental studies in conflict. In J. McV. Hunt (Ed.), *Personality and the behavior disorders* (pp. 431–465). New York: Ronald.

Pegg, J. (1970). *The personality integration of early adolescents.* Unpublished doctoral dissertation, George Peabody College, Nashville, TN.

Portnoy, B., & Stacey, C. L. (1954). A comparative study of Negro and white subnormals on the children's form of the Rozenzweig Picture Frustration Test. *American Journal of Mental Deficiency,* **59,** 272–278.

Reuveni, S. (1975). *The impact of background traits, motivational orientation, and vocational aspiration on rating the status of vocations in a group of adolescents.* Unpublished master's thesis, Bar-Ilan University, Ramat-Gan, Israel.

Ringness, T. A. (1961). Self-concept of children of low, average, and high intelligence. *American Journal of Mental Deficiency,* **65,** 453–462.

Rogers, C. (1947). Some observations on the organization of personality. *American Psychologist,* **2,** 358–368.

Rosenzweig, S. (1945). The picture-association method and its application in a study of reactions to frustration. *Journal of Personality,* **15,** 3–23.

Rotter, J. (1954). *Social learning and clinical psychology.* New York: Prentice-Hall.

Ryan, T. J., & Watson, P. (1968). Frustrative nonreward theory applied to children's behavior. *Psychological Bulletin,* **69,** 111–125.

Seeman, J. (1983). *Personality integration: studies and reflections.* New York: Human Sciences Press.

Silon, E. L., & Harter, S.(1985). Assessment of perceived competence, motivational orientation, and anxiety in segregated and mainstreamed educable mentally retarded children. *Journal of Educational Psychology,* **77,** 217–230.

Skinner, B. F. (1953). *Science and human behavior.* New York: Macmillan.

Snygg, D., & Combs, A. V. (1949). *Individual behavior: A new frame of reference for psychology.* New York: Harper.

Spradlin, J. E. (1962). Effects of reinforcement schedules on extinction in severely retarded children. *American Journal of Mental Deficiency,* **66,** 634–640.

Stevenson, H. W. (1961). Social reinforcement with children as a function of CA, sex of experimenter, and sex of subject. *Journal of Abnormal and Social Psychology,* **63,** 147–154.

Stevenson, H. W., & Zigler, E. (1957). Discrimination learning and rigidity in normal and feebleminded individuals. *Journal of Personality,* **25,** 699–711.

Stevenson, H. W., & Zigler, E. (1958). Probability learning in children. *Journal of Experimental Psychology,* **56,** 185–192.

Switzky, H. N., & Haywood, H. C. (1974). Motivational orientation and the relative efficacy of self-monitored and externally imposed reinforcement schedules. *Journal of Personality and Social Psychology,* **30,** 360–366.

Switzky, H. N., & Haywood, H. C. (1984). A biosocial ecological perspective on mental retardation. In N. S. Endler & J. McV. Hunt (Eds.), *Personality and the behavioral disorders* (2nd ed., Vol. 2). New York: Wiley.

Switzky, H. N., & Haywood, H. C. (1985a, March). *Self-reinforcement schedules in the mildly mentally retarded: Effects of motivational orientation and instructional demands.* Presented at the eighteenth annual Gatlinburg Conference on Research and Theory in Mental Retardation and Developmental Disabilities, Gatlinburg, TN.

Switzky, H. N., & Haywood, H. C. (1985b). *Self-reinforcement schedules in young children: Effects of motivational orientation and instructional demands.* Unpublished manuscript, Northern Illinois University, De Kalb.

Switzky, H. N., Haywood, H. C., & Isett, R. (1974). Exploration, curiosity, and play in young children: Effects of stimulus complexity. *Developmental Psychology, 10,* 321–329.

Switzky, H. N., Ludwig, L., & Haywood, H. C. (1979). Exploration and play in retarded and nonretarded preschool children: Effects of object complexity and age. *American Journal of Mental Deficiency, 86,* 637–646.

Switzky, H. N., & Rotatori, A. F. (1981). Assessment of perceptual cognitive functioning in nonverbal severely and profoundly handicapped children. *Early Child Development and Care, 7,* 29–44.

Tahia, R. (1977). *Modifiability of bedouin children.* Unpublished manuscript, School of Education, Bar-Ilan University, Ramat-Gan, Israel.

Taylor, J. (1951). The relationship of anxiety to the conditioned eyelid response. *Journal of Experimental Psychology, 41,* 81–92.

Thorndike, E. L. (1932). *The fundamentals of learning.* New York: Teachers College Press.

Tzuriel, D., & Haywood, H. C. (1984). Exploratory behavior as a function of motivational orientations and task conditions. *Personality and Indivudal Differences, 5,* 67–76.

Viney, L. L., Clarke, A. M., & Lord, J. (1973). Resistance to extinction and frustration in retarded and nonretarded children. *American Journal of Mental Deficiency, 78,* 308–315.

Wachs, T. D. (1968). *Free-recall learning in children as a function of directional motivation orientation, intelligence, and chronological age.* Unpublished doctoral dissertation, George Peabody College, Nashville, TN.

Weiner, B. (1974). Achievement motivation as conceptualized by an attribution theorist. In B. Weiner (Ed.), *Achievement motivation and attribution theory.* Morristown, NJ: General Learning Press.

Weiner, B. (1976). An attributional model for educational psychology. In L. Schulman (Ed.), *Review of research in education* (Vol. 4). Itasca, IL: Peacock.

Weiner, B., Frieze, I., Kukla, A., Reed, S., Rest, S., & Rosenbaum, R. N. (1972). Perceiving the causes of success and failure. In E. E. Jones, D. E. Kanouse, H. H. Kelley, R. E. Nisbett, S. Valins, & B. Weiner (Eds.), *Attribution: Perceiving the causes of behavior.* Morristown, NJ: General Learning Press.

Weiner, B., & Sierad, J. (1975). Misattribution for failure and the enhancement of achievement strivings. *Journal of Personality and Social Psychology, 31,* 415–421.

White, R. W. (1959). Motivation reconsidered: The concept of competence. *Psychological Review, 66,* 297–333.

Woodworth, R. S. (1918). *Dynamic psychology.* New York: Columbia University Press.

Wooldridge, R. (1966). *Motivation-hygiene orientation and school achievement in mentally subnormal children.* Unpublished EdS Study, George Peabody College, Nashville, TN.

Zigler, E. (1961). Social deprivation and rigidity in the performance of feebleminded children. *Journal of Abnormal and Social Psychology, 92,* 413–421.

Zigler, E. (1962). Rigidity in the feebleminded. In E. P. Trapp & P. Himelstein (Eds.), *Readings on the exceptional child.* New York: Appleton-Century-Crofts.

Zigler, E. (1966). Research on personality structure in the retardate. In N. R. Ellis (Ed.), *International review of research in mental retardation* (Vol. 1, pp. 77–108). New York: Academic Press.

Zigler, E. (1969). Developmental versus difference theories of mental retardation. *American Journal of Mental Deficiency, 73,* 536–556.

Zigler, E. (1973). The retarded child as a whole person. In D. K. Routh (Ed.), *The experimental psychology of mental retardation* (pp. 231–322). Chicago: Aldine.

Zigler, E., & Balla, D. (1981). Issues in personality and motivation in mentally retarded persons. In M. J. Begab, H. C. Haywood, & H. L. Garber (Eds.), *Psychosocial influences in retarded performance: Vol. 1. Issues and theories in development* (pp. 197–218). Baltimore: University Park Press.

Zigler, E., & Balla, D. (Eds.). (1982). *Mental retardation: The developmental-difference controversy.* Hillsdale, NJ: Erlbaum.

Zigler, E., Balla, D., & Styfco, S. (1984). Investigation of the effects of institutionalization on learning and other behaviors. In P. H. Brooks, R. Sperber, & C. McCauley (Eds.), *Learning and cognition in the mentally retarded* (pp. 129–140). Hillsdale, NJ: Erlbaum.

Zigler, E., Hodgden, L., & Stevenson, H. W. (1958). The effect of support and non-support on the performance of normal and feebleminded children. *Journal of Personality, **26,** 106–122.*

The Rehearsal Deficit Hypothesis

NORMAN W. BRAY

SPARKS CENTER FOR DEVELOPMENTAL AND LEARNING DISORDERS
AND
DEPARTMENT OF PSYCHOLOGY
UNIVERSITY OF ALABAMA AT BIRMINGHAM
BIRMINGHAM, ALABAMA 35294

LISA A. TURNER

DEPARTMENT OF PSYCHOLOGY
UNIVERSITY OF NOTRE DAME
NOTRE DAME, INDIANA 46556

I. INTRODUCTION

One of the major contributions of cognitive research in mental retardation has been the identification of strategy deficits and the demonstration that retarded individuals may be trained to use strategies to improve their memory performance. Since the late 1960s, numerous studies have shown that mildly mentally retarded individuals are less likely to use mnemonic strategies than are nonretarded individuals of the same chronological age (see reviews in Belmont & Butterfield, 1977; Borkowski & Cavanaugh, 1979; Bray, 1979; Brown, 1974; Campione, Brown, & Ferrara, 1982; Turnure, 1985). The general finding has been that retarded individuals are less likely than nonretarded individuals to use an intentional strategy for (1) maintaining information for short intervals (rehearsal), (2) organizing items to be remembered, (3) elaborating relations among stimuli to render them more memorable, (4) using imagery in an attempt to recall, or (5) using other types of mnemonic strategies.

Strategy deficits have assumed an important role in the study of cognitive processes in mental redardation because the influence of such deficits may be very general. Failure to use effective mnemonic strategies has been viewed as a

INTERNATIONAL REVIEW OF RESEARCH IN
MENTAL RETARDATION, Vol. 14

failure to solve the "problem of remembering"—organizing behavior in order to cope with limitations of the memory system (Belmont & Mitchell, 1985; Bray, 1985; Spitz & Borys, 1984). As mentioned by Brown (1974):

> By the appropriate exploitation of various strategies we organize and transform the random input of information into manageable information-rich units. . . . It is economical to employ such strategies and plans in order to make the most efficient use of a limited-capacity memory system. [pp. 55–56]

Strategy deficits result in less than optimal use of processing capacity. This view has considerable importance for psychological theories of mental retardation because the consistently ineffective use of processing capacity may contribute to the initial and cumulative development of an inadequate knowledge base.

Strategies also have general theoretical importance because their use requires planning. Planning is seen by several theorists as a central aspect of intelligence (Das, 1984; Spitz & Borys, 1984). For instance, Das (1984) notes that "what qualifies as intelligence may be the ability to plan or structure one's behavior with an end in view. The more efficient and parsimonious the plan is, the more intelligent the resulting behavior" (p. 116). Thus, understanding the extent and nature of deficits in the use of strategies may contribute to an understanding of intelligence in general and mental retardation in particular.

Although strategies derive their importance from their role in coping with limited processing capacity and from their reflection of planfulness, there may be other important deficits in cognition. It is well recognized that structural aspects of the cognitive system may also be deficient (Ellis, Meador, & Bodfish, 1985). These structural deficits are important in part because they may contribute to strategy deficiencies. Further work on structural deficits and their relationship to strategy adoption is necessary. Such relationships, however, are likely to be clearer if based on an understanding of the extant findings on strategy deficiencies in retarded individuals. Thus, the focus of this chapter is on issues related to strategy use.

A. Historical Background

1. DEFINITIONS OF REHEARSAL

The initial study of rehearsal in retarded individuals was influenced greatly by theory and research on memory processes in nonretarded adults (college students). Among the most influential developments was the information processing model of memory described by Atkinson and Shiffrin (1968). In this model, structural features are presumably fixed aspects of the information processing system, and control processes are flexible routines under the volition of the person. In Atkinson and Shiffrin's (1968) terms:

Control processes are selected, constructed, and used at the option of the subject and may vary dramatically from one task to another even though superficially they may appear very similar. The use of a particular control process in a given situation will depend on such factors as the nature of the instructions, the meaningfulness of the material, and the individual subject's history. [p. 190]

Rehearsal was defined as the control process used to maintain information in short-term store. It was recognized that there could be ambiguity in how this maintenance function was executed. Atkinson and Shiffrin (1968) noted: "Indeed, almost any kind of operation on an array of information (such as coding) can be viewed as a form of rehearsal, but this paper reserves the term only for the duration-lengthening process" (p. 111).

Subsequently, some investigators attempted to distinguish two types of rehearsal: maintenance and elaborative rehearsal (Craik & Watkins, 1973). Maintenance rehearsal involves the repetition of to-be-remembered information for short-term recall (e.g., immediate recall of a series of numbers). Elaborative rehearsal includes strategies for categorizing or otherwise grouping to-be-remembered items or using meaningful relationships among items in order to render them more memorable. This type of rehearsal would be useful when the number of to-be-remembered items exceed the capacity of working memory or when the use of previously learned information in long-term memory renders the material meaningful.

In research on strategies used by retarded individuals, two approaches have emerged that differ in their emphasis on maintenance rehearsal and elaborative processes. The studies focusing on maintenance rehearsal have used relatively short sequences of digits, letters, or pictures to be recalled either immediately or after short intervals (Belmont & Butterfield, 1969). Studies on elaboration strategies have typically used lists of paired associates that greatly exceed the capacity of working memory and require the use of elaboration for high performance (Rowher, 1973; Turnure, 1985; Taylor & Turnure, 1979).

This chapter will focus on theory and research most directly related to maintenance rehearsal. In many of the memory tasks reviewed herein it would be possible, of course, to use elaborative strategies, but, in most cases, the tasks seem better suited to the use of maintenance rehearsal.[1] Turnure (1985) provides a current review of elaborative strategies used by retarded individuals.

2. DEFINITIONS OF A REHEARSAL DEFICIT

The study of rehearsal was a new, exciting topic during the late 1960s and early 1970s. Although several investigators suggested that retarded individuals

---

[1]Ellis (1970) and Detterman (1979) defined rehearsal to include both maintenance and elaborative aspects of rehearsal. However, this statement seems to apply to most of the studies reported and reviewed by these authors.

were deficient in their use of strategies, the "rehearsal deficit hypothesis" was not explicitly defined. For instance, Belmont and Butterfield (1969) presented the results of several experiments, and their discussions of these experiments described the range of rehearsal activity that would be expected of retarded individuals. The range was from the failure to use rehearsal to the use of strategies that are "less active" than those used by nonretarded individuals. For instance, in discussing pause-time patterns in a sequential memory task, Belmont and Butterfield (1969) noted: "retardates hesitated less . . . than did the highly intelligent college students. Indeed, it is clear from the low, flat curve . . . that retardates thought hardly at all as they progressed through the lists" (p. 75). While this statement implies a failure to use rehearsal, considering other data they reached the conclusion that, in contrast to the retarded individuals, "more intelligent *S*s employ more active acquisition strategies" (p. 78).

Ellis (1970) noted that "retardates suffer a deficit in rehearsal strategies, a mechanism of central importance in short-term storage" (p. 3). Discussion of the results from specific experiments indicated that retarded individuals would not be expected to use a rehearsal strategy in some situations. For instance, following an experiment showing no primacy effect in the serial position curves of mentally retarded adolescents, Ellis (1970) concluded: "it would appear that the retardate does not rehearse, even under spaced conditions, therefore his memory for items exceeding the initial capacity of [primary memory] is poor" (p. 10).

In other parts of his paper, however, Ellis broadened the range of meaning for a rehearsal deficit to include the use of a strategy, but one that was "inadequate" when compared to the strategies of nonretarded individuals: "It seems clear that retardates and normals differed markedly in [secondary memory]. We believed this to be due to inadequate rehearsal strategies" (p. 18). Thus, a rehearsal deficit might range from the failure to use any strategy to using an inadequate strategy.

A similar range in the definition of a rehearsal deficit can be found in the papers of Brown (1974) and Campione and Brown (1977). Brown (1974) implies that the rehearsal deficit hypothesis refers to the failure to use a rehearsal strategy: "The evidence for a rehearsal deficit in retarded children is quite convincing, although the generality of the deficit may depend on the particular task and situation. . . . However, in general, it appears that retardates fail to attempt active acquisition patterns of rehearsal" (p. 68). Campione and Brown (1977) imply a broader definition of a rehearsal deficit in noting: "The conclusion that retarded adolescents *never* rehearse is obviously incorrect. . . . However, it is clear that retarded adolescents are much less likely to employ an efficient rehearsal strategy than are their equal-CA nonretarded counterparts" (p. 376).

While Belmont and Butterfield (1969), Ellis (1970), and Campione and Brown (1977) established the possibility that mentally retarded individuals may use "less active" or "inadequate" rehearsal strategies or may be "less likely" to use rehearsal, the emphasis in subsequent studies seems to have been on the lack of rehearsal. For instance, in the spate of "production deficiency" studies on rehearsal that followed the early papers, the assumption was made that a "mediating process" (rehearsal) is available but not used. These studies seemed to assume that mentally retarded individuals fail to use rehearsal, and not that they use rehearsal in some less-than-optimal manner. How this emphasis on the lack of rehearsal rather than a range of rehearsal activities evolved requires a closer examination of the production deficiency hypothesis. As noted by Brown (1974):

> A production deficiency is said to be operating when potential mediators are *not produced* and hence do not aid performance. Thus the [production deficient] subject would perform poorly on a memory task requiring rehearsal because he *does not* spontaneously employ the rehearsal strategy, although he can be shown capable of doing so if he were instructed. [p. 62] [italics added]

In this context the production deficiency hypothesis influenced thinking about the use of rehearsal strategies by mentally retarded individuals. Numerous training studies were designed. Brown, Bransford, Ferrara, and Campione (1983) noted:

> Prototypical experiments of this genre consisted of an assessment phase and a training phase. It was readily shown that young or slow [i.e., mentally retarded] children tended *not* to produce mnemonic strategies in the assessment phase but could readily be trained to do so. . . . We would like to stress that this prototypical finding has been replicated many times and is one of the most robust findings in the developmental literature (Belmont & Butterfield, 1977; Brown, 1975, 1978; Flavell, 1970). [p. 87] [italics added]

As has been summarized by several reviewers (Brown *et al.,* 1983; Borkowski & Cavanaugh, 1979), these training studies led to studies of maintenance and generalization of trained strategies. As is well documented for mentally retarded groups, maintenance of strategy training has been relatively easily obtained, but strategy generalization has not (Campione *et al.,* 1982).

It should be noted that the production deficiency hypothesis overlaps but is *not* equivalent to the early positions describing rehearsal deficits in retarded individuals. However, the production deficiency concept, meaning a failure to produce a strategy, is an emphasis that has greatly influenced the subsequent strategy research. For the purpose of this chapter and consistent with the original usage, the "rehearsal deficit hypothesis" will be defined as a range of strategic behavior that extends from the failure to use rehearsal to the use of rehearsal strategies that differ from those used by nonretarded comparison groups.

3. QUANTITATIVE AND QUALITATIVE ASPECTS OF REHEARSAL

Several dimensions of this definition of a rehearsal deficit deserve elaboration. One important aspect is that a "range" of behavior implies a continuum. In this case the continuum begins with a lack of rehearsal and extends to some indefinite amount or type of rehearsal that differs from the strategies used by nonretarded individuals. Thus, the rehearsal deficit hypothesis would have both quantitative and qualitative aspects that differ in varying degrees along a continuum.

To address the quantitative aspects of the continuum, measures of the frequency of repetition would be needed. For instance, rehearsal has been operationally defined as the number of overt verbal repetitions (Fischler, Rundus, & Atkinson, 1970; Ornstein & Naus, 1978) and the number of times each item is viewed in a self-paced task (Turner & Bray, 1985a,b). Moreover, there are other measures that are highly correlated with frequency of repetition (e.g., measures of self-pacing between items in a sequence, Belmont & Butterfield, 1969, 1971; Ellis & Dugas, 1968). An evaluation of the quantitative aspects of the rehearsal deficit hypothesis might indicate that for a given type of rehearsal strategy (e.g., cumulative rehearsal), retarded individuals may use "less active" rehearsal (fewer repetitions) than some reference groups such as nonretarded individuals of the same chronological age.

Qualitative aspects of the rehearsal deficit hypothesis refer to the type of rehearsal strategy used. These types would include cumulative rehearsal (Butterfield & Belmont, 1977), rehearsal of subsets of items (Ornstein & Naus, 1978), repetition of all items in a sequence (Ferguson & Bray, 1976), or other repetition strategies. Although strategy types may differ quantitatively (in the frequency of repetition required in each), Ferguson and Bray (1976) showed that when the frequency of repetition is held constant, the type of repetition still influences recall. The importance of qualitative differences in strategies for the rehearsal deficit hypothesis is that different repetition strategy types represent different organizational schemes.

B. Scope of the Review

The purpose of this chapter is to review the entire range of research on the use of rehearsal strategies by mentally retarded individuals while assessing the quantitative and qualitative aspects of the rehearsal deficit hypothesis. Most of the previous reviews of this literature have been (self admittedly) "selective reviews" (Bray, 1979; Brown, 1974; Campione *et al.*, 1982; Detterman, 1979). None has focused on quanitative and qualitative aspects of the rehearsal deficit hypothesis.

We have attempted to locate every study that has been published using measures bearing on the use of rehearsal by mentally retarded individuals. The only studies omitted were those in which clear conclusions about the use of rehearsal could not be reached because of incomplete statistical reports or because the measures used were nonstandard (e.g., self-report). There may, of course, have been oversights, but an effort was made to be comprehensive. This included a review of all issues of the *American Journal of Mental Deficiency, Child Development, Journal of Experimental Child Psychology, Journal of Experimental Psychology,* and the *International Review of Research in Mental Retardation* from 1969 to 1985, as well as chapters published in books related to this area and our own work.

Although the original descriptions of the rehearsal deficit in retarded individuals indicated a range of rehearsal activity, from a failure to use a strategy to the "less active" use of a strategy, the measures of rehearsal have varied. Some measures allow an assessment of the quantitative and qualitative aspect of a rehearsal strategy and others do not. Also, some studies have included a comparison group allowing an assessment of differences between retarded and non-retarded individuals and others have not.

The results of studies using quantitative measures of repetition will be described along with the qualitative differences (to the extent possible). These will include studies using observational measures of repetition and self-pacing measures correlated with repetition. For each type of measure, studies providing a comparison of rehearsal strategies used by retarded and nonretarded individuals (by inclusion of a comparison group) will be reviewed in chronological order. For a given measure, these studies will be followed by those not including a comparison group, also reviewed in their chronological order. The discussion of studies using measures of repetition will be followed by a review of studies using measures less directly related to repetition. These include primacy effects, the effect of presentation rate, and the effect of filled versus unfilled retention intervals. Finally, we will discuss our conclusions about the issue of strategy adoption by mentally retarded individuals and the implications of our review for the rehearsal deficit hypothesis.

II. THE RESEARCH ON REHEARSAL STRATEGIES

A. Observational Measures of Repetition

Observation of either spontaneous or elicited verbal behavior during the presentation of to-be-remembered items can provide at least three quantitative measures of repetition. The first is the use of lipreading of to-be-remembered words selected to have distinct mouthing patterns (Flavell, Beach, & Chinsky, 1966; Flavell, Friedrichs, & Hoyt, 1970). The second is the use of elicited verbal repetitions during the presentation of the to-be-remembered items. The participant is asked to repeat the items aloud as they are studied (Fischler *et al.*, 1970; Ornstein & Naus, 1978; Rundus, 1971). The third method is to allow the participant to control the exposure sequence and number of re-presentations of to-be-remembered items and to record the number of times each item is repeated (Turner & Bray, 1985a,b).

Although the lipreading technique has not yet been used with mentally retarded groups, it provides an operational definition of rehearsal used with nonretarded groups. Flavell and his associates (Flavell *et al.*, 1966, 1970) showed that, following extensive training in lipreading, spontaneous lip movements can be unobtrusively observed to determine the number of repetitions used by children. Reliability checks indicate that this method can be used with a high degree of agreement among observers.

The use of elicited verbalization during the presentation of to-be-remembered items derives from studies with nonretarded adults (Fischler *et al.*, 1970; Rundus, 1971) and with nonretarded children (Bray, Justice, Ferguson, & Simon, 1977; Ornstein & Naus, 1978; Naus & Ornstein, 1983). The studies with adults showed that the early items in a sequence tend to be repeated more than the middle and late items. This pattern of repetition has contributed to the interpretation of primacy effects as an indicator of rehearsal. The studies of elicited overt repetition in nonretarded children have shown a developmental increase in the sophistication of the repetition strategy. Children in the early school years use simple repetition, repeating only the current item. Older children use repetition strategies that include the current and prior items in the rehearsal set (Bray *et al.*, 1977; Naus & Ornstein, 1983).

Kellas, Ashcraft, and Johnson (1973, Experiment 1) used a similar overt rehearsal procedure with retarded adolescents. Their results were similar to those for young nonretarded participants. Early items were repeated more than late items. The rehearsal set size (the number of different items repeated prior to receiving another item) increased slightly across serial positions (from 1 to 1.7 items), but this difference was not statistically significant.

The method of allowing the participant to control the presentation sequence and the number of re-presentations of the to-be-remembered items provides an additional measure of item repetition. Turner and Bray (1985a) used this measure to test retarded and nonretarded children and adolescents in a recall readiness task similar to that used by Flavell *et al.* (1970). Participants in the any-order condition could view the items as many times as desired in any order. Those in the forward-order condition could view the items as many times as desired, but only in a forward (left-to-right) order. The mean number of repetitions did not differ for the any-order and forward-order conditions for either intelligence group. Overall, however, the nonretarded groups repeated the items more often than the retarded group (means of 5.8 and 3.9, respectively). Further, the types of strategies used by retarded and nonretarded children differed. In the any-order condition, both intelligence groups tended to repeat the entire set in sequence, but the nonretarded children were more likely than the retarded children to repeat the items within a sequence in small groups ("chunking?"). Thus, under these conditions, retarded children used repetition strategies but the strategy types reflected less sophisticated organization schemes than the strategies used by nonretarded children of the same chronological age.

Turner and Bray (1985b) tested retarded children and adolescents on a recall readiness task similar to the any-order condition they had used previously (Turner & Bray, 1985a). Participants were shown supraspan lists of common objects in a self-paced task in which they were allowed to study the items in any order as many times as desired. The average number of repetitions was 3.8, 4.3, and 6.2 for 10-, 12-, and 14-year-old groups, respectively. Although nonretarded comparison groups were not included, these results indicate that under these conditions most retarded children use repetition strategies.

B.   Self-Pacing Measures

Using a procedure adapted from Ellis and Dugas (1968), Belmont and Butterfield (1969) suggested that participants be allowed to pace themselves through a list of to-be-recalled items and that pause times between items be recorded. Also in a self-paced task, Kellas et al. (1973) used the exposure duration of each item as a measure of study time. If pause-time or study-time patterns across successive items have a positive slope, it is inferred that participants are repeating previous items. If the times are equal and brief throughout the sequence, producing a flat pattern, it is inferred that the participants are not repeating previous items. Belmont and Butterfield (1969) reported four sources of evidence supporting the reliability and validity of the pause-time measure: (1) patterns often differed between individuals but were usually consistent within individuals; (2) patterns corroborated college students' verbal report of strategy adoption; (3) patterns were sensitive to strategy changes induced by either instruction or repetition of well-learned lists; and (4) patterns were related to recall accuracy. Other investigators have shown that pause time increases as the number of repetitions (overt or covert) increases (Bray, Goodman, & Justice, 1982) and that study-time patterns are flat across serial positions when simple labeling is used (Bray et al., 1977).

Belmont and Butterfield (1971) used pause time as a measure comparing nonretarded and retarded adolescents on a self-paced position probe task. In this study each trial consisted of a six-letter list in which the individual viewed one letter at a time at his/her own pace. After seeing the sixth letter, the participant exposed the probe letter and attempted to indicate where in the list it had occurred. The nonretarded participants increased their pause times between successive items. There was a strong primacy effect in recall accuracy. These results were taken as evidence for the use of a cumulative rehearsal strategy. In contrast, a relatively flat pause-time pattern and no primacy effect in recall accuracy was found for the retarded individuals. Apparently, under these conditions retarded individuals did nothing more than label the to-be-remembered items.

Butterfield and Belmont (1977) recorded pause time in a self-paced circular recall task for mentally retarded and nonretarded adolescents. This task required that recency items be recalled first, followed by primacy times (e.g., serial positions 4, 5, 6, then 1, 2, 3). For nonretarded adolescents, there was a long pause between items 3 and 4, followed by short pauses to the end of the sequence. Subjects later reported that they repeated the first three items during the long pause and they quickly named the last few items. For retarded subjects, however, pause-time patterns were flat.

Two additional studies found flat pause-time patterns for retarded groups but did not include nonretarded comparison groups. Butterfield, Wambold, and Belmont (1973) tested retarded adolescents with the task used by Butterfield and Belmont (1977). Bray *et al.* (1982) recorded pause times for retarded adolescents in a selective remembering task using pictures of common objects. The pause-time patterns for untrained groups of retarded adolescents in both studies were consistently flat.

The results from these pause-time studies indicate that, at most, simple labeling was used by retarded groups. On the same tasks, nonretarded comparison groups usually have pause-time patterns that increase or have peaks optimally placed within the sequence. These patterns are related to repetition of the to-be-remembered items. Thus, these studies indicate that retarded individuals apparently failed to use rehearsal under these conditions.

There are, however, several studies using pause-time and study-time measures that have found evidence for some spontaneous use of rehearsal by the retarded individuals. Belmont, Ferretti, and Mitchell (1982) recorded pause-time patterns of mentally retarded adolescents given a circular recall task similar to that used by Butterfield and Belmont (1977) and Butterfield *et al.* (1973). In this experiment, however, considerable pretraining and practice on the task (but no strategy instruction) was given. Pause-time patterns were compared to an ''ideal pattern'' defined as the patterns employed by nonretarded adults. The degree of similarity between the pause-time patterns of the retarded participants and the ''ideal pattern'' was signficantly correlated with recall. Although the proportion of retarded adolescents showing a pattern similar to the ideal was not reported, these results indicate that some retarded adolescents use rehearsal strategies similar to those used by nonretarded comparison groups.

Turner and Bray (1985a) tested retarded and nonretarded children and adolescents on either a standard sequential memory task or a recall readiness task. Although the study-time patterns indicated less rehearsal in the retarded groups, both intelligence groups were more likely to rehearse in the recall readiness task than in the sequential memory task. However, the study-time patterns of the retarded children did not seem to be well adapted to the task demands, especially in the sequential memory task.

Several other studies have found evidence for increases in study time across serial positions for retarded individuals but have not included a nonretarded comparison group. Kellas *et al.* (1973, Experiment 1) examined study-time patterns of retarded adolescents in either a free or serial recall task. Stimuli were pictures of nine easily labeled objects. Twenty percent of the participants had increasing study-time patterns.

Bray, Turner, and Hersh (1985) recorded pause times in a self-paced selective remembering task similar to that used by Bray *et al.* (1982). The subjects were 11-, 15-, and 18-year-old retarded students. Although there was considerable variability in the type of pause-time patterns observed, 23% of the patterns indicated the use of rehearsal. In a similar study with nonretarded adolescents, 52% of the participants had pause-time patterns indicating the use of rehearsal (Bray, Hersh, & Turner, 1985). By comparison, the strategies used by retarded adolescents were not as well suited to the task requirements as those used by the nonretarded groups in the latter study.

Turner and Bray (1985b) reported the spontaneous use of rehearsal by 97% of the retarded children and adolescents tested on the recall readiness task. Almost all patterns were characterized by a pause on the final item that was significantly longer than that on other items. Patterns for participants with long (7–8 item) spans occasionally showed long pauses spaced throughout the list, possibly indicating chunking of the items. We concluded that almost all participants rehearsed, and we attributed this to the use of the recall readiness task, which allows considerable variation in study behavior.

These studies show that retarded individuals use rehearsal strategies on several types of tasks, although their strategies are generally not as well adapted to the task requirements as the strategies used by nonretarded comparison groups. In studies that reported individual data, from about 20% to nearly all of the retarded participants used some type of rehearsal strategy. There is considerable variation between studies due to differences in tasks and differences in the dependent measures employed. It appears that mentally retarded individuals are more likely to use a repetition strategy when they are free to study the items in any manner as compared to tasks in which study behavior is relatively constrained (Turner & Bray, 1985a,b).

C. Primacy Effects

One of the most frequently used methods for inferring the use of rehearsal is the presence of a primacy effect in recall accuracy. A primacy effect obtains when recall of the initial items in a sequence is greater than recall of the middle items. The inference of rehearsal is based on the assumption that the initial items have a greater likelihood of being repeated and, therefore, are recalled with higher accuracy than items in the middle of the sequence (Bruce & Papay, 1970; Crowder, 1969; Rundus, 1971).

There are a number of studies that have found no primacy effects in recall accuracy with retarded individuals. Three of these have included a comparison group. In the first, Ellis (1970, Experiment 1) gave retarded adolescents and nonretarded adults a position probe task. Nine digits were presented per trial with one item probed after each trial. The participants then pointed to the spatial location in which the probed item had appeared. There were two sessions with a different inter-item interval used in each (0.5 and 2.0 seconds). There was clear primacy for the nonretarded adults but no primary for the retarded adolescents.

Belmont and Butterfield (1971) tested retarded and nonretarded adolescents on a six-item position probe task. There was no primacy for the retarded group and marked primacy for the nonretarded group. The participants were subsequently either trained to rehearse or prevented from rehearsing. Recall of primacy items increased for retarded individuals trained to rehearse and decreased for non-retarded participants prevented from rehearsing. This supported the conclusion that recall of primacy items was dependent on rehearsal and that the retarded individuals were not spontaneously rehearsing.

Brown, Campione, Bray, and Wilcox (1973) tested retarded and nonretarded adolescents on a keeping-track task similar to the probe task. A set of four to-be-remembered items, one from each of four categories (e.g., clothing, food), was shown, followed by a probe test that required the participant to recall the most recent example of a specific category. Each category contained two, four, or six examples. The most effective strategy for the keeping-track task is to rehearse each set of to-be-remembered items. Recall accuracy for rehearsing participants is not affected by the number of examples of a category. For the nonretarded adolescents, keeping-track accuracy was not influenced by the number of category examples and accuracy was high at all serial positions. Brown *et al.* (1973) found that accuracy for untrained retarded adolescents decreased as the number of examples of a category increased, and there was no primacy in the serial position curves. These data were taken as further evidence for a lack of rehearsal in retarded adolescents.

Two additional studies found no primacy for retarded groups but did not include a comparison group. Ellis (1970, Experiment 3) tested retarded adolescents and adults using a probe task with three to nine digits. Conroy (1978), also using the probe task, tested retarded adolescents using common objects, nonsense figures, and geometric shapes as stimuli. There was no primacy in the recall accuracy of untrained retarded adolescents in either study.

Several experiments have found primacy in the recall accuracy of retarded individuals, and three of these have included a nonretarded comparison group. In the first of these, Ellis and Munger (1966, Experiment 1) tested retarded adolescents and adults and nonretarded preschool children on a position probe task with sequences of eight familiar pictures. The slopes of the primacy portion of the serial position curves were similar.

In a similar study using the position probe task, Ellis (1969) presented nine-digit sequences to nonretarded adolescents and seven-digit sequences to retarded-adolescents and adults. Half of the participants were required to label each stimulus as it was presented. The slopes of the primacy portion of the serial position curves were similar in both intelligence groups. Labeling resulted in a decrease in primacy effects for both, indicating that labeling may have disrupted rehearsal.

Dugas (1975) varied presentation rate in testing nonretarded and retarded adults on a probe task presented at either 1 second per item or a subject-determined pace. There were five and eight items per sequence for the retarded and nonretarded groups, respectively. Nonsense figures were used as stimuli. Primacy was greater in the self-paced condition for both intelligence groups. In both presentation conditions, however, primacy was greater for the nonretarded than for the retarded groups.

Twelve additional studies found primacy for retarded groups, but these studies did not include nonretarded comparison groups. In the first of these, Ellis and Munger (1966, Experiment 2) tested retarded adolescents and adults on a position probe task with eight familiar pictures. On half of the trials the pictures were presented in a left-to-right sequence, and on the other half they were presented in a right-to-left sequence. Marked primacy effects were present in both presentation conditions and there were no significant differences between presentation orders.

Ellis (1970, Experiment 2) used a similar position probe task with retarded adults, presenting nine digits per sequence for 36 trials per session for 12 sessions. Three rates of presentation (0.5, 1.0, and 2.0 seconds) were used. There were primacy effects for all three presentation rates. Primacy effects were present during the first 4-day block of trials, and their magnitude increased thereafter.

Glidden (1972) presented a paired-associates task to retarded adolescents using line drawings as stimuli. Each pair was presented for 2 seconds and one pair was tested by presenting one stimulus and the four response items. Participants pressed a button to indicate their choice. In addition to the typical recency effect, there was also a marked primacy effect.

Bray (1973) conducted three experiments on selective remembering in retarded adolescents. This task was a modified sequential memory task in which the person recalled a picture name in response to a probe light indicating the position of the item to be recalled. In each of the experiments there were primacy effects in the group and individual data.

Kellas *et al.* (1973) presented retarded adolescents pictures of easily labeled objects in either a free or a serial recall task. They found marked primacy effects in the accuracy data.

Detterman (1974, Experiment 1) tested retarded adults in a probe task with nine pictures of common objects per sequence. The stimuli were presented at rates of 2, 4, or 6 seconds per item. There were primacy effects at each presentation rate.

Turnbull (1974) gave retarded children a pretest of four sessions with seven trials each on a seven-item position probe task. The stimuli were drawn from a set of 63 easily identified common objects. Following the pretest there were 14 sessions of 7 trials each. Half of the subjects were given rehearsal training and the other half were not. In a four-session posttest, there were marked primacy effects in both groups, with increases in primacy for both.

Hagen, Streeter, and Raker (1974) tested retarded 9- and 11-year-old children on a position probe task with seven-item sequences of pictures. Half in each age group were required to overtly label each item as it was presented and half were given no special instructions. There were primacy effects for each age and condition. Labeling did not have a systematic effect on the 9-year-old group, but resulted in reduced primacy for the 11-year-olds. This is comparable to the effect a labeling strategy has on 10-year-old nonretarded children (Hagen & Kingsley, 1968). Hagen *et al.* (1974) concluded that the reduction in primacy for the 11-year-old labeling group implied that labeling interfered with spontaneous rehearsal.

Wambold, Jedlinski, and Brown (1976) presented trainable mentally retarded children with a serial ordering task. Participants were required to reproduce the order of two to five pictures of common objects. There were primacy effects in the recall data.

Butterfield and Belmont (1977, Experiment 1) tested 12-year-old retarded children on a self-paced free recall task. The to-be-remembered items were sequences of six letters. A primacy effect in recall accuracy was found.

To summarize the research on primacy, in studies that included a control group, primacy effects were usually not as marked for retarded individuals as they were for nonretarded individuals. However, primacy occurred frequently with retarded individuals.

Many studies that found primacy for retarded individuals were designed to investigate implications of the rehearsal deficit hypothesis for various aspects of memory performance in retarded individuals and, for this purpose, did not require a nonretarded comparison group. Although the degree of primacy obtained in these studies cannot be compared to the primacy that might be obtained with nonretarded comparison groups, the studies do suggest situational variables that may contribute to the use of rehearsal in retarded individuals. Among these would be the use of careful pretraining procedures to assure the comprehension of task demands (Bray, 1973) and a slow presentation rate (Detterman, 1974; Dugas, 1975).

There is also some suggestion that primacy increases with practice for retarded individuals. Two studies found that when the task is held constant from trial to trial and across sessions, there is a tendency for primacy to increase with practice (Ellis, 1970, Experiment 2; Turnbull, 1974). In contrast, when relatively little practice is given on a task (e.g., 18 trials as in Belmont & Butterfield, 1971) it is unlikely that primacy will be observed even though primacy is observed when nonretarded groups are given the same amount of practice. This latter result would suggest that for retarded individuals the amount of experience required in a given situation before use of rehearsal may be greater than for nonretarded individuals.

D. Presentation Rate

Another method used to infer the use of rehearsal is to measure the effect of presentation rate on recall accuracy. Since a decrease in presentation rate allows more time for rehearsal, accuracy should increase if rehearsal is used. If there is no improvement in recall when items are presented at a slower rate, it is inferred that rehearsal was not used.

As mentioned in the section on primacy effects, Ellis (1970, Experiment 1) varied presentation rate in a position probe task given to retarded adolescents and nonretarded adults. The task consisted of remembering nine digits, each present-ed for 0.5 seconds, with an inter-item interval of either 0 or 2 seconds. For the nonretarded group, the 2-second inter-item interval facilitated performance and resulted in substantially higher recall for the primacy items than for the middle positions. The marked primacy for the 2-second inter-item interval was in-terpreted as evidence for the use of rehearsal. In contrast, the performance of a group of retarded adolescents and retarded adults was not affected by rate. At both rates there was recency but no primacy. The lack of an effect due to rate for retarded individuals was replicated in a second study in which retarded adults were given a probe task using presentation rates of 0.5, 1, and 2 seconds (Ellis, 1970, Experiment 2).

Several other studies with retarded groups, however, have found that recall accuracy varies with presentation rate. Of these studies, the only one to include a nonretarded control group was Dugas (1975). As mentioned previously, she tested retarded and nonretarded adults on a probe task with nonsense figures presented at 1 second per item or presented at a subject-determined pace. For both intelligence groups there were primacy effects, and recall accuracy was greater in the subject-paced task.

Three additional studies found that recall accuracy for retarded individuals varies with presentation rate, but these studies did not include nonretarded comparison groups. In the first of these, Haynes (1970) presented familiar words to retarded adolescents at a rate of either 1 or 4 seconds per word. Participants were given repeated trials in which they attempted to recall each word before it was presented. Recall was better at 4 seconds per item than at 1 second per item.

As mentioned in the section on primacy, Detterman (1974, Experiment 1) found primacy for retarded adults at each of three presentation rates. Detterman also found that overall recall accuracy was significantly higher at 6 seconds than at 2 and 4 seconds per item.

Detterman (1974, Experiment 2) provided a replication of these findings. Stimuli were sets of pictures presented at 4, 6, or 8 seconds per item. For retarded adults, recall accuracy was significantly greater with a presentation rate of 8 seconds per item than with 4 or 6 seconds per item.

On speeded tasks, nonretarded individuals may use rehearsal strategies that take advantage of slight differences in presentation rate and retarded individuals may not. The accuracy patterns for retarded individuals may reflect a lack of rehearsal or the use of a type of strategy that does not result in improved levels of recall at relatively fast rates. As the overall pace of the task is slowed, however, the recall accuracy of retarded individuals is likely to indicate the use of rehearsal.

E. Effect of Filled and Unfilled Retention Intervals

An additional method used to infer the use of rehearsal strategies is based on the effect of filled and unfilled retention intervals. It is assumed that an unfilled retention interval allows participants to rehearse items until they must be recalled and that a filled retention interval disrupts rehearsal by requiring participants to perform an unrelated cognitive task.

Anders (1971) tested retarded and nonretarded adults on a probe task with either filled or unfilled intervals of 0, 5, 10, and 20 seconds. The retarded participants counted backward by ones and the nonretarded participants counted backward by threes in the filled interval condition. Stimuli were 8-letter and 12-letter lists for the retarded and nonretarded groups, respectively. The presentation rate was 1 second per item. For both intelligence groups recall accuracy was lower for groups receiving the filled intervals. This result indicates that the interpolated task interfered with rehearsal in both groups. Although the interaction of retention interval and filler was not statistically significant for the retarded group, the decrease in recall across retention intervals in the unfilled condition was most apparent for the recency items. If rehearsal was used, as indicated by the significant main effect of filler activity, it did not appear to be sufficient for high recall levels on the recency items.

Fagan (1968) used filled and unfilled retention intervals in a free recall task with delayed recall. Retarded 12-year-old children and nonretarded 8-year-old children were given sequences of five digits presented aurally at a rate of 2 seconds per item. Recall was required after either 2 or 10 seconds. The 10-second delay was either filled with a humming noise or with color names which participants were required to repeat. Recall accuracy at the 10-second interval was significantly greater in both groups when the delay was filled with noise than when it was filled with color names. Repeating color names may have interfered with rehearsal.

Belmont (1972) tested mildly retarded adolescents and MA-matched nonretarded children in a task requiring memory for a sequence of colored lights. All participants were given 4-, 8-, and 12-second retention intervals either unfilled or filled with the repetition of spoken numbers. Recall was greater in the unfilled condition at each interval and there were no interactions with intelligence. The filler activity may have interfered with rehearsal.

Borys and Spitz (1976) reported the use of rehearsal by moderately and mildly mentally retarded adolescents in a free recall task with delayed recall. Participants were shown slides of easily labeled objects, in sets of 2, 3, 4, or 5 pictures. A study period of 5 seconds was allowed for each picture within a set. Following stimulus presentation, participants had either a filled or an unfilled interval of 0, 18, 36, or 140 seconds. In the filled intervals, slides were presented consisting of 9 to 14 circles that participants were required to count. Each filler slide was exposed for 5 seconds. In the unfilled intervals, individuals simply looked at a blank screen. In the filled-interval condition, immediate recall was signficantly greater than recall at all other intervals. In contrast, delay interval did not have a reliable effect on recall in the unfilled interval condition with 2, 3, and 4 pictures. However, recall declined after 18 seconds with 5 pictures. Also, a comparison of early and late trial blocks indicated proactive interference in the filled interval conditions as measured by recall accuracy and intralist intrusions. There was no indication of proactive interference in the unfilled interval condition. Borys and Spitz (1976) reached the following conclusions:

> When no distracting activity was interposed there was no forgetting for up to 4 pictures relative to the amount of material acquired at 0 sec delay. This suggests that retarded Ss, as do nonretarded Ss, adopt a rehearsal strategy to maintain information in short-term store, thereby resisting not only simple decay but also the effects of proactive interference. With 5 pictures, however, forgetting occurred beyond 18 sec of uninterrupted delay, probably because five objects exceed the rehearsal set size of retarded individuals. [p. 214]

Winters and Semchuk (1982) reported similar findings. They presented three familiar words per trial to moderately and mildly mentally retarded adolescents. Half of the participants named colored lights presented during retention intervals of 0, 30, and 60 seconds. The other participants received an unfilled retention interval. Participants receiving the unfilled retention interval recalled more items than those receiving a filled interval. This indicates that the filler task may have disrupted rehearsal.

Each of the studies varying the type of filler activity during retention intervals have found that overall recall is lower with filled than with unfilled intervals. The finding that recall of recency items tends to decrease across unfilled retention intervals may indicate that, if rehearsal is used, it is not used very effectively. There is some indication that the effectiveness of rehearsal may be limited by rehearsal set size (Borys & Spitz, 1976).

III. CONCLUSIONS AND IMPLICATIONS

There is clear evidence to support the rehearsal deficit hypothesis in mentally retarded individuals. Strategic behavior ranges from a failure to use rehearsal to the use of strategies that differ from those used by nonretarded individuals. The use of rehearsal seems to be a more fragile phenomenon in retarded groups than in comparable nonretarded groups. Both younger retarded and nonretarded individuals are less likely to use a repetition strategy when the task constrains the number of times the items may be viewed before recall, but the effect of this type of limitation is more severe for retarded individuals than nonretarded adolescents (Turner & Bray, 1985a). Similarly, under some conditions study-time patterns similar to those used by nonretarded groups may be found for retarded groups, but only after exquisitely clear task instructions (Belmont *et al.*, 1982). Retarded individuals may show evidence of primacy effects, but in some cases a large number of trials on one task must be given (Turnbull, 1974), whereas primacy is evident in nonretarded groups with relatively few trials (Belmont & Butterfield, 1971). When accuracy on sequences presented at different rates is compared for retarded groups, rate has an effect when relatively slow rates are included (Haynes, 1970), whereas differences due to presentation rate are evident for nonretarded groups even when the rates are relatively fast (Ellis, 1970, Experiment 1). Retarded groups may maintain information during an unfilled retention interval, but their maintenance may not be as effective as in nonretarded groups (Anders, 1971), and it is apparently restricted by a small rehearsal set size (Borys & Spitz, 1976).

This overall picture of fragile strategic abilities is only partially congruous with the production deficiency hypothesis. This hypothesis maintains that individuals fail to use strategic abilities even though they are capable of doing so (Flavell, 1970). This appears to be the case in some situations, but it also seems that retarded individuals will use rehearsal without being trained to do so if the conditions for strategy use are ''supportive.'' Such supportive conditions may include relatively few constraints on study behavior, a careful explanation of the task requirements, extensive practice, and slow presentation with relatively few items. Thus, the overall evidence for the rehearsal deficit hypothesis indicates that retarded individuals will not use rehearsal under some conditions but may use a rehearsal strategy under supportive conditions.

In order to understand the nature of the supportive condition necessary for strategy adoption by retarded individuals, both the quantitative and the qualitative aspects of the rehearsal strategies used by nonretarded and retarded individuals would need to be assessed. The clearest assessments of quantitative aspects of rehearsal strategies have been provided by studies measuring repetition. In the relatively few studies that have used such measures, it appears that when retarded individuals use a repetition strategy they repeat the items fewer times than nonretarded individuals (Kellas *et al.*, 1973; Turner & Bray, 1985a). In studies using measures known to be correlated with use of repetition (e.g., pause time) there is also reason to suspect quantitative differences in the use of repetition by nonretarded and retarded individuals (Belmont & Butterfield, 1971; Turner & Bray, 1985a).

Conclusions about qualitative differences in the strategies used by nonretarded and mentally retarded individuals are also limited. In studies that have used measures of repetition, nonretarded individuals have tended to repeat subsets within a longer sequence, whereas mentally retarded individuals have been most likely to repeat the entire sequence in order (Turner & Bray, 1985a).

Studies using pause time and study time have indicated that nonretarded individuals will use a cumulative rehearsal strategy in a sequential memory task, whereas mentally retarded individuals seemingly label each item only once (Belmont & Butterfield, 1971). In other studies using pause time, nonretarded individuals have used a "cumulative rehearsal fast finish" strategy under some conditions, whereas retarded individuals, again, seemingly merely labeled each item once (Butterfield & Belmont, 1977).

Although there is some evidence for quantitative and qualitative differences in the rehearsal strategies used by nonretarded and mentally retarded individuals, there is much to be learned about the nature of these differences. The differences reflect a deficiency in strategy use, but they also reflect some degree of strategic competence. Elsewhere, strategic competence has been defined as the knowledge that influences strategy adoption (Bray, 1985). As indicated by the studies reviewed, the competence of the mentally retarded seems to be more "fragile" than the competence of nonretarded individuals in the sense that more supportive conditions are required before strategies will be adopted. An understanding of the nature of strategic deficiencies will require a clearer understanding of the nature of this strategic competence. It is to such issues that we now direct our attention.

Nearly all studies reviewed tested either adolescents or young adults and did not include age as a dimension of the study. However, strategic competence changes with age in nonretarded children (Brown *et al.*, 1983), and it is likely to have an identifiable developmental course in retarded individuals. For instance, Bray, Turner, and Hersh (1985) found that the proportion of retarded individuals spontaneously using a rehearsal strategy in a selective remembering task increased from 19 to 31% between the ages of 11 and 18 years, indicating that strategic competence does change with age in mentally retarded individuals. Further, the nature of the selective remembering strategies adopted by 15- and 18-year-old retarded individuals tended to be more sophisticated than the strategies used by the 11-year-old retarded children.

In a similar study with nonretarded children and adolescents, the proportion of individuals using rehearsal strategies increased from 25 to 75% across the same age range (Bray, Hersh, & Turner, 1985). Additionally, differences in recall accuracy between rehearsing and nonrehearsing subgroups were larger for nonretarded children and adolescents than for retarded individuals the same age. In this particular situation, the rate of developmental change and the likelihood of using a strategy both appear to be greater for nonretarded than for retarded children and adolescents. More complete explication of the comparative trends in quantitative and qualitative aspects of strategy adoption would provide a richer understanding of the strategic competence of retarded individuals.

One important aspects of cognition related to strategic competence is comprehension. The use of a strategy such as rehearsal requires that the task be understood to the extent that a strategy can be devised to cope with the problem of remembering. Bray (1979) has shown that, in the context of a selective remembering task, retarded individuals will spontaneously adopt effective strategies, but only when they thoroughly understand the procedures and requirements of the task. When either retarded or nonretarded individuals do not comprehend the task requirements, they do not adopt effective strategies (Bray, Justice, & Simon, 1978).

This finding is not limited to research on selective remembering. Whereas previous studies using a circular recall task had failed to find rehearsal in retarded individuals, Belmont *et al.* (1982) found spontaneous strategy adoption in many retarded adolescents using this task. They attributed this discrepancy in the results to their use of careful pretraining on the task requirements for circular recall in their 1982 study. As with the selective remembering studies, no strategy training was given. Comprehension of the task demands was apparently a necessary and sufficient condition for adoption of a strategy for some retarded individuals. Although task comprehension may not always be a sufficient condition for strategy adoption, it will always be necessary. Thus, in efforts to understand the strategic competence of retarded individuals, we must know more about the role of comprehension in strategy adoption (Bray, 1979, 1985).

Another promising approach to strategic competence is to examine the influence of task context. It has been recognized for some time that young nonretarded children may be more likely to spontaneously use rehearsal when the memory task is placed within a naturalistic context. In a somewhat more laboratory-based series of experiments, Turner and Bray (1985a,b) found that most retarded children and adolescents will use rehearsal when given a task that does not constrain the number of times or the order in which they are allowed to study the items to be recalled. Traditional sequential memory tasks restrict both of these aspects of study behavior. It may be that the removal of these constraints results in a task which is easily placed in a familiar context. This may increase comprehension so as to reveal the necessity for and the possibility of strategy use.

As noted herein and previously (Bray, 1979, 1985; Turner, 1985), the success of strategy training has been dramatic. Retarded individuals can be trained readily to use strategies they do not adopt spontaneously. Considerably less success has been obtained in strategy generalization studies (Campione et al., 1982). One reason for the relatively modest success of the strategy generalization studies may be that the nature of strategic competence has not been considered. This may be due, in part, to the production deficiency hypothesis with its emphasis on the lack of strategy use. Strategy generalization studies may be more successful if the training capitalizes on the person's strategic capabilities, no matter how "fragile."

Finally, because there is considerable evidence that the likelihood of spontaneous strategy adoption varies depending on the type of task used, it becomes important to understand the contribution of the task to strategy adoption. It seems that investigators of rehearsal in retarded individuals began by studying strategic abilities in a very limited task domain, namely sequential memory. However, the findings from this task do not always generalize to other types of memory tasks. This leads to overgeneralization of legitimate conclusions from sequential memory tasks (Brown, 1974). Retarded individuals may be "nonstrategic" in the context of a sequential memory task (though our review indicates that in some cases even this is not true), but many retarded individuals are clearly "strategic" in other situations (Turner & Bray, 1985a,b). Thus, the issue is not to determine whether the person is "strategic" or "nonstrategic," but to understand the nature of the strategic competence of mentally retarded individuals, its developmental course, and its relation to strategic competence in nonretarded individuals.

ACKNOWLEDGMENTS

The preparation of this chapter was supported by Grant HD 15669 from the National Institute of Child Health and Human Development. We are grateful to John M. Belmont, Norman R. Ellis, Elaine M. Justice, and Martin D. Murphy for their many helpful comments on this chapter.

REFERENCES

Anders, T. R. (1971). Short-term memory for serially presented supraspan information in non-retarded and mentally retarded individuals. *American Journal of Mental Deficiency, 75,* 571–578.

Atkinson, R. C., & Shiffrin, R. M. (1968). Human memory: A proposed system and its control processes. In K. W. Spence & J. T. Spence (Eds.), *The psychology of learning and motivation* (Vol. 2, pp. 90–195). New York: Academic Press.

Belmont, J. M. (1972). Relations of age and intelligence to short-term color memory. *Child Development, 43,* 19–29.

Belmont, J. M., & Butterfield, E. C. (1969). The relations of short-term memory to development and intelligence. In L. P. Lipsitt & H. W. Reese (Eds.), *Advances in child development and behavior* (Vol. 4, pp. 30–82). New York: Academic Press.

Belmont, J. M., & Butterfield, E. C. (1971). Learning strategies as determinants of memory deficiencies. *Cognitive Psychology, 2,* 411–420.

Belmont, J. M., & Butterfield, E. C. (1977). The instructional approach to developmental cognitive research. In R. V. Kail & J. W. Hagen (Eds.), *Perspectives on the development of memory and cognition* (pp. 437–481). Hillsdale, NJ: Earlbaum.

Belmont, J. M., Ferretti, R. P., & Mitchell, D. W. (1982). Memorizing: A test of untrained retarded children's problem solving. *American Journal of Mental Deficiency, 87,* 197–210.

Belmont, J. M., & Mitchell, D. W. (1985, March). The general strategies hypothesis as applied to cognitive theory in mental retardation. In N. W. Bray (Chair), *Why are the mentally retarded strategically deficient?* Symposium conducted at the Gatlinburg Conference on Research in Mental Retardation/Developmental Disabilities, Gatlinburg, TN.

Bjork, R. A. (1970). Positive forgetting: The non-interference of items intentionally forgotten. *Journal of Verbal Learning and Verbal Behavior, 9,* 255–268.

Borkowski, J. G., & Cavanaugh, J. C. (1979). Maintenance and generalization of skills and strategies by the retarded. In N. R. Ellis (Ed.), *Handbook of mental deficiency, psychological theory and research* (2nd ed., pp. 569–617). Hillsdale, NJ: Erlbaum.

Borys, S. V., & Spitz, H. H. (1976). Short-term retention in retarded adolescents as a function of load, delay, and interpolated activity. *Journal of Psychology, 94,* 207–216.

Bray, N. W. (1973). Controlled forgetting in the retarded. *Cognitive Psychology, 5,* 288–309.

Bray, N. W. (1979). Strategy production in the retarded. In N. R. Ellis (Ed.), *Handbook of mental deficiency, psychological theory and research* (2nd ed., pp. 699–726). Hillsdale, NJ: Erlbaum.

Bray, N. W. (1985, March). An overview of strategy deficiencies: A case for production anomalies and strategic competence. In N. W. Bray (Chair), *Why are the mentally retarded strategically deficient?* Symposium conducted at the Gatlinburg Conference on Research in Mental Retardation/Developmental Disabilities, Gatlinburg, TN.

Bray, N. W., Goodman, M. A., & Justice, E. M. (1982). Task instructions and strategy transfer in the directed forgetting performance of mentally retarded adolescents. *Intelligence, 6,* 187–200.

Bray, N. W., Hersh, R. E., & Turner, L. A. (1985). Selective remembering during adolescence. *Developmental Psychology, 21,* 290–294.

Bray, N. W., Justice, E. M., Ferguson, R. P., & Simon, D. L. (1977). Developmental changes in the effects of instructions on production deficient children. *Child Development, 48,* 1019–1026.

Bray, N. W., Justice, E. M., & Simon, D. L. (1978). The sufficient conditions for directed forgetting in normal and educable mentally retarded adolescents. *Intelligence, 2,* 153–167.

Bray, N. W., Turner, L. A., & Hersh, R. E. (1985). Developmental progressions and regressions in the selective remembering strategies of EMR individuals. *American Journal of Mental Deficiency, 90,* 198–205.

Brown, A. L. (1974). The role of strategic behavior in retardate memory. In N. R. Ellis (Ed.), *International review of research in mental retardation* (Vol. 7, pp. 55–111). New York: Academic Press.

Brown, A. L. (1975). The development of memory: Knowing, knowing about knowing, and knowing how to know. In H. W. Reese (Ed.), *Advances in child development and behavior* (Vol. 10, pp. 104–152). New York: Academic Press.

Brown, A. L. (1978). Knowing when, where, and how to remember: A problem of metacognition. In R. Glaser (Ed.), *Advances in instructional psychology* (Vol. 1, pp. 77–165). Hillsdale, NJ: Erlbaum.

Brown, A. L., Bransford, J. D., Ferrara, R. A., & Campione, J. C. (1983). Learning, remembering and understanding. In J. H. Falvell & E. M. Markman (Eds.), *Handbook of child psychology* (4th ed., pp. 77–166). New York: Wiley.

Brown, A. L., Campione, J. C., Bray, N. W., & Wilcox, B. L. (1973). Keeping track of changing variables: Effects of rehearsal training and rehearsal prevention in normal and retarded adolescents. *Journal of Experimental Psychology, 101,* 123–131.

Bruce, D., & Papay, J. P. (1970). Primacy effects in single-trial free recall. *Journal of Verbal Learning and Verbal Behavior, 9,* 473–486.

Butterfield, E. C., & Belmont, J. M. (1977). Assessing and improving the executive cognitive functions of mentally retarded people. In I. Bialer & M. Sternlicht (Eds.), *Psychological issues in mental retardation* (pp. 277–318). New York: Psychological Dimensions.

Butterfield, E. C., Wambold, C., & Belmont, J. M. (1973). On the theory and practice of improving short-term memory. *American Journal of Mental Deficiency, 77,* 654–669.

Campione, J., & Brown, A. (1970). Memory and metamemory development in educable retarded children. In R. V. Kail & J. W. Hagen (Eds.), *Perspectives on the development of memory and cognition* (pp. 367–406). Hillsdale, NJ: Erlbaum.

Campione, J. C., Brown, A. L., & Ferrara, R. A. (1982). Mental retardation and intelligence. In R. J. Sternberg (Ed.), *Handbook of human intelligence* (pp. 392–490). London: Cambridge University Press.

Conroy, R. L. (1978). Facilitation of serial recall in retarded children and adolescents: Verbal and kinesthetic strategies. *American Journal of Mental Deficiency, 82,* 410–413.

Craik, F. I. M., & Watkins, M. J. (1973). The role of rehearsal in short-term memory. *Journal of Verbal Learning and Verbal Behavior, 12,* 599–607.

Crowder, R. G. (1969). Behavioral strategies in immediate memory. *Journal of Verbal Learning and Verbal Behavior, 8,* 524–528.

Das, J. P. (1984). Cognitive deficits in mental retardation: A process approach. In P. H. Brooks, R. Sperber, & C. McCauley (Eds.), *Learning and cognition in the mentally retarded* (pp. 115–128). Hillsdale, NJ: Erlbaum.

Detterman, D. K. (1974). Primacy effects in short-term memory with the mentally retarded. *Child Development, 45,* 1077–1082.

Detterman, D. K. (1979). Memory in the mentally retarded. In N. R. Ellis (Ed.), *Handbook of mental deficiency, psychological theory and research* (2nd ed., pp. 727–760). Hillsdale, NJ: Erlbaum.

Dugas, J. (1975). Effects of stimulus familiarity on the rehearsal transfer mechanism in retarded and nonretarded individuals. *American Journal of Mental Deficiency, 80,* 349–356.

Ellis, N. R. (1969). Evidence for two storage processes in short-term memory. *Journal of Experimental Psychology, 80,* 390–391.

Ellis, N. R. (1970). Memory processes in retardates and normals. In N. R. Ellis (Ed.), *International review of research in mental retardation* (Vol. 4, pp. 1–32). New York: Academic Press.

Ellis, N. R., & Dugas, J. (1968). The serial position effect in short-term memory under E- and S-paced conditions. *Psychonomic Science, 12,* 55–56.

Ellis, N. R., Meador, D. M., & Bodfish, J. W. (1985). Differences in intelligence and automatic memory processes. *Intelligence, 9,* 265–273.

Ellis, N. R., & Munger, M. (1966). Short-term memory in normal children and mental retardates. *Psychonomic Science, 6,* 381–382.

Fagan, J. F. (1968). Short-term memory processes in normal and retarded children. *Journal of Experimental Child Psychology, 6,* 279–296.

Ferguson, R. P., & Bray, N. W. (1976). Component processes of an overt rehearsal strategy in young children. *Journal of Experimental Child Psychology, 21,* 490–506.

Fischler, I., Rundus, D., & Atkinson, R. C. (1970). Effects of overt rehearsal processes on free recall. *Psychonomic Science, 19,* 249–250.

Flavell, J. H. (1970). Developmental studies of mediated memory. In H. W. Reese (Ed.), *Advances in child development and behavior* (Vol. 5, pp. 181–211). New York: Academic Press.

Flavell, J. H., Beach, D. R., & Chinsky, J. M. (1966). Spontaneous verbal rehearsal in a memory task as a function of age. *Child Development, 37,* 283–299.

Flavell, J. H., Friedrichs, A. G., & Hoyt, J. D. (1970). Developmental changes in memorization processes. *Cognitive Psychology, 1,* 324–340.

Glidden, L. M. (1972). Meaningfulness, serial position, and retention interval in recognition short-term memory. *Journal of Experimental Child Psychology, 13,* 154–164.

Hagen, J. W., & Kinglsey, P. R. (1968). Labeling effects in short-term memory. *Child Development, 39,* 113–121.

Hagen, J. W., Streeter, L. A., & Raker, R. (1974). Labeling, rehearsal, and short-term memory in retarded children. *Journal of Experimental Child Psychology, 18,* 259–268.

Haynes, J. R. (1970). Effects of white noise and presentation rate on serial learning in mentally retarded individuals. *American Journal of Mental Deficiency, 74,* 574–577.

Kellas, G., Ashcraft, M. H., & Johnson, N. S. (1973). Rehearsal processes in the short-term memory performance of mildly retarded adolescents. *American Journal of Mental Deficiency, 77,* 670–679.

Naus, M. J., & Ornstein, P. A. (1983). Development of memory strategies: Analysis, questions, and issues. In M. T. H. Chi (Ed.), *Trends in memory development research* (pp. 1–30). New York: Karger.

Ornstein, P. A., & Naus, M. J. (1978). Rehearsal processes in children's memory. In P. A. Ornstein (Ed.), *Memory development in children* (pp. 69–99). Hillsdale, NJ: Erlbaum.

Rowher, W. D. (1973). Elaboration and learning in childhood and adolescence. In H. W. Reese (Ed.), *Advances in child development and behavior* (Vol. 8, pp. 2–57). New York: Academic Press.

Rundus, D. (1971). Analysis of rehearsal processes in free recall. *Journal of Experimental Psychology, 89,* 63–77.

Spitz, H. H., & Borys, S. (1984). Depth of search: How far can the retarded search through an internally represented problem space? In P. H. Brooks, R. Sperber, & C. McCauley (Eds.), *Learning and cognition in the mentally retarded* (pp. 333–358). Hillsdale, NJ: Erlbaum.

Taylor, A. M., & Turnure, J. E. (1979). Imagery and verbal elaboration with retarded children: Effects on learning and memory. In N. R. Ellis (Ed.), *Handbook of mental deficiency, psychological theory and research* (2nd ed., pp. 659–697). Hillsdale, NJ: Erlbaum.

Turnbull, A. P. (1974). Teaching retarded persons to rehearse through cumulative overt labeling. *American Journal of Mental Deficiency, 79,* 331–337.

Turner, L. A. (1985, March). Effects of constraint and context on strategy adoption. In N. W. Bray (Chair), *Why are the mentally retarded strategically deficient?* Symposium conducted at the

Gatlinburg Conference on Research in Mental Retardation/Develpomental Disabilities, Gatlinburg, TN.

Turner, L. A., & Bray, N. W. (1985a). *Effects of task constraint on strategy adoption in mentally retarded and nonretarded children and adolescents.* Unpublished manuscript.

Turner, L. A., & Bray, N. W. (1985b). Spontaneous rehearsal in mildly mentally retarded children and adolescents. *American Journal of Mental Deficiency,* **90,** 57–63.

Turnure, J. E. (1985). Communication and cues in the functional cognition of the mentally retarded. In N. R. Ellis & N. W. Bray (Eds.), *International review of research in mental retardation* (Vol. 13, pp. 43–77). New York: Academic Press.

Wambold, C. L., Jedlinski, K., & Brown, L. (1976). Improving the sequential memory performance of trainable mentally retarded youngsters: A learning strategies approach. *Journal of Special Education,* **10,** 41–46.

Winters, J. J., & Semchuk, M. T. (1982). Proactive inhibition by mentally retarded persons: Effects of distractor vocalization. *American Journal of Mental Deficiency,* **87,** 231–233.

Zeaman, D., & House, B. J. (1963). The role of attention in retardate discrimination learning. In N. R. Ellis (Ed.), *Handbook of mental deficiency* (pp. 159–223) New York: McGraw-Hill.

Molar Variability
and the Mentally Retarded

STUART A. SMITH[1]

SELINSGROVE CENTER
SELINSGROVE, PENNSYLVANIA

PAUL S. SIEGEL

DEPARTMENT OF PSYCHOLOGY
UNIVERSITY OF ALABAMA
UNIVERSITY, ALABAMA 35486

This chapter will examine in depth the molar variability of the mentally retarded. As used here, molar variability, sometimes called intraindividual response variability, refers to some index of the extent to which the individual varies his or her successive choices between or among gross molar acts requiring equal effort and providing equal effectiveness in accomplishing a common end. Variations in topography are of no concern in the same sense that successive lever presses made by the rat are not distinguished one from the other by the observer of molar behavior. To illustrate, Siegel and Foshee (1960) required mentally retarded subjects to turn off a light by throwing any one of four switches. The switches were arranged in a semicircle in such a fashion as to make them equally easy to reach and to manipulate. Variability was indexed by variation within the pattern of response choices (switch 1, 2, 3, or 4) yielded over a series of 33 trials. They found the mentally retarded to be less variable (expressing greater "stereotypy" or "rigidity") than normal control subjects. Some readers will recognize this type of variability to be that labeled "Type 2" by Fiske and Rice (1955) and referred to as "reactive variability."

Molar variability has been directly or indirectly addressed within a number of different theoretical arenas. Particularly apposite have been studies of the learn-

---

[1]Present address: Director of Psychology, Polk Center, Polk, Pennsylvania 16342.

73

ing processes, inhibition, satiation, and disinhibition, studies of personality "rigidity," the orienting reflex, and distraction. This chapter will first review general theoretical accounts of this behavior and will then review research that has directly addressed normal–mentally retarded differences.

I. THEORIES OF MOLAR RESPONSE VARIABILITY

Molar response variability began to attract serious attention in the 1950s. At that time, most learning theorists endorsed the view that the mechanism behind motivated behavior was a drive state initiated by tissue needs and that learning was strengthened through need or drive reduction. However, then-developing experiments on curiosity and exploratory behavior strongly challenged these traditional beliefs. Some claimed that organisms "seek" novel stimulation and that new behaviors could be reinforced with stimuli that were not necessarily need reducing. These behaviors appeared to be "autonomously motivated" (Nissen, 1954) and strengthened by the introduction of novel and unfamiliar stimuli or, more generally, by a change in current stimulation. Further, this property of novel stimuli did not appear to be linked to prior association with primary drives (Harlow, Blazek, & McClearn, 1956). Hence, the common view that apparently novel stimuli have a history and act as secondary or learned drives (Dashiell, 1928; Nissen, 1930) was seriously questioned (Butler, 1953; Harlow, 1953; Hebb, 1955; Montgomery, 1954; Nissen, 1954). As attention to such behaviors increased, motivational theorists found the tissue need conception to be wanting, and they turned to operational definitions of drive. Defining drive as an intervening variable related to antecedent environmental events and to consequent behavioral acts paved the way for a broader acceptance of curiosity and exploration theories.

Early theorists often found themselves supporting one of two opposing motivational constructs, curiosity or boredom (Fowler, 1965). Curiosity theories proposed that novel stimulation, defined as a change in the environmental stimulus complex, acted as an unconditioned stimulus (UCS), and, if not too intense, elicited investigatory behavior; the organism exhibited "curiosity" about the novel stimuli. In contrast, boredom theorists viewed exploratory behavior as reflecting an effort to escape a familiar, unchanging, monotonous, hence aversive, stimulus situation. The organism had become satiated. Rather than energizing or driving behavior, novel stimuli served a reinforcing function, acting to relieve boredom. In short, for the curiosity theorist, the unconditioned response (UCR) of exploratory behavior was elicited by the "change in stimulation," whereas for the boredom theorist, it was elicited by a "deprivation of change in stimulation" (Fowler, 1965). The latter conception fitted neatly with the then popular drive notion of deprivation states, with drive reduction continuing as the source of reinforcement.

Influenced by research on the arousal system (Hebb, 1955; Leuba, 1955; Olds & Milner, 1954), an influential third camp of behavior theorists developed later, holding that increases in drive could also be reinforcing. Organisms were viewed as behaving in such a way as to "optimize" arousal and the experience of stimulation. We shall review this position in a moment.

A. Curiosity

Harlow (1953) was one of the first prominent theorists to reject the notion that behavior was necessarily motivated by internal drives associated with tissue need and that reinforcement must necessarily be associated with need reduction. Exposure to novel stimulation appeared to strengthen learning and exploratory responses in his monkeys. Traditional drive theorists attempted to account for Harlow's findings by appealing to secondary drives and to prior conditioning— arguments that were countered immediately by experimentation with naive infant monkeys lacking such experience (Harlow et al., 1956).

In a related theory, Montgomery (1953) proposed that initial contact with a novel stimulus served to arouse an exploratory drive. The strength of the exploratory drive was assumed to decrease with continued exposure, to recover in its absence, and to follow the principle of stimulus generalization. Later, Montgomery (1955), in an effort to explain why organisms tend to avoid extremely novel stimuli, appealed to "fear of novel stimulation," a state that also decreased with continued exposure and increased in its absence.

Criticism followed: (1) The definition of exploratory drive in terms of exploratory behavior was circular. (2) The theory could not reliably predict whether a novel stimulus would elicit an exploratory drive and subsequent approach, or fear and avoidance. (3) Traditional drive theorists continued to be opposed to the suggestion that drive induction could be reinforcing.

In an attempt to remain within a more nearly traditional drive reduction formulation, Berlyne (1950, 1955) hypothesized that novel stimulation acts as a UCS and elicits a "curiosity response," which in turn produces drive and approach behavior. Continued exposure to novel stimulation reduces the curiosity drive and thus reinforces associated exploratory behavior. Berlyne explained the subsequent decrement in exploratory behavior by assuming the operation of reactive and condition inhibition (Hull, 1943).

The major criticism directed at the time toward Berlyne and other curiosity theorists was that they focused on experiments in which the organism learned to perform an instrumental response to experience novel stimulation as a consequence. In such situations, the novel stimulus, absent until the instrumental response occurred, could not be reasonably viewed as producing the drive that motivated the animal to respond in the first place (Brown, 1961).

B. Boredom

A number of investigators avoided the conceptual problems plaguing the curiosity theorists by developing a more nearly traditional drive account. Intraindividual response variability and exploratory behavior were viewed as escape from a too familiar or boring stimulus complex. Thus, Myers and Miller (1954) proposed that exposure to a homogeneous, constant surround generated stimulus satiation and a "boredom drive." A change in the stimulus complex reduced this drive, reinforcing the instrumental response that brought it about. Drive theorists welcomed this conception since it not only retained the notion of drive reduction as the source of reinforcement and learning, but it also accounted for the occasional failure of the organism to approach extremely novel stimulation. Such stimulation was assumed to be drive inducing, aversive, and, hence, to be avoided.

Glanzer (1953) also developed a boredom-like theory but accounted for exploratory behavior without referring to an energizing drive mechanism. Rather, he emphasized the inhibitory influence of the familiar stimulus complex. Briefly, Glanzer proposed that, whenever a stimulus is perceived, a temporary quantity of "stimulus satiation" (sI) accumulates and reduces responsiveness to that particular stimulus. The longer the stimulus is present, the greater the accumulation of inhibition. When the stimulus is withdrawn, sI dissipates spontaneously.

Although Glanzer (1953) presented a number of experiments to support his hypothesis, several problems soon became evident: (1) the suggestion that all responses should decrease with continued exposure to novel stimulation and increase in its absence implied that avoidance responses would be affected similarly—a patently ridiculous implication; (2) although Glanzer could predict the avoidance of a familiar stimulus, he could not explain why the organism chose the alternative unfamiliar one; (3) neglect of energization led some drive theorists to ask why an organism would not choose to do nothing, rather than approach a novel stimulus; and (4) Glanzer's neglect of the reinforcement principle left him unable to explain why organisms learn an instrumental response when stimulus change is arranged as a contingency. He could explain a response "to" change but not a response "for" change (Fowler, 1965).

Fowler (1965) argued that the motivation for performing the instrumental response that leads to novel stimulation arises from two sources, drive and incentive. Thus, continued exposure to unchanging stimulation ("deprivation of change in stimulation") results in the energizing drive state of boredom. Novel stimulation then serves to elicit the consummatory goal response of exploratory behavior. This serves to reduce the boredom drive and thus reinforces the approach response that leads to change. The incentive effect (curiosity) enters as a "learned anticipation" of the novel stimulation (incentive) that is experienced as a contingency. Interestingly, Fowler assumes that the organism is not inherently curious. At least one trial with a novel stimulus is required before curiosity is experienced; the anticipatory mechanism cannot take place until the exploratory response has occurred at least once.

C. Optimal Stimulation

A third group of theorists placed intraindividual response variability and exploratory behavior in a homeostatic context. They adopted the views of Hebb (1955) and Leuba (1955), who stated that organisms behave in ways that result in or maintain an "optimal (usually intermediate)" level of total stimulation. Hence, an increase in stimulation, perhaps through "exploration," is sought when the momentary level of stimulation is too low, a decrease when too high. It should be noted that advocates of this position held that both drive reduction and drive induction may motivate and reinforce behavior. Some influential experimental results (Olds & Milner, 1954; Sheffield & Roby, 1950; Sheffield, Wulff, & Backer, 1951) have provided support. But, ultimately, serious definitional and measurement problems loomed large.

One of the more comprehensive theories of intraindividual response variability was offered by Fiske and Maddi (1961), who perceived the organism as striving to attain an intermediate or optimum level of activation through overall stimulation. Performance became an inverted U-shaped function of "level of activation" or total "stimulus impact." The latter refers to the "intensity," "meaningfulness," and "novelty" of all internal and external stimuli impinging upon the organism at any given moment. Meaningfulness refers to the perceived significance of the stimulus, whereas novelty gauges the extent to which the current stimulus provides variation from previous stimulation. Fiske and Maddi have also suggested that, at a given moment, the organism experiences a particular level of activation that varies with its sleep–wakefulness cycle. When not performing a specific task, the organism behaves in such a way as to maintain the level of activation characteristic of that particular point in its sleep–wakefulness cycle. Responses for change refer to responses instrumental in bringing about a moderate change in stimulation and are presumably influenced by "affective states." Low arousal that follows low stimulus impact is affectively negative and results in the motivation to increase it. As the activation level approaches a more nearly optimal level, positive affect results and serves to reinforce associated instrumental responses.

Criticism was immediate. It was objected that the theory explained much but predicted little. Accurate a priori levels of arousal could not be estimated nor could one predict reliably whether a particular behavior would increase or decrease them. Further, several experiments yielded embarrassing outcomes (Fowler, Blond, & Dember, 1959; Fowler, 1965).

Berlyne (1960, 1963) held that activation or arousal is a U-shaped function of stimulus impact. Stimulus properties such as "novelty," "surprisingness," and "complexity" were assumed to be motivational and to help determine the probability, vigor, and direction of exploratory responses. High levels of activation are produced by exposure either to extremely novel stimuli or to stimuli that have become very familiar, hence monotonous.

Assuming that departures from an intermediate level of activation are aversive, Berlyne accounted for exploratory behavior by invoking a "curiosity drive." When initially experienced, novelty elicits a curiosity drive. This is aversive and the organism engages in exploratory behavior. To explain why an organism continues to explore and thus experience an increase in activation, Berlyne postulated the "arousal jag": a temporary increase in activation is tolerated because of the ensuing pleasure of activation reduction. Berlyne ultimately linked curiosity to "information" constructs.

Later Berlyne (1967) proposed two major theoretical changes. First, reference to specific physiological mechanisms of activation was discarded. Second, influenced by experiments such as those of Olds and Milner (1954) in which rats increased their instrumental responding for brain stimulation, he offered a modified drive induction hypothesis: if the organism is not already highly excited, small or moderate increases in activation could be viewed as reinforcing.

Glanzer (1958) explained intraindividual response variability by appealing to an information processing system that demands a certain (optimal) amount of "information" input per unit of time. Approach or avoidance behavior was then related to the discrepancy between the rate of information flow to which the organism was accustomed and the current rate of input offered by the environment. If a high flow of information had been experienced in the past, a high flow of information would be required. If a low "standard" had been experienced, such as that created by an impoverished environment, a low input would suffice. Exploratory behavior and exposure to stimulus variation regulate the discrepancy. "Information" relates to the concept introduced by Shannon and Weaver (1949), who defined information as a reduction of "uncertainty." When stimulus events are redundant, repetitive, or completely familiar, there is total "certainty," and no information can be gained. When stimulus events are changing, unfamiliar, and relatively random, there is uncertainty and more information to be gained. The greater the range of alternative possibilities that exist with respect to stimulus or response events, the greater the uncertainty and potential information gain. Maximum uncertainty exists when alternatives are equiprobable. The information theorist views exploratory behavior as an attempt to gain information and reduce uncertainty. And the organism is often assumed to be seeking the optimal amount.

In 1963, Berlyne linked information theory to curiosity, exploratory behavior, and his "collative" variables (stimulus "novelty," "surprisingness," and "complexity") by hypothesizing a relation between the concepts of "conflict" and "uncertainty." He held that a motivational effect common to collative variables is the generation of conflict and that uncertainty is a form of conflict. Conflict refers specifically to competing responses that are elicited simultaneously by various stimuli. Through stimulus generalization from past experience, apparently novel stimuli elicit similar, yet incompatible, response tendencies. Thus, conflict is related to the number and strength of competing responses that are elicited by a novel, a surprising, or a complex stimulus pattern. Similarly, uncertainty is related to the number of possible response alternatives and is taken to be a variable that can produce the curiosity drive. Exploratory behavior may be a way to gain information in order to reduce uncertainty and conflict.

Dember and Earl (1957) also agreed that behavior is directed toward optimizing stimulus variability or complexity. However, they disagreed with Berlyne's assumption that exploratory behavior may lower activation to an optimum level by reducing conflict. To them, a stimulus situation was explored in order to raise the organism's "complexity value" to the optimum level. They argued that, at any given moment, the organism entertains a preferred or "ideal" complexity value for each stimulus attribute. The ideal is the maximum complexity of a stimulus that can be comfortably tolerated. It varies among stimulus attributes and is affected by experience. Most importantly, it relates to a "pacer" stimulus which defines the complexity value that is "just above" the ideal.

A. Jones (1961) attempted to integrate information theory into a more nearly traditional drive framework by proposing that an "information drive" exists that is similar to primary drives and that instrumental responses will be strengthened if they reduce "information deprivation." Some experimental support was found by A. Jones, Wilkinson, and Braden (1961), who subjected college students to sensory isolation and recorded the pressing of a button that delivered random light patterns. Increasing randomness of light patterns was assumed to relate directly to uncertainty. The rate of button pressing was found to be directly related to hours of information deprivation, as was the preferred amount of information contained in the light pattern.

D. Response Variability in Type 2 Situations

Fiske and Rice (1955) defined intraindividual response variability in general as a difference between two responses at two different points in time. They recognized three types. Type 1, or the "pure" case, was termed spontaneous variability and was defined as the difference between two responses at two points in time when the eliciting stimuli were objectively indistinguishable. All external factors affecting the response were taken to be constant. It was assumed that the order of the two responses was of no consequence and that the responses would exhibit no systematic trend over time due to such processes as learning and fatigue. Hence, the second response was affected by neither the first response nor the first stimulus presentation. Because of the required constancy of the external environment, spontaneous variability was assumed to be a product of some internal condition of the organism. They also recognized that the required similarity between stimulus situations might be impossible to realize in reality.

Type 2, or reactive variability, differed from Type 1 only in that a change in the second response was partly due to reaction to the first stimulus and/or the preceding response. The sequence of responses suggests a pattern, or an order effect. Theories that stress a need for variety are generally concerned with reactive variability, as are the experiments on spontaneous alternation.

In Type 3 variability, responses are observed either when objectively different stimuli are presented on the two occasions or when the background situation changes. Type 3 experiments are usually concerned with the appropriateness of a response that occurs with a change in stimulus conditions. An example is the "rigidity" paradigm, in which the subject's failure to change adaptively to successive, objectively different stimuli becomes the focus.

Fiske and Rice (1955) have argued that intraindividual response variability relates to factors such as the nature of the task and response required, the number of trials, the amount of time between responses, the structure of instructions, behavioral rigidity, motivational level, and certain physiological conditions.

E. Reactive Inhibition and Stimulus Satiation

Hull (1943) seems to have developed the construct of reactive inhibition (Ir) largely to account for work decrement. But it also accounted nicely for other facts, including spontaneous alternation. Reactive inhibition was described as a temporary, response-produced, negative drive state similar to fatigue, accumulating over trials and, upon cessation of responding, dissipating spontaneously. Reactive inhibition accumulation is independent of reinforcement and is influenced directly by the effort required as well as the number of trials experienced. All things being equal, then, when a response occurs it is somewhat less likely to reoccur immediately because of Ir buildup. Intraindividual response variability and spontaneous alternation could be caused by the accumulation of Ir on each preceding trial.

Dember (1961) and Dember and Fowler (1958) have reviewed the negative evidence with major attention given the failure of Ir to account for maze-reversal findings (Glanzer, 1953; Montgomery, 1952). When a rat in a cross-shaped maze is started on its way toward a goal box from the opposite direction on the second of two trials, it tends to repeat the first response, seemingly alternating stimulus exposure as opposed to responses. This prompted Glanzer (1953) to opt for stimulus satiation as the determinant of behavior variability. He argued that whenever a stimulus is observed, satiation to that stimulus accumulates to reduce responsiveness to that stimulus, hence, subsequent response change.

There are problems. For example, the somewhat crucial deduction of stimulus generalization has received inconsistent support (Dember, 1961). Glanzer also fails to tell us why a very novel or incongruous stimulus is avoided (Eisenberger, 1972). The theory predicts the avoidance of a previously experienced stimulus but not the choice of an alternative.

F. Cortical Satiation

Spitz (1963) accounted for intraindividual response variability within a Gestalt framework, viewing performance as determined by the way the environment is perceived. Perception depends upon cortical organizing functions such as goodness of figure, perceptual closure, and figure–ground structuring. He asserted that "cortical satiation" occurs with the repeated stimulation of the same area of the cortex. Variability in behavior results. Cortical satiation theory accounts well for perceptual processes such as visual figural after-effects and figure–ground reversals (Spitz, 1958; Spitz & Blackman, 1959), but intraindividual response variability has not been directly addressed. Studies that do relate to behavioral "rigidity" will be discussed in a later section.

Several theorists have perceived strong similarities among the concepts of reactive inhibition, stimulus satiation, and cortical satiation. Dember (1961) noted that both reactive inhibition and stimulus satiation accumulate over trials, dissipate over time, and are "peripheral" mechanisms. Both adopt the view that behavioral variability expresses avoidance of the preceding response or experience. Dember also suggested that stimulus satiation could readily incorporate reactive inhibition by recognizing response feedback as another stimulus dimension. Quite early, Solomon (1948) suggested that reactive inhibition might be viewed as response-produced, kinesthetic stimulation. Reactive inhibition and cortical satiation were taken to be possibly identical processes by Duncan (1956, 1957) and by Lipman and Spitz (1961).

G. Action Decrement

Walker (1958) emphasized the importance of central events. He suggested that any psychological action results in "action decrement," a lowered capacity for immediate arousal. It persists for a limited time, dissipates, and is followed by increased habit strength. Action decrement theory generates a number of predictions similar to those made by stimulus satiation theory but also finds a role for motivation and reinforcement. Support for the theory has been inconsistent (Dember, 1961).

II. RESPONSE VARIABILITY AND
THE MENTALLY RETARDED

A. Personality Theory

Lewin (1936) and later Kounin (1941a,b) argued that the cognitive structure of the familial retarded individual is more "rigid" and "less differentiated" than is that of the nonretarded. This story has been told many times and needs not be repeated here. Suffice it to say rigidity was offered as a construct that could account for such behaviors as the inability to change sets or shift cognitive strategies. Clearly these relate to stereotypy, perseveration, and lack of variability. The theorizing of Lewin and Kounin generated considerable controversy and, ultimately, other theories of behavioral rigidity. We shall look at these now.

Werner (1940, 1948) agreed that the retarded behave more rigidly because of inherent factors and he presented supportive observations. He criticized the Lewin–Kounin explanations and theorized that rigidity among the retarded results from the oversimplification of situations and problems; the retarded seize on resemblances to problems previously encountered and continue to apply strategies that are simply no longer applicable. For the most part, Werner presented as evidence impressions and descriptive statements. Zigler and Balla (1982) offer a more thorough critique of Werner's position and his confusion over Kounin's definition of rigidity.

Goldstein (1943), in his observations of individuals with organic brain damage, proposed two types of rigidity. "Primary rigidity" was assumed to be independent of higher mental processes and to reflect subcortical damage and defective "einstellung." There resulted an inability to change sets when faced with an unrelated task. "Secondary rigidity" was assumed to be associated with impaired cortical pathways and was viewed as implicating higher mental processes. There resulted a problem in abstraction, a preponderance of concrete behavior, and lessened ability to cope adaptively with the world. This occurs most often with difficult tasks and serves to decrease tension. Goldstein claimed that the retarded individual finds many problems beyond his grasp. Rather than take a chance on failure when confronted with a new and difficult task, the individual persists with maladaptive behaviors that were successful in the past.

Zigler (1962) has criticized Goldstein for ignoring etiology, for viewing the retarded as a homogeneous group. And he has argued that Goldstein's failure to distinguish the organic from familial retardation poses substantial difficulties for his position. A more extensive critique of Goldstein's position can be found in Zigler and Balla (1982).

Disagreeing that the retarded behave more rigidly or inflexibly because of "rigid boundaries," "lesser degree of differentiation," and/or subcortical or cortical defect, Stevenson and Zigler (1957) have presented a motivational explanation of Kounin's experimental findings. Previously, Plenderleith (1956) had used response-switching and discrimination tasks and failed to confirm Kounin's findings of greater rigidity in the retarded. Similar results were obtained by Stevenson and Zigler when they used even more difficult tasks (to avoid Plenderleith's ceiling effects). They pointed to a serious sampling bias that may have affected Kounin's data. Kounin permitted over half of his retarded subjects to refuse to participate. This was done to eliminate insecurity as a possible confounding element. However, normal subjects were not offered the opportunity to withdraw. Zigler (1962) suggested that there remained a subgroup of institutionalized retarded subjects who were strongly motivated to prolong social contact with the adult experimenter. Thus, their greater persistence on satiation and cosatiation tasks gained them increased adult attention and approval. This need to maintain social contact was assumed to be related to greater preinstitutional "social deprivation," as suggested by previous investigators (Clark, 1933; Sarason, 1953; Skeels, Udegraff, Wellman, & Williams, 1938).

Zigler, Hodgden, and Stevenson (1958) presented motor tasks similar to those used by Kounin under two motivational conditions. In one the experimenter was nonsupportive, while in the other he was warm and encouraging. Although normals performed similarly under both conditions, the retarded not only responded longer on both motor tasks, but were influenced more strongly by the warm social condition.

Later Green (1960) and Zigler (1961) rated detailed social histories of institutionalized retarded children for the amount of preinstitutional social deprivation and found that those rated high performed longer.

Although considerable support for the motivational theory has accumulated (Gayton & Bassett, 1972; Green & Zigler, 1962; Weaver, Balla, & Zigler, 1971; Zigler, 1966), a recent critical review by Mercer and Snell (1977) appeals for more research before firm conclusions are drawn. They recommend a stronger systematic examination of such related variables as level of retardation, age of retarded subjects, magnitude of reinforcement, and task difficulty. Added to this might be such questions as: Is the behavioral rigidity of "noninstitutionalized," socially deprived retarded individuals affected similarly? Do many "less strongly" socially deprived institutionalized retarded display rigid behavior? If so, why? Do many "strongly" socially deprived institutionalized retarded fail to display rigid behavior? Again, why? Perhaps groups of subjects from high and low socially depriving environments should be followed longitudinally before the verdict is brought in.

B. Response Variability and Learning Theory

Gerjuoy and Winters (1968) in a review of developmental studies have argued that the individual may exhibit three "preferences" in a choice situation: (1) "stimulus preference," which derives from the characteristics of the individual

stimuli in the array and often expresses a learned bias, (2) "response preference," which relates to stimulus location commonly seen in a position preference, and (3) "choice–sequence preference," which refers to a response pattern
in a series of trials, with each response influenced by previous responses. Examples of this last include perseveration, or the tendency to fixate on a particular
choice, and alternation of choices more often than expected by chance.

Stimulus and response preferences may be additive or competitive in determining the final effective response. If the preferred stimulus is in the preferred
location, frequency of choice of the preferred stimulus increases. If the two
conflict, the probability of a response to the preferred stimulus decreases.

Gerjuoy and Winters (1968) report that response strategies change with development and relate to intellectual level, schedule of reinforcement, and task
difficulty. Normal children younger than 4 years tend to perseverate (fixate),
unaffected by the reinforcement schedule. From then until about 6 years, they
tend to alternate invariably, again uninfluenced by reinforcement schedule.
Choice–sequence effects appear strongest at this time. As age increases, task
variables and reinforcement schedules begin to enter as influences, but response
alternation continues higher than chance. During adolescence, alternation tendencies disappear and performance reflects task and reinforcement demands.
Similar developmental trends were observed among the retarded, with response
strategies closely related to MA. Compared to CA-matched normals, their response strategies are less advanced developmentally. And they also exhibit more
within-group variability. Finally, when faced with tasks that are difficult, the
retarded may "regress" more readily to earlier response strategies.

1. INHIBITION-RELATED THEORIES AND THE
MENTALLY RETARDED

Heal and Johnson (1970) view inhibition as a hypothetical construct, inferred
from response decrement, following a change in the environment. And they have
distinguished between "response inhibition" and "stimulus inhibition." The
former they likened to Pavlov's "internal inhibition"; it produces suppression of
a learned response and is seen in extinction and discrimination reversal. In
contrast, stimulus inhibition refers to an inhibition of attention to extraneous
stimuli and is similar to Pavlov's "external inhibition." "Distraction" relates
strongly to their stimulus inhibition.

Heal and Johnson (1970) have reported that weaker response inhibition in the
retarded is seen in transfer suppression experiments that focus on discrimination
reversal and classification shifts, proactive interference findings, and experiments featuring differentiation and extinction. The fact that the retarded extinguish more slowly has long been established, and since the spontaneous recov-

ery of extinguished responses suggests the operation of an inhibitory process, extinction will be discussed in some detail.

One of the earliest extinction studies was conducted by Mateer (1918). He conditioned classically 14 retarded children (MA, 1 to 7 years) and 50 normal children who were roughly matched for CA (3 to 8 years). Subjects were blind-folded (CS), waited 10 seconds, and then had chocolate candy (UCS) placed in their mouths. Criterion for acquisition was two consecutive conditioned responses (CRs), defined by an opening of the mouth before the 10 seconds had elapsed. After a 24-hour delay, conditioning was again conducted, followed immediately by extinction, defined as the failure to make the CR twice in succession. Although no differences in acquisition were found between groups, the retarded extinguished more slowly.

Later, Denny (1964) also concluded that, although an appetitive conditioned response may be acquired by the retarded as quickly as normals, it extinguishes more slowly. Differences in extinction rates between retarded and normal peers have been reported in delayed conditioning and conditioned inhibition (Luria, 1963), the eyelid response (Ross, Headrick, & MacKay, 1967; Ross, Koski, & Yaeger, 1964), and the galvanic skin response (Lobb, 1967). Lobb suggested that differences in extinction rate may have been due to a failure of the retarded to recognize the stimulus change accompanying nonreinforcement, as opposed to a failure of inhibition. Estes (1970) has offered a similar account, reminding us that the stimulus context changes markedly from acquisition to extinction. That the retarded have more difficulty attending to the relevant dimensions of a stimulus complex has been strongly supported in the discrimination learning experiments of Zeaman and House (1963) and Fisher and Zeaman (1973).

Another explanation for the slower extinction rate of the retarded was offered by Viney, Clarke, and Lord (1973) using an operant conditioning procedure. Moderately retarded children with brain damage or Down's syndrome (mean CA, 13 years; mean MA, 35 months) and MA-matched normal children performed a matching-to-sample, button-pressing task. Although retarded and normal subjects were similar in acquisition rate, the former were more resistant to extinction. Of 60 observations, 27 retarded subjects failed to extinguish; only 8 normals so failed. Viney et al. (1973) placed their results in the context of Amsel's (1958) frustrative nonreward hypothesis. After an organism learns to "anticipate" reward during acquisition trials, extinction trials produce frustration. Fractional components of frustration may occur early and introduce responses competitive with approach. According to Viney et al., greater resistance to extinction by the retarded follows from a partial reinforcement effect linked to a past characterized by more intermittent failure and frustration. This has resulted in stronger frustration tolerance, therefore less competition from frustration during extinction and a tendency to continue at the task longer.

2. NORMAL-RETARDED DIFFERENCES
   IN STIMULUS INHIBITION

Weaker stimulus inhibition in the retarded has been tied to a slower buildup of satiation to the stimuli present, generating less intraindividual response variability. Several theories of stimulus inhibition have been presented already. The following discussion will review the associated research that compares the retarded and nonretarded.

Appealing to the sI theory of Glanzer (1953), Terdal (1967a) suggested that the less variable behavior of the retarded may be due to a slower rate of sI accumulation. He hypothesized that this would be reflected in weaker attention to new stimuli as well as greater attention to repetitive and background stimuli. The major comparisons were made between institutionalized adult retarded subjects (mean CA, 20 years; mean MA, 10–14 years) and CA-matched adult and MA-matched preadolescent normals. Preadolescent retarded subjects (mean CA, 11 years; estimated mean MA, 4–10 years) and MA-matched preschool normals were also included to determine whether or not the younger subjects would exhibit slower stimulus satiation than their older counterparts. Subjects were shown a series of 24 slides, each consisting of two multicolored checkerboard designs. Throughout the series, one of the checkerboard designs remained constant, while the other varied. Although the various retarded groups did not differ significantly among themselves, they attended visually to the unfamiliar varied designs significantly less than both CA- and MA-matched normals, and they also looked away from the slides more often. These findings are consistent with the hypothesis of slower satiation to familiar as well as irrelevant stimuli. Older normal and retarded subjects satiated more quickly than their younger counterparts.

In a subsequent experiment with the same subjects, Terdal (1967b) modified the above procedure by pairing varying designs with one of four constant designs. Two of the constant designs were judged to be "simple" in stimulus configuration, and two "complex." Both the retarded and CA-matched normals viewed the complex checkerboard designs longer, but they satiated at different rates to the two types of constant designs. Normals decreased their viewing time to the simple designs more rapidly than to the complex, whereas the retarded decreased viewing time equally to both types. These results are consistent with the hypothesis of weaker inhibition and slower buildup of sI in the retarded.

3. CORTICAL SATIATION AND THE
   MENTALLY RETARDED

Spitz (1959, 1963) held that prolonged exposure to a constant stimulus results in cortical satiation that accumulates and then dissipates more slowly in retarded than in normal peers of equal CA and possibly MA. He offered four postulates that characterize the retarded: (1) in response to stimulation, cortical cells change their state more slowly in the retarded; (2) once stimulation has begun, the return to a normal state of cortical cellular activity is slower in the retarded; (3) with a change in stimulation, the retarded change previously established cortical patterns into new patterns more slowly; and (4) there is less spread of activity from stimulated cortical cells to surrounding cortical fields in the retarded.

Support for the above postulates comes from experiments measuring the rate of reversing figures and the extent of visual figural after-effects (Spitz & Blackman, 1959). In a test of the former, institutionalized, mildly retarded adolescent males (mean CA, 17 years; mean IQ, 62) and CA-matched, local high school males were exposed to the Rubin Vase-Profile Reversible Figure. Spitz and Blackman interpreted the significantly fewer figure–ground shifts among the retarded as reflecting greater perceptual rigidity associated with weaker cortical satiation. Similar groups of institutionalized, mildly retarded adolescent males (mean CA, 17 years; mean IQ, 66) and CA-matched, local high school males were also administered the Visual Figural After-Effect Test. Items consist of an "Inspection Figure" that is observed first and a subsequent "Test Figure." Visual after-effect distortion is measured by comparing the visual fixation point of the Inspection Figure to that of the Test Figure. Theoretically, observation of an Inspection Figure results in cortical satiation and temporary impedance in the affected cortical area. Since excitation cannot enter this area of impedance, the Test Figure appears distorted from the previous fixation point. Consistent with the Spitz (1963) postulates, the retarded exhibited significantly fewer visual after-effects than normal peers. Further, those experiencing after-effects tended to experience slower dissipation.

The Spitz and Blackman (1959) experiments are certainly suggestive. However, Estes (1970) has criticized cortical satiation theory for its failure to relate the assumed cortical phenomena to more specific kinds of behavior.

4. REACTIVE INHIBITION AND THE MENTALLY RETARDED

A relatively large amount of research has examined normal–retarded differences in Ir (Hull, 1943) accumulation. A slower rate of accumulation would result in less intraindividual response variability because of a weaker tendency to avoid a recent response. In the following experiments, Ir elicitation was generally examined in pursuit rotor performance and measured in reminiscence scores. The typical experimental procedure was that of giving subjects two sets of massed trials separated by a short rest period. Reminiscence scores were generally collected during the third postrest trial and the performance increment attributed to the dissipation of Ir during the rest period. However, this interpretation of reminiscence has been challenged by several investigators (Eysenck, 1965; M. B. Jones, 1968; Peters, 1972; Wright & Willis, 1969), some of whom claim that differences in reminiscence scores simply reflect different skill levels.

Further, Eysenck (1965) cautions against the hasty acceptance of reminiscence scores as a valid measure of inhibition because such effects may be task specific.

Ellis, Pryer, and Barnett (1960) observed the pursuit rotor performance of institutionalized, mentally retarded adolescents and young adults (mean IQ, 61; range, 38 to 75) and CA-matched, local high school students. The posttest reminiscence scores of the latter were facilitated relatively more by the 5-minute rest period, and this held up at retests 1 and 28 days later. The authors suggested that normals accumulate Ir at a faster rate and that their higher reminiscence scores reflect a greater dissipation of Ir per unit of time during the rest period. It was suggested that the slower buildup of Ir by the retarded might be due to disinhibition, as proposed by Siegel and Foshee (1960). Siegel and Foshee hypothesized that the retarded accumulate less total inhibition when making a particular response because of greater disinhibition occasioned by the inability to shut out distraction.

In a subsequent experiment, R. Jones and Ellis (1962) reasoned that, if normals build up Ir at a faster rate than retarded peers, then they should show relatively greater reminiscence score differences when performing motor tasks that schedule "spaced" as opposed to "massed" practice. The pursuit rotor performance of institutionalized, mildly retarded adolescents and young adults (IQ range, 60 to 75) and local high school students matched roughly for CA were again observed. As before, normals exhibited more reminiscence. Further, the hypothesized differential buildup of Ir under spaced versus massed practice approached statistical significance. Unfortunately, differences in reminiscence were not shown to be independent of skill level.

Wright and Hearn (1964) asked whether normal retarded differences in reminiscence scores could be due to differential skill level, buildup rate of Ir, or dissipation of Ir. To control for differences in skill level, institutionalized mildly retarded males (mean CA, 22 years; mean IQ, 58) and CA-matched, normal male students were brought to a common level of prerest performance on the pursuit rotor. Despite performing many more trials to reach criterion, retarded subjects still yielded significantly lower reminiscence scores, suggesting a slower Ir buildup rate as opposed to differential skill level. The observation of Ir dissipation added further support. Subjects were given either a 3- or a 6-minute rest period. Since previous results had indicated that most Ir dissipates within 3 minutes (Ammons, 1950; Kimble & Horenstein, 1948), Wright and Hearn reasoned that a slower dissipation rate in the retarded would result in a relatively larger reminiscence difference between their two retarded groups than in the two normal groups. However, the interaction of intelligence with rest period duration was found to be nonsignificant.

Methodological problems can be identified. First, tangible motivational incentives were provided only to the retarded subjects. Second, a sampling bias may have occurred in that 38% of the subjects were eliminated, either for reaching criterion too quickly to build up Ir or for failing to reach criterion within 40 trials. The former criterion resulted in a rejection of scores from 16 normal subjects but only 1 retarded subject; the latter yielded a rejection of scores from no normal subjects but 8 retarded.

To control for these weaknesses, Wright and Willis (1969) again equated prerest level of performance but avoided the problem of motivational confounding by offering tangible incentives to neither group. They also included more intelligent retarded subjects (mean CA, 15 years; mean IQ, 71), which permitted a common prerest performance criterion of 63% on target for any two trials. This produced the much smaller elimination rate of 15% for the retarded and 0% of the CA-matched normals. Again, their retarded subjects required more trials to reach the common level of prerest performance but yielded significantly smaller reminiscence scores. And once again, it was concluded that Ir buildup is independent of skill level and is slower for the retarded.

Wright (1970) assessed the generality of past findings by using a different manipulandum, a hand crank. He also varied conditions in order to determine the role of stronger motivation in normal subjects during prerest trials. Institutionalized retarded (mean CA, 15 years; mean IQ, 70) and CA-matched normal subjects were divided into "control-exerted" and "no-control-exerted" conditions. In the former, prerest performance was equalized by the experimenter, who directly instructed subjects to speed up or slow down their hand-crank performance. The latter groups were permitted to crank at their own speed. Results indicated that, whereas the reminiscence scores of the two control-exerted groups were similar, normals displayed significantly more reminiscence in the no-control-exerted condition. They cranked more and were presumably more strongly motivated. Wright concluded that normal–retarded differences in reminiscence were not independent of prerest level of performance; differential prerest performances due to motivational factors seemed implicated. This contradicted his previous findings (Wright & Hearn, 1964; Wright & Willis, 1969), but resolution may be found in the data analysis. Even though there was no significant difference in the mean reminiscence scores of the two control-exerted groups (mean difference = 1.72), the scores were almost as large as those seen in the no-control-exerted condition (mean difference = 1.85). Wright departed from his previous procedure of excluding the first posttest trial from the calculation of reminiscence scores. Since the no-control-exerted group of normals had a substantially higher initial posttest score than their retarded peers, the reminiscence score mean difference may have been enhanced just enough to attain significance. The conclusion that Ir accumulation is dependent upon prerest performance level and motivational factors certainly invites further scrutiny.

Although the consensus appears to be that retarded subjects build up Ir more slowly than normal peers, unanimity is lacking. Baumeister, Hawkins, and Holland (1967) observed the pursuit rotor performance of institutionalized retarded males (mean CA, 14 years; IQ, 79) and CA-matched normal public school students and failed to find significant reminiscence score differences. Wright (1970) suggested that this contradictory finding resulted from experimental design differences, such as a longer intertrial interval and a different number of prerest trials. In turn, Baumeister *et al.* countered that others had included retarded subjects with motor disabilities. It must be noted that most of the previous investigators did report that subjects were free or relatively free of such motor and sensory defects (Ellis *et al.*, 1960; R. Jones & Ellis, 1962; Wright & Hearn, 1964). And interestingly, Baumeister *et al.* presented no evidence indicating that their subjects were any freer. Perhaps a more plausible explanation of the discrepant findings lies with their subject samples. Their two groups were much more similar in intelligence than those used by other experimenters and might even have overlapped in some degree. In fact, some of their "retarded" subjects clearly were not retarded (mean IQ, 79; SD, 9.3). Their normal subjects were described as being "enrolled in regular classes."

In conclusion, it appears that the evidence from inhibition studies does support the hypothesis of weaker inhibition and/or slower satiation in the retarded. Stronger support would be forthcoming if the inhibition-related areas of the orienting reflex and distraction also agreed. However, as indicated in Section IV, support from these areas is tenuous.

III. DISINHIBITION

A process that may help explain the weaker response variability of the retarded is that of "disinhibition," or the temporary reappearance of a suppressed or inhibited response when an extraneous stimulus is presented (Brimer, 1970a). Disinhibition was initially reported by Pavlov (1927), who noticed that, during extinction of a conditioned salivary response, the presentation of an extraneous stimulus together with the CS resulted in a temporary return of the CR. The evocation of a formerly inhibited response was found again in delayed conditioning experiments when the extraneous stimulus was introduced during the early presentation of the CS. Pavlov suggested that extinction, spontaneous recovery, and disinhibition all imply inhibition.

Although he conducted no strong studies of disinhibition, Pavlov proposed the following (Brimer, 1972): (1) every unusual environmental stimulus is a potential disinhibitor; (2) the restorative effect on the CR is probably temporary; (3) an inverted U-shaped function appears to characterize the relation between stimulus intensity and disinhibition, as well as between the inhibitory and disinhibitory capacity of stimuli; (4) the extraneous stimulus need not be present at the time of testing (disinhibitory effects could last from seconds to even days); and (5) the same extraneous stimulus that facilitates an extinguished CR can inhibit an excitatory CR if presented with the CS during acquisition.

Using an operant conditioning approach, Brimer (1970a) drew several conclusions that contradict Pavlov: (1) both inhibition and disinhibition appear to be relatively insensitive to stimulus intensity; (2) the relation between the magnitudes of the inhibitory and disinhibitory stimuli appears to be monotonic; and (3) stimulus novelty seems to play an important role in inhibition but not in disinhibition. The decrement in disinhibition during repeated testing appears to be due to the growth of inhibition during responding rather than to adaptation to the extraneous stimulus.

With little exception (Rexroad, 1937; Skinner, 1936; Warren & Brown, 1943), disinhibition has proved to be a reliable phenomenon in both classical conditioning (Hunter, 1935; Razran, 1939; Switzer, 1933; Wenger, 1936) and operant conditioning experiments (Baumeister & Hawkins, 1966; Brimer, 1970a,b, 1972; Brimer & Kamin, 1963; Brimer & Wickson, 1971; Flanagan & Webb, 1964; Gagne, 1941; Hinrichs, 1968; Horns & Heron, 1940; Melvin & Baumeister, 1969; Singh & Wickens, 1968; Winnick & Hunt, 1951; Yamaguchi & Ladioray, 1962).

Operant conditioning and disinhibition have been studied in depth by Brimer (1970a,b), who observed the effect of introducing extraneous stimulation on the lever-pressing response of rats. He found disinhibition to have substantial generality and to occur during inhibition-related experiments involving conditioned suppression and discrimination learning (Brimer & Wickson, 1971), food satiation, punishment, and, most commonly, extinction (Brimer, 1970a,b). The strength of disinhibition was dramatically illustrated by Brimer and Kamin (1963), who used unsignaled electric shock to inhibit lever pressing in rats but still found recurrence of the response when novel white noise was introduced during extinction.

Disinhibition-related variables include (1) "type of disinhibitor," with effective stimuli being related to several sensory modalities (buzzers, white noise, lights, vibration, and even shock), (2) "duration of the disinhibitor," (from 1.5 seconds to 3 minutes), (3) "intensity of stimulation," [generally, according to Yamaguchi and Ladioray (1962), an effective disinhibiting stimulus can be weaker than that required for external response inhibition during acquisition], (4) "timing of the introduction of the disinhibitor within an FI schedule," with the extraneous stimulus disinhibiting during the early part of an FI schedule but inhibiting during the latter part (Flanagan & Webb, 1964; Hinrichs, 1968; Singh & Wickens, 1968), and (5) "type of reinforcement schedule," with disinhibition occurring more readily with VR and FI schedules than with a CRF schedule (Baumeister & Hawkins, 1966; Flanagan & Webb, 1964; Hinrichs, 1968; Melvin & Baumeister, 1969; Singh & Wickens, 1968). The significance of this last finding has been emphasized by investigators in explaining occasional failures to obtain disinhibition. For example, Baumeister and Hawkins (1966) placed severely and moderately retarded adolescents into CRF as well as VR schedules in which reinforcement followed upon 25, 50, or 75% of the subject's responses. Both the greatest resistance to extinction and the most disinhibition (loud buzzer) occurred with the lowest ratio of reinforcement offered during acquisition. Almost no disinhibition occurred with the CRF schedule. These findings were replicated in an analogous experiment by Melvin and Baumeister (1969), who required rats to bar press for food. Again, their CRF group exhibited virtually no disinhibition. Melvin and Baumeister speculated that a higher VR results in more Ir and thus susceptibility to greater disinhibition.

Pavlov (1927) believed that, during extinction, the extraneous stimulus interferes with a dominant, active inhibitory central state. The resulting response increment reflects the release of the CR from "internal inhibition." In effect there occurs an "inhibition of inhibition." When the same extraneous stimulus is presented during acquisition it may weaken the CR. Pavlov viewed the latter effect as an "inhibition of excitation." The extraneous stimulus, then, always inhibits. That an active inhibition process is involved in disinhibition has been demonstrated by Brimer (1970a,b), who found that disinhibition occurred only when the previously reinforced response rate had been reduced from a high to a critically low rate.

Hull (1943) proposed that the introduction of a novel stimulus during acquisition trials changes the stimulus complex and thus weakens habit strength (the CR). Presenting a novel stimulus during extinction trials also changes the stimulus situation, but Hull assumed that it was sIr (learned inhibition) that is weakened. This generates disinhibition and a temporary recurrence of the CR.

IV. DISINHIBITION AND THE MENTALLY RETARDED

Several investigators have argued that the mentally retarded may disinhibit more readily than normal peers (Denny, 1964; Estes, 1970; Luria, 1959). This possibility was advanced formally by Siegel and Foshee (1960), who observed the molar response variability of retarded subjects on a Type 2 (Fiske & Rice, 1955) task. Over a series of 33 massed trials, normal and retarded subjects pressed any one of four switches to turn off a light. Switches were positioned to equalize the effort used to reach each of them. The dependent measure was the 33-trial response pattern. Their results indicated that the retarded display significantly less response variability than normals. And as a post hoc hypothesis, Siegel and Foshee speculated that the retarded may experience greater disruption of inhibition (disinhibition) because of a "lessened capacity to shut out even minor distraction." This could lead to response repetition or less variability.

Jackson (1959) presented CA-matched experimental and control groups of moderately retarded subjects (mean CA, 22 years; range, 11 to 51 years) with essentially the same apparatus and procedure used by Siegel and Foshee (1960). However, Jackson's subjects experienced the brief presentation of a slide (a landscape scene) shortly before the signal light appeared. A control group received no slide (simple delay). The hypothesis of reduced response variability with the occurrence of novel stimulation was supported. Further, with respect to generalization, their subjects were both younger and more intelligent than those used by Siegel and Foshee. Unfortunately, normal subjects were not run as a control.

Some support for the Siegel–Foshee hypothesis is found in an early study by Luria (1959). Luria presented a differential conditioning task in which the child was trained to press a balloon when a green light appeared and to "not press" the balloon when a red light appeared. Luria reported that differential responding was disrupted by the introduction of a loud bell, but neither details of the procedure nor supportive data were presented.

Using a variety of tasks, Smith (1984) examined the Siegel–Foshee hypothesis in some detail. On each of a series of trials, normal and retarded subjects were required to accomplish a common outcome by choosing among equally effective, equally effortful, topographically similar responses. Variability was defined in terms of various measures of the extent to which successive response choices varied (the Type 2 variability of Fiske and Rice, 1955). Only limited support of the hypothesis was found, together with a number of contradictions. Particularly troubling was the problem of disentangling inhibition and disinhibition.

That disinhibition and distraction may be closely linked is supported by a number of previously mentioned studies. For example, Brimer (1970a) showed that the most effective response inhibitors during acquisition were, later, the most potent disinhibitors. But, is there convincing experimental evidence that the retarded are more distractible than normal peers? We shall review this literature in a later section, but first the "orienting reflex" (OR) will be examined. This process has been related closely to attention and distractibility, and normal–retarded differences have been researched.

A. The OR in the Mentally Retarded

Although Pavlov (1927) first drew attention to the OR and described it as a normal, investigatory, reflex-like behavior in response to novel stimuli, it was Sokolov (1963) who studied it in depth. He reported it to be composed of sensory, muscular, and vegetative changes elicited by a meaningful change in the stimulus situation. Its purpose appeared to be that of alerting the organism and of increasing receptor sensitivity in order to maximize information input and filter out task-irrelevant stimuli. If the stimulus is of little significance, the OR quickly extinguishes.

Offering a neurophysiological explanation, Sokolov (1960) proposed that incoming stimulus patterns leave cortical traces of their characteristics such as quality, intensity, frequency, and duration. A "neuronal model" is thus formed, and features of subsequent stimuli are compared to it. If different, an OR is elicited, and new information is added to the model. The magnitude of the OR is proportional to the degree of stimulus discrepancy from the model.

Luria (1963) and Lynn (1966) have listed various indices of the OR as ceasing ongoing activity, increasing muscle tone, changing body orientation, turning the head and eyes, decreasing respiration rate, decreasing cortical alpha activity, and changes in the galvanic skin response. Also reported have been a deceleration of heart rate and a constriction of blood vessels in the extremities, accompanied by a dilation of blood vessels in the head.

Repeated stimulation results in "habituation" of the OR. And this is presumed to be a function of increasing congruence between the neuronal model and features of the relevant stimuli. When there is close congruence, the stimuli are no longer arousing and the OR extinguishes. As is true of conditioned responses, an extinguished OR can be disinhibited by the presentation of novel stimulation.

In a series of studies by Luria (1963), mentally retarded children failed to develop an OR that was readily elicited in normal children of equal CA. Even when the OR did occur, it was weaker and habituated more rapidly. The retarded children were also more likely to display an OR to an extraneous stimulus, prompting Luria to link their weaker OR to attention problems or greater distractibility.

A weaker OR in retarded subjects has also been reported by Vogel (1961), who used a tone and cold water with mildly retarded subjects. They recovered their GSR baseline more quickly and exhibited less cerebral dilation and peripheral constriction of arteries than did CA-matched normal peers. Berkson, Hermelin, and O'Connor (1961) presented light flashes and found institutionalized, adult retarded subjects to be less responsive than CA-matched normals in skin potential changes. Baumeister, Spain, and Ellis (1963) have reported that institutionalized, moderately retarded young adults yield a significantly shorter alpha block duration to light stimuli than CA-matched normal staff members. Finally, Clausen and Karrer (1968) delivered a series of tones and light flashes to groups of "organic" and "nonorganic" retarded subjects as well as to CA-matched normals. Their organic retarded subjects made the fewest ORs, the normals the most. The nonorganic retarded subjects fell in between. Dependent measures included divergent hand–finger blood volume response, changes in systolic blood pressure, and changes in the galvanic skin response.

In contrast, other investigators have failed to find a weaker OR in the retarded. Wolfensberger and O'Connor (1965) presented light stimuli to institutionalized, mildly retarded young adults and CA-matched normals. The former yielded greater GSR changes. Pilgrim, Miller, and Cobb (1969) introduced high-intensity light stimulation to mildly retarded children and to CA and MA-matched normals and found no differences in GSR latency, amplitude, or duration. Elliott and Johnson (1971) presented tone and light to mildly retarded male adolescents and to CA-matched normals and found no differences in digital blood volume. Finally, Klein, Klein, Oskamp, and Patnode (1972) presented a discrimination learning task to mildly retarded children and CA-matched normals. A novel colored cue card introduced intermittently as a distractor failed to elicit differences in vasomotor reactions.

Discrepant results prompted Karrer, Nelson, and Galbraith (1979) to conclude a recent summary of the literature by stating that "virtually every conceivable finding has been reported." They speculate that the inconsistency reflects a lack of commonality among studies: stimulus situations have varied, response measures have differed, the etiology of retardation has been ignored, duration of institutionalization has varied, and medication effects have been disregarded.

Normal–retarded differences in OR habituation have also been reported. Although Luria (1963) claimed that the retarded habituate to stimuli more rapidly than nonretarded peers, evidence gathered since then has not been supportive. Many of the previously described experiments on the OR also tested for habituation and found no normal–retarded differences (Berkson et al., 1961; Clausen & Karrer, 1968; Elliott & Johnson, 1971; Pilgrim et al., 1969; Siddle & Glenn, 1974; Wolfensberger & O'Connor, 1965). Other investigators have found the retarded to habituate more slowly than normal peers (Baumeister et al., 1963; Fenz & McCabe, 1971). The latter have been criticized by Karrer et al. (1979) on the grounds that the authors failed to give proper attention to the weaker initial responsiveness of the mentally retarded. Karrer et al. feel that habituation should be evaluated only in relation to initial responsiveness.

B. OR Habituation and Intellectual Performance

Borrowing from the "serial habituation" theory of Jeffrey (1968), Furby (1974) proposed that a slower rate of OR habituation causes low-IQ individuals to attend longer per unit of time to the more salient cues of a percept. The longer time spent scanning and habituating results in the formation of relatively fewer "schemata" than in higher IQ peers and a consequent lower MA. Furby's primary assumption of a strong relation between speed of OR habituation and IQ appears to invite verification or at least qualification, since the findings of normal–retarded OR habituation differences are contradictory.

In conclusion, the occasional finding of a weaker OR and slower habituation to novel stimuli among the retarded offers qualified support to the hypothesis of weaker stimulus inhibition. This would gain strength if the retarded were also found to be more readily distracted by task-irrelevant or extraneous stimuli. Such a finding would tend to confirm the assumption that a weaker OR reflects a weaker filtering system and thus permits extraneous stimuli to evoke their own ORs. Whether or not the retarded are really more distracted by task-irrelevant, extraneous stimuli is the question that we now turn to.

C. Distraction by Task-Irrelevant Stimuli

Crosby and Blatt (1968) have observed that the retarded are often viewed as "distractible," defined as "attending to task-irrelevant stimuli instead of or in addition to task-relevant ones." But, after reviewing much of the distraction literature, they have concluded that such a description may require a great deal of qualification.

Luria (1959) reported that the retarded commonly lack a balance between excitatory and inhibitory processes, with the former dominating, resulting in distraction and impulsive behavior. He also proposed that a weak OR, coupled with a deficit in OR habituation, results in continued elicitation of the OR, whether or not the stimuli are relevant to the task at hand (Luria, 1963). Goldstein (1943) tied distractibility to cortical damage and the impairment of abstract ability. Thus, the brain-injured individual shifts attention from one stimulus to another to avoid the discomfort of inadequate responding. Zigler (1966) has suggested that distractibility may reflect the outer-directed, problem-solving style of the retarded. This is characterized by looking to others for helpful cues and results in scattered attention. Cromwell (1963) also hypothesized that the retarded are more attentive to extra task cues but linked this to a tendency toward external locus of control. It should be noted that the above theories of distraction have not been well researched and, at the present time, can only be viewed as suggestive.

A review of studies that have compared retarded and nonretarded individuals turns up only two that support strongly the view that the retarded are more distractible (Follini, Sitkowski, & Stayton, 1969; Klein *et al.,* 1972) and two that provide qualified support (Hetherington & Ross, 1967; Krupski, 1979). The rest have either failed to find significant differences or have found normals to be slightly more distractible (Crosby, 1972; Ellis, Hawkins, Pryer, & Jones, 1963; Forehand, Calhoun, Peed, & Yoder, 1973; Girardeau & Ellis, 1964; Turnure, 1970; Whitman & Sprague, 1968).

The experimental tasks used in distraction studies have included discrimination learning (Crosby, 1972; Klein *et al.,* 1972; Whitman & Sprague, 1968), oddity learning (Ellis *et al.,* 1963; Turnure, 1970), recall tasks (Girardeau & Ellis, 1964), incidental learning (Forehand *et al.,* 1973), and the performance of academic and nonacademic assignments (Krupski, 1979). Task-irrelevant, extraneous stimuli have been directed at one or more sensory modalities, have been intense and nonintense, and have been "meaningful" and "meaningless." Auditory stimulation has included loud white noise (Forehand *et al.,* 1973), interfering metronome beats (Follini *et al.,* 1969), the names of alphabetical letters (Crosby, 1972), familiar environmental sounds (Girardeau & Ellis, 1964), and the telling of a children's story (Forehand *et al.,* 1973). Visual stimulation has been provided by a mirror placed before the subject (Ellis *et al.,* 1963; Turnure,

1970), alphabet letters (Crosby, 1972), various toys and objects (Whitman & Sprague, 1968), and colored figures (Klein *et al.*, 1972). Some studies have used a combination of visual and auditory stimulation as distractors (Crosby, 1972; Whitman & Sprague, 1968). And, a wide variety of dependent measures have been used, including trials-to-criterion (Ellis *et al.*, 1963; Girardeau & Ellis, 1964), number of correct and/or incorrect responses (Forehand *et al.*, 1973; Klein *et al.*, 1972; Whitman & Sprague, 1968), accuracy of subjective estimates (Follini *et al.*, 1969), and number and duration of extra task glances (Krupski, 1979; Turnure, 1970). Crosby and Blatt (1968) remind us that inconsistent results must follow from the lack of commonality in the methodologies used. They have also criticized the practice of comparing institutionalized and non-institutionalized subjects, pointing out that the former may well have been institutionalized because of maladaptive behaviors, one of which could readily have been distractibility. Finally, they have proposed that experimental tasks requiring sustained attention be used, the distractors be "meaningful," and that experimental procedures follow from a clearly stated theoretical rationale. In a more recent review of the distraction literature, Doleys (1976) has reached similar conclusions and has recommended standard distracting stimulus conditions and common dependent measures.

V. SUMMARY

The scattered nature of the studies we have reported makes it almost impossible to draw firm conclusions about the molar response variability (or rigidity) of the retarded. Too many of these experiments are isolated, are of limited methodological sophistication, or possess little generalization value. As reflected in the use of dissimilar tasks, dissimilar populations, and differing dependent variables, this research is nonsystematic and has yielded a tangle of ambiguous and sometimes unreliable data. As difficult as it has been to answer the basic question of whether the retarded display more or less molar response variability than do normals of equal CA or MA, the effort to discover "why" such might exist has encountered even thornier problems. And the failure to tie constructs into a meaningful theoretical package must lead us to the humbling conclusion that we know little about response variability and not a great deal more about mental retardation itself. The contradictions and inconsistencies found in these research findings simply permit no compelling conclusions. Our promising theories seem inadequately tested and our experiments seem to have generated far more questions than answers.

The usual "more research is needed" caveat is certainly in order; more insistently, "more rigorous basic research is needed." The list of theoretical constructs encountered in this research clearly contains redundancies. What conceptual properties that are possessed by "distraction" are found wanting in "inhibition"? Can "disinhibition" and "inhibition" be reduced to some common process? What about "habituation" and "satiation"? How do they differ logically? It appears to the present investigators that advances in our understanding of the molar variability of the mentally retarded must await the development of theory and method at a level that achieves some integration of currently popular constructs and procedures. Perhaps we have gathered enough scattered "facts" and honored too many isolated constructs.

REFERENCES

Ammons, R. B. (1950). Acquisition of motor skill: III. Effects of initially distributed practice on rotor pursuit performance. *Journal of Experimental Psychology,* **40,** 777–787.

Amsel, A. (1958). The role of frustrative nonreward in noncontinuous reward situations. *Psychological Bulletin,* **55,** 102–119.

Baumeister, A. A., & Hawkins, W. F. (1966). Extinction and disinhibition as a function of reinforcement schedule with severely retarded children. *Journal of Experimental Child Psychology,* **3,** 343–347.

Baumeister, A. A., Hawkins, W. F., & Holland, J. (1967). Motor learning and knowledge of results. *American Journal of Mental Deficiency,* **70,** 590–594.

Baumeister, A. A., Spain, C. J., & Ellis, N. R. (1963). A note on Alpha Block duration in normals and retardates. *American Journal of Mental Deficiency,* **67,** 723–725.

Berkson, G., Hermelin, B., & O'Connor, N. (1961). Physiological responses of normals and institutionalized mental defectives to repeated stimuli. *Journal of Mental Deficiency Research,* **5,** 30–39.

Berlyne, D. E. (1950). Novelty and curiosity as determinants of exploratory behaviour. *British Journal of Psychology,* **41,** 68–80.

Berlyne, D. E. (1955). The arousal and satiation of perceptual curiosity in the rat. *Journal of Comparative and Physiological Psychology,* **48,** 238–246.

Berlyne, D. E. (1960). *Conflict, arousal, and curiosity.* New York: McGraw-Hill.

Berlyne, D. E. (1963). Motivational problems raised by exploratory and epistemic behavior. In S. Koch (Ed.), *Psychology: A study of a science* (Vol. 5). New York: McGraw-Hill.

Berlyne, D. E. (1967). Arousal and reinforcement. In D. Levine (Ed.), *Nebraska Symposium on Motivation* (Vol. 15). Lincoln: University of Nebraska Press.

Brimer, C. J. (1970a). Disinhibition of an operant response. *Learning and Motivation,* **1,** 346–371.

Brimer, C. J. (1970b). Inhibition and disinhibition of an operant response as a function of the amount and type of prior training. *Psychonomic Science,* **21,** 191–192.

Brimer, C. J. (1972). Disinhibition of an operant response. In R. A. Boakes & M. S. Halliday (Eds.), *Inhibition and learning.* New York: Academic Press.

Brimer, C. J., & Kamin, L. J. (1963). Disinhibition, habituation, sensitization, and the conditioned emotional response. *Journal of Comparative and Physiological Psychology,* **56,** 508–516.

Brimer, C. J., & Wickson, S. (1971). Shock frequency, disinhibition, and conditioned suppression. *Learning and motivation,* **2,** 124–137.

Brown, J. S. (1961). *The motivation of behavior.* New York: McGraw-Hill.

Butler, R. A. (1953). Discrimination learning by Rhesus monkeys to visual-exploration motivation. *Journal of Comparative and Physiological Psychology,* **46,** 95–98.

Clark, L. P. (1933). *The nature and treatment of amentia.* Baltimore: Wood.

Clausen, J., & Karrer, R. (1968). Orienting response-frequency of occurrence and relationships to other autonomic variables. *American Journal of Mental Deficiency, 73*, 455–464.

Cromwell, R. L. (1963). A social learning approach to mental retardation. In N. R. Ellis (Ed.), *Handbook of mental deficiency*. New York: McGraw-Hill.

Crosby, K. G. (1972). Attention and distractibility in mentally retarded and intellectually average children. *American Journal of Mental Deficiency, 77*, 46–53.

Crosby, K. G., & Blatt, B. (1968). Attention and mental retardation. *Journal of Education, 150*(3), 67–81.

Dashiell, J. F. (1928). *Fundamentals of objective psychology*. Boston: Houghton Mifflin.

Dember, W. N. (1961). Alternation behavior. In D. Fiske & S. Maddi (Eds.), *Functions of varied experience*. Homewood, IL: Dorsey Press.

Dember, W. N., & Earl, R. W. (1957). Analysis of exploratory, manipulatory, and curiosity behaviors. *Psychological Review, 64*, 91–96.

Dember, W. N., & Fowler, H. (1958). Spontaneous alternation behavior. *Psychological Bulletin, 55*, 412–428.

Denny, M. R. (1964). Research in learning and performance. In H. Stevens & R. Heber (Eds.), *Mental retardation*. Chicago: University of Chicago Press.

Doleys, D. M. (1976). Distractibility and distracting stimuli: Inconsistent and contradictory results. *Psychological Record, 26*, 279–287.

Duncan, C. P. (1956). On the similarity between reactive inhibition and neural satiation. *American Journal of Psychology, 69*, 227–235.

Duncan, C. P. (1957). Visual and kinesthetic components of reactive inhibition. *American Journal of Psychology, 70*, 616–619.

Eisenberger, R. (1972). Explanation of rewards that do not reduce tissue needs. *Psychological Bulletin, 27*, 319–339.

Elliott, L., & Johnson, J., Jr. (1971). The orienting reflex in intellectually average and retarded children to a relevant and an irrelevant stimulus. *American Journal of Mental Deficiency, 76*, 332–336.

Ellis, N. R., Hawkins, W. F., Pryer, M. W., & Jones, R. W. (1963). Distraction effects in oddity learning by normal and mentally defective humans. *American Journal of Mental Deficiency, 67*, 576–583.

Ellis, N. R., Pryer, M. W., & Barnett, C. D. (1960). Motor learning and retention in normals and defectives. *Perceptual and Motor Skills, 10*, 83–91.

Estes, W. K. (1970). *Learning theory and mental development*. New York: Academic Press.

Eysenck, H. J. (1965). A three-factor theory of reminiscence. *British Journal of Psychology, 56*, 163–181.

Fenz, W. D., & McCabe, M. W. (1971). Habituation of the GSR to tones in retarded children and nonretarded subjects. *American Journal of Mental Deficiency, 75*, 470–473.

Fisher, M. A., & Zeaman, D. (1973). An attention–retention theory of retardate discrimination learning. In N. R. Ellis (Ed.), *International review of research in mental retardation* (Vol. 6). New York: Academic Press.

Fiske, D. W., & Maddi, S. R. (1961). A conceptual framework. In D. Fiske & S. Maddi (Eds.), *Functions of varied experience*. Homewood, IL: Dorsey Press.

Fiske, D. W., & Rice, L. (1955). Intra-individual response variability. *Psychological Bulletin, 52*, 217–250.

Flanagan, B., & Webb, W. B. (1964). Disinhibition and external inhibition in fixed interval operant conditioning. *Psychonomic Science, 1*, 123–124.

Follini, P., Sitkowski, C., & Stayton, S. E. (1969). The attention of retardates and normals in distraction and non-distraction conditions. *American Journal of Mental Deficiency, 74*, 200–205.

Forehand, R., Calhoun, K., Peed, S., & Yoder, P. (1973). The effects of intelligence quotient and extraneous stimulation on incidental learning. *Journal of Mental Deficiency Research, 17,* 24–27.

Fowler, H. (1965). *Curiosity and exploratory behavior.* New York: Macmillan.

Fowler, H., Blond, J., & Dember, W. N. (1959). Alternation behavior and learning: The influence of reinforcement magnitude, number, and contingency. *Journal of Comparative and Physiological Psychology, 52,* 609–614.

Furby, L. (1974). Attentional habituation and mental retardation. *Human Development, 17,* 118–138.

Gagne, R. M. (1941). External inhibition and disinhibition in a conditioned operant response. *Journal of Experimental Psychology, 29,* 104–116.

Gayton, W. F., & Bassett, J. E. (1972). The effect of positive and negative reaction tendencies on receptive language development in mentally retarded children. *American Journal of Mental Deficiency, 76,* 499–508.

Gerjuoy, I. R., & Winters, J., Jr. (1968). Development of lateral and choice-sequence preferences. In N. R. Ellis (Ed.), *International review of research in mental retardation* (Vol. 3). New York: Academic Press.

Girardeau, F. L., & Ellis, N. R. (1964). Rote verbal learning by normal and mentally retarded children. *American Journal of Mental Deficiency, 68,* 525–532.

Glanzer, M. (1953). Stimulus satiation: An explanation of spontaneous alternation and related phenomena. *Psychological Review, 60,* 257–268.

Glanzer, M. (1958). Curiosity, exploratory drive, and stimulus satiation. *Psychological Bulletin, 55,* 302–315.

Goldstein, K. (1943). Concerning rigidity. *Character and Personality, 11,* 209–226.

Green, C. G. (1960). *Social interaction in feebleminded children.* Unpublished master's thesis, University of Missouri, Columbia.

Green, C., & Zigler, E. (1962). Social deprivation and the performance of retarded and normal children on a satiation type task. *Child Development, 33,* 499–508.

Harlow, H. F. (1953). Motivation as a factor in the acquisition of new responses. In *Current theory and research in motivation* (pp. 24–49). Lincoln: University of Nebraska Press.

Harlow, H. F., Blazek, N. C., & McClearn, G. (1956). Manipulatory motivation in the infant rhesus monkey. *Journal of Comparative and Physiological Psychology, 49,* 444–448.

Heal, L. W., & Johnson, J., Jr. (1970). Inhibition deficits in retardate learning and attention. In N. R. Ellis (Ed.), *International review of research in mental retardation* (Vol. 4). New York: Academic Press.

Hebb, D. O. (1955). Drives and the C.N.S. (conceptual nervous system). *Psychological Review, 62,* 243–254.

Hetherington, E. M., & Ross, E. (1967). Discrimination learning by normal and retarded children under delay of reward and interpolated task conditions. *Child Development, 38,* 639–647.

Hinrichs, J. V. (1968). Disinhibition of delay in fixed-interval instrumental conditioning. *Psychonomic Science, 12,* 313–314.

Horns, H. L., & Heron, W. T. (1940). A study of disinhibition in the white rat. *Journal of Comparative Psychology, 30,* 97–102.

Hull, C. L. (1943). *Principles of behavior.* New York: Appleton-Century-Crofts.

Hunter, W. S. (1935). The disinhibition of experimental extinction in the white rat. *Science, 81,* 77–78.

Jackson, D. E. (1959). *The effect of controlled "distraction" on molar variability in the mental defective.* Unpublished master's thesis, University of Alabama, University.

Jeffrey, W. E. (1968). The orienting reflex and attention in cognitive development. *Psychological Review, 75,* 323–334.

Jones, A. (1961). Supplementary report: Information deprivation and irrelevant drive as determiners of an instrumental response. *Journal of Experimental Psychology*, **62**, 310–311.

Jones, A., Wilkinson, H., & Braden, I. (1961). Information deprivation as a motivational variable. *Journal of Experimental Psychology*, **62**, 126–137.

Jones, M. B. (1968). Intertrial correlations under variations in effort. *Ergonomics*, **11**, 175–181.

Jones, R., & Ellis, N. R. (1962). Inhibitory potential in rotary pursuit acquisition by normal and defective subjects. *Journal of Experimental Psychology*, **63**, 534–537.

Karrer, R., Nelson, M., & Galbraith, G. (1979). Psychophysiological research with the mentally retarded. In N. R. Ellis (Ed.), *Handbook of mental deficiency* (2nd ed.). Hillsdale, NJ: Erlbaum.

Kimble, G. A., & Horenstein, B. R. (1948). Reminiscence in motor learning as a function of length of interpolated rest. *Journal of Experimental Psychology*, **38**, 239–244.

Klein, H., Klein, G., Oskamp, L., & Patnode, C. (1972). Color distractors in discrimination with retarded and nonretarded children. *American Journal of Mental Deficiency*, **77**, 328–331.

Kounin, J. S. (1941a). Experimental studies of rigidity I. The measurement of rigidity in normal and feeble-minded persons. *Character and Personality*, **9**, 251–273.

Kounin, J. S.(1941b). Experimental studies of rigidity II. The explanatory power of the concept of rigidity as applied to feeble-mindedness. *Character and Personality*, **9**, 273–282.

Krupski, A.(1979). Are retarded children more distractible? Observational analysis of retarded and nonretarded children's classroom behavior. *American Journal of Mental Deficiency*, **84**, 1–10.

Leuba, C. (1955). Toward some integration of learning theories: The concept of optimal stimulation. *Psychological Reports*, **1**, 27–33.

Lewin, K. (1936). *A dynamic theory of personality*. New York: McGraw-Hill.

Lipman, R. S., & Spitz, H. H. (1961). The relationship between kinesthetic satiation and inhibition in rotary pursuit performance. *Journal of Experimental Psychology*, **62**, 468–475.

Lobb, A. (1967, May). *Attention of trace electrodermal conditioning by benzedrine in mentally defective and normal adults*. Paper presented at the annual convention of the American Association on Mental Deficiency, Denver.

Luria, A. R. (1959). Experimental study of the higher nervous activity of the abnormal child. *Journal of Mental Deficiency Research*, **3**, 1–22.

Luria, A. R. (1963), *The mentally retarded child*. Oxford: Pergamon.

Lynn, E. (1966). *Attention, arousal, and the orientation reaction*. Oxford: Pergamon.

Mateer, F. (1918). *Child behavior*. Boston: Gorham Press.

Melvin, K. B., & Baumeister, A. A. (1969). Effects of size of variable ratio schedule on disinhibition. *Psychological Record*, **19**, 33–37.

Mercer, C. D., & Snell, M. E. (1977). *Learning theory research in mental retardation: Implications for teaching*. Columbus, OH: Merrill.

Montgomery, K. C. (1952). Exploratory behavior and its relation to spontaneous alternation in a series of maze exposures. *Journal of Comparative and Physiological Psychology*, **45**, 50–57.

Montgomery, K. C. (1953). The effect of activity deprivation upon exploratory behavior. *Journal of Comparative and Physiological Psychology*, **46**, 438–441.

Montgomery, K. C. (1954). The role of the exploratory drive in learning. *Journal of Comparative and Physiological Psychology*, **47**, 60–64.

Montgomery, K. C. (1955). The relation between fear induced by novel stimulation and exploratory behavior. *Journal of Comparative and Physiological Psychology*, **48**, 254–260.

Myers, A. K., & Miller, N. E. (1954). Failure to find a learned drive based on hunger: Evidence for learning motivated by "exploration." *Journal of Comparative and Physiological Psychology*, **47**, 428–436.

Nissen, H. W. (1930). A study of exploratory behavior in the white rat by means of the obstruction method. *Journal of Genetic Psychology*, **37**, 361–376.

Nissen, H. W. (1954). The nature of the drive as innate determinant of behavioral organization. In M. R. Jones (Ed.), *Nebraska Symposium on Motivation.* Lincoln: University of Nebraska Press.

Olds, J., & Milner, P. (1954). Positive reinforcement produced by electrical stimulation of septal area and other regions of the rat brain. *Journal of Comparative and Physiological Psychology,* **47,** 419–427.

Pavlov, I. P. (1927). *Conditioned reflexes.* New York: Dover.

Peters, E. N. (1972). Nonexistent individual differences in reminiscence. *Psychological Bulletin,* **78,** 375–378.

Pilgrim, D., Miller, F., & Cobb, H. (1969). GSR strength and habituation in normal and nonorganic mentally retarded children. *American Journal of Mental Deficiency,* **74,** 27–31.

Plenderleith, M. (1956). Discrimination learning and discrimination reversal learning in normal and feebleminded children. *Journal of Genetic Psychology,* **88,** 107–112.

Razran, G. H.(1939). Decremental and incremental effects of distracting stimuli upon the salivary CRs of 24 adult human subjects (inhibition and disinhibition?). *Journal of Experimental Psychology,* **24,** 647–652.

Rexroad, C. (1937). Reaction time and conditioning: Extinction, recovery, and disinhibition. *Journal of Experimental Psychology,* **20,** 468–476.

Ross, L., Headrick, M., & MacKay, P. (1967). Classical eyelid conditioning of young Mongoloid children. *American Journal of Mental Deficiency,* **72,** 21–29.

Ross, L., Koski, C., & Yaeger, J. (1964). Classical eyelid conditioning of the severely retarded. *Psychonomic Science,* **1,** 253–254.

Sarason, S. B. (1953). *Psychological problems in mental deficiency* (2nd ed.). New York: Harper.

Shannon, C. E., & Weaver, W. (1949). *The mathematical theory of communication.* Urbana: University of Illinois Press.

Sheffield, F., & Roby, T. (1950). Reward value of a non-nutritive sweet taste. *Journal of Comparative and Physiological Psychology,* **43,** 471–481.

Sheffield, F., Wulff, J., & Backer, R. (1951). Reward value of copulation without sex drive reduction. *Journal of Comparative and Physiological Psychology,* **44,** 3–8.

Siddle, D., & Glenn, S. (1974). Habituation of the orienting response to simple and complex stimuli. *American Journal of Mental Deficiency,* **78,** 688–693.

Siegel, P. S., & Foshee, J. G. (1960). Molar variability in the mentally defective. *Journal of Abnormal and Social Psychology,* **61,** 141–143.

Singh, D., & Wickens, D. (1968). Disinhibition in instrumental conditioning. *Journal of Comparative and Physiological Psychology,* **66,** 557–559.

Skeels, H., Udegraff, R., Wellman, B., & Williams, H. (1938). A study of environmental stimulation, an orphanage preschool project. *University of Iowa Studies on Child Welfare,* **15,** No. 4.

Skinner, B. F. (1936). A failure to obtain "disinhibition." *Journal of General Psychology,* **14,** 127–133.

Smith, S. A. (1984). *The effect of disinhibition on the molar response variability of the mentally retarded.* Unpublished doctoral dissertation, University of Alabama, University.

Sokolov, E. N. (1960). Neuronal models and the orienting reflex. In M. A. Brazier (Ed.), *The central nervous system and behavior.* New York: Josiah Macy.

Sokolov, E. N. (1963). *Perception and the conditioned reflex.* New York: Pergamon.

Solomon, R. L. (1948). The influence of work on behavior. *Psychological Bulletin,* **45,** 1–40.

Spitz, H. H. (1958). The present status of the Kohler–Wallach theory of satiation. *Psychological Bulletin,* **55,** 1–28.

Spitz, H. H. (1959). Cortical satiation as a common factor in perception and abstraction: Some postulated relationships based on the performance of atypical groups. *American Journal of Mental Deficiency,* **63,** 633–638.

Spitz, H. H. (1963). Field theory in mental deficiency. In N. R. Ellis (Ed.), *Handbook of mental deficiency*. New York: McGraw-Hill.

Spitz, H. H., & Blackman, L. D. (1959). A comparison of mental retardates and normals on visual figure aftereffects and reversible figures. *Journal of Abnormal and Social Psychology*, **58**, 105–110.

Stevenson, H., & Zigler, E. (1957). Discrimination learning and rigidity in normal and feebleminded individuals. *Journal of Personality*, **25**, 699–711.

Switzer, S. A. (1933). Disinhibition of a conditioned response. *Journal of General Psychology*, **9**, 77–100.

Terdal, L. G. (1967a). Stimulus satiation and mental retardation. *American Journal of Mental Deficiency*, **71**, 881–885.

Terdal, L. G. (1967b). Complexity and position of stimuli as determinants of looking behavior in retardates and normals. *American Journal of Mental Deficiency*, **72**, 384–387.

Turnure, J. E. (1970). Children's reactions to distractors in a learning situation. *Developmental Psychology*, **2**, 115–122.

Viney, L., Clarke, A., & Lord, J. (1973). Resistance to extinction and frustration in retarded and nonretarded children. *American Journal of Mental Deficiency*, **78**, 308–315.

Vogel, W. (1961). The relationship of age and intelligence to autonomic functioning. *Journal of Comparative and Physiological Psychology*, **54**, 133–138.

Walker, E. (1958). Action decrement and its relation to learning. *Psychological Review*, **65**, 129–142.

Warren, A., & Brown, R. (1943). Conditioned operant response phenomena in children. *Journal of General Psychology*, **28**, 181–207.

Weaver, S., Balla, D., & Zigler, E. (1971). Social approach and avoidance tendencies of institutionalized retarded and noninstitutionalized retarded and normal children. *Journal of Experimental Research in Personality*, **5**, 98–110.

Wenger, M. (1936). External inhibition and disinhibition produced by duplicate stimuli. *American Journal of Psychology*, **48**, 446–456.

Werner, H. (1940). *Comparative psychology of mental development*. New York: Harper.

Werner, H. (1948). The concept of rigidity: A critical evaluation. *Psychological Review*, **53**, 43–53.

Whitman, M., & Sprague, R. (1968). Learning and distractibility in normals and retardates. *Training School Bulletin*, **65**, 89–101.

Winnick, W., & Hunt, J. (1951). The effect of an extra stimulus upon strength of response during acquisition and extinction. *Journal of Experimental Psychology*, **41**, 205–215.

Wolfensberger, W., & O'Connor, N. (1965). Stimulus intensity and duration effects on EEG and GSR responses of normals and retardates. *American Journal of Mental Deficiency*, **70**, 21–37.

Wright, L. (1970). Prerest performance levels of nonretardates and retardates, and reminiscence on a manual crank task. *American Journal of Mental Deficiency*, **75**, 304–308.

Wright, L., & Hearn, C., Jr. (1964). Reactive inhibition in normals and defectives as measured from a common performance criterion. *Journal of General Psychology*, **71**, 57–64.

Wright, L., & Willis, C. (1969). Reminiscence in normals and defectives. *American Journal of Mental Deficiency*, **73**, 700–702.

Yamaguchi, H. G., & Ladioray, G. L. (1962). Disinhibition as a function of extinction trials and stimulus intensity. *Journal of Comparative and Physiological Psychology*, **55**, 572–577.

Zeaman, D., & House, B. (1963). The role of attention in retardate discrimination learning. In N. R. Ellis (Ed.), *Handbook of mental deficiency*. New York: McGraw-Hill.

Zigler, E. (1961). Social deprivation and rigidity in the performance of feebleminded children. *Journal of Abnormal Social Psychology*, **62**, 413–421.

Zigler, E. (1962). Rigidity in the feebleminded. In E. Trapp & P. Himmelstein (Eds.), *Readings on the exceptional child*. New York: Appleton-Century-Crofts.

Zigler, E. (1966). Research on personality structure in the retardate. In N. R. Ellis (Ed.), *International review of research on mental retardation* (Vol. 1). New York: Academic Press.

Zigler, E., & Balla, D. (1982). *Mental retardation: The developmental-difference controversy.* Hillsdale, NJ: Erlbaum.

Zigler, E., Hodgden, L., & Stevenson, H. (1958). The effect of support on the performance of normal and feebleminded children. *Journal of Personality, 26,* 106–122.

Computer-Assisted Instruction for the Mentally Retarded

FRANCES A. CONNERS

DEPARTMENT OF PSYCHOLOGY
CASE WESTERN RESERVE UNIVERSITY
CLEVELAND, OHIO 44106

DAVID R. CARUSO

DEPARTMENT OF PSYCHOLOGY
YALE UNIVERSITY
NEW HAVEN, CONNECTICUT 06520

DOUGLAS K. DETTERMAN

DEPARTMENT OF PSYCHOLOGY
CASE WESTERN RESERVE UNIVERSITY
CLEVELAND, OHIO 44106

I. INTRODUCTION

A difficulty in teaching mentally retarded students is that they vary so widely in their needs and abilities (Robinson & Robinson, 1976). For this reason, a major goal in the education of mentally retarded students has been to maximize the amount of individual attention each student receives from the teacher (Polloway, Payne, Patton, & Payne, 1985; Robinson & Robinson, 1976). The ideal situation might be one-to-one tutoring, and, in fact, research shows that retarded students usually benefit from one-to-one instruction compared with group instruction, even if tutors are peer or cross-age tutors (Jenkins, Mayhall, Peschka, & Jenkins, 1974; Russel & Ford, 1983; Wagner, 1974). It is difficult, however, for teacher to work individually with students when there are several students to teach. One solution to this problem is to develop computer-assisted instruction

INTERNATIONAL REVIEW OF RESEARCH IN
MENTAL RETARDATION, Vol. 14

(CAI) to perform some individualized instructional functions (Bennet, 1982; Hannaford & Taber, 1982).

The purpose of this chapter is to investigate the applications and research on CAI for the mentally retarded and to evaluate the extent to which individualization has been addressed. First, we will discuss some current trends in thinking and research on CAI, mainly with the nonretarded. Next, we will consider one-to-one teaching as a model for individualizing CAI. Finally, we will discuss CAI applications for the mentally retarded—the rationale, the literature, and future directions.

II. TRENDS AND FINDINGS IN CAI

In this chapter, we will refer to CAI as instruction which is implemented by a computer. CAI can be short, cartoonlike educational games or semester-long, text-based question-and-answer instruction. We will not discuss learning environments (e.g., Edison Responsive Environment) or programming languages for children (e.g., LOGO) because they do not instruct, but rather make knowledge available to users. Information on such uses of the computer can be found in Geoffrion and Goldenberg (1981), Moore (1966), and Papert (1980).

Little empirical evidence has been reported regarding the educational components of CAI. However, three factors are often cited as reasons that CAI should be educationally effective. These are individualization (Atkinson, 1967; Byrne, 1983; Cooley & Glaser, 1969; Glaser, 1970; Piele, 1983), motivation (Budoff & Hutten, 1982; Hannaford & Taber, 1982; Lepper, 1985), and active learning (Gallini, 1983; Glaser, 1970; Ward, Sewell, Rostron, & Phillips, 1983). Computer-assisted instruction software can be classified according to its primary approach to educational effectiveness. One type of CAI is designed primarily to afford individualized instruction. It may not use color or graphics, but it attempts to deliver instruction at a variable pace and includes remedial branches where they are needed on an individual basis. Another type of CAI attempts to present instruction or drill within the context of a game, with the belief that the game will motivate students to learn. Students may also proceed at their own pace, but this is secondary to the gaming aspect. A third type of CAI requires active learning by making the student discover concepts rather than teaching them to the student explicitly. This type of CAI is based on the theory that discovery learning results in a higher quality of learning than directed learning (Bruner, 1961).

A. Effectiveness

Several literature reviews and meta-analyses have been carried out in order to determine whether or not CAI enhances learning. The conclusions drawn concerning supplementary CAI have been consistently favorable (Burns & Boze-man, 1981; Jamison, Suppes, & Wells, 1974; Vinsonhaler & Bass, 1972). There have been mixed conclusions, however, regarding the effectiveness of CAI that is used in place of traditional instruction. Two reviews compared supplementary and substitution CAI. Edwards, Norton, Taylor, Weiss, and Dusseldorp (1975) reported positive findings for supplementary CAI but mixed findings for CAI used as a substitute. J. A. Kulik, Bangert, and Williams (1983), however, reported a higher effect size for substitution computer-based instruction (CBI) (including CAI) than for supplementary CBI (.36 and .21, respectively). Regardless of whether CAI supplemented or substituted, it reduced lesson time compared to traditional instruction (Edwards *et al.*, 1975; Jamison *et al.*, 1974; J. A. Kulik, Kulik, & Cohen, 1980). In the most general sense, then, evidence indicates that CAI is educationally worthwhile.

Reviews and meta-analyses provide general conclusions from a literature, but often do not provide the crucial information—what is it that makes a CAI program succeed or fail? Are the believed-to-be attributes of CAI actually beneficial? Are they actually implemented? In the next few sections we will discuss some evidence bearing on whether individualized instruction, motivation, and discovery are related to learning. We will also review the CAI literature to determine whether the three attributes have been incorporated successfully into CAI software to enhance learning. We will discuss one attribute at a time, leaving individualized instruction for last, as it will be the focus of the remainder of the chapter.

B. Motivation

Motivation is believed to be a powerful variable affecting learning. In early learning studies, motivation or drive was important in explaining learning (Hull, 1943). Today's conception of motivation, however, deals less with hunger and thirst and more with stimulus properties such as novelty and complexity (Dember, 1974), goal-directed behavior, and control (Harter, 1978). Lepper (1985) has pointed out that, although we assume that motivation plays a role in learning, there is surprisingly little evidence that this is so (cf. Koehler, 1975; Lane, 1973; Sheeran, 1982). However, to the extent that intrinsic motivation can be measured by one's persistence with a task (Deci, 1971; Greene, Sternberg, & Lepper, 1976; Kersh, 1962; Rosenfeld, Folger, & Adelman, 1980), and to the extent that time engaged with a task effects learning (Cobb, 1972; Fisher, Marliave, & Filby, 1979; Fredrick & Walberg, 1980), motivation may lead to greater learning.

Is there any evidence that CAI programs have successfully incorporated motivating elements in such a way as to enhance learning? Recently, there has been some attention given to the motivational aspects of video games, which have proven to be extremely enjoyable and even addictive for children and adults. This attention has been focused on extracting the motivational components of video games so that they might be used in CAI (Bowman, 1982; Chaffin, Maxwell, & Thompson, 1982; Driskell & Dwyer, 1984; Lesgold, 1982; Swenson & Anderson, 1982). Malone (1981) has studied the effects of various components of arcade games on game preference as indicated by ratings and time spent playing. Although not conclusive, his results suggest that arcade game preference is affected by the amount of challenge (the presence of a goal, scorekeeping, and randomness or uncertainty), fantasy, and sensory curiosity (visual and auditory effects) in the game. Malone and others (Bowman, 1982; Chaffin *et al.*, 1982; Driskell & Dwyer, 1984) have suggested other possible motivating factors of video games, such as (1) a goal hierarchy with goals that are difficult, but within reach, and with a ceiling that is seemingly unlimited, (2) high response rates that demand undivided attention, and (3) immediate response-by-response feedback, allowing improvement indicated by more global feedback. Some people have attempted to apply these elements to educational software by embedding the instruction within a game (Chaffin *et al.*, 1982; Lesgold, 1982).

Thus, attempts have been made to incorporate motivational elements into CAI. Is there any evidence that CAI actually is motivating to students? Little if any evidence is available to determine whether educational games have been successful motivationally or educationally. To the extent that motivation fosters positive attitudes, however, we can examine the literature on the effects of CAI on students' attitudes. First, do students enjoy CAI? Evidence suggests that students who use CAI have more positive attitudes toward it than those who do not use it (Mathis, Smith, & Hansen, 1970) and have slightly more positive attitudes toward CAI than control students have toward conventional instruction (J. A. Kulik *et al.*, 1980, 1983). Other positive effects include self-responsibility for success and academic self-confidence (Griswold, 1984). Although attitudes toward CAI are positive, CAI does not seem to strongly affect enjoyment of the subject a student studies using CAI. Griswold found no relationship between CAI use and attitudes toward school or mathematics. J. A. Kulik *et al.* (1980, 1983) found smaller (but positive) effect sizes for attitudes toward subject matter than for attitudes toward instructional mode. Thus, there is some evidence supporting CAI as a motivating form of instruction, though CAI may not increase motivation for learning subject matter.

C. Active Learning

Active participation in learning, or learning by discovery, is believed by some to be a more meaningful type of learning than other types and therefore somehow more lasting. According to Bruner (1961), discovery learning has four advantages over expository learning: (1) increased "intellectual potency," because children learn to organize concepts and knowledge, (2) increased intrinsic motivation, assuming that we have a need to control the environment and demonstrate competence, (3) generalized skill in learning through discovery, such as might be useful in scientific exploits, and (4) increased memory, insofar as the key to retrieval is organization. Others agree that children gain from exploratory learning beyond what they learn when they are taught explicitly (Holt, 1964, 1967; Papert, 1980; Suchman, 1961).

From a sampling of studies, some discussed by Kersh and Wittrock (1962), it is evident that the effectiveness of discovery learning has not been confirmed. Discovery learning was found to be better than (Andrews, 1984), worse than (Kersh, 1958), and equivalent to (Kittel, 1957) directed learning, as measured by immediate posttests of rule application. On retention measures, discovery learning was found to be better than (Kersh, 1958) and worse than (Guthrie, 1967) directed learning. Finally, on transfer measures, discovery learning was found to be equivalent to (Kittel, 1957) and better than (Gagne & Brown, 1961) directed learning. Guided discovery learning, a compromise between discovery learning and directed learning, was found in two studies to be the best alternative (Gagne & Brown, 1961; Kittel, 1957). According to Strike (1975), the reason for inconsistencies in the literature is that there is no clear conceptualization of discovery learning.

The type of CAI that is based on discovery learning is referred to as simulation. This type of CAI gives the student a goal to reach or a problem to solve and requires the student to learn concepts through trial and error. For example, the ongoing simulation "Oligopoly" (R. M. Miller, 1981) requires business students to operate a chocolate firm in an oligopolistic market, given certain market conditions and business choices. The goal of the game is to maximize profits. The goal of the simulation is to learn business concepts such as supply and demand, the operation of stocks and bonds, and so on.

There is little empirical evidence concerning the educational value of computerized simulations. In a review of noncomputerized simulation games, Reiser and Gerlach (1977) painted a bleak picture. There were no differences between subjects who used simulations and those who used an alternative method of instruction in measures of learning, intellectual skills (e.g., problem solving), social attitudes, or interest in the subject matter. The only positive effects of simulations were interest in and skill in simulations. Reiser and Gerlach suggested that the major problem in the literature is in defining the purpose of the individual simulation games and choosing dependent variables accordingly. Even if simulation games are only as good as other instructional methods, however, they may have an advantage if they are more interesting.

D. Individualized Instruction

Individualized instruction is believed to be very successful as a method of instruction. Many studies have investigated the instructional effects of individualized instruction programs such as Personalized System of Instruction (PSI), Individual System of Instruction (ISI), Programmed Instruction (PI), and instruction by tutor. Kulik and Kulik and their colleagues have synthesized the effectiveness literature on each of these types of individualized instruction (Bangert, Kulik, & Kulik, 1983; Cohen, Kulik, & Kulik, 1982; J. A. Kulik & Jaska, 1977; Kulik et al., 1980; Kulik, Kulik, & Smith, 1976; C.-L. C. Kulik, Shwalb, & Kulik, 1982). The average gains in achievement experienced by groups receiving individualized instruction ranged from .10 to .66 standard deviations, depending on the type of instruction and the level of education of the students. Some average gains were minimal, but average differences favored individualized instruction in each meta-analysis. Bloom (1984a,b) reported that instruction by tutor is the most effective type of instruction known, raising student achievement 2.0 standard deviations over conventional instruction.

Atkinson and his associates and Tennyson and his associates have studied individualized aspects of CAI. Their findings indicate that CAI is most effective when the instructional method is adapted to the abilities and responses of the individual.

Atkinson's work has dealt with finding the optimal allocation of computer time among students, of instructional "strands" within a lesson, and of items within a strand. Much of the work has concerned the latter, most specific type of optimization and has dealt with list learning, such as beginning word recognition (Atkinson, 1974; Atkinson & Fletcher, 1972). Atkinson's approach has been to design instruction around a model of the learning process. Atkinson and Paulson (1972) discussed three models describing possible processes for list learning. The linear model maintains that people learn items gradually, and the more exposure one has to an item, the greater the probability of having mastered it. The all-or-none model contends that every item is either learned or not learned, and the more consecutive correct responses to the item, the greater is the probability that the item has been mastered. When an incorrect response is made the probability drops to zero. Finally, the random-trial increments model is a variant of the linear model in which learning depends on two parameters, such as ability and item difficulty. Atkinson and Crothers (1964) tested model fit for several models, including the three discussed by Atkinson and Paulson. They found the random-trial increments to fit the data better than the all-or-none model or the linear model.

Each of the three models can be converted to an algorithm which allocates the order of items according to its probability of not being learned, or probability of error. In each case, the item with the highest probability of error is chosen to be presented next. The three models' presentation strategies determine which item this is in different ways. In the linear strategy, the item with the highest error probability is the one which has been presented the least number of times. This strategy results in an initial presentation of all items in random order, followed by a second presentation of all items in random order, and so on. In the all-or-none strategy, the item chosen is the one which has the fewest number of cumulative correct responses. When an incorrect response is made, that item's counter is reset to zero, and it has presentation priority. Finally, in the random-trial increment strategy, the probability of error is determined algebraically from the student's ability (determined by his history of error across words) and the word's difficulty (determined by its history of error across students). These values are updated and become more precise as more responses are given by the student and more students encounter each of the words. All three strategies use student responses to determine a unique series of items for each student. Thus, all three are individualized strategies.

Which instructional strategy is most successful? The all-or-none strategy was found superior to the linear strategy (Lorton, 1973), and the random-trial increment strategy was found superior to both the all-or-none strategy and the linear strategy (Laubsh, 1971). Thus, the strategy that considered individual differences in student ability and word difficulty was more successful than those that only considered individual differences in learning speed.

Tennyson has further explored the variables of individualization. His research has dealt with the Minnesota Adaptive Instructional System (MAIS), primarily examining concept acquisition in high school and college students. Like Atkinson's random-trial increment instruction, Tennyson's instruction is based on a mathematical model that determines the instructional sequence a student receives. Unlike Atkinson's instruction, Tennyson's considers pretask measures as well as on-task response patterns.

Tennyson has used a Bayesian probability model to determine how much instruction a student will need based on the student's responses. Two pretask measures are taken, an ability measure and a knowledge measure. The knowledge measure is a sample of items like those in the learning task and is used to estimate the student's probability of having mastered the concepts (''prior probability''). The ability measure is a reasoning test, used to set a ''loss ratio'' of false advances to false retainments. The higher the student's ability, the higher this ratio is allowed to be. A learning criterion is set, reflecting the probability of mastery needed to conclude that the student has mastered the concept. The Bayesian model calculates the number of instructional examples (instances) needed by the student by considering the prior probability and the loss ratio. The student then completes that number of instances and an operating level is computed based on his responses. The operating level expresses a probability that the student has mastered the concept and replaces the prior probability. The operating level is compared with the criterion to determine whether the student needs more instruction. If necessary, another instance is presented, followed by evaluation. Thus, the program offers an individualized prescription of instruction. It should be pointed out that, in the standard program, the order of instances is uniform for all students.

Tennyson and Rothen (1977) tested the Bayesian model of adaptive instruction by comparing it with a nonadaptive version and a partially adaptive version of concept acquisition instruction. The partially adaptive version differed from the adaptive version in that it used only pretask information to prescribe instruction and did not use on-task information to adjust it. The nonadaptive version presented a uniform number of exercises to each student. The adaptive version proved better than the other two in terms of posttest performance and time needed to reach criterion.

Park and Tennyson (1980) found no differences in posttest performance between instruction adapted on the basis of only pretask, only on-task, or both pretask and on-task information. However, adaptation based on both pretask and on-task information resulted in the shortest learning time. In the same study, Park and Tennyson tested the effect of prescribing the order of instances according to response history. After an incorrect response, an instance or example of the answer given was provided. This "response-sensitive" method produced higher posttest scores and quicker learning than the standard method. These studies suggest that the greater extent of individualization, the more powerful the instruction.

E. Conclusion

Obviously, more research is needed in the motivational, discovery, and individualized aspects of CAI. The motivational approach to CAI is to make boring instruction fun by making it a game, which will keep students engaged in instruction longer. Some concern has been expressed, however, that the extrinsic motivation provided by the computer game might undermine any intrinsic interest a student might have in the subject matter (Lepper, 1985). Simulation CAI has not received very much research attention, but the mixed results in the discovery learning literature and the negative results in the noncomputerized simulation literature raise questions about the effectiveness of the simulation approach. Individualized CAI, on the other hand, not only has been studied, but also has been supported by empirical evidence. Thus, individualization in CAI seems most promising at this point, if only because there are data supporting it. While we advocate research in all three areas, we encourage thinking, research, and program development to emphasize individualization in CAI.

III. A LESSON FROM ONE-TO-ONE TUTORING

If CAI is to provide individualized instruction, then it might benefit from what is known about one-to-one tutoring, an individualized form of instruction which, according to Bloom (1984a,b), is the most effective form of instruction. Two meta-analyses reported that the average achievement gain resulting from tutorial instruction over traditional instruction is .40 standard deviations (Cohen *et al.,* 1982; Walberg, 1984). Walberg grouped tutorial instruction among the largest instructional effects. Both meta-analyses included studies on peer tutoring and cross-age tutoring, reflecting the finding that one-to-one instruction is often superior to group instruction even when elementary or junior high tutors are compared with experienced classroom and resource room teachers (B. Chiang, Thorpe, & Darch, 1980; Devin-Sheehan, Feldman, & Allen, 1976; Jenkins *et al.,* 1974; Russel & Ford, 1983; Trovato & Bucher, 1980). Bloom (1984a,b), however, reported that with a *good* tutor the effect of tutorial instruction is 2.0 standard deviations. His students have demonstrated this effect in four samples of different grades and different topics of study (Anania, 1982; Burke, 1984). Since mentally retarded students require "more directive, intensive, and highly individualized instruction" than they can get through traditional methods (Polloway *et al.,* 1985, p. 2), they stand to benefit from one-to-one tutoring.

Why is the tutorial method of teaching more effective in increasing student achievement? Bloom suggested some reasons by comparing it with classroom instruction. The reasons largely have to do with the amount of attention students receive from the teacher. In the classroom, the teacher's attention tends to be directed toward a small number of students who are typically achieving in the top third of the class. As a result, a majority of students may not (1) be directly engaged in learning, (2) receive much corrective feedback, and (3) receive much encouragement and reinforcement.

In a tutoring situation, the student must be directly engaged in learning. The student cannot rely on others to answer questions, but must pay attention and respond often. Research has shown that the more time students spend directly engaged in learning, the greater their achievement (Cobb, 1972; Fisher *et al.,* 1979; Fredrick & Walberg, 1980). Good and Beckerman (1978) found that low-achieving sixth graders tended to spend a lower percentage of their time engaged in learning activities than high-achieving sixth graders. Although the direction of causality was not explicit, an environment which fosters involvement must be especially important for those who start out with low ability.

Corrective feedback and reinforcement can be more direct and relevant to the student's performance in a one-to-one situation than in other situations. Corrective feedback is feedback which explains the correct answer or leads the student to the correct answer rather than only indicating the correct or incorrect status of the student's answer. When corrective feedback is constant, the need for extra review or the ability to accelerate may be more readily recognized. Research has shown that the use of corrective feedback is related to student achievement (Thompson, 1977; Walberg, 1984). Because the tutor pays close attention to the student's performance, it is possible to reinforce the student whenever a correct answer is given and to encourage the student to do well. Reinforcement has perhaps the greatest effect on achievement of all manipulable educational factors

(Walberg, 1984). By using feedback as a corrective process and encouraging correct answers, the tutor can produce a high rate of success in the student. Special education students' progress in academic subjects has been found to be related to their teachers' use of feedback (Englert, 1983).

Finally, in a tutoring situation, attention is given to the special needs of individual students. According to Burke (1984), one reason for low achievement is that teachers' time is divided among many students and they cannot meet the needs of individual students. In one-to-one teaching, the teacher knows or can assess the student's abilities and learning style and can instruct in such a way that will capitalize on strong points and give extra attention to weak points. Egan and Archer (1985) found that teachers can assess these abilities quite accurately. Also, the teacher can guess the thinking behind errors made by the student and present appropriate remediation. For example, A. Miller and Miller (1971) found that, in sight word instruction, some students learned more words using a picture-accentuated method, whereas others learned more using a picture-pairing method. The students' ability to use a reference effectively determined which method was better for them. A tutor might choose between instructional methods based on the student's ability to use a reference.

Because students are directly engaged in learning and proceed at their own pace and because instruction is focused on their individual needs, the tutorial method provides the optimal use of student time. However, most often the teacher also must teach many other students, and tutorial instruction does not make the best use of the teacher's time (Bennet, 1982; Hannaford & Taber, 1982).

Types of instruction such as small group instruction, classroom instruction, and instruction by filmstrip vary along a continuum of student–teacher interaction. Beginning with small group instruction and progressing along the continuum, each type of instruction demands less student activity and attention, allows less opportunity for extra practice or speeding ahead, and gives less attention to student characteristics. As a result, each affords less efficient learning time for the student, but more efficient teaching time for the teacher than the one before. If CAI were modeled after the tutoring situation, it could serve to increase efficiency of student time without decreasing efficiency of teacher time.

CAI potentially can include components of tutorial instruction. It can require students to respond often, commanding their attention and involvement. It can give corrective feedback and branch to remedial sequences which break a problem down into small steps. It can reinforce good performance with pictures, games, or other stimuli and can do so on a relative basis, such that "good performance" is defined differently for each student. Finally, it can use knowledge of student abilities or past performance to present instruction in an optimal way for each individual.

The CAI programming developed thus far for mentally retarded users contains some of the elements of one-to-one teaching. It maintains the activity and the attention of the student and gives opportunity for review or acceleration. It allows individual pacing, but not individualized presentation of instruction. What is missing in the CAI programming is attention to student characteristics and types of errors made, and adjustment of instruction accordingly. This is precisely the role we believe CAI can best fill in the instruction of mentally retarded students.

IV. CAI FOR MENTALLY RETARDED PERSONS

Until now we have discussed issues in CAI and in one-to-one instruction which are applicable to the general population. We have stressed the value of individualized instruction and have used one-to-one instruction as the best model for individualized CAI. We turn now to the use of CAI with mentally retarded students. In this section, we will present a rationale for using CAI in the education and training of mentally retarded individuals based on what is known about mentally retarded people and the capacities of the computer for CAI. Then we will give an overview of the types of CAI programs that have been developed specifically for retarded students and the results of these studies. Finally, we will evaluate the literature in terms of how well it has addressed the individualized instruction issue.

A. Rationale

Although the number of computer applications for handicapped people has increased (Goldenberg, 1977), few applications have been developed for mentally retarded learners. Yet, the need of mentally retarded students for individual attention in instruction and for drill is great (Robinson & Robinson, 1976). Individual attention and drill are aspects of instruction that CAI can easily provide and are indeed the two most commonly cited advantages of CAI.

Several authors have noted that CAI seems particularly suited to mentally retarded students. Certain characteristics of mentally retarded students which are tedious for teachers or trainers to deal with can be addressed simply and tirelessly by a computer. An initial problem among mentally retarded students is distractibility (Crosby & Blatt, 1968; Ellis, Hawkins, Pryer, & Jones, 1963; Krupski, 1979). Computer-assisted instruction can use various visual and auditory techniques to draw attention to the learning task. Contrast, for example, could be used to direct attention toward a stimulus. McLesky (1982) found that contrast increased retention of stimuli for mentally retarded children. Moving graphics, music, and color may also attract attention (Allen, 1975).

A second problem experienced by mentally retarded individuals is low expectancy for success (Bialer, 1961). This may be caused by frequent failure experiences and may result in a low level of motivation (Wong, 1980). Zigler (1969) has emphasized the importance of motivational factors in mentally retarded people's performance. To address this expectancy/motivation problem, the computer can present material within the range of a student's competence, reinforcing correct answers and allowing for and emphasizing successes. Reinforcement in the form of music (Holloway, 1980; D. M. Miller, 1976) and verbal praise (Levy, 1974; Stevenson & Cruse, 1961; Stevenson & Fahel, 1961; Zigler, 1963) has been found to increase task performance and achievement of mentally retarded individuals. The computer could administer such reinforcement consistently.

Mentally retarded students seem to require a great deal of review of the same material. They can review the material to whatever extent necessary with CAI. Finally, because retarded students often cannot read, they need modes of presentation of instruction other than text. The computer can present material pictorially, using graphics, slides, or videotapes, or auditorily, using a speech synthesizer or a tape recorder.

As we have emphasized, mentally retarded students are individuals who vary widely in their needs and abilities. Finn (1983) argued that, in evaluating educational programs for mentally retarded students, "enormous variability among children in prior learning or more specific functional needs" should be considered, and he suggests that investigators "characterize each subject of a study by a multivariate profile of functional needs" (p. 264). Perhaps the most useful role CAI can play in teaching or training mentally retarded students is in presenting instruction which is adapted to these individual needs and abilities.

B.   Overview of the Literature

This section provides an overview of the programming and research in CAI for mentally retarded students. The CAI programs developed for the mentally retarded will be described in terms of instructional sequencing and methods of student–computer interaction. Then, studies of effectiveness, program parameter effects, and subject characteristic effects will be presented.

Our literature search on CAI programming for mentally retarded students and research studies involving CAI applications for mentally retarded people located descriptions of 16 CAI programs and 17 research studies. Fourteen of the 16 CAI programs were the object of one of the research studies. The CAI programs used in two of the research studies were not described in detail. One CAI program was used in two studies.

1. PROGRAMMING

Two aspects of CAI programming that are particularly important for handicapped students are the degree of individualization present in the instructional sequencing and the ease with which students can interact with the computer. We will discuss these two aspects of CAI programming and conclude that individualization is lacking, whereas ergonomics are relatively advanced.

a. Individualization. There are at least four degrees of individualization in CAI. First, CAI can present the same sequence of instruction to each student at a pace that is comfortable for the student (individual pacing). Next, it can give a certain amount of instruction, test, and then advance only those who have attained a level of mastery (progression based on competence). It can analyze the errors made by a student and give special help based on what is difficult for the individual (remedial branching). Finally, it can present items in a different way based on the student's personality or cognitive characteristics (assessment of characteristics for instructional modification). Each increasingly individualized category subsumes the categories before it. We will describe one CAI program from each of the categories except the fourth, because no CAI programs that we found fit that category.

An example from the first category (individual pacing) is a budget-balancing program designed by England (1979). In this program, mentally retarded adults practiced spending "Joe Confused's" salary on typical monthly purchases. Slides were shown, giving a choice of purchases to the trainees, who typed in an amount of money if they wished to purchase the depicted item. If the trainee had overspent Joe's salary at any time or had underspent it at the end of the session, a warning was given and the trainee had an opportunity to start over. No attempt was made to understand the reasons behind errors made. No explanation or remediation was given by the computer after errors were made.

The second type of program demands demonstrated competence before more difficult material is introduced. Vitello and Bruce (1977) developed a program called "Add" to present addition problems involving numbers from 1 to 99, arranged in increasingly difficult formats. The three formats included two response alternatives, three response alternatives, and a blank for the student to fill in. Each format was divided into number levels, or "decades" (1 to 10, 11 to 20, etc.). Students started in the easiest format with the lowest decade. They had to respond correctly to ten consecutive problems in order to advance to a more difficult format, and only after ten consecutive trials in the most difficult format could they move on to a higher decade. Programs that are criterion-based or competency-based are a step more individualized than those merely offering repeated error trials because they keep a student at an appropriate level of difficulty until the student is ready to proceed.

The most highly individualized CAI programs we found focused on errors made. Remedial sequences appropriate to specific errors were presented in order to help students understand their errors. Strain's (1974) social arithmetic program is an example of programs with remedial branching. Designed to increase speed and accuracy in the buying situation, it included sections on the skills necessary to do so, such as knowledge of coin values and subtraction. It was a competency-based program in which trainees had to demonstrate proficiency in each necessary skill before going on to the next section. The program presented slides of price tags and coin combinations. It asked "key step" questions such as, "Can you buy this item with the money available?" and "Is the change correct?" When errors were made, the program branched to more specific questioning, meant to deliver the information or logic necessary to answer the key step question. Those students not making an error would not receive the remedial sequence, but would instead go on to other material, getting extra help where they needed it. Though this CAI program represents the most highly individualized programs that we found, still there was no assessment of student characteristics. Outside of special remediation, each student received the same instruction, in much the same way as small group instruction with homework might function.

b. Ergonomics. The second important aspect of CAI programming for special students is its degree of simplicity of use. It is particularly important for mentally retarded users that the computer–user interaction be as straightforward as possible, in order to minimize thinking which is irrelevant to the learning task and to maximize attention to the learning task. Students should forget that they are working on a computer. Attention to three aspects of the programming can be crucial to achieving this goal. First, instructions should be minimal and easy to understand. Hughson and Brown (1983) found that mentally retarded adults performed best on nonverbal tasks when instructions were brief, slow, and nonredundant. Often a demonstration is effective in getting the idea across to mentally retarded individuals without a lot of verbal explanation (Sedlak, Doyle, & Schloss, 1982).

Second, tasks the student is asked to complete should be uncomplicated and straightforward and should make minimal assumptions about the student's knowledge. This requirement has become apparent from our own experience testing mentally retarded students on computers.

Finally, the most direct method of response should be adopted (Spelt, 1984). Many methods of response can be tasks in themselves; for example, students asked to type "Y" for yes and "N" for no must either know how to spell "yes" and "no" or associate the letters with the words. To give their response, they must translate it into a letter and then find that letter on the keyboard. Simple, brief instructions, easily executed tasks, and direct response methods should result in maximizing learning efficiency.

The CAI programs developed for mentally retarded students have made great progress in ergonomics. Instructions are generally simple and often presented auditorily, with random access tape recorders or speech synthesizers. One program used four demonstrations of the instructed task, aided by audio messages (Vitello & Bruce, 1977). Although none of the other programs used demonstrations, half of them used speech. Knutson and Prochnow (1970) succeeded in simplifying verbal instructions by using a dialogue format, in which the students "conversed" (in English or in Spanish) with a girl or boy who guided them through the exercise.

In most cases, the students' task was also simple. Vitello and Bruce (1977) had students choose one of two stimuli in their shape discrimination program. Children working on Eaton's (1975) letter and word discrimination program touched a letter, digraph, or word as directed by audio messages. A telephone dialing program (Lally & Macleod, 1983) required only telephone dialing. Word recognition programs of Holz (1976) and Lally (1981) called for finding words and touching or pressing them.

By far the greatest strides have been made in response methods. Before describing some good methods, we will discuss two examples of very cumbersome response methods. First, Luyben's (1973) students were required to find a word or a picture which matched a target word. The CAI program was carried out on a teletype machine, and, to give their response, students typed a number which corresponded to the response alternative they had chosen. Thus, the students first had to find the matching word or picture, then determine its "code" number and find that number on the keyboard. Nelon's (1972) students, learning word recognition and spelling, had to retype words presented to them for short periods of time. Needless to say, finding the correct letters on the keyboards may have resulted in forgetting the spelling of some words. The task of remembering spelling was compounded by the task of retyping the word.

Contrast Luyben's or Nelon's response methods with that of Grocke (1983, 1984). Grocke's CAI program was an exercise in reading text, using a cloze procedure. The students were presented with a sentence or two of text with some words missing. They were to read the text and choose from two, three, or four words at the top of the screen to complete the blanks. A touch-sensitive screen was attached to the display monitor, and the students gave responses by touching the word they thought should go in the blank. As the students proceeded, they could at any time touch a "HELP" indicator in the corner of the screen, touch any unfamiliar word, and hear the speech synthesizer pronounce that word. In this way, unfamiliar words were not an impediment to the cloze task.

Holz (1976) and Eaton (1975) also used touch-sensitive screens. Holz fixed one screen over the display monitor and another over a rear-projection slide screen. Other direct response methods include large, simplified buttons to press (Lally, 1980, 1981; Macleod & Overheu, 1977; Knutson & Prochnow, 1970), light pens to indicate choices on the display monitor (Nolan & Ryba, 1984; Vitello & Bruce, 1977), a digitizer handwriting pen and graphics tablet (Lally, 1982, 1983), and a telephone dial (Lally & Macleod, 1983).

2. RESEARCH

Most of the research studies on CAI with mentally retarded groups have investigated the effectiveness of an individual CAI program. A minority of studies has also investigated the effects of program parameters and student characteristics on learning. Both types of findings will be reviewed.

a. Effectiveness Studies. Effectiveness studies are studies designed to determine whether a CAI program is successful in increasing knowledge or skill in the students who use it. In the mental retardation literature, CAI has almost always been evaluated as a supplement to, rather than a replacement of, conventional class instruction. We found only one exception (Nolan & Ryba, 1984). Most of the 15 effectiveness studies found that the CAI program in question was indeed effective for the sample tested (see Table I). However, the samples were often small and select, and control groups were often not employed.

Studies using control group comparisons all reported that the experimental group performed significantly better on posttests than the control group, with the exception of three studies. Significant differences were found in spelling (Nelon, 1972), money handling (Holz, 1979), number conservation (Lally, 1980), word recognition (Lally, 1981), text reading (Grocke, 1983, 1984), handwriting (Lally, 1982), and visual discrimination (Eaton, 1975).

In one of the studies that found no differences (A. Chiang, 1978), teachers authored CAI arithmetic and reading lessons for each student according to their Individual Education Plans. The frequency, time, and subject of the CAI lessons varied from student to student. Several teachers were involved in authoring the lessons. It is difficult to know if the lessons were ineffective because of poor software, poor authoring by teachers, poor prescription, or because of the low ability level of the students. Because similar samples of mildly retarded students succeeded in learning from other CAI programs in reading (Lally, 1981; Grocke, 1983, 1984) and in arithmetic (Richardson, 1974), the failure must be attributed to one or a combination of the first three possibilities.

The other two studies that found no differences both examined sight word learning in severely and moderately retarded persons (Caruso, Conners, & Detterman, 1984; Nolan & Ryba, 1984). The low intelligence level of the students may have impeded learning. These were the only two control studies of word recognition using subjects in the 30 to 55 IQ range.

The study described by Nolan and Ryba, however, used a tutored control group. The finding may mean that CAI was just as effective as one-to-one instruction. This is psychologically significant if learning occurred in both CAI and tutored groups. The report we were able to obtain, however, did not provide this information.

Although control group studies were generally successful in demonstrating the effectiveness of CAI, only a few of them investigated transfer or retention. Three studies considered transfer. Eaton (1975) used a standardized test to evaluate his visual discrimination program. This can be considered a transfer test, as it was not a sample of the CAI training. In this study, retarded students matched on mental age to kindergarteners performed significantly better than their control

TABLE I
Effectiveness Studies

Reference	Instruction	Number of weeks	Age	IQ	Group size	Control group	P[a]	T	R	RT
Knutson & Prochnow (1970)	Making change	—	12–18	45–80	21	No	S	S	S	NS
Nelon (1972)	Spelling	<1	5–7	—	6	Yes	S	—	—	—
Richardson (1974)	Arithmetic	16	High school	73.9	10	Yes	S	S	—	—
Strain (1974)	Money handling	1	—	21–107	17	No	S[b]	S[b]	S[c]	S[c]
Eaton (1975)	Visual discrimination	3	—	—	—	Yes	—	S	—	—
Holz (1976)	Vocabulary	2	11–20	38–69	19	No	—	S	—	—
A. Chiang (1978)	Arithmetic and reading	20	Elementary and jr. high	50–80	18	Yes	—	NS	—	—
England (1979)	Budgeting	4	Adult	—	10	No	S[d],NS[e]	NS[d,e]	—	—
			Adult	—	14	No	NS			
Holz (1979)	Money handling	6	7–21	31–53	16	Yes	S	S	—	—
Lally (1980)	Number conservation	4	9–14	40–72	9	Yes	S	S	NS	NS
Lally (1981)	Word recognition	4	9–16	40–74	8	Yes	S	—	—	NS
Lally (1982)	Handwriting	5	7–15	40–72	9	Yes	S	—	—	—
Grocke (1983)	Text reading	5	11–16	45–77	10	Yes	S	—	S	—
Caruso, Conners, & Detterman (1984)	Word recognition	6[f]	9–22	35–50	19	Yes	NS	—	NS	—
Nolan & Ryba (1984)	Word recognition	—	15–56	30–55	13	Yes[g]	NS	NS	NS	NS

[a]Abbreviations: P, posttest on lesson content; T, posttest of transfer; R, retention test on lesson content; RT, retention test of transfer; S, significant difference, $p < .05$; NS, no significant difference.

[b]Time.

[c]Accuracy.

[d]Subjects' actual spending.

[e]Subjects' beliefs of how money should be spent.

[f]Approximately.

[g]Tutored control group.

group. Another effectiveness study (Lally, 1980), involving a CAI number conservation program, tested conservation of volume, weight, and length as well as number. Although significantly more training group subjects than control group subjects demonstrated conservation of number immediately after training and 9 weeks after training (we performed Fisher Exact Probabilities Tests on the data Lally reported), no transfer was evidenced. Nolan and Ryba (1984) also found no effects on transfer tests.

Retention was examined in three studies. Lally (1981) tested retention at intervals up to 23 weeks after the end of the CAI word recognition training period. The analyses indicate that, relative to a control group, the improvement in sight word vocabularies stopped after the training period. However, students appeared to have retained the gains made during the training session. Caruso *et al.* (1984) and Nolan and Ryba (1984) found no retention differences in experimental and control groups. Although transfer and retention resulting from CAI remain questionable, the evidence from control group studies of at least immediate benefit is rather strong.

Five effectiveness studies did not use control groups, but instead compared pretest and posttest performance to determine effectiveness. A problem with these studies is that, without control group information, it is not certain that the CAI intervention actually caused the increase in performance. Especially with supplementary CAI, gains could occur as a result of other instruction. Knutson and Prochnow (1970), Richardson (1974), and Holz (1976) found significant gains on transfer tests in money handling, arithmetic, and vocabulary, respectively. Strain (1974) and England (1979), however, both had mixed results.

Strain's (1974) money handling program produced increased accuracy for a transfer task which employed actual items and money, but not for the task on which the subjects were trained. On the other hand, subjects took less time to complete the training task, but not the transfer task. The important skill (the transfer task), however, was improved. In England's (1979) CAI budgeting study, retarded adults living in the community and holding full-time jobs indicated personal spending patterns which approximated a desirable standard more closely than the pattern they indicated before the CAI training. They did not improve in indicating how much they "should" spend on various categories of items and did not maintain improved spending patterns 1 month after the end of the CAI training period. Retarded adults in residence with part-time jobs had no improvement at all.

Although the no-control studies were flawed, they presented positive evidence for the effectiveness of CAI for mentally retarded users, particularly on immediate transfer tasks. Again, effects on retention are questionable.

b. Program Parameters. Four studies examined versions or parameters of CAI programs in order to determine the better technique. These are detailed in Table II. Luyben (1973) compared two methods of teaching sight words—matching words with words and matching words with pictures. On each trial a word was

TABLE II
PROGRAM PARAMETER AND COMPARATIVE STUDIES

Reference	Instruction	Number of weeks	Age	IQ	Group size	Comparison	Significance	Group favored
				A. Program parameter studies				
Luyben (1973)	Word recognition	—	9.5	—	11	Pairing words with words vs. pictures	S[a]	Pictures
Holz (1976)	Vocabulary	2	11–20	38–69	10	Supplementary audio vs. no audio	S	Audio
Lally (1983)	Handwriting	4	9–16	41–61	6	Small vs. large vs. reducing cursor box	S	Reducing
Nolan & Ryba (1984)	Word recognition	—	15–56	30–55	13	Picture pairing vs. errorless discrimination	NS	—
				B. Subject characteristic studies[b]				
Nelon (1972)	Spelling	<1	5–7	—	6	Retarded vs. non-retarded	NS	—
Eaton (1975)	Discrimination	3	—	—	14	Retarded vs. non-retarded	NS	—

[a] Abbreviations: S, significant difference, $p < .05$; NS, no significant difference.
[b] See also Conners & Detterman (1984) for a correlational study of subject characteristics and CAI performance.

typed out by a teletype terminal. Two, three, or four response alternatives were then offered. In the word–word condition response alternatives were words typed by the computer, whereas in the word–picture condition they were pictures xeroxed and bound in booklets. Students were to choose the matching alternative. The word–picture method proved to be more effective than the word–word method in increasing word recognition and reading comprehension, as measured by standardized tests.

Nolan and Ryba (1984) also compared two methods of teaching sight words. They compared a paired-associate method, which matched words with pictures, with an errorless discrimination method, which gradually increased the difficulty of the discriminations the trainees were required to make. Severely and moderately retarded adults attempted to learn two sets of eight words in ten CAI sessions. An audio system accompanied the CAI program so that the trainees could hear the words pronounced. No differences were found between the two methods on either immediate or delayed tests.

A handwriting CAI program was described in its early stages by Macleod and Overheu (1977). Since then, pilot data and effectiveness data have been published, as well as a study examining three alternative ways of presenting the handwriting instruction (Macleod & Procter, 1979; Lally, 1982, 1983), In its current form, the handwriting apparatus includes a graphics tablet equipped with a digitizer pen interfaced to a microcomputer. Student commands are given by pressing the pen on a menu affixed to the tablet, and students can "write" on the tablet and see the lines they draw appear on the display monitor. In the lessons, students "track" the model of a letter, number, or word, prompted by a blinking spot. Accurate tracking results in the computer filling in the lines of the model; line filling ceases if the tracking is inaccurate. The allowable margin of error can be increased or decreased. This margin is indicated by the size of a cursor box on the monitor, which indicates the position registered by the digital pen. Lally (1983) tested the effect of gradually reducing the cursor box size by comparing this method with methods using small and large cursor boxes. Based on teachers' ratings of handwriting samples, he concluded that reducing the cursor box was indeed the best method of the three. This finding supports the use of a behavior-shaping approach for handwriting instruction.

The fourth study which examined a CAI program parameter was carried out by Holz (1976). Holz's program was meant to teach social sight vocabulary, or recognition of important survival words, such as DANGER. A fade-in procedure was used, in which discriminations became increasingly difficult. Slides containing a target word or representation were presented to the student. Then the display monitor offered from one to four response alternatives. The student was to find the matching word, touch the target, and touch the match. As the task became more difficult, the target word was depicted on a sign, at varying distances, or in pictorial representation. Half of the students received audio messages along with the presentation of the target word, telling them what the word was and what it meant. Holz found that the students receiving audio messages identified more words in a posttest than did those completing the task in silence. The results from Holz's study support the notion that multiple modality presentation can aid in teaching mentally retarded individuals.

Although the four studies described above are more informative than the typical effectiveness studies, still no attention was given to individual differences in students and how they might interact with various program techniques.

c. Subject Characteristics. Three studies examined the effect of subject characteristics on CAI performance (see Table II). Both Nelon (1972) and Eaton (1975) investigated the effect of intelligence on CAI learning. They both compared retarded and nonretarded subjects of equal mental age on performance in CAI spelling and visual discrimination, respectively. Both found no significant differences. Since significant gains over control groups were also found in both studies, the results suggest that mentally retarded children can profit as much from CAI as can nonretarded children.

We examined the relationship of cognitive abilities to on-line measures of CAI performance (Conners, 1985; Conners & Detterman, 1984). Our sight word recognition CAI program presented students four words at a time. First, the students were allowed to hear words pronounced by a speech synthesizer in the order and with the frequency they desired. Then the students were asked to find words pronounced by the speech synthesizer from among the set of four words. The students had to correctly indicate each word three times before starting four new words. At the end of each 10-minute session, an on-line test was given covering the words encountered in the session. The number of word sets completed in 10 sessions, the median number of trials to criterion, and the percent correct on the 10 session tests combined were correlated with seven measures of simple cognitive abilities. Correlations ranged from .03 to .66. The cognitive abilities correlated most highly with the three measures were stimulus discrimination, probed recall, and simple learning. Further research will explore ways the instruction can be modified to complement or compensate for high or low abilities in these tasks. Choice reaction time, inspection time, relearning, and recognition memory correlated minimally with the three measures.

C. Evaluation of the Literature

Four observations of programming and research techniques lead us to conclude that CAI for the mentally retarded is not very individualized. The first two observations pertain to the categorization of programs. First, there were no programs in the most individualized category. That is, no program made an assessment of any individual difference measure for the purpose of modifying instruction according to that measure. Instead, all of the programs fell into the first three, less individualized, categories.

Second, half of the CAI programs reviewed represented the simplest and least individualized type of program. These included individual pacing with repetition of error trials. This form of CAI need not even use a computer. In fact, individual pacing and repetition was the purpose of the most rudimentary teaching machines (Pressey, 1926), principles of which were later adapted and expanded for programmed instruction (Skinner, 1968). This analogy suggests that, with respect to individualization, half of the CAI programs developed for mentally retarded students to use have not progressed beyond the 1960s in sophistication.

The last two observations supporting our contention that CAI for mentally retarded users has not made progress in presenting individualized instruction come from the research studies. In many studies, programs were only appropriate for a narrow class of mentally retarded students, and program evaluation considered only these students. Most studies were designed with a particular group in mind, which was then screened for necessary entering skills. Only those demonstrating proficiency in one skill but not another were allowed to participate in the study. For example, Holz (1979) and Knutson and Prochnow (1970) excluded those individuals with too much or too little knowledge of numbers and money from participating in their CAI money handling studies. Strain (1974) first required correct solving of a subtraction problem with borrowing and then pretrained his subjects for his social arithmetic CAI program. Finally, Eaton (1975) went to great lengths to find students with just the right mental age and who possessed behavioral skills necessary for his CAI program. Thus, attempts were made to homogenize a group of students rather than to present instruction appropriate to each student's skill level.

Finally, the nature of the research studies in CAI applications for mentally retarded students was also disappointing in terms of individualization. Fifteen out of 17 studies were designed to determine general effectiveness of a CAI program. Whereas CAI is touted for its individualized instruction, the trend in the literature concerning mentally retarded students has been to select a narrow class of students whose skills are appropriate to the CAI program, deliver flash cards electronically, and determine whether or not the program is effective for the group of students as a whole.

D. Suggestions for Further Research

Research in CAI programming for mentally retarded people is needed in two main areas—methods for individualizing CAI and methods which address group characteristics of the mentally retarded.

First, research must begin to investigate the important variables in making CAI adaptive and individualized, much like a good tutor. Thus, interactions between student variables and instructional variables must be explored. There are several ways a good tutor is likely to adapt teaching to the student. Corresponding to these, there are several approaches that may be taken to studying interactions between student and instructional variables. A large literature on Aptitude

X Treatment Interactions (ATI) and Trait X Treatment Interactions (TTI) already exists (see Cronbach & Snow, 1977). Little of it, however, has involved either mentally retarded learners or variables of CAI.

Interactions between student characteristics, such as personality and cognitive style, and type of instruction could be investigated. Malone (1981) found that girls like extrinsic fantasy (fantasy that is only weakly related to the skill in a video game) whereas boys like intrinsic fantasy (fantasy that is very closely related to the skill in the game). He suggested that such preference depends on many factors besides gender.

Another approach to individualized CAI is to examine the interaction of student characteristics with parameters of the CAI program. Student characteristics could be personality traits, such as impulsivity/reflectivity and attention span, or cognitive abilities, such as memory, encoding, and stimulus discrimination. Instructional parameters could relate to the amount of instruction or length of a session, the difficulty level of the material, or the reinforcement schedule. Tennyson and his associates (Park & Tennyson, 1980; Tennyson & Rothen, 1977) used a reasoning ability measure to adjust the number of instances a student would presumably need to learn a concept. Boyson and Thomas (1980) found that elementary students who were more field dependent achieved most when feedback was given only at the end of an equation-solving problem, whereas those who were more field independent achieved most when they received feedback at every step of the solving process. Other such studies could be carried out.

We are especially interested in interactions between basic cognitive abilities or information processing measures and specific variables of instruction (Conners, 1985; Conners & Detterman, 1984). Many studies of more global aptitude and treatments have been undertaken with nonrelated students, and generally, results have been disappointing (see Cronbach & Snow, 1977). A more specific analysis of aptitudes and treatments, based on a theoretical framework, is likely to yield more useful information.

A third approach is to look at the effect of adjusting parameters of the instruction based on the student's current or past performance. Atkinson and his colleagues (Atkinson & Fletcher, 1972; Atkinson & Paulson, 1972) used student responses to determine the order and frequency of items prescribed and found the instruction to be effective. Similarly, Tennyson and his associates found that students understood concepts better when response data were used to adjust the number (Tennyson & Rothen, 1977) and order (Park & Tennyson, 1980) of items. The response data could also be used to shorten or lengthen the session time. For example, if students' responses were significantly worse than usual, they might not be paying adequate attention and instruction would be painful and wasteful. On the other hand, if students were succeeding beyond their own averages, instruction might be lengthened in order to prolong the successful learning experience.

The second main area of research needed is in instruction aimed to address the group characteristics of mentally retarded students. Deficits in strategy use, rehearsal, transfer of learning, motivation, and attention should be addressed in CAI programming. Techniques could be developed to either compensate for or induce strategy use, rehearsal, or transfer. Program parameters could be examined in order to find out what instructional elements can be added or modified to draw and hold attention and to motivate mentally retarded students to learn. For example, effects of color, motion, and sound should be explored. Malone (1981) found that sound was a strong determinant of video game preference among girls and suggested that visual effects affected video game preference in college students. Also, components of computer games, such as goals, high response rates, scorekeeping, and fantasy should be analyzed in terms of their applicability in serious instruction for mentally retarded students. Various schedules of reinforcement and feedback should be investigated in terms of their capacity for motivating students and their conduciveness to retention of material. Several authors have found that feedback schedules affect CAI learning (Rankin & Trepper, 1978; Shaw, 1968; Tait, Hartley, & Anderson, 1973; Thompson, 1977). Finally, the effects of various degrees of student control over the lesson could be examined in relation to attention and motivation.

   In order for research in CAI for the mentally retarded to proceed at a reasonable rate, methods must be established for sampling CAI learning. The current thinking seems to be that CAI research should consist of long classroom experiments for the sake of ecological validity. However, if CAI research proceeds only in this fashion, it will proceed very slowly, particularly with slow-learning mentally retarded students. We have found that learning measures from 3 sessions of our CAI program are very good estimates of measures from 10 sessions, correlating .92, .86, and .91 (Conners, 1985). We expect that studies longer than ours also could be approximated using a relatively small number of sessions. Therefore, we suggest that most work in CAI could be carried out in microexperiments, using samples of CAI learning to infer effects of various instructional and student variables. Field studies could be implemented only after several important variables have been identified in microexperiments. In this way, time-efficient laboratory experiments could be combined with ecologically valid classroom experiments such that research proceeds swiftly and meaningfully.

ACKNOWLEDGMENTS

   This paper was facilitated by a training grant from the National Institute of Child Health and Human Development (HD07176) supporting the first author and by a grant from the Case Western Reserve University Alumni Association to the first author. Some of the research described in the paper was supported by a grant from the Apple Education Foundation (2092) to the second and third authors.

We would like to thank Iain Macleod for supplying us with manuscripts from The Australian National University and for his helpful comments on an earlier draft of the paper.

REFERENCES

Allen, W. H. (1975). Intellectual abilities and instructional media design. *Audio Visual Communication Review*, **23**, 139–140.

Anania, J. (1982). The effects of quality of instruction on the cognitive and affective learning of students. *Dissertation Abstracts International*, **42**, 4269A.

Andrews, J. D. W. (1984). Discovery and expository learning compared: Their effects on independent and dependent students. *Journal of Educational Research*, **78**, 80–89.

Atkinson, R. C. (1967). CAI: Learning aspects. In R. W. Gerard (Ed.), *Computers in education* (pp. 11–33). New York: McGraw-Hill.

Atkinson, R. C. (1974). Teaching children to read using a computer. *American Psychologist*, **29**, 169–178.

Atkinson, R. C., & Crothers, E. J. (1964). A comparison of paired associate learning models having different acquisition and retention axioms. *Journal of Mathematical Psychology*, **1**, 285–315.

Atkinson, R. C., & Fletcher, J. D. (1972). Teaching children to read with a computer. *Reading Teacher*, **25**, 319–327.

Atkinson, R. C., & Paulson, J. A. (1972). An approach to the psychology of instruction. *Psychological Bulletin*, **78**, 49–61.

Bangert, R., Kulik, J. A., & Kulik, C.-L. C. (1983). Individualized systems of instruction in secondary schools. *Review of Educational Research*, **53**, 143–158.

Bennet, R. E. (1982). Applications of microcomputer technology to special education. *Exceptional Children*, **49**, 106–113.

Bialer, I. (1961). Conceptualizations of success and failure in mentally retarded and normal children. *Journal of Personality*, **31**, 258–270.

Bloom, B. S. (1984a). The search for methods of group instruction as effective as one-to-one tutoring. *Educational Leadership*, **41**(8), 4–17.

Bloom, B. S. (1984b). The 2 sigma problem: The search for methods of group instruction as effective as one-to-one tutoring. *Educational Researcher*, **13**(6), 4–16.

Bowman, R. F. (1982). A Pac-Man theory of motivation: Tactical implications for classroom instruction. *Educational Technology*, **22**(9), 14–17.

Boyson, V. A., & Thomas, R. A. (1980). Interaction of cognitive style with type of feedback used in computer-assisted equation solving. *Proceedings of the 18th Annual Convention of the Association for Educational Data Systems*, **18**, 31–36. (ERIC Document Reproduction Service No. ED 192 718)

Bruner, J. (1961). The act of discovery. *Harvard Educational Review*, **31**, 21–32.

Budoff, M., & Hutten, L. R. (1982). Microcomputers in special education: Promises and pitfalls. *Exceptional Children*, **49**, 123–128.

Burke, A. J. (1984). Students' potential for learning contrasted under tutorial and group approaches to instruction. *Dissertation Abstracts International*, **44**, 2025A.

Burns, P. K., & Bozeman, W. C. (1981). Computer-Assisted Instruction in mathematics achievement: Is there a relationship? *Educational Technology*, **21**(10), 32–39.

Byrne, D. M. (1983). Computer uses in social studies. In M. T. Grady & J. D. Gawronski (Eds.), *Computers in curriculum and instruction* (pp. 124–126). Alexandria, VA: Association for Supervision and Curriculum Development.

Caruso, D. R., Conners, F. A., & Detterman, D. K. (1984). *Sight-word vocabulary acquisition by mentally retarded students using Computer-Assisted Instruction.* Unpublished manuscript.

Chaffin, J. D., Maxwell, & B., & Thompson, B. (1982). Arc-Ed curriculum: The application of video game formats to educational software. *Exceptional Children*, **49,** 173–178.

Chiang, A. (1978). *Demonstrations of the use of Computer-Assisted Instruction with handicapped children* (Report No. 446-AH-60076A). Arlington, VA: RMC Research Corp. (ERIC Document Reproduction Service No. ED 166 913)

Chiang, B., Thorpe, H. W., & Darch, C. B. (1980). Effects of cross-age tutoring on word-recognition performance of learning disabled students. *Learning Disability Quarterly*, **3**(4), 11–19.

Cobb, J. A. (1972). Relationship of discrete classroom behaviors to fourth-grade academic achievement. *Journal of Educational Psychology*, **63,** 74–80.

Cohen, P. A., Kulik, J. A., & Kulik, C.-L. C. (1982). Educational outcomes of tutoring: A meta-analysis of findings. *American Educational Research Journal*, **19,** 237–248.

Conners, F. A. (1985). *Cognitive determinants of Computer-Assisted Instruction outcome in mentally retarded adolescents.* Unpublished master's thesis, Case Western Reserve University, Cleveland.

Conners, F. A., & Detterman, D. K. (1984, July). *Individual differences in Computer-Assisted Instruction performance: Underlying cognitive abilities.* Paper presented at the Gettysburg College Summer Practicum on Computing in Undergraduate Psychology, Gettysburg, PA.

Cooley, W. W., & Glaser, R. (1969). An information and management system for individually prescribed instruction. In R. C. Atkinson & H. H. Wilson (Eds.), *Computer-Assisted Instruction: A book of readings* (pp. 95–117), New York: Academic Press.

Cronbach, L. J. & Snow, R. E. (1977). *Aptitudes and instructional methods.* New York: Irvington.

Crosby, K. G., & Blatt, B. (1968). Attention and mental retardation. *Journal of Education*, **150,** 67–81.

Deci, E. L. (1971). Effects of externally mediated rewards on intrinsic motivation. *Journal of Personality and Social Psychology*, **18,** 105–115.

Dember, W. N. (1974). Motivation and the cognitive revolution. *American Psychologist*, **29,** 161–168.

Devin-Sheehan, L., Feldman, R. S., & Allen, V. L. (1976). Research on children tutoring children: A critical review. *Review of Educational Research*, **46,** 355–385.

Driskell, J. E., & Dwyer, D. J. (1984). Microcomputer video game based training. *Educational Technology*, **24**(2), 11–16.

Eaton, P. (1975). *Visual discrimination and computer-assisted learning.* Unpublished doctoral dissertation, University of Calgary.

Edwards, J., Norton, S., Taylor, S., Weiss, M., & Dusseldorp, R. (1975). How effective is CAI? A review of the research. *Educational Leadership*, **33,** 147–153.

Egan, O., & Archer, P. (1985). The accuracy of teachers' ratings of ability: A regression model. *American Educational Research Journal*, **22,** 25–34.

Ellis, N. R., Hawkins, W. F., Pryer, M. W., & Jones, R. W. (1963). Distraction effects in oddity learning by normal and mentally defective humans. *American Journal of Mental Deficiency*, **67,** 576–583.

England, G. (1979). *A study of computer-assisted budgeting among the developmentally handicapped.* Unpublished doctoral dissertation, University of Calgary.

Englert, C. S. (1983). Measuring special education teacher effectiveness. *Exceptional Children*, **50,** 247–254.

Finn, J. D. (1983). Multivariate approaches to the evaluation of programs for mentally retarded persons. *American Journal of Mental Deficiency*, **88,** 263–269.

Fisher, C. W., Marliave, R. S., & Filby, N. N. (1979). Improving teaching by increasing "academic learning time". *Educational Leadership*, **37**(1), 52–54.

Fredrick, W. C., & Walberg, H. (1980). Learning as a function of time. *Journal of Educational Research,* **73,** 183–194.

Gagne, R. M., & Brown, L. T. (1961). Some factors in the programming of conceptual learning. *Journal of Experimental Psychology,* **62,** 313–321.

Gallini, J. K. (1983). What Computer-Assisted Instruction can offer toward the encouragement of creative thinking. *Educational Technology,* **23**(4), 7–11.

Geoffrion, L. D., & Goldenberg, E. P. (1981). Computer-based exploratory learning systems for communication-handicapped children. *Journal of Special Education,* **15,** 325–332.

Glaser, R. (1970). Psychological questions in the development of Computer-Assisted Instruction. In W. H. Holtzman (Ed.), *Computer-assisted instruction, testing, and guidance* (pp. 74–93). New York: Harper & Row.

Goldenberg, E. P. (1977). *Special technology for special children: Computers to serve communication and autonomy in the education of handicapped children.* Baltimore: University Park Press.

Good, T. L., & Beckerman, T. M. (1978). Time on task: A naturalistic study in sixth-grade classrooms. *Elementary School Journal,* **78,** 193–201.

Greene, D., Sternberg, B., & Lepper, M. R. (1976). Overjustification in a token economy. *Journal of Personality and Social Psychology,* **34,** 1219–1234.

Griswold, P. A. (1984). Elementary students' attitudes during two years of Computer-Assisted Instruction. *American Educational Research Journal,* **21,** 737–754.

Grocke, M. A. (1983). Computers in the classroom: How can they teach reading? *Australian Journal of Reading,* **6,** 175–185.

Grocke, M. A. (1984, March). *Computer-based reading instruction using a modified cloze procedure.* Paper presented at the 17th annual Gatlinburg Conference on Research in Mental Retardation and Developmental Disabilities, Gatlinburg, TN.

Guthrie, J. T. (1967). Expository instruction versus a discovery method. *Journal of Educational Psychology,* **58,** 45–49.

Hannaford, A. E., & Taber, F. M. (1982). Microcomputer software for the handicapped: Development and evaluation. *Exceptional Children,* **49,** 137–144.

Harter, S. (1978). Effectance motivation reconsidered: Toward a developmental model. *Human Development,* **1,** 34–64.

Holloway, M. S. (1980). A comparison of passive and active music reinforcement to increase preacademic and motor skills in severely retarded children and adolescents. *Journal of Music Therapy,* **17,** 58–69.

Holt, J. (1964). *How children fail.* New York: Pitman.

Holt, J. (1967). *How children learn.* New York: Pitman.

Holz, E. (1976). *A study of the use of Computer-Assisted Instruction for teaching a social sight vocabulary to mentally handicapped adolescents.* Unpublished master's thesis, University of Calgary.

Holz, E. (1979). *Computer-Assisted Instruction for teaching basic money handling skills to mentally handicapped students at Christine Meikle School in Calgary.* Edmonton, Alberta: Alberta Department of Education, Planning and Research Branch. (ERIC Document Reproduction Service No. ED 212 101)

Hughson, E. A., & Brown, R. I. (1983). Some effects of verbal instruction on learning by developmentally handicapped adults. *Australia and New Zealand Journal of Developmental Disabilities,* **9,** 107–115.

Hull, C. (1943). *Principles of behavior.* New York: Appleton-Century-Crofts.

Jamison, D., Suppes, P., & Wells, S. (1974). The effectiveness of alternative instructional media: A survey. *Review of Educational Research,* **44,** 1–67.

Jenkins, R., Mayhall, W. F., Peschka, C. M., & Jenkins, L. M. (1974). Comparing small group and tutorial instruction in resource rooms. *Exceptional Children,* **40,** 245–250.

Kersh, B. Y. (1958). The adequacy of "meaning" as an explanation of the superiority of learning by independent discovery. *Journal of Educational Psychology, 49*, 282–292.

Kersh, B. Y. (1962). The motivating effect of learning by directed discovery. *Journal of Educational Psychology, 53*, 65–71.

Kersh, B. Y., & Wittrock, M. C. (1962). Learning by discovery: An interpretation of recent research. *Journal of Teacher Education, 13*, 461–468.

Kittel, J. E. (1957). An experimental study of the effect of external direction during learning on transfer and retention of principles. *Journal of Educational Psychology, 48*, 391–405.

Knutson, J. M., & Prochnow, R. R. (1970). *Computer-Assisted Instruction for vocational rehabilitation of the mentally retarded* (Monograph No. 2). Austin: University of Texas, Austin College of Education. (ERIC Document Reproduction Service No. ED 044 039)

Koehler, V. (1975). The theory of achievement motivation, and grades and occupational aspirations. *Dissertation Abstracts International, 35*, 1083B.

Krupski, A. (1979). Are retarded children more distractible? Observational analysis of retarded and nonretarded children's classroom behavior. *American Journal of Mental Deficiency, 84*, 1–10.

Kulik, C.-L. C., Shwalb, B. J., & Kulik, J. A. (1982). Programmed Instruction in secondary school. *Journal of Educational Research, 75*, 133–138.

Kulik, J. A. Bangert, R. L., & Williams, G. W. (1983). Effects of computer-based teaching on secondary school students. *Journal of Educational Psychology, 75*, 19–26.

Kulik, J. A., & Jaska, P. (1977). PSI and other educational technologies in college teaching. *Educational Technology, 17*(9), 12–14.

Kulik, J. A., Kulik, C.-L. C., & Cohen, P. A. (1980). Effectiveness of computer-based college teaching: A meta-analysis of findings. *Review of Educational Research, 50*, 525–544.

Kulik, J. A., Kulik, C.-L. C., & Smith, B. B. (1976). Research on the Personalized System of Instruction. *Programmed Learning and Educational Technology, 13*, 23–30.

Lally, M. (1980). Computer-assisted development of number conservation in mentally retarded school children. *Australian Journal of Developmental Disabilities, 6*, 131–136.

Lally, M. (1981). Computer-assisted teaching of sight-word recognition for mentally retarded school children. *American Journal of Mental Deficiency, 85*, 383–388.

Lally, M. (1982). *A skills approach to the learning of handwriting by retarded school children.* Unpublished manuscript, Australian National University, Canberra.

Lally, M. (1983). Computer-assisted handwriting instruction and visual–kinaesthetic feedback processes. *Applied Research in Mental Retardation, 3*, 397–405.

Lally, M., & Macleod, I. (1983, March). *Computer-Assisted Instruction in telephone dialling skills.* Paper presented at the 16th annual Gatlinburg Conference on Research in Mental Retardation and Developmental Disabilities, Gatlinburg, TN.

Lane, P. R. (1973). Motivation to achieve in school, intellectual achievement responsibility, and academic achievement in urban black third grade students. *Dissertation Abstracts International, 34*, 397B.

Laubsch, J. H. (1971). An adaptive teaching system for optimal item allocation. *Dissertation Abstracts International, 31*, 3961A.

Lepper, M. R. (1985). Microcomputers in education: Motivational and social issues. *American Psychologist, 40*, 1–18.

Lesgold, A. M. (1982). Computer games for the teaching of reading. *Behavior Research Methods and Instrumentation, 14*, 224–226.

Levy, J. (1974). Social reinforcement and knowledge of results as determinants of motor performance among EMR children. *American Journal of Mental Deficiency, 78*, 752–758.

Lorton, P. V., Jr. (1973). Computer-based instruction in spelling: An investigation of optimal strategies for presenting instructional material. *Dissertation Abstracts International, 34*, 3147A.

Luyben, P. D. (1973). *The effects of pictures on the acquisition of a sight vocabulary in rural EMR children.* Tallahassee: Florida State University, Computer-Assisted Instruction Center. (ERIC Document Reproduction Service No. ED 074 752)

Macleod, I., & Overheu, D. (1977). Computer-aided assessment and development of basic skills. *Exceptional Child,* **24,** 19–35.

Macleod, I., & Procter, P. S. (1979). A dynamic approach to teaching handwriting skills. *Visible Language,* **13,** 29–42.

Malone, T. W. (1981). Toward a theory of intrinsically motivating instruction. *Cognitive Science,* **4,** 333–369.

Mathis, A., Smith, T., & Hanson, D. (1970). College students' attitudes toward computer-assisted instruction. *Journal of Educational Psychology,* **61,** 46–51.

McLesky, J. (1982). Procedures for ameliorating attentional deficits of retarded children through instructional media design. *Education and Training of the Mentally Retarded,* **17,** 227–233.

Miller, A., & Miller, E. E. (1971). Symbol accentuation, single track functioning and early reading. *American Journal of Mental Deficiency,* **76,** 110–117.

Miller, D. M. (1976). Effects of music-listening contingencies on arithmetic performance and music preference of EMR children. *American Journal of Mental Deficiency,* **81,** 371–378.

Miller, R. M. (1981). Oligopoly: A multipurpose computer simulation game. *Simulation and Games,* **12,** 393–416.

Moore, O. K. (1966). Autotelic responsive environments and exceptional children. In O. J. Harvey (Ed.), *Experience, structure, and adaptability* (pp. 169–216). New York: Springer.

Nelon, E. M. (1972). *An evaluation of computer-assisted vocabulary instruction with mentally retarded children* (Report No. 7322). Syracuse, NY: Syracuse City School District. (ERIC Document Reproduction Service No. ED 090 964)

Nolan, P., & Ryba, K. (1984). The microcomputer as a learning system. *New Zealand Journal of Educational Studies,* **19**(1), 24–33.

Papert, S. (1980). *Mindstorms: Children, computers, and powerful ideas.* New York: Basic Books.

Park, O., & Tennyson, R. D. (1980). Adaptive design strategies for selecting number and presentation order of examples in coordinate concept acquisition. *Journal of Educational Psychology,* **72,** 362–370.

Piele, D. (1983). Computer-assisted mathematics. In M. T. Grady & J. D. Gawronski (Eds.), *Computers in curriculum and instruction* (pp. 118–123). Alexandria, VA: Association for Supervision and Curriculum Development.

Polloway, E. A., Payne, J. S., Patton, J. R., & Payne, R. A. (1985). *Strategies for teaching retarded and special needs learners* (3rd ed.). Columbus, OH: Merrill.

Pressey, S. L. (1926). A simple apparatus which gives tests and scores—and teaches. *School and Society,* **23,** 373–376.

Rankin, R. J., & Trepper, T. (1978). Retention and delay of feedback in a computer-assisted instructional task. *Journal of Experimental Education,* **46**(4), 67–70.

Reiser, R. A., & Gerlach, V. S. (1977). Research on simulation games in education: A critical analysis. *Educational Technology,* **17**(12), 13–18.

Richardson, W. M. (1974). Research and implementation of CAI in elementary and secondary schools. *Viewpoints in Teaching and Learning,* **50**(4), 39–51.

Robinson, N. M., & Robinson, H. B. (1976). *The mentally retarded child* (2nd ed.). New York: McGraw-Hill.

Rosenfield, D., Folger, R., & Adelman, H. F. (1980). When rewards reflect competence: A qualification of the overjustification effect. *Journal of Personality and Social Psychology,* **39,** 368–376.

Russel, T., & Ford, D. F. (1983). Effectiveness of peer tutors vs. resource teachers. *Psychology in the Schools,* **20,** 436–441.

Sedlak, R. A., Doyle, M., & Schloss, P. (1982). Video games: A training and generalization demonstration with severely retarded adolescents. *Education and Training of the Mentally Retarded,* **17,** 332–336.

Shaw, C. N. (1968). Effects of three instructional strategies on achievement in a remedial arithmetic program. *Dissertation Abstracts International,* **29,** 1479–1480A.

Sheeran, J. (1982). The relationship of achievement motivation and competition to school achievement in Samoan high school students. *Dissertation Abstracts International,* **43,** 562B.

Skinner, B. F. (1968). *The technology of teaching.* Englewood Cliffs, NJ: Prentice-Hall.

Spelt, P. F. (1984, July). *Human factors considerations in designing and or selecting courseware.* Paper presented at the Gettysburg College Practicum on Computing in Undergraduate Psychology, Gettysburg, PA.

Stevenson, H., & Cruse, D. (1961). The effectiveness of social reinforcement with normal and feeble-minded children. *Journal of Personality,* **29,** 124–135.

Stevenson, H., & Fahel, L. (1961). The effectiveness of social reinforcement on the performance of institutionalized and noninstitutionalized normal and retarded children. *Journal of Personality,* **29,** 136–147.

Strain, A. R. (1974). *Computer-Assisted Instruction in social arithmetic for the retarded.* Unpublished master's thesis, University of Calgary.

Strike, K. A. (1975). The logic of learning by discovery. *Review of Educational Research,* **45,** 461–483.

Suchman, J. R. (1961). Inquiry training: Building skills for autonomous discovery. *Merrill-Palmer Quarterly,* **7,** 147–169.

Swenson, R. P., & Anderson, P. (1982). The role of motivation in Computer-Assisted Instruction. *Creative Computing,* **8**(10), 134–139.

Tait, K., Hartley, J. R., & Anderson, R. C. (1973). Feedback procedures in computer-assisted arithmetic instruction. *British Journal of Educational Psychology,* **43,** 161–171.

Tennyson, R. D., & Rothen, W. (1977). Pretask and on-task adaptive design for selecting number of instances in concept acquisition. *Journal of Educational Psychology,* **69,** 586–592.

Thompson, G. E. (1977). A comparative study of the effectiveness of four types of feedback in a CAI unit on achievement in mathematics of elementary education majors. *Dissertation Abstracts International,* **38,** 2634–2635A.

Trovato, J., & Bucher, B. (1980). Peer tutoring with or without home-based reinforcement, for reading remediation. *Journal of Applied Behavior Analysis,* **13,** 129–141.

Vinsonhaler, J. F., & Bass, R. K. (1972). A summary of ten major studies on CAI drill and practice. *Educational Technology,* **12**(7), 29–32.

Vitello, S. J., & Bruce, P. (1977). Computer-assisted programs to facilitate mathematical learning among the handicapped. *Journal of Computer-Based Instruction,* **4,** 26–29.

Wagner, P. (1974). Children tutoring children. *Mental Retardation,* **12,** 52–55.

Walberg, H. J. (1984). Improving the productivity of America's schools. *Educational Leadership,* **41**(8), 4–17.

Ward, R. D., Sewell, D. F., Rostron, A. B., & Phillips, R. J. (1983). Interactive computer learning for the classroom: Problems and principles. *Programmed Learning and Educational Technology,* **20,** 269–275.

Wong, B. (1980). Motivation for learning in mildly handicapped adolescents and young adults: A review of related theories [Special issue on Education for Adolescents and Young Adults]. *Exceptional Education Quarterly,* **1,** 37–45.

Zigler, E. (1963). Rigidity and social reinforcement in the performance of institutionalized and noninstitutionalized normal and retarded children. *Journal of Personality,* **31,** 258–270.

Zigler, E. (1969). Development versus difference theories of mental retardation and the problem of motivation. *American Journal of Mental Deficiency,* **73,** 536–556.

Procedures and Parameters of Errorless Discrimination Training with Developmentally Impaired Individuals

GIULIO E. LANCIONI

INSTITUTE OF ORTHOPEDAGOGICS
UNIVERSITY OF NIJMEGEN
6500 HD NIJMEGEN, THE NETHERLANDS

PAUL M. SMEETS

DEPARTMENT OF DEVELOPMENTAL PSYCHOLOGY
UNIVERSITY OF LEIDEN
2312 KM LEIDEN, THE NETHERLANDS

I. INTRODUCTION

Experimental work conducted between the 1940s and 1960s demonstrated that a difficult discrimination can be more easily and efficiently established if subjects are first exposed to simpler discriminations involving similar stimulus material (Baker & Osgood, 1954; House & Zeaman, 1960; Lawrence, 1952, 1955; Schlosberg & Solomon, 1943). Building upon this experimental evidence, over two decades ago Terrace (1963a,b) conducted his classical studies on errorless discrimination learning. The studies were carried out with infrahumans (pigeons) and involved different visual discriminations. In the first experiment (aimed at teaching a red versus green discrimination), for example, the subjects were initially trained to respond to a key when it was illuminated by a red light and to refrain from responding to it when it was dark. The intervals in which the key was dark were very short. Subsequently, those intervals were gradually extended, and then substituted with a short and progressively brighter green light. Eventually, the durations of the red and green lights were equated. In essence,

INTERNATIONAL REVIEW OF RESEARCH IN
MENTAL RETARDATION, Vol. 14

Terrace arranged a sequence of discriminative stimuli which led to the final (more difficult) discrimination gradually, and prevented the subjects from making errors. His approach was in clear contrast with trial-and-error training. According to the latter paradigm, the red and green lights would be presented at full brightness and equal duration from the beginning of the program. At first, the subjects would respond to both of them. After a certain number of errors (varying across subjects), responding to the green light (S− stimulus) would extinguish.

Terrace's work has had a wide resonance principally for two reasons. First, his data were a definite challenge to the assumptions of traditional theories of discrimination learning (Hull, 1950; Spence, 1936). These theories had attributed an active role to the incorrect choice (S−) within a discrimination task, contending that errors (responses to the S−) are an essential component of discrimination acquisition. Second, the possibility of devising strategies that can establish discrimination without relying on errors appeared of great value for human subjects affected by severe developmental disorders. Many of those individuals, in fact, may fail to acquire even fairly simple discriminations by means of trial-and-error training (Barrett, 1965; Ellis, Girardeau, & Pryer, 1962; House & Zeaman, 1958). Errors seem to create a deterioration of their performance rather than helping them to acquire the discrimination (Sidman & Stoddard, 1966, 1967; Touchette, 1968).

From those early days, a relatively large number of studies have been carried out with humans. These studies have been aimed at (1) developing new techniques of errorless discrimination training, (2) extending their use over different discrimination tasks, and (3) testing their efficacy with a variety of developmentally impaired (mentally retarded, autistic, and multihandicapped) individuals. Five different procedures are now available; that is, stimulus fading, stimulus shaping, superimposition and fading, superimposition and shaping, and delayed cue. All procedures share the general objective of errorless training (which may be interpreted as training with error rates lower than 10% of the responses). They also share two specific rules. First, the initial responding is easy. That is, the subject is not immediately presented with the final (criterion) discrimination (as it occurs in trial-and-error training), but with a discrimination appropriate to his/her current level of functioning. Second, progress toward the final discrimination is gradual. Despite the commonalities, the aforementioned procedures show various differences among them.

Stimulus fading involves the manipulation of one or more dimensions of at least one of the stimuli to be discriminated, for example, duration, size, intensity (Moore & Goldiamond, 1964; Terrace, 1963a). If the final discrimination is to be between a circle and an ellipse, stimulus fading along the dimension of intensity could start with one of the two stimuli (e.g., the correct choice, S+) drawn at the criterion level, while the S− is invisible (i.e., a white card). Progressively, the shape of the S− would appear on the white card. Eventually, the intensity of both stimuli is equated. If the final discrimination is to be between a smaller and a larger square, stimulus fading along the dimension of size could start with a very large square and a very small one. Progressively, the small square is increased in size (i.e., until it reaches its final level). Then, the size of the very large square is reduced to its final level.

Stimulus shaping involves manipulations along the topography (configuration) of the stimuli to be discriminated. Thus, the initial level of the stimuli (or of one of them) often does not resemble their final level (Etzel & LeBlanc, 1979; Sidman & Stoddard, 1966). For example, if the final discrimination is to be between a circle and a triangle, stimulus shaping could start with the drawings of an apple and of a tree (stimuli that the subject can easily discriminate). Subsequently, the configuration of the apple is changed into the circle. Finally, the configuration of the tree is altered into the triangle.

Superimposition and fading involves the use of known stimuli as prompts for the discrimination of new stimuli (Koegel & Rincover, 1976; Terrace, 1963b). For the discrimination of two letters of the alphabet, superimposition and fading could start by pairing them (or only the S+) with colors already discriminated by the subject. Subsequently, the colors are gradually faded out. Eventually, only the two letters are presented. Similarly, for the discrimination of words, the starting point could consist of pairing the words with the drawings of the corresponding objects (known to the subject). Subsequently, the drawings are faded out and responding is totally dependent on the words. As opposed to the previous two procedures, here the program manipulations are not dealing with the stimuli to be discriminated but with those used as prompts (e.g., colors or familiar drawings).

Superimposition and shaping is similar to superimposition and fading. Yet, the manipulation of the prompts leads to embedding them into the stimuli to be discriminated (Etzel, LeBlanc, Schilmoeller, & Stella, 1981; Smeets, Lancioni, & Hoogeveen, 1984b). For the discrimination of two letters of the alphabet, for example, the program could start by superimposing the drawings of familiar objects on the letters. The configurations of drawings and letters are similar. Then, the drawings are modified in their size and configuration until they completely overlap with the related letters.

Delayed cue requires that one of the stimuli to be discriminated (normally the S+) is paired with a conspicuous prompt (e.g., finger pointing). The appearance of the prompt is then postponed with regard to the presentation of the stimuli (Touchette, 1971; Touchette & Howard, 1984). For the discrimination of different shapes, the delayed-cue procedure could start with the experimenter pointing to the S+ at each presentation of the stimuli. When the subject responds correctly, the experimenter's pointing starts to be gradually delayed. Once the subject can respond before the occurrence of the prompt (the experimenter's pointing) this is discontinued.

II. APPLICATIONS OF ERRORLESS DISCRIMINATION TRAINING PROCEDURES[1]

A. Stimulus Fading

The stimulus-fading procedure first delineated by Terrace (1963a) has been used to teach the discrimination of length, size and numerosity, spatial relations, letters and words, shapes or other configurations, and sounds.

1. LENGTH, SIZE, AND NUMEROSITY

Studies in this area have been reported by Gold and Barclay (1973), Richmond and Bell (1983), and Zawlocki and Walls (1983). Gold and Barclay taught mentally retarded subjects to discriminate bolts of different lengths. At each trial, the experimenter provided two bolts. The subjects were to match them with bolts of the same lengths. At the first step of the program, the bolts measured $1\frac{1}{2}$ inches and $\frac{3}{4}$ inch, respectively. At the second step, the measures were 1 inch and $\frac{3}{4}$ inch. Finally, the measures were 1 inch and $\frac{7}{8}$ inch. The program was successful with 14 of 16 subjects who had no previous training at the criterion level. It also succeeded with six of eight subjects who had previously failed with trial-and-error training at the criterion level. No individual error rates are available.

Richmond and Bell (1983) taught mentally retarded subjects to discriminate between two circles of similar dimensions by manipulating the S−. That is, the S+ (a circle of 8.89 cm in diameter) was held constant throughout the program. The size of the S− was progressively increased until it reached the diameter of 7.62 cm. This was accomplished in 12 steps. Data show that the five subjects exposed to the program acquired the discrimination with percentages of correct responding of 82–96. Subjects exposed to finger prompting (which was gradually removed) or trial-and-error training had much higher percentages of errors.

Zawlocki and Walls (1983) trained 12 mentally retarded subjects on size as well as on numerosity discriminations. Their fading procedures involved manipulations of the S−, of the S+, or of both stimuli. In each case, the manipulations were carried out along the dimension crucial for the final discrimination (i.e., size or number of stimuli on the cards). For every condition, training consisted of 40 trials. Testing was then implemented with 40 additional trials. Their group data suggest that none of the procedures was errorless. Yet, all of them were superior to trial-and-error training. When training performance and test performance were combined, no substantial differences were found among the fading strategies. When the training performance was analyzed independently, conditions in which fading involved the S− or both the S+ and S− seemed superior to the condition in which fading involved the S+.

---

[1]This section reviews only studies involving developmentally impaired individuals. The definition of the procedures does not always coincide with the terminology used in the studies being cited.

2. SPATIAL RELATIONS

Research in this context has been conducted by Touchette (1971), Dixon, Spradlin, Girardeau, and Etzel (1974), Irvin and Bellamy (1977), Newsom and Simon (1977), and Mosk and Bucher (1984). For example, Dixon *et al.* taught mentally retarded subjects the "in front" spatial relation. At the start of the 70-step program, the subjects were presented with the drawing of an animal or of a human in a profile view. They had to point to the figure's front. Subsequently, the aforementioned (referent) figures were represented in combination with relational objects. The relational object was first drawn in contact with the referent (e.g., a girl with a leaf immediately before her face). The subjects were to (1) touch the front of the referent, (2) move the finger to the object in front, and then (3) point to the object in front. Next, the relational object was gradually distanced from the referent's front. This was accompanied by the fading in of relational objects in S− positions (i.e., over, under, and behind the referent). Finally, fading was used to divide the stimulus cards into four quadrants, each of which reported the same referent with the relational object in front, over, under, and behind. Data show that the nine subjects exposed to the program had (virtually) errorless acquisition. By contrast, poor performance was shown by eight control subjects exposed to trial-and-error training. Subsequently, seven of the latter subjects succeeded with the program.

Irvin and Bellamy (1977) taught 26 mentally retarded subjects the correct orientation (which allowed a correct assembly response) of nuts having slightly different faces. The training procedure involved the manipulation of the face of the nuts that had to be up. That is, the dimensions of that face were initially increased and then brought back to normal. The entire procedure involved four steps. Data indicate that 7 of the 26 subjects failed to acquire the discrimination within the maximum number of trials allowed. The acquisition performance and failures obtained with this procedure seemed to compare unfavorably with those obtained through superimposition and fading (i.e., color cues were used) and through a combined procedure (i.e., color and dimension cues were used).

Mosk and Bucher (1984) programmed either one of two similar tasks for two groups of six mentally retarded children. The first task consisted of inserting pegs into two specific holes of a pegboard. At the start, the pegboard contained only those holes (S+). Subsequently, four new holes (S−) were faded in (one at a time) in various parts of the board. Each of these holes was very small at the first step, to achieve full size within the following two steps. The second task consisted of hanging a familiar object on a specific peg of a board. The location of the correct peg was maintained constant while three other pegs (S−) were faded in (one at a time) in other positions of the board. Each peg was very short at the first step, to achieve criterion length on the following two steps. Both programs established discrimination responding more effectively than a simple prompt-plus-reinforcement procedure. Yet, relatively high error rates were occasionally observed.

3. LETTERS AND WORDS

Research with this type of stimulus material has been carried out by Guralnick (1975), LaVigna (1977), and Wolfe and Cuvo (1978). For example, LaVigna taught three autistic subjects to associate printed words with the corresponding objects (edible reinforcers). The procedure started with the display of one of the edibles. The subjects had to match it with the card (the only one available) which reported the printed word of the edible. Subsequently, a distracting card was introduced. At the beginning, this card was white. Then, the name of a second edible was faded in. This occurred in six steps, during which the word was brought from a very faint outline to full intensity. Afterward, the second word was associated with its object. Finally, a third card was introduced according to the strategy previously described. Data show that the discrimination of the first two words was acquired with percentages of correct responding of 87–93. The percentage of correct responding for the acquisition of all three words was 89–91.

Wolfe and Cuvo (1978) taught 24 mentally retarded subjects to discriminate upper-case letters.[2] Three different discrimination tasks, each including one S+ and two S− letters, were programmed. At first, every S+ letter was made easily discriminable. That is, a component of it appeared very thick, while the distracting letters were at a normal level of intensity. The increased thickness of the S+ was then faded out in three steps. No individual acquisition data were reported. Posttraining (group) data indicate that the aforementioned procedure was more effective than finger prompting (which also was gradually faded out).

4. SHAPES OR OTHER CONFIGURATIONS

Within this area, studies have been performed by Sidman and Stoddard (1967), Lambert (1975), Schreibman (1975), Schreibman and Charlop (1981), and Aeschleman and Higgins (1982). For example, Sidman and Stoddard devised a program to teach mentally retarded subjects to discriminate between circle (S+) and ellipses (S−). They used a nine-key (3 × 3) matrix in which only the eight external keys were operative. At the start of the program, the subjects were presented with a bright key showing a circle. The other keys were dark. Then fading began, with the incorrect keys becoming progressively brighter (six steps). From that point, fading involved the gradual appearance of ellipses in the incorrect keys. By step 17, the ellipses and the circle were equally distinct. Data show that 7 of the 10 subjects who received the program immediately after the

---

[2]This study is listed under stimulus fading. However, the description of the procedure does not exclude that it could be interpreted as a study of superimposition and fading.

initial test acquired the discrimination. Of the seven, only four could be considered strictly errorless. Two subjects who were exposed to the program after repeated failures on trial-and-error testing did not succeed in acquiring the discrimination.

Schreibman and Charlop (1981) taught eight autistic children the discrimination of two sets of stimuli. At the criterion level, the stimuli of one set resembled a manikin with both arms down and a manikin with one arm down and one up. The stimuli of the other set consisted of an X combined with two dots in horizontal line and of an X with two dots in vertical line. The same stimuli had already been used by Schreibman (1975). Two fading procedures were compared. The first procedure started with the presentation of the relevant component of the S+. This component consisted of one of the two arm positions for the manikin stimuli and of one of the dots arrangements for the other set of stimuli. Then, the procedure involved the fading in of the relevant component of the S− (i.e., the arm position or dots arrangement not used as S+). This fading (concerning the intensity dimension) was carried out in five steps. The procedure continued with the reduction in the size of the aforementioned components (steps 6–10). Finally, the component common to both the S+ and the S− (i.e., the stick and head to complete the manikins or the Xs) was introduced through five additional steps.

The second fading procedure was identical to the first with one exception. That is, it started with the relevant component of the S− presented at the criterion level. Thus, the initial fading involved the relevant component of the S+. This procedure was found to be more effective than the first, with some of the children apparently displaying very low error rates.

5. SOUNDS

Only one study (Schreibman, 1975) has been addressed to this type of discrimination. The final sounds of similar words (i.e., magōō versus magō, nolē versus nolä) were used to start discrimination training. At first, the subjects were presented with one of these sounds (e.g., gōō) as the S+. Then, the S− (e.g., gō) was faded in. That is, from nonaudible it reached full intensity (in six steps). Finally, the common component of the S+ and S− (e.g., ma) was faded in. The six autistic children participating in the study (all exposed to the discrimination magōō versus magō, two also to the discrimination nolē vs nolä) were able to learn. Responding, however, was mostly interspersed with errors.

B. Stimulus Shaping

This procedure, first introduced by Sidman and Stoddard (1966), has been used to teach the discrimination of shapes or other configurations, letters and words, and body positions.

1. SHAPES OR OTHER CONFIGURATIONS

Programs have been developed by Sidman and Stoddard (1966), Bijou (1968), and Stella (1980). Sidman and Stoddard introduced the stimulus-shaping procedure to teach a discrimination reversal. That is, after establishing the discrimination between circle (S+) and ellipses (S−), they brought the subjects to respond to an ellipse as the new S+ stimulus. At the beginning, they shaped the circle into a square (S+). Then, they shaped the ellipses into circles (S−). Subsequently, they shaped the square into a flat rectangle (S+). Eventually, the rectangle was modified into an ellipse. The entire program included 43 steps, two of which served as test trials. The two retarded subjects exposed to the program (as well as a young normal child) were successful in acquiring the discrimination reversal. Of the two retarded subjects, one exhibited errorless performance.

Stella (1980) exposed three retarded preschool children to either one of two comparable tasks. Each task required the discrimination between two Kanji (Japanese) symbols which consisted of several strokes or lines. The configurations of the symbols involved in each pair were highly similar. This made the discrimination very difficult. For every task, the program started with the presentation of familiar drawings (e.g., a cowboy and a dog). The drawings were then shaped, one at a time, into the target symbols. Shaping was accomplished in 60 steps. Data indicate that two subjects were successful in acquiring the discrimination while one failed.

2. LETTERS AND WORDS

Studies have been conducted by Guralnick (1975) and Smeets, Lancioni, and Hoogeveen (1984a). Guralnick used stimulus shaping (supplemented with stimulus fading) for pairs of letters such as V–U and C–O. Shaping involved distinctive elements of the letters and was carried out in three steps. All eight retarded children succeeded in acquiring the discriminations. Smeets *et al.* (1984a) taught mentally retarded children to sight-read a set of three words. At the beginning, three familiar pictures were presented. Each picture was then transformed into the letters (one letter at a time) of the corresponding word. Shaping was carried out on all three words simultaneously and consisted of 28 steps. The seven subjects were successful in acquiring the discrimination. Data suggest that several of them had errorless performance. The same procedure with an increased number of steps (i.e., 37) proved effective also to teach four of the subjects words that they had not acquired under superimposition and fading.

3. BODY POSITIONS

Two studies have been concerned with this topic (Lancioni, 1983; Lancioni, Smeets, & Oliva, 1984). The first study involved pictorial stimuli. The second study (in which two blind subjects and one sighted subject participated) involved three-dimensional stimuli. In each study, the subjects (all retarded) were initially trained on arm positions. The procedure started with the introduction of the first S+ at the criterion level (i.e., a doll or the drawing of a child with arms up). Subsequently, an S− doll or drawing (i.e., with arms unshaped) was introduced. Throughout the following 9 or 11 steps, the second arm position was brought to criterion level. Then, the subjects were taught to perform it. The same procedure was repeated to introduce (one at a time) five new arm positions. A comparable strategy was also used for teaching different leg positions in combination with the previously established arm positions. While no specific error rates are available, all six subjects were found to be successful in acquiring the discriminations.

C. Superimposition and Fading

This procedure, which finds its origins in Terrace's (1963b) work, has been used to teach the discrimination of spatial relations, words and mathematical problems, shapes, letters, and sounds.

1. SPATIAL RELATIONS

Research in this context has been conducted by Touchette (1968), Sherman and Webster (1974), and Irvin and Bellamy (1977). Touchette has been the first author to apply superimposition and fading (supplemented with stimulus fading/shaping) with human subjects. He taught mentally retarded individuals to press whichever of two external panels (in a three-panel apparatus) had a black square closer to it. Initially, each subject was trained to press either one of the external panels on the basis of a red light projected in it. The central panel as well as the other external panel were dark. Subsequently, a horizontal bar was superimposed on the red panel. Then, the other two panels changed from darkness to full brightness. In this process, part of the black bar started to project itself into the central panel. Next, the red was faded out. Eventually, the black bar was shortened from the outside until all that was left of it was a small black square in either side of the central panel. The six subjects who received the 60 steps of the program followed by 40 test trials immediately after pretraining (i.e., after being taught to respond to red) made no more than 11 errors. Only four of the six subjects who had first undergone trial-and-error training had similar success.

Sherman and Webster (1974) used Touchette's procedure with three groups of children (normal, autistic, and mentally retarded). Their findings suggest that the procedure was relatively successful with the normal children. Yet, it involved various errors or failed with many of the other children.

2. WORDS AND MATHEMATICAL PROBLEMS

Studies have been performed by Dorry and Zeaman (1973, 1975), Dorry (1976), Rincover (1978), Walsh and Lamberts (1979), McGee and McCoy (1981), Smeets et al. (1984a,b), and Smeets, Lancioni, Striefel, and Willemsen

(1984c). For example, Dorry and Zeaman (1975) trained mentally retarded subjects to discriminate groups of four words. The procedure was similar to that used by the same authors in a previous study (Dorry & Zeaman, 1973) and by Dorry (1976). It started with the presentation of each word combined with the picture of the corresponding object. Then, the pictures were faded out (on all words simultaneously) over the following six steps. Data indicate that, although the procedure was more effective than control strategies, the subjects' criterion performance contained several errors. Poor performance was also reported by Walsh and Lamberts (1979). These authors used a procedure similar to that of Dorry and Zeaman, with the difference that the subjects (30 mentally retarded students) were to discriminate a group of 10 words.

Rincover (1978) trained eight autistic children to discriminate pairs of words. The procedure started with the teaching of prompts (i.e., exaggerated single features of letters). Each prompt was then superimposed to one word (the S+) of a pair, according to four different conditions. That is, the prompt could emphasize a distinctive feature (an element of a letter not contained by the letters of the S− word) or a nondistinctive feature (an element of a letter contained also by the letters of the S− word). Moreover, the prompt could be on top or spatially separated from the corresponding feature of the S+ word. Subsequently, the prompt was faded out in six steps. The results show that when the prompt emphasized a distinctive feature by appearing on top of it, acquisition of discrimination was successful. No error rates are available. When the prompt had the shape of a distinctive feature but did not overlap with the feature of the word, failure occurred in seven of the eight subjects. Apparently, in this situation the prompt failed to call attention to the distinctive feature of the word. This seems confirmed also by the fact that the results did not substantially differ from those obtained with prompts of nondistinctive features.

Smeets *et al.* (1984c) taught nine mentally retarded children to discriminate (and finally to solve as well) mathematical problems. The S+ was represented by missing minuend problems (e.g., $-3 = 5$). The S− stimuli were other missing number problems (e.g., $+3 = 5$; $5- = 3$; $3+ = 5$) and standard addition and subtraction problems. A prompt shaped like a pan was superimposed on the S+ problems (e.g., $\llcorner 3 = 5$). The prompt was then faded out in seven steps. The subjects were first required to reproduce (trace over) the prompt. Eventually, they were to produce the prompt independently. Acquisition of discrimination was found to occur in errorless fashion.

3. SHAPES, LETTERS, AND SOUNDS

Experimental evidence has been provided by Guralnick (1975) and Koegel and Rincover (1976). Guralnick taught eight mentally retarded children to discriminate three pairs of letters. For each pair, different color cues were used to emphasize the distinctive features of the letters. The cues were eventually faded out. All subjects were able to learn the discriminations.

Koegel and Rincover (1976) exposed normal and autistic children to four different two-choice discrimination tasks. Two color cues constituted the background for the new pairs of stimuli to be discriminated (i.e., an O and an X, a hexagon and an octagon, a low-frequency and a high-frequency tone, a quiet and a moderate noise). In each of the tasks, the fading out of the color cues could take up to 16 steps. Data concerning the eight autistic subjects show that (1) six learned to discriminate between O and X, (2) only two learned to discriminate between hexagon and octagon, (3) two also learned to discriminate between high- and low-frequency tone, and (4) none learned to discriminate between quiet and moderate noise.

D. Superimposition and Shaping

This procedure, introduced by Etzel et al. (1981), has found application in a study of Smeets et al. (1984b). In this study, 15 mentally retarded children were taught the discrimination (sight-reading) of a group of three words written in Roman letters as well as of a group of three words written in Hebrew letters. In each group, the procedure started with the superimposition of words and pictures of the corresponding objects. Then, the pictures were reduced in size and shaped into a distinctive feature (i.e., a letter) of the related words. The procedure was carried out on all three words of the group simultaneously, and involved 32 steps. All subjects succeeded (often errorlessly) in the acquisition of both groups of words.

E. Delayed Cue

This procedure, first defined by Touchette (1971), has been used to teach the discrimination of spatial relations and shapes, verbal instructions and manual signs, letters, words, and numerals.

1. SPATIAL RELATIONS AND SHAPES

This area includes the original study of Touchette (1971) as well as studies by Smeets and Lancioni (1981), Aeschleman and Higgins (1982), and Zane, Handen, Mason, and Geffin (1984). Touchette carried out two experiments. In the first one, he began by teaching three mentally retarded subjects to respond to a red key. Then, an E letter with legs down (S+) was superimposed on the red key, while an E letter with legs up (S−) was superimposed on a white key. Subsequently, the red color of the former key started to be delayed with regard to the appearance of the S+. The delay increased in steps of .5 seconds following correct responses. Once the subjects had learned the discrimination (i.e., responded before the red cue appeared), the same procedure was used to teach discrimination reversals. The results show that subjects had errorless performance.

In the second experiment, Touchette substituted the E letters with tilted lines. Two subjects were able to acquire the new discrimination errorlessly. One failed to switch from the red cue to the S+ line. That is, he kept on waiting for the red cue even when the delay of this cue in regard to the line had increased to 17.5 seconds. Subsequently, this subject was successfully trained to discriminate between the lines by means of a stimulus-fading procedure.

Smeets and Lancioni (1981) trained 10 mentally retarded subjects to discriminate between an X and a + sign (easy discrimination) and/or between circles differing with regard to the positions of four alternating white and black quadrants (difficult discrimination). The cue consisted of finger pointing. At the beginning, this was simultaneous with the presentation of the stimuli to be discriminated. Then, it was delayed (following correct responses) in steps of 1 second until a maximum of 10 seconds. Four of the five subjects exposed to the simple discrimination were successful in acquiring it. By contrast, only 2 of the 10 subjects acquired the difficult discrimination.

2. VERBAL INSTRUCTIONS AND MANUAL SIGNS

Two studies have been reported in this area (Smeets & Striefel, 1976; Striefel, Bryan, & Aikins, 1974). Striefel *et al.* taught three mentally retarded subjects to perform a series of simple activities on the basis of the appropriate verbal instructions. After the subjects had learned to imitate the activities, a verbal instruction was presented immediately before the modeling. Correct responding was followed by a delay between the verbal instruction and the modeling. The procedure was applied to one activity at a time. Data show that all three subjects were able to transfer control to verbal instructions. Their error rates showed medians of 6 to 12%.

With a procedure similar to that previously described, Smeets and Striefel (1976) taught a mentally retarded deaf girl 10 manual signs corresponding to as many different colors. The results indicate that the girl learned with error rates never exceeding 11%.

3. LETTERS, WORDS, AND NUMERALS

Research has been carried out by Johnson (1977), McGee and McCoy (1981), and Touchette and Howard (1984). Johnson has been the first author to apply the "4-second delay" procedure. This procedure requires that the experimenter wait 4 seconds after the presentation of the stimuli to be discriminated. If the subject does not respond within that interval, the cue is presented. Moreover, the interval is kept constant rather than being extended (as normally done in the conventional delayed cue strategy). Johnson used the 4-second delay procedure with a mentally retarded subject over three different tasks. Each task required the subject to identify and point to one of five or six stimuli. All stimuli of a task were trained simultaneously (trials were randomly distributed across them). For two of the tasks, successful acquisition was reported. For the other task, no conclusion can be drawn.

Touchette and Howard (1984) used three similar tasks, each of which involved several stimuli. Within every task, one stimulus at a time was treated as S+. The prompt consisted of finger pointing and was delayed in steps of .5 seconds. The findings show that all three subjects had errorless performance during the training on the single stimulus. During posttraining probes, in which all stimuli of a task were randomly treated as S+, errors were observed.

III. BASIC PARAMETERS OF ERRORLESS DISCRIMINATION TRAINING

The previous review of studies indicates that errorless discrimination training has been used for a variety of tasks. It also indicates that, although this training has proven overall effective, the results have not always matched the expectations. Together with findings of errorless acquisition, error performance and failures to learn have also been reported. In general, it can be observed that studies using stimulus shaping and superimposition and shaping have been successful with all but one of the subjects treated. By contrast, studies using stimulus fading and (more commonly) studies using superimposition and fading and delayed cue have reported several cases of failure. The reasons for the differential outcomes are not immediately perceivable. The fact that discrepant results have occurred across as well as within programs makes it difficult to isolate specific variables as determinants of success or lack thereof. On the other hand, a better understanding of the factors that may be responsible for the differential findings appears of great importance for anyone interested in the use of these procedures. In view of the above, this section of the chapter attempts to review the basic procedural parameters involved in errorless discrimination training, that is, type of stimulus manipulations, error criteria and positive responses per step, nature of the task, number of steps in the program, and manipulations along the S+ and/or S− stimuli. At the same time, an effort is made to relate these parameters to the results obtained.

A.   Type of Stimulus Manipulations

To a large extent, differences in this parameter are connected with the procedure used. For example, stimulus shaping and stimulus fading involve manipulations that are directly concerned with the stimuli to be discriminated (i.e., within-stimulus manipulations). Superimposition and fading and delayed cue (and superimposition and shaping also) involve manipulations of the prompts, that is, manipulations of stimuli other than those to be discriminated (i.e., extra-stimulus manipulations). Among the within-stimulus manipulations, differentiation can be made between those that are criterion related and those that are noncriterion related (Etzel & LeBlanc, 1979; Schilmoeller & Etzel, 1977). The former ones involve changes along a dimension of the stimuli (e.g., shape, size, or length) that is present at the final discrimination (Richmond & Bell, 1983; Sidman & Stoddard, 1966; Stella, 1980). The latter ones involve changes along a dimension of the stimuli that is not present at the final discrimination. That is, changes may be carried out along the dimension of intensity, while the final discrimination is based on shape (Aeschleman & Higgins, 1982; Schreibman & Charlop, 1981; Sidman & Stoddard, 1967).

Among the extra-stimulus manipulations, differentiation can be made between those connected and those nonconnected with a distinctive feature of the stimuli to be discriminated (Rincover, 1978). The former ones involve changes along a prompt(s) that emphasizes a relevant (differentiating) portion of the stimuli to be discriminated. Examples of these strategies could be (1) the fading out of a pretrained cue (color or black mark) superimposed on the leg of the R in a P–R discrimination, or (2) the embedding of a picture into a distinctive letter of the corresponding word (Rincover, 1978; Smeets *et al.*, 1984b). The latter ones involve changes of a prompt(s) not related to any relevant portion of the stimuli to be discriminated. One such situation could be represented by the fading out or delaying of a red background used to prompt responding to R in a P–R discrimination (Koegel & Rincover, 1976; McGee & McCoy, 1981; Touchette, 1971).

These different types of manipulations have been considered most important in determining variations in program outcome. For example, Schilmoeller and Etzel (1977), Etzel and LeBlanc (1979), and Etzel *et al.* (1981) have suggested that truly errorless procedures are those that involve within-stimulus criterion-related manipulations. In fact, these are the only manipulations that do not require transfer of stimulus control. That is, subjects do not need to switch their attention and responding from the dimension of the stimulus (or from the stimulus) manipulated to the dimension (or stimulus) necessary for the final discrimination.

Schreibman (1975), Koegel and Rincover (1976), Rincover (1978), Wolfe and Cuvo (1978), and Lambert (1980) have maintained that extra-stimulus nondistinctive-feature manipulations (i.e., manipulations of a prompt not connected with differentiating elements of the stimuli) can easily end in failure. This contention has also found support in some literature on compound conditioning (Feldman, 1975; Mackintosh, 1971; Mackintosh & Honig, 1970; Rescorla & Wagner, 1972). According to this literature, the prompts being manipulated could often be considered the salient aspect of the stimulus compound, while the stimuli to be discriminated could represent the nonsalient aspect of such compound. When a situation of this kind is given, the risk exists that the salient aspect overshadows the nonsalient aspect, blocking or reducing any attention to it. It can therefore follow that discrimination of the nonsalient aspect does not occur.

If one reviews the different types of stimulus manipulations adopted in the studies in terms of total "training instances" and "failures," a more comprehensive picture may be obtained (see Table I). A training instance here refers to one subject trained on a specific task.[3] It has to be noted that in many studies the same subjects were used in more than one task. Therefore, the number of training instances exceeded the number of subjects. In the table, studies in which this occurred are marked with an asterisk.

Of the 10 studies involving within-stimulus criterion-related manipulations (first category in the table), the one by Zawlocki and Walls (1983) does not allow conclusions. No information about individual performance is given. The other nine studies involved a total of 85 training instances. In five of those instances (Gold & Barclay, 1973; Stella, 1980), failures were recorded. Thus, in the other 80 instances, discrimination was established (although not necessarily in errorless fashion). If the latter instances were called "successes," one could conclude that failures represented 6% while successes represented 94% of the total training instances.

With regard to the studies involving within-stimulus noncriterion-related manipulations (second category in the table), two clarifications are in order. First, the study of Wolfe and Cuvo (1978) cannot be included in the computation of failures and successes because no information on individual performance is available. Second, the study of Dixon et al. (1974) cannot be considered strictly to belong to this category. While the stimulus manipulations were noncriterion related, the response the subjects were initially taught was criterion related (i.e., they were to indicate, by pointing and moving the finger, the parts of the stimulus determining the spatial relation under training). This response could have (1) bridged the gap between criterion-related and noncriterion-related stimulus manipulations, and (2) acted as a self-cueing strategy. In view of the above, the study of Dixon et al. is also excluded from the computation. An inspection of the remaining 10 studies indicates that a total of 115 training instances were available. Of those, 19 ended in failure. Thus, the failures represented 17% while the successes represented 83% of the total training instances.

The studies using extra-stimulus distinctive-feature manipulations (third category in the table) reported no failures. Thus, the percentage of successes is to be rated at 100. Finally, of the 21 studies involving extra-stimulus nondistinctive-feature manipulations (fourth category in the table), five cannot be considered for the computation. Four of them (Dorry, 1976; Dorry & Zeaman, 1973, 1975; Walsh & Lamberts, 1979) do not provide individual data. The fifth (Smeets et

---

[3]A task could involve from two to over ten stimuli (see Section III,C). Discrimination reversals involving the same procedure were not considered separate tasks.

TABLE I

STUDIES GROUPED ACCORDING TO TYPE OF STIMULUS MANIPULATIONS, WITH
TRAINING INSTANCES, FAILURES, ERROR CRITERIA AND RESPONSES
PER STEP, AND TASKS

Stimulus manipulations[a]	Reference	Training Instances	Failures	Error criteria responses[b]	Tasks[b]
Within-stimulus criterion-related manipulations	Sidman & Stoddard (1966)	2	0	C	II
	Bijou (1968)	10	0	/[c]	III
	Gold & Barclay (1973)	24	4	D	III
	Guralnick (1975)	24*[d]	0	/	III
	Stella (1980)	3	1	F	I
	Lancioni (1983)	3	0	E	V
	Richmond & Bell (1983)	5	0	D	I
	Zawlocki & Walls (1983)	36*	/	D	I
	Lancioni, Smeets, & Oliva (1984)	3	0	E	V
	Smeets, Lancioni, & Hoogeveen (1984a)	11*	0	D, F	IV
Within-stimulus noncriterion-related manipulations	Sidman & Stoddard (1967)	12	5	C	II
	Touchette (1971)	1	0	C	I
	Dixon, Spradlin, Girardeau, & Etzel (1974)	17	1	F	II
	Lambert (1975)	8	0	D	I
	Schreibman (1975)	18*	1	B	I
	Irvin & Bellamy (1977)	26	7	D	I
	LaVigna (1977)	3	0	E	V
	Newsom & Simon (1977)	11	3	F	I
	Wolfe & Cuvo (1978)	72*	/	D	II
	Schreibman & Charlop (1981)	16*	0	E	I
	Aeschleman & Higgins (1982)	8	3	D	VI
	Mosk & Bucher (1984)	12	0	E	II
Extra-stimulus distinctive-feature manipulations	Guralnick (1975)	24*	0	/	III
	Rincover (1978)	8	0	A	I
	Smeets, Lancioni, & Hoogeveen (1984b)	30*	0	D	IV

(continued)

TABLE I—*Continued*

Stimulus manipulations	Reference	Training Instances	Failures	Error criteria responses[a]	Tasks[a]
Extra-stimulus non-distinctive-feature manipulations	Touchette (1968)	12	2	C	I
	Touchette (1971)	6*	1	D	I
	Dorry & Zeaman (1973)	9	/	F	IV
	Sherman & Webster (1974)	16	6	C	I
	Striefel, Bryan, & Aikins (1974)	3	0	F	V
	Dorry & Zeaman (1975)	18*	/	F	IV
	Dorry (1976)	24*	/	F	IV
	Koegel & Rincover (1976)	32*	22	A	I
	Smeets & Striefel (1976)	1	0	F	V
	Irvin & Bellamy (1977)	25	4	D	I
	Johnson (1977)	2*	0	F	VI
	Rincover (1978)	24*	19	A	I
	Walsh & Lamberts (1979)	30	/	/	IV
	McGee & McCoy (1981)	16*	0	C,F	IV
	Smeets & Lancioni (1981)	15*	9	D	I
	Aeschleman & Higgins (1982)	8	5	D	VI
	Smeets, Lancioni, & Hoogeveen (1984a)	18*	4	D,F	IV
	Smeets, Lancioni, & Hoogeveen (1984b)	30*	4	D	IV
	Smeets, Lancioni, Striefel, & Willemsen (1984c)	9	0	E	II
	Touchette & Howard (1984)	9*	0	F	VI
	Zane, Handen, Mason, & Geffin (1984)	4	1	D	VI

[a]The studies are listed according to the classification system used here, not necessarily that of their authors.

[b]See text for full explanation.

[c]Slash indicates that the number of failures or the error criterion and responses per step cannot be determined.

[d]Asterisk indicates that the number of training instances exceeds the number of subjects.

al., 1984c) presents important procedural variations. Extra-stimulus nondistinctive-feature manipulations were integrated with a self-cueing strategy. That is, the subjects were to reproduce (and eventually produce independently) the cue superimposed on the S+. The drawing of the cue (given its configuration) would easily prevent or inform the child of any errors. The remaining 16 studies included 221 training instances. Of those, at least 77 were failures.[4] Thus, the failures represented (at least) 35% while the successes represented (at most) 65% of the total training instances. If the 16 studies are divided according to the procedure used, one finds that those based on superimposition and fading had a higher percentage of failures (i.e., 37) than those based on delayed cue (i.e., 29).

The percentages reported above have been computed on all training instances of each study, that is, also on those in which the subjects had a history of failure (e.g., previous trial-and-error training) on the task. Although in some of those instances the negative history seemed to correlate with the ineffectiveness of the subsequent training program (Sidman & Stoddard, 1967; Touchette, 1968), in others no such link could be identified (Dixon *et al.*, 1974; Schreibman, 1975; Schreibman & Charlop, 1981; Smeets *et al.*, 1984a). In view of the conflicting evidence (maybe related to differences in procedural parameters), the exclusion of those instances from the computation of the percentages did not seem necessary at this stage.

On the basis of the aforementioned percentages, the following summary points could be made. First, studies using within-stimulus or extra-stimulus distinctive-feature manipulations appear to be much more effective (i.e., to have higher percentages of successes) than studies involving extra-stimulus nondistinctive-feature manipulations. Second, among the latter studies, those involving superimposition and fading appear less successful than those using delayed cue. Third, the difference in percentages of failures and successes between the studies using within-stimulus criterion-related manipulations and those using within-stimulus noncriterion-related manipulations may appear somewhat smaller than would have been expected on the basis of data collected with nonretarded subjects (Etzel & LeBlanc, 1979; Etzel *et al.*, 1981; Gollin & Savoy, 1968; Schilmoeller, Schilmoeller, Etzel, & LeBlanc, 1979).

Before any conclusion can be drawn on the previous points, a number of issues should be considered. For example, the aforementioned percentages (failures and successes) do not provide any information as to the error criteria used for determining the failures (see next section). Nor do they account for any possible effects of other procedural parameters on the findings. For instance, the number of positive responses per step of the program and the nature of the tasks used could have had a very significant impact on the successes reported as well as on

[4]The group data provided by Sherman and Webster (1974) do not exclude the possibility that the number of failures was higher than that computed.

the fashion in which they were obtained (i.e., errorlessly or with errors). Last, although not much emphasis has been placed on the subjects' level of functioning, this might also have played a role in determining the program outcomes.

B. Error Criteria and Positive Responses Per Step

Studies have varied widely with regard to these procedural parameters. For example, Rincover (1978) used a procedure that could prove rather restrictive as to the number of errors allowed. Within this procedure, correct responding on the five trials available at any given step of the program allowed the child to advance to the next step. If an error occurred, the subject was immediately returned to the previous step (where he/she had already responded correctly). Again, five correct responses allowed the subject to move forward. Yet, if the subject made errors on two consecutive presentations of the same step, training was ended in failure. This procedure and the somewhat similar one used by Koegel and Rincover (1976) are indicated in Table I with the letter *A*.

The procedure used by Schreibman (1975) is identified by the letter *B*. This author provided the opportunity for five positive responses at each level of stimulus manipulation. If the subject made an error at a particular step, he/she was returned to the previous step for another five consecutive correct trials. If the subject made again an error when advanced, he/she was once more returned to the previous step. From that point, the following step was broken into substeps. If the subject failed on two consecutive attempts at the smallest possible substep, training was ended in failure.

The letter *C* in the table identifies studies that did not set an error criterion (and/or allowed several consecutive errors on the same step), providing only one opportunity for correct responding per step. The letter *D* identifies studies that did not set an error criterion, but a trial limit (usually high) for ending training. Mostly, these studies allowed more than one positive response per step. The letter *E* identifies studies that did not establish error criteria for ending training and, at the same time, allowed multiple responses at each step of the program. Finally, the letter F identifies delayed-cue studies that applied virtually no restrictions as to errors or trials, as well as other studies (not based on delayed cue) that did not conform with the previous categories.

The first (methodological) observation one can make in view of the above is that studies frequently allowed more than one positive response per step. This strategy (''sequencing,'' see Etzel & Schilmoeller, 1977; Touchette & Etzel, 1977) represents a diversion from the classical conception of errorless programming (Gollin & Savoy, 1968; Moore & Goldiamond, 1964; Schilmoeller & Etzel, 1974, 1977; Schilmoeller *et al.*, 1979; Sidman & Stoddard, 1966, 1967; Touchette, 1968). According to this conception, subjects should be allowed only one response per step, that is, they should be required to move continuously toward the final discrimination.

In light of the new classification of the studies (i.e., based on error criteria and positive responses per step), additional considerations are possible as to the percentages of successes and failures discussed in the previous section. For example, it may be noticed that procedures which could be quite restrictive as to the errors allowed (i.e., A) have been adopted in 56 training instances involving extra-stimulus nondistinctive-feature manipulations. The same procedures were not applied in studies involving within-stimulus manipulations. Although Rincover (1978) has demonstrated (through within-subject comparisons) that the type of stimulus manipulations rather than the error criterion was responsible for failure, one might argue that (1) a less rigid criterion (e.g., *B* or *D*), or (2) a different approach to the errors (Stella, LeBlanc, & Etzel, 1981) would have produced better results. That is, fewer failures would have been obtained by Rincover (1978) and perhaps by Koegel and Rincover (1976) as well.

If this hypothesis is accepted, implications could be twofold. First, the overall percentage of successes observed with the studies using extra-stimulus nondistinctive-feature manipulations (i.e., 65) could have been higher. In spite of any increase, however, the efficacy of those manipulations would have remained inferior to that of within-stimulus or extra-stimulus distinctive-feature manipulations (Etzel & LeBlanc, 1979; Rescorla & Wagner, 1972; Schilmoeller & Etzel, 1974, 1977; Schreibman, 1975; Smeets *et al.,* 1984a,b). Second, since the restrictive error criterion concerned studies of superimposition and fading, an increase in their percentage of successes would have reduced the previously reported difference (in efficacy) between these studies and those using delayed cue.

The new classification of the studies may also serve as a basis for critical comments on the issue of errorless learning. One may argue that studies that allow multiple positive responses per step or substep of the program are more likely to obtain high percentages of correct responding even when the stimulus manipulations are not very successful in precluding errors. In coincidence with errors, for example, those studies offer the subjects (through the repetition of steps) a variety of extra-response opportunities. These may significantly contribute to a high percentage of correct responding. By contrast, studies that allow only one positive response per step do not offer as many extra opportunities to make up for errors. A high percentage of correct responding within these studies may therefore be taken as a more direct evidence of the effectiveness of the program in preventing errors.

Finally, in view of the new classification of the studies, two hypotheses may be formulated on the relatively small success differences found between the within-stimulus criterion-related and the within-stimulus noncriterion-related manipulations. On the one hand, it could be argued that the transfer of control (from the dimension manipulated to the one relevant for discrimination) required by noncriterion-related procedures is not as difficult as expected (Goetz & Etzel, 1977). On the other hand, it may be speculated that the frequent availability of multiple responses per step combined with nonstringent error criteria has inflated success rates. This in turn has reduced the possibility of observing differences based on the two diverse types of stimulus manipulations.

C. Nature of the Task

Another parameter that needs to be considered for a better appraisal of the influence of different stimulus manipulations is the nature of the task used. Among the studies reviewed, six types of tasks can be identified. In Table I these are indicated with roman numerals. The first type of task (I) identified is a two-choice discrimination requiring a standard response (e.g., pointing) to the S+. The second task (II) is similar to the first one, except that more than one S− stimulus is available. The third type of task (III) consists of match-to-sample strategies, where two or more stimuli are alternately or simultaneously used as samples and as many or more stimuli are used as matches. The fourth type of task (IV) involves three or more stimuli that function as S+ at each single step of the program. Each of these stimuli requires a specific response (e.g., sight reading different words). The fifth type of task (V) also involves various S+ stimuli (from three to over ten) requiring different responses. In contrast with the fourth type of task, however, the stimuli are learned one at a time. The sixth type of task (VI) represents an extension of the second (the training paradigm is repeated across stimuli) or a variation of the fourth (the same pointing response is used for each of the two to six stimuli available).

An inspection of the tasks in relation to the different forms of stimulus manipulations suggests that the fourth type of task has been employed rather extensively in studies based on extra-stimulus nondistinctive-feature manipulations. Since this type of task may be considered more difficult than others (e.g., two-choice tasks), it could be argued that the task difficulty influenced the results obtained with those studies. This argument would seem to apply if one looks at studies such as those of Dorry and Zeaman (1973, 1975), Dorry (1976), and Walsh and Lamberts (1979), which reported rather poor results. It has to be noted, however, that these studies involved many stimuli (i.e., 4 to 10 S+ stimuli) and short training programs. Thus, they maximized the difficulties of the task while providing a weak training context. A somewhat different picture could be drawn if one analyzes the results of the studies using three S+ stimuli within an apparently more elaborate training program (McGee & McCoy, 1981; Smeets et al., 1984a,b). The success rate (i.e., training instances in which discrimination was achieved) for these studies is 87%. At the same time, the success rate of studies using extra-stimulus nondistinctive-feature manipulations in combination with two-choice tasks is 52%. These percentages seem to suggest that the fourth type of task does not result directly in a larger number of failures to learn. Yet, before the aforementioned conclusion can be accepted, two issues are to be considered. First, the fourth type of task (normally concerned with sight reading) may frequently have involved better functioning subjects, that is, subjects with better learning skills and fewer behavioral problems (compared to the subjects exposed to two-choice tasks). Second, many of the failures in two-choice tasks have been reported under restrictive error criteria (Koegel & Rincover, 1976; Rincover, 1978).

With regard to the other types of tasks used by the studies, data available do not allow specification of any differential effects. Based on this observation and on the previous discussion, it can be maintained that, although the type of task used may play a role, this is not immediately obvious or unequivocal. The nature of stimulus manipulations, the error criteria, and the number of positive responses per step, for instance, can all contribute to shadow the specific impact of the task. Important variations within the same type of task, concerning the complexity and/or similarity of the stimuli involved, may further confound the differential role of diverse tasks (Smeets & Lancioni, 1981; Stella, 1980; Touchette & Howard, 1984). Finally, the characteristics of the subjects or, more specifically, the discrepancy between the subjects' abilities and the task requirements can be considered another very influential (confounding) variable (Etzel, Bickel, Stella, & LeBlanc, 1982; Walls, Dowler, Haught, & Zawlocki, 1984).

D. Number of Steps in the Program

This parameter has been largely debated (Bijou, 1968; Schilmoeller & Etzel, 1974; Sidman & Stoddard, 1966; Terrace, 1966). It applies only marginally to studies using the delayed-cue procedure (i.e., only with regard to the steps taken to postpone the cue). With regard to studies using the other procedures, the number of steps for accomplishing the stimulus manipulations is normally preset according to two general rules. The steps are to be small so that the subjects can continue to respond correctly throughout the program. The steps are not to be too many, otherwise the program may become unnecessarily long and/or subjects may lose motivation in responding (Sidman & Stoddard, 1966; Sulzer-Azeroff & Mayer, 1977). Despite the rules, studies have varied considerably on the number of steps devised. As an example, it may be sufficient to say that the number of steps devised for two-choice tasks has varied between 4 and 60. The number of steps for tasks of the fourth type has varied between 5 and 37.

In light of the results obtained and of the discrepancies mentioned above, two considerations can be formulated. First, a high number of steps does not seem to have detrimental effects on learning (Schilmoeller & Etzel, 1977; Schilmoeller *et al.*, 1979; Stella & Etzel, 1979, 1983). The use of a high number of steps, however, may not always be sufficient for successful training when extra-stimulus nondistinctive-feature manipulations are carried out (Sherman & Webster, 1974; Touchette, 1968).

Second, the number of steps involved in a program perhaps should not be considered independent of the nature of stimulus manipulations, type of stimuli, subjects' abilities, and positive responses per step. For example, programs that manipulate both stimuli of a two-choice discrimination task (Stella & Etzel, 1979) would tend to involve more steps than programs manipulating only one stimulus. Programs that involve three-dimensional stimuli (Lancioni *et al.*, 1984; Mosk & Bucher, 1984) may tend to use fewer steps, since the manipulation of the stimuli could be laborious and difficult. Similarly, the availability of higher functioning subjects or relatively simple stimuli (or combinations of the program with self-cueing strategies) may induce one to devise fewer steps (Smeets *et al.*, 1984c).

E. Manipulations along the S−, the S+, or Both Stimuli

In two-choice discrimination tasks taught through stimulus shaping or stimulus fading, manipulations have often been carried out only on one of the stimuli. Studies that have manipulated both stimuli include those of Sidman and Stoddard (1966), Stella (1980), and Zawlocki and Walls (1983). In two-choice discrimination tasks taught through superimposition and fading, manipulations have been carried out on one of the stimuli (Irvin & Bellamy, 1977; Rincover, 1978) or on both of them (Koegel & Rincover, 1976; Sherman & Webster, 1974; Touchette, 1968). In tasks taught through delayed-cue procedures, manipulations are normally carried out on one of the stimuli.

Whether manipulations of one or both stimuli make a difference in the outcome of the program is not easy to decide based on the evidence available. Only two studies have attempted to shed some light on this issue. Stella and Etzel (1978) have reported that normal children had a better performance when exposed to a program in which both stimuli were shaped than when exposed to a program in which only one stimulus was shaped. The data, however, have to be interpreted with some caution. In fact, in the first program, subjects received more training trials than in the second program. Zawlocki and Walls (1983) have found no substantial differences between conditions in which fading was carried out along the S− and conditions in which fading was carried out along both stimuli. Although the number of steps varied between conditions, the number of training trials was held constant.

In connection with the manipulation of only one of the two stimuli, the issue has been raised of whether changes along the S+ could be more effective than changes along the S− (the latter changes being conventional). Studies aimed at clarifying this issue have provided conflicting evidence. With normal preschool children, Cheney and Stein (1974) found a slight difference favoring the fading procedure in which the S− was manipulated. With mentally retarded subjects,

Zawlocki and Walls (1983) found that fading along the S− produced better results than fading along the S+. By contrast, Schreibman and Charlop (1981) and Stella and Etzel (1986) have reported data favoring fading or shaping along the S+. Autistic and normal children were involved in the studies. These authors have suggested that the better results obtained with the manipulation of the S+ are due to the fact that the subjects' attention is more heavily drawn on the S+ (i.e., the changing stimulus). This suggestion, which Stella and Etzel have documented with data on the subjects' visual orientation, seems to find support also in previous work of the same authors (Stella & Etzel, 1978, 1979). The importance and implications of these findings as well as of those concerning the manipulation of one or both stimuli of the task certainly deserve further investigation. This investigation should also take into account the characteristics of the subjects and should possibly control for the impact of other relevant procedural parameters.

IV. CONCLUSION

On the basis of the review of studies and procedural parameters, it can be argued that a number of questions need to be answered before a real appreciation, and eventually a more effective use of errorless training procedures, can be achieved. In order to summarize some of the basic issues involved in the chapter, the following points could be made. First, errorless training procedures have not always been as successful as expected. Error performance and failures have also been reported. Nevertheless, the results obtained with the procedures have, with sporadic exceptions (Koegel & Rincover, 1976), compared favorably with those obtained with trial-and-error training (Dixon et al., 1974; Gold & Barclay, 1973; Richmond & Bell, 1983; Sidman & Stoddard, 1967; Touchette, 1968; Zawlocki & Walls, 1983).

Second, procedures involving within-stimulus manipulations and extra-stimulus distinctive-feature manipulations have appeared more effective than procedures based on extra-stimulus nondistinctive-feature manipulations. Third, studies involving within-stimulus criterion-related manipulations, which do not require transfer of stimulus control (Etzel & LeBlanc, 1979), have shown mostly positive outcomes. The differences between these studies and those using within-stimulus noncriterion-related manipulations (at least with regard to the percentages of successes), however, have seemed somewhat smaller than would have been expected on the basis of data collected with normal subjects (Etzel & LeBlanc, 1979; Gollin & Savoy, 1968; Schilmoeller et al., 1979). It may be that the transfer of control across dimensions of the target stimuli (required in studies using noncriterion-related manipulations) is not always as difficult as one might anticipate (Goetz & Etzel, 1977). It may also be plausible that procedural parameters, such as multiple responses per step of the program and nonrestrictive error criteria, have contributed to increase the success rate of the latter studies and have thus shadowed the differential impact of the diverse (criterion-related versus noncriterion-related) stimulus manipulations.

Fourth, with regard to the studies using extra-stimulus distinctive-feature manipulations, two viewpoints may be expressed. On the one hand, it can be argued that an extra-stimulus prompt connected to a relevant dimension of the stimuli to be discriminated is likely to attract the subjects' attention to that dimension (Guralnick, 1975; Meador, 1984) rather than block attention away from it, as may occur with nondistinctive-feature prompts (Nelson, Gergenti, & Hollander, 1980). This appropriate attention may be sufficient for the subjects to achieve discrimination (as observed in the studies reviewed; Guralnick, 1975; Rincover, 1978; Smeets et al., 1984b). On the other hand, one may also argue that an extra-stimulus prompt (contrary to within-stimulus criterion-related manipulations) locates the relevant dimension of the stimuli to be discriminated rather than "informing" the subject of it. Thus, the risk may exist that the subject fails to perceive the critical difference between the stimuli, particularly if the difference is small or embedded in common features (Etzel & LeBlanc, 1979; Etzel et al., 1982). The consequence could be that the elimination of the prompt is followed by errors.

Fifth, among the procedural parameters reviewed, the type of stimulus manipulations, the error criteria, and the number of positive responses per step have appeared most influential. However, the contrasting results obtained in several studies (especially in those using superimposition and fading and delayed cue) seem to suggest that other procedural parameters as well as the stimuli used for the discrimination tasks and the characteristics of the subjects may also play a role (Doran & Holland, 1979; Smeets & Lancioni, 1981; Smeets et al., 1984b; Walls et al., 1984).

In view of the aforementioned considerations, two points could be made. First, although errorless training procedures are normally demanding in terms of ingenuity, preparation, and time investment, their use may be warranted and decisive in situations in which conventional teaching methods have failed or are considered unlikely to work. Second, further research is needed to ensure an overall improvement in the efficiency of the procedures. With regard to this point, a better understanding is required (1) of the role of the procedural parameters, and (2) of the possible interactions between procedural parameters, subjects, and stimuli used for the discrimination tasks. Moreover, investigations should be designed to assess the effects of errorless training on generalization. Thus far, studies have concentrated on the acquisition of the discrimination, paying very little attention, if any, to the issue of generalization across stimuli or settings. The early suggestion of Gollin and Savoy (1968) that errorless procedures may attenuate the transfer from a single discrimination to a conditional discrimination task did not seem substantiated by subsequent data (Schilmoeller *et al.*, 1979). Similarly, the negative findings of Guralnick (1975) with regard to generalization across stimuli do not seem supported by more recent research (Aeschleman & Higgins, 1982).

In conclusion, it can be argued that, until new experimental evidence is available, guidelines for the selection and use of the errorless procedures will remain somewhat general. Procedures involving within-stimulus criterion-related manipulations could be indicated as likely to be effective across subjects and situations. At the same time, procedures using extra-stimulus distinctive-feature manipulations may also be found highly successful (as previously discussed). Procedures involving within-stimulus noncriterion-related manipulations may provide better results if combined with criterion-related (self-cueing) motor responses (Dixon *et al.*, 1974). The use of a large number of training steps is unlikely to be detrimental for learning. Yet, the availability of many steps may not be a sufficient condition for success if the program involves extra-stimulus nondistinctive-feature manipulations and low-functioning subjects.

ACKNOWLEDGMENTS

The authors would like to thank Dr. Barbara C. Etzel for her most helpful comments on a previous version of this paper. Their appreciation is also extended to Dr. Aloysius J. Goossens.

REFERENCES

Aeschleman, S. R., & Higgins, A. F. (1982). Concept learning by retarded children: A comparison of three discrimination learning procedures. *Journal of Mental Deficiency Research,* **26,** 229–238.

Baker, R. A., & Osgood, S. W. (1954). Discrimination transfer along a pitch continuum. *Journal of Experimental Psychology,* **48,** 241–246.

Barrett, B. H. (1965). Acquisition of operant differentiation and discrimination in institutionalized retarded children. *American Journal of Orthopsychiatry,* **35,** 863–885.

Bijou, S. W. (1968). Studies in the experimental development of left–right concepts in retarded children using fading techniques. In N. R. Ellis (Ed.), *International review of research in mental retardation* (Vol. 3, pp. 65–96). New York: Academic Press.

Cheney, T., & Stein, N. (1974). Fading procedures and oddity learning in kindergarten children. *Journal of Experimental Child Psychology,* **17,** 313–321.

Dixon, L. S., Spradlin, J. E., Girardeau, F. L., & Etzel, B. C. (1974). Development of a programmed stimulus series for training *in front* discrimination. *Acta Symbolica,* **5,** 1–21.

Doran, J., & Holland, J. G. (1979). Control by stimulus features during fading. *Journal of the Experimental Analysis of Behavior,* **31,** 177–187.

Dorry, G. W. (1976). Attentional model for the effectiveness of fading in training reading-vocabulary with retarded persons. *American Journal of Mental Deficiency,* **81,** 271–279.

Dorry, G. W., & Zeaman, D. (1973). The use of a fading technique in paired-associate teaching of a reading vocabulary with retardates. *Mental Retardation,* **11**(6), 3–6.

Dorry, G. W., & Zeaman, D. (1975). Teaching a simple reading vocabulary to retarded children: Effectiveness of fading and nonfading procedures. *American Journal of Mental Deficiency,* **79,** 711–716.

Ellis, N. R., Girardeau, F. L., & Pryer, M. W. (1962). Analysis of learning sets in normal and severely defective humans. *Journal of Comparative and Physiological Psychology*, **55**, 860–865.

Etzel, B. C., Bickel, W. K., Stella, M. E., & LeBlanc, J. M. (1982). The assessment of problem-solving skills of atypical children. *Analysis and Intervention in Developmental Disabilities*, **2**, 187–206.

Etzel, B. C., & LeBlanc, J. M. (1979). The simplest treatment alternative: The law of parsimony applied to choosing appropriate instructional control and errorless-learning procedures for the difficult-to-teach child. *Journal of Autism and Developmental Disorders*, **9**, 361–382.

Etzel, B. C., LeBlanc, J. M., Schilmoeller, K. J., & Stella, M. E. (1981). Stimulus control procedures in the education of young children. In S. W. Bijou & R. Ruiz (Eds.), *Contributions of behavior modification to education* (pp. 3–37). Hillsdale, NJ: Erlbaum.

Etzel, B. C., & Schilmoeller, K. J. (1977). *A review of errorless learning procedures.* (Working Paper No. 100). Lawrence: University of Kansas, Bureau of Child Research, John T. Stewart Children's Center.

Feldman, J. M. (1975). Blocking as a function of added cue intensity. *Animal Learning and Behavior*, **3**, 98–102.

Goetz, E. M., & Etzel, B. C. (1977). *Review of recent examples of discrimination learning research with children in which various manipulations of the S+ (correct choice) or S− (incorrect choice), or both, facilitated or failed to facilitate correct criterion-level (final) responding.* Unpublished manuscript. Lawrence: University of Kansas.

Gold, M. W., & Barclay, C. R. (1973). The learning of difficult visual discriminations by moderately and severely retarded. *Mental Retardation*, **11**(2), 9–11.

Gollin, E. S., & Savoy, P. (1968). Fading procedures and conditional discrimination in children. *Journal of the Experimental Analysis of Behavior*, **11**, 443–451.

Guralnick, M. J. (1975). Effects of distinctive-feature training and instructional technique on letter and form discrimination. *American Journal of Mental Deficiency*, **80**, 202–207.

House, B. J., & Zeaman, D. (1958). Visual discrimination learning in imbeciles. *American Journal of Mental Deficiency*, **63**, 447–452.

House, B. J., & Zeaman, D. (1960). Transfer of a discrimination from objects to patterns. *Journal of Experimental Psychology*, **59**, 298–302.

Hull, C. L. (1950). Simple qualitative discrimination learning. *Psychological Review*, **57**, 303–313.

Irvin, L. K., & Bellamy, G. T. (1977). Manipulation of stimulus features in vocational-skill training of severely retarded individuals. *American Journal of Mental Deficiency*, **81**, 486–491.

Johnson, C. M. (1977). Errorless learning in a multihandicapped adolescent. *Education and Treatment of Children*, **1**, 25–33.

Koegel, R. L., & Rincover, A. (1976). Some detrimental effects of using extra stimuli to guide learning in normal and autistic children. *Journal of Abnormal Child Psychology*, **4**, 59–71.

Lambert, J.-L. (1975). Extinction by retarded children following discrimination learning with and without errors. *American Journal of Mental Deficiency*, **80**, 286–291.

Lambert, J.-L. (1980). Stimulus fading procedures and discrimination learning by retarded children. In J. Hogg & P. J. Mittler (Eds.), *Advances in mental handicap research* (pp. 83–128). Chichester, England: Wiley.

Lancioni, G. E. (1983). Using pictorial representations as communication means with low-functioning children. *Journal of Autism and Developmental Disorders*, **13**, 87–105.

Lancioni, G. E., Smeets, P. M., & Oliva, D. S. (1984). Teaching severely handicapped adolescents to follow instructions conveyed by means of three-dimensional stimulus configurations. *Applied Research in Mental Retardation*, **5**, 107–123.

LaVigna, G. W. (1977). Communication training in mute autistic adolescents using the written word. *Journal of Autism and Childhood Schizophrenia*, **7**, 135–149.

Lawrence, D. H. (1952). The transfer of a discrimination along a continuum. *Journal of Comparative and Physiological Psychology,* **45,** 511–516.

Lawrence, D. H. (1955). The applicability of generalization gradients to the transfer of a discrimination. *Journal of General Psychology,* **52,** 37–48.

Mackintosh, N. J. (1971). An analysis of overshadowing and blocking. *Quarterly Journal of Experimental Psychology,* **23,** 118–125.

Mackintosh, N. J., & Honig, W. K. (1970). Blocking and enhancement of stimulus control in pigeons. *Journal of Comparative and Physiological Psychology,* **73,** 78–85.

McGee, G. G., & McCoy, J. F. (1981). Training procedures for acquisition and retention of reading in retarded youth. *Applied Research in Mental Retardation,* **2,** 263–276.

Meador, D. M. (1984). Effects of color on visual discrimination of geometric symbols by severely and profoundly mentally retarded individuals. *American Journal of Mental Deficiency,* **89,** 275–286.

Moore, R., & Goldiamond, I. (1964). Errorless establishment of visual discrimination using fading procedures. *Journal of the Experimental Analysis of Behavior,* **7,** 269–272.

Mosk, M. D., & Bucher, B. (1984). Prompting and stimulus shaping procedures for teaching visual–motor skills to retarded children. *Journal of Applied Behavior Analysis,* **17,** 23–34.

Nelson, D. L., Gergenti, E., & Hollander, A. C. (1980). Extra prompts versus no extra prompts in self-care training of autistic children and adolescents. *Journal of Autism and Developmental Disorders,* **10,** 311–321.

Newsom, C. D., & Simon, K. M. (1977). A simultaneous discrimination procedure for the measurement of vision in nonverbal children. *Journal of Applied Behavior Analysis,* **10,** 633–644.

Rescorla, R. A., & Wagner, A. R. (1972). A theory of Pavlovian conditioning: Variations in the effectiveness of reinforcement and nonreinforcement. In A. H. Black & W. F. Prokasy (Eds.), *Classical conditioning II: Current theory and research* (pp. 64–99). New York: Appleton-Century-Crofts.

Richmond, G., & Bell, J. (1983). Comparison of three methods to train a size discrimination with profoundly mentally retarded students. *American Journal of Mental Deficiency,* **87,** 574–576.

Rincover, A. (1978). Variables affecting stimulus fading and discriminative responding in psychotic children. *Journal of Abnormal Psychology,* **5,** 541–553.

Schilmoeller, G. L., Schilmoeller, K. J., Etzel, B. C., and LeBlanc, J. M. (1979). Conditional discrimination after errorless and trial-and-error training. *Journal of Experimental Analysis of Behavior,* **31,** 405–420.

Schilmoeller, K. J., & Etzel, B. C. (1974). *The effect of criterion- and non-criterion-related cues on response latency during a programmed discrimination task.* Paper presented at the 82nd annual convention of the American Psychological Association, New Orleans.

Schilmoeller, K. J., & Etzel, B. C. (1977). An experimental analysis of criterion-related and non-criterion-related cues in "errorless" stimulus control procedures. In B. C. Etzel, J. M. LeBlanc, & D. M. Baer (Eds.), *New developments in behavioral research* (pp. 317–347). Hillsdale, NJ: Erlbaum.

Schlosberg, H., & Solomon, R. L. (1943). Latency of response in a choice discrimination. *Journal of Experimental Psychology,* **33,** 22–39.

Schreibman, L. (1975). Effects of within-stimulus and extra-stimulus prompting on discrimination learning in autistic children. *Journal of Applied Behavior Analysis,* **8,** 91–112.

Schreibman, L., & Charlop, M. H. (1981). S+ versus S− fading in prompting procedures with autistic children. *Journal of Experimental Child Psychology,* **31,** 508–520.

Sherman, T. W., & Webster, C. D. (1974). The effects of stimulus-fading on acquisition of a visual position discrimination in autistic, retarded, and normal children. *Journal of Autism and Childhood Schizophrenia,* **4,** 301–312.

Sidman, M., & Stoddard, L. T. (1966). Programming perception and learning for retarded children.

In N. R. Ellis (Ed.), *International review of research in mental retardation* (Vol. 2, pp. 151–208). New York: Academic Press.

Sidman, M., & Stoddard, L. T. (1967). The effectiveness of fading in programming a simultaneous form discrimination for retarded children. *Journal of the Experimental Analysis of Behavior,* **10,** 3–15.

Smeets, P. M., & Lancioni, G. E. (1981). The efficacy of three procedures for teaching easy and difficult discriminations in severely retarded adolescents. *Behavior Research of Severe Developmental Disabilities,* **2,** 191–201.

Smeets, P. M., Lancioni, G. E., & Hoogeveen, F. R. (1984a). Effects of different stimulus manipulations on the acquisition of word recognition in trainable mentally retarded children. *Journal of Mental Deficiency Research,* **28,** 109–122.

Smeets, P. M., Lancioni, G. E., & Hoogeveen, F. R. (1984b). Using stimulus shaping and fading to establish stimulus control in normal and retarded children. *Journal of Mental Deficiency Research,* **28,** 207–218.

Smeets, P. M., Lancioni, G. E., Striefel, S., & Willemsen, R. J. (1984c). Training EMR children to solve missing minuend problems errorlessly: Acquisition, generalization, and maintenance. *Analysis and Intervention in Developmental Disabilities,* **4,** 379–402.

Smeets, P. M., & Striefel, S. (1976). Acquisition of sign reading by transfer of stimulus control in a retarded deaf girl. *Journal of Mental Deficiency Research,* **20,** 197–205.

Spence, W. W. (1936). The nature of discrimination learning with and without errors. *Psychological Review,* **43,** 427–449.

Stella, M. E. (1980). *Training visual discriminations: An analysis of errorless learning procedures and visual attention patterns with normal and atypical children.* Unpublished doctoral dissertation, University of Kansas, Lawrence.

Stella, M. E., & Etzel, B. C. (1978). *Procedural variables in errorless discrimination learning: Order of S+ and S− manipulation.* Paper presented at the 86th annual convention of the American Psychological Association, Toronto.

Stella, M. E., & Etzel, B. C. (1979). *Manipulation of visual orientation on correct (S+) stimuli during acquisition.* Lawrence: University of Kansas, Kansas Research Institute for the Early Childhood Education of the Handicapped. (ECI Document No. 129)

Stella, M. E., & Etzel, B. C. (1983). Effects of criterion-level probing on demonstrating newly acquired discriminative behavior. *Journal of the Experimental Analysis of Behavior,* **39,** 479–498.

Stella, M. E., & Etzel, B. C. (1986). Stimulus control of eye orientations: Shaping S+ only versus shaping S− only. *Analysis and Intervention in Developmental Disabilities,* **6,** 137–153

Stella, M. E., LeBlanc, J. M., & Etzel, B. C. (1981). *The effectiveness of criterion-related instructions as a correction procedure.* Paper presented at the 7th annual convention of the Association of Behavior Analysis, Milwaukee.

Striefel, S., Bryan, K. S., & Aikins, D. A. (1974). Transfer of stimulus control from motor to verbal stimuli. *Journal of Applied Behavior Analysis,* **7,** 123–135.

Sulzer-Azeroff, B., & Mayer, G. R. (1977). *Applying behavior-analysis procedures with children and youth.* New York: Holt, Rinehart & Winston.

Terrace, H. S. (1963a). Discrimination learning with and without errors. *Journal of the Experimental Analysis of Behavior,* **6,** 1–27.

Terrace, H. S. (1963b). Errorless transfer of a discrimination across two continua. *Journal of the Experimental Analysis of Behavior,* **6,** 223–232.

Terrace, H. S. (1966). Stimulus control. In W. K. Honig (Ed.), *Operant behavior: Areas of research and application* (pp. 271–344). New York: Appleton-Century-Crofts.

Touchette, P. E. (1968). The effects of graduated stimulus change on the acquisition of a simple discrimination in severely retarded boys. *Journal of the Experimental Analysis of Behavior,* **11,** 39–48.

Touchette, P. E. (1971). Transfer of stimulus control: Measuring the moment of transfer. *Journal of the Experimental Analysis of Behavior,* **15,** 347–354.

Touchette, P. E., & Etzel, B. C. (1977). *Errorless acquisition: Research and methodology.* Paper presented at the Gatlinburg Conference on Research in Mental Retardation, Gatlinburg, TN.

Touchette, P. E., & Howard, J. S. (1984). Errorless learning: Reinforcement contingencies and stimulus control transfer in delayed prompting. *Journal of Applied Behavior Analysis,* **17,** 175–188.

Walls, R. T., Dowler, D. L., Haught, P. A., & Zawlocki, R. J. (1984). Progressive delay and unlimited delay of prompts in forward chaining and whole task training strategies. *Education and Training of the Mentally Retarded,* **19,** 276–284.

Walsh, B. F., & Lamberts, F. (1979). Errorless discrimination and picture fading as techniques for teaching sight words to TMR students. *American Journal of Mental Deficiency,* **83,** 473–479.

Wolfe, V. F., & Cuvo, A. J. (1978). Effects of within-stimulus and extra-stimulus prompting on letter discrimination by mentally retarded persons. *American Journal of Mental Deficiency,* **83,** 297–303.

Zane, T., Handen, B. L., Mason, S. A., & Geffin, C. (1984). Teaching symbol identification: A comparison between standard prompting and intervening response procedures. *Analysis and Intervention in Developmental Disabilities,* **4,** 367–377.

Zawlocki, R. J., & Walls, R. T. (1983). Fading on the S+, the S−, both, or neither. *American Journal of Mental Deficiency,* **87,** 462–464.

Reading Acquisition and Remediation in the Mentally Retarded

NIRBHAY N. SINGH AND JUDY SINGH

DEPARTMENT OF PSYCHOLOGY
UNIVERSITY OF CANTERBURY
CHRISTCHURCH 1, NEW ZEALAND

I. INTRODUCTION

Reading is an essential skill for daily living. It is a particularly important skill for mentally retarded persons if they are to live and achieve some degree of independence in the community. Reading skills are not only useful when competing for employment, but also for domestic and leisure-time activities such as using the bus, shopping, cooking, using the telephone directory, and reading for pleasure. Moreover, with the current emphasis on mainstreaming and community integration of mentally retarded persons, the need for them to be able to read is greater than ever.

Historically, the concept of teaching reading to mentally retarded persons has received a mixed reception. At the turn of the century, reading was not considered to be necessary or even a desirable skill for the mentally retarded. Although this view prevailed until the 1950s and 1960s, some effort was made to teach reading to those classified either as borderline or educable mentally retarded. The aim was to teach them a sight vocabulary of functional words, characterized as "protective" words, which included street signs (e.g., stop, walk, wait), convenience signs (e.g., toilet, men, women, ladies), cautionary words (e.g., danger, do not enter, private, dogs) and names of common objects (Ingram, 1953; Wallin, 1924).

Early reading research indicated that educable mentally retarded (EMR) children were able to read at mental age (MA) expectancy levels (Bennett, 1929; MacIntyre, 1937; Merrill, 1924). However, later studies showed that mentally retarded children read below their MA expectancy levels, especially if they had been placed in special classes (Bliesmer, 1954; Dunn, 1954; Quay, 1963). More-

INTERNATIONAL REVIEW OF RESEARCH IN
MENTAL RETARDATION, Vol. 14

over, it was suggested that, given adequate instruction, the most that EMR children could be taught to read was at the second- or third-grade level (Perry, 1960).

Virtually no reading research was conducted with trainable mentally retarded (TMR) children until about 15 years ago. This was mainly due to the prevailing notion that the TMR could not be taught academic skills such as counting and reading. This view was reinforced by leading authorities in the field (Kirk & Johnson, 1951) and still continues to be the view of many professionals (Burton, 1974; Gearhart & Litton, 1975; Kirk, 1972). The assumption behind this view is that the TMR simply do not possess the mental abilities necessary for acquiring reading skills beyond a few simple words, and those who do have probably been misdiagnosed as TMR (Kirk, 1972).

Despite this pessimistic view, a few reports were published indicating that the TMR could indeed be taught to read more than a few simple words (Davy, 1962; Riese, 1956). Subsequently, more optimistic views appeared in the literature (Cawley & Pappanikou, 1967; D'Amelio, 1971; Nietupski, Williams, York, Johnson, & Brown, 1976), which led to a reassessment of our expectations of the TMR and resulted in the development of appropriate instructional technology for teaching them to read.

A. Reading and the Slow Learner

Persons with an IQ from 68 to 85 are usually referred to as slow learners. Until the 1973 revision of the AAMD definition (Grossman, 1973) this group was defined as *borderline* mentally retarded. This population falls between those who are considered "average" and those who are classified as mentally retarded. Most children who are slow learners are pupils in regular classrooms and are taught with their mentally "normal" peers. Since the primary focus of this article is on reading in the mentally retarded (i.e., those with an IQ of 67 or less), reading research related to the slow learner will not be covered. Readers interested in this area should consult Kirk, Kleibhan, and Lerner (1978), Gillespie and Johnson (1974), and Hargis (1982).

B. Reading in the Mentally Retarded

This article covers reading acquisition and remediation in mentally retarded persons, mainly children. The focus is on instructional and remediation techniques, supported by a review of the available empirical literature evaluating or demonstrating the use of these techniques. The bulk of the research reviewed used two groups of mentally retarded persons as subjects, those labeled EMR, or the mildly mentally retarded (Stanford–Binet IQ of 52 to 67), those labeled TMR, or the moderately mentally retarded (Stanford–Binet IQ of 36 to 51). Only a few studies included subjects classified as severely mentally retarded (Stanford–Binet IQs 20 to 35). No studies could be located that used profoundly mentally retarded children as subjects.

In terms of the research literature in reading, studies dealing with word recognition, comprehension, and oral reading are covered. The literature on reading readiness or prereading skills was deemed beyond the scope of this article. It was assumed that children being taught word recognition skills would have had prior instruction in appropriate prereading skills. These skills would include an oral vocabulary of meaningful words, auditory discrimination of letter sounds, visual discrimination of written symbols, and left-to-right, top-to-bottom orientation (for reading written English). Readers interested in this area should consult Duffy, Sherman, and Roehler (1977), Duffy and Sherman (1977), and Snell (1978) for a description of these skills and ways to teach them.

The research literature will be discussed in the context of the reading process which is briefly outlined in Section II. The various approaches used to teach word recognition skills to mentally retarded persons are described in Section III. Comprehension is discussed in Section IV, and remediation techniques for oral reading errors are considered in Section V. Finally, Section VI summarizes the current state of reading research in this area and identifies a number of areas in need of further research.

II. THE READING PROCESS

Reading has been defined in many ways. However, most definitions emphasize the importance of correctly recognizing the written word or symbol and an understanding of its meaning. For example, D. A. Brown (1982) has suggested that ''reading is the product of the process by which we gain understanding of the thoughts someone has communicated in writing'' and that the reader is required to ''perceive, recognize, comprehend, and react to the author's message.'' Operationally, reading can be conveniently considered as consisting of two interrelated stages: word recognition and comprehension. Although there is no consensus on the definition of word recognition, the term is usually thought to imply the process of determining the pronounciation of a written word, and it is often assumed that some degree of meaning is also attached to the word. Comprehension is basically the understanding of what is read, and this can be achieved at different levels.

A. Word Recognition

The beginning reader usually has a sizable oral vocabulary before being able to read. One of the first things the reader learns is that for every spoken word there is a corresponding written word. There are two ways in which the beginning reader can identify and verbally label a written word, namely instantly and through mediation (Duffy *et al.*, 1977). Those words the child recognizes instantly are called sight words and form his sight vocabulary.

1. INSTANT RECOGNITION OF WORDS

Instantly recognized words are those the child is familiar with, and this familiarity has been acquired through paired associate learning. The child is able to associate a spoken word with its written form and remember this association over time. This association is acquired through discrimination learning which enables the child to visually discriminate the configuration of the word in terms of its letters, letter sequences, and left-to-right, beginning-to-end orientation. In time, the child uses these visual cues to instantly recognize the written word.

2. MEDIATED RECOGNITION OF WORDS

If the child is faced with a word which is not in his sight vocabulary (i.e., is new or unfamiliar), then one of a number of mediating strategies can be used to determine its pronounciation. These strategies have been variously labeled as decoding, word attack, word analysis, and word identification techniques. The utility of these strategies can be evaluated across several dimensions, the four most important of which (as determined in Duffy *et al.* 1977) are (1) *independence,* or the ability of the child to use the mediating strategy without assistance from teacher or parent, (2) *accuracy,* or the degree to which the mediating strategy will lead to the correct identification of a new word, (3) *speed,* or the amount of time taken by the child to figure out the pronounciation of a new word, and (4) *generalizability,* the extent to which the mediating strategy can be used to figure out other unknown words. These criteria will be used to evaluate some of the more common mediational strategies used with beginning readers.

a. Whole-Word or Look-and-Say Methods. There are a large number of instructional techniques covered by these approaches. Typically a new word is presented and the teacher directs the child's attention to the word, verbally labels the word, and gets the child to label it until mastery is achieved. Each new word is taught individually since this strategy does not lead either to independence in reading or to generalization to other unknown words. However, it does produce rapid and accurate identification of the target word. The whole-word approach is more commonly used in the early stages of reading instruction and later with those words that do not easily lend themselves to phonic analysis.

b. Phonic Analysis. This technique, also known as sounding out, enables the child to pronounce a new word on the basis of letter–sound (grapheme–phoneme) relationships. Unfamiliar words are broken into their letter constituents, the sounds of the letters are identified, and then the sounds are synthesized to pronounce the word. For the child with some initial reading skills, syllabication skills are also taught. The child is taught to recognize and divide a word into syllables (or vowel phonograms), sound out each syllable, and then telescope the sounds to pronounce the word. Phonic analysis is an extremely useful technique for mediating word recognition since it teaches independence in reading, assists the child to decode a word very rapidly, and provides a high degree of accuracy on most words that can be sounded out. Additionally, it teaches the child a set of skills which can be used to decode other unknown words. However, it does not assist the reader to work out the meaning of the word.

   c. *Structural Analysis.* Structural analysis techniques are also useful for working out the pronounciation of unfamiliar words. These techniques can be seen as a combination of phonic analysis and instant sight word recognition. Children are taught to recognize four basic grammatical systems: prefixes, suffixes, contractions, and compound words. Once the child learns the affixes (e.g., un-, -ed, -ing) by sight, then pronounciation of a new word is reduced to sounding out the root word. Knowing the affixes by sound and position produces faster mediation of the unknown word. The strengths of this technique are similar to those of phonic analysis. Meanings of words can be derived through this technique only if the reader understands the meaning of the word parts.

   d. *Contextual Analysis.* Context clues are usually better used by proficient readers than by those just beginning to read, since they rely heavily on the reader's ability to understand the bulk of what he or she is reading. Thus, contextual clues become increasingly important as the reader becomes more proficient. Two ways of using contextual clues are (1) by looking at the function of the word (e.g., does it act as an adjective, adverb, noun, verb, or connective?) and (2) by analyzing the relationship of the unknown word to other known words in the context of the passage or sentence read. Contextual clues usually provide an idea of the meaning of the unknown word through syntax and structure. However, both the meaning and the pronounciation of the word can be derived by pairing this technique with phonic analysis, thereby making this a very powerful mediating strategy for the proficient reader.

   e. *Dictionary Skills.* Although this technique would prove to be of little benefit to the beginning reader, increasingly proficient readers can look up the pronounciation and meaning of unknown words in the dictionary.

   f. *Picture Clues.* The reader can often guess an unfamiliar word by looking at the picture associated with the text. For proficient readers, pictures and illustrations (e.g., charts, diagrams) may lead to a better comprehension of the written material. However, excessive reliance on picture clues may hinder the beginning reader's development of other mediating strategies which would lead to independence in reading (Samuels, 1970).

   Once the reader is able to figure out the pronounciation of an unfamiliar word, repeated reading of the word will lead to increasingly faster recognition. Eventually the word will be recognized instantly and become a part of the reader's sight vocabulary. The actual sight words taught vary from teacher to teacher, depending in part on the basal reading text being used, but most of these words are contained in standard word lists, notably that of Dolch (1936). Lists of sight words for borderline retarded persons are also available (Borreca, Burger, Goldstein, & Simches, 1953).

In summary, instant and mediated word recognition skills assist the reader to pronounce and to some extent to understand the meaning of new and unfamiliar words. The actual mediating strategy used will depend on a variety of factors, including reading proficiency, the reading material, and teacher preference of different techniques.

B. Comprehension

Reading comprehension has been defined in several ways, but most definitions include the understanding of word meanings and reasoning with verbal concepts as crucial requirements for comprehension. Reading passages can be understood or comprehended at various levels depending, in part, on the language ability of the reader. Smith (1969), for example, divides reading comprehension into four cumulative categories: literal comprehension, interpretation, critical reading, and creative reading. Literal comprehension is thought to operate at a low level of understanding and relies heavily on the information actually provided by the text. This would be the level at which the trainable mentally retarded child would best be able to comprehend most reading material.

At a slightly higher level of comprehension, interpretation would involve the ability to understand abstract ideas and to understand what is only suggested or implied in the text rather than directly stated. The third level is that of critical reading, which requires the reader to make judgments about what is read. For example, the reader should be able to understand the difference between scientific writing and science fiction. In the final level, creative reading, the reader is not only able to read critically, but also to think creatively about what is read. For example, if reading detective fiction, the reader is able to solve the mystery before the author does or provide alternative solutions. Thus, comprehension can be seen as a skill which can be achieved at various levels and, therefore, should be tested for at these levels of understanding.

III. WORD RECOGNITION

Several methods have been used to teach word recognition skills to mentally retarded children. These can be broadly categorized into four general approaches, those using whole words, phonics, modified alphabets, and programmed instruction and automated techniques. With the exception of the studies by Sidman (1977), which used severely retarded children, most of the other studies used EMR and TMR children as subjects.

A. Whole-Word Approaches

As the name implies, words are taught as meaningful wholes and not segmented into syllables or sounds. Initially, high-frequency words are taught, usually by pairing them with pictures. Almost all reading books used with beginning readers, called basal readers (Williams, 1979), use one of the whole-word approaches. The teaching of sounds or phonics is delayed until the child has learned a substantial sight-word vocabulary. The whole-word methods have proved most popular for teaching word recognition skills to the mentally retarded.

1. STIMULUS FADING

Complex discriminations can be taught by beginning with easy-to-discriminate stimuli and then gradually introducing more complex or difficult stimuli. One technique for achieving this is through errorless discrimination training (Terrace, 1963a,b). For example, with pigeons it is usually simpler to establish color discrimination (e.g., red, green) than line discrimination (horizontal, vertical). Thus, one way of teaching line discrimination is to establish color discrimination between red and green and then superimpose the lines on the colors (e.g., vertical line on green and horizontal on red). Gradually the color dimension can be faded out, resulting in the transfer of discrimination from color to the lines.

This technique has been used to teach oral reading of basic sight words. Beginning readers are often introduced to new words through an association with pictures. For example, if the written word is ORANGE, the teacher uses the picture of an orange as a cue or prompt. Once the association between the picture and the written word has been established with repeated pairings, the child's attention is shifted from the picture to the word, until the word controls the oral reading response in the absence of the picture.

In a series of studies, picture fading has been used to teach sight words to mentally retarded children. In the first study, Dorry and Zeaman (1973) tested the comparative efficacy of picture fading and a standard nonfading procedure using a paired-associate methodology. Two groups of nine TMR children received training on a word list. One group received training with the fading technique, and the other, a standard technique in which a picture and word were presented simultaneously throughout training. The fading procedure was similar to the standard procedure except that the picture was gradually faded over trials. Each group had four presentations of the word list. The fading group learned 3.6 words from a list of 8 words, compared to 1.2 words learned by the nonfading group. This finding replicated that of an earlier study with nonretarded kindergarten children (Corey & Shamow, 1972). Similar results were obtained in a later study by Dorry and Zeaman (1975). Finally, Dorry (1976) found picture fading-out and picture fading-out plus word fading-in to be superior to word fading-in alone and the standard procedure in sight-word learning by TMR children.

These studies suggest that there was a transfer of control from the picture to the written word as a result of the gradual picture-fading procedure. Walsh and Lamberts (1979) compared the effects of the Dorry and Zeaman picture fading and errorless discrimination (Edmark Reading Program) training on the learning of sight words by TMR children. In the errorless procedure, the focus is strictly upon the word and no pictures are used. The new word is first presented by itself and the child is required to point to the word which is orally read by the teacher. Then, the child is required to read and point to the word, which is presented together with other words grossly dissimilar to the target word. Over successive trials, the target word is presented with words increasingly similar to it. On the final trial, only the target word is presented and the child is asked to read it. Walsh and Lamberts (1979) found the errorless discrimination procedure to be more effective than the picture-fading procedure.

In a recent study, McGee and McCoy (1981) evaluated the comparative effects of three training procedures on the sight-word learning of four TMR adults. The Dorry and Zeaman fading procedure was compared to trial-and-error and delay procedures. In the trial-and-error procedure, all correct oral reading responses to written words were reinforced and errors were not reinforced. The delay procedure was similar to the fading procedure except that instead of the intensity dimension of the picture being faded, this procedure required an increasing temporal delay between the presentation of the word and the picture, with longer delays being systematically programmed over successive trials (Touchette, 1971). The fading and the delay procedures produced greater acquisition and retention than the trial-and-error procedure.

The evidence for the efficacy of the fading procedure in the acquisition of sight words by mentally retarded children appears to be reasonably well documented. However, more data are needed regarding the delay procedure. In practical terms, it is feasible that the fading procedure can be used in the regular classroom, although the equipment needed to present the materials easily (e.g., two slide projectors) can be rather cumbersome. Of course, flash cards and photographs can be used instead of slides, but guidelines to assist the teacher regarding the rate at which the photographs should be faded will need to be established. Certainly future research should focus on this aspect of the procedure so that broad guidelines on the rate of fading can be drawn from hard data.

2. TRIAL-AND-ERROR METHODS

In the teaching of sight words through trial-and-error methods, the child would typically be reinforced for correctly vocalizing the written words and errors would not be attended to. A small number of studies have attempted to document the efficacy of this technique in teaching sight words to mentally retarded children. Some of the earlier studies indicated that, in terms of acquisition and retention of sight words, the trial-and-error method either led to equivalent performance when compared to errorless learning (Blackman & Holden, 1963; Hawker, Geertz, & Shrago, 1964; Hawker, 1968) or was less effective for acquisition but superior for retention of sight words (Stolurow, 1961). However, in a recent study, McGee and McCoy (1981) found that, in comparison to fading and delay procedures, trial-and-error was the least effective procedure, both in terms of acquisition and retention of sight words.

While there are inadequate data to judge the general utility of the trial-and-error procedure for teaching word recognition skills, the vast discrimination learning literature would suggest that this method may not be as effective as others (e.g., fading, errorless discrimination learning, delay). For example, there is good evidence to suggest that errorless discrimination procedures produce better acquisition and retention in the mentally retarded than trial-and-error techniques (Lambert, 1975; Touchette, 1968). Additionally, how useful this procedure is for learning new and more difficult words once basic words are learned remains to be determined.

3. BEHAVIORAL APPROACHES

A number of studies have used behavioral procedures to teach sight words to retarded children. One of the first was a study by L. Brown, Hermanson, Klemme, Haubrick, and Ora (1970). The teacher presented a flash card, modeled the correct label (word), instructed the subject to match the label provided, and finally reinforced the subject for doing so. The utility of this approach was demonstrated with a 12-year-old TMR girl who learned 51 new words in 26 20- to 25-minute teaching sessions. Moreover, six TMR boys were subsequently trained as a group using a similar procedure.

In a related study, L. Brown, Fenrick, and Kleeme (1971) used similar techniques to teach two TMR children 20 sight words each. The two sets of 20 words had 10 words in common. Subsequently, each subject taught the 10 words the other did not know using the same procedures the teachers had used with them. Once they had mastered the additional 10 words, they used the same teaching procedures to instruct five or their TMR peers and successfully taught them five of the words from their own repertoire. This study showed that the L. Brown *et al.* (1970) methods could be used not only to teach the TMR a number of sight words, but also that these children in turn could teach their retarded peers to read a number of words.

L. Brown and Perlmutter (1971) taught functional reading to seven TMR children, with reading being defined as "discrete and observable motor responses to printed stimuli." Functionally, this meant that the subjects had to label the printed stimuli and then do what the printed stimuli (i.e., sentences) instructed them to do. The instructional program was divided into three parts, with each part being subdivided further. The components were:

1. *Baseline*. This phase was used to determine how well each subject could (a) label the words in sentence order, (b) respond differentially to the sentence after labeling the words, and (c) respond differentially to the sentences after listening to the teacher label the words.

2. *Training*. In this phase the children were taught those skills they lacked during baseline, that is, (a) to label the printed words, and (b) to label the words in sentence order. They were evaluated on their ability to label the words in the order in which they occurred in sentences. The actual teaching procedure was adapted from Brown *et al.* (1970).

3. *Training to respond differentially to printed stimuli*. In this phase the children were tested during baseline on their ability to respond differentially to printed stimuli and were then trained to make differential location responses to the verbal stimuli. Subsequently, the children were evaluated on their ability to listen and respond differentially to sentences the teacher read orally.

As this description indicates, the teaching program was progressional, with children being required to respond at or close to 100% efficiency at each step before being taught the next one. The results showed that all seven nonreaders were able to read and comprehend nine sentences after 60 instructional hours.

Variations of the L. Brown *et al.* (1970) and L. Brown and Perlmutter (1971) teaching models have been employed in other related studies by the same group of researchers. L. Brown *et al.* (1972) taught two young TMR children to read and comprehend 12 adjective–noun phrases. Comprehension was tested by asking each child to touch the object to which the phrase referred. L. Brown, Huppler, Pierce, York, and Sontag (1974) taught three TMR children to read unconjugated words. Finally, similar techniques were used by another group of researchers to teach basic sight words to three Down's syndrome girls (Folk & Campbell, 1978).

In all these studies, correlational data were presented to attest to the efficacy of the teaching procedures. However, further research using robust single-subject designs is needed to better evaluate the usefulness of these procedures. Moreover, measures of long-term maintenance need to be included as well as generalization across other subjects and reading materials. One of the problems of this approach is that it teaches the child a certain number of words but does not provide the child a skill by which he/she can work out the verbal response to a new printed word. This procedure may be more effective if it is paired with other procedures which concentrate on word-attack skills.

In another series of studies, MacAulay (1968) used behavioral procedures to teach beginning reading to nonverbal TMR, EMR, and slow learners. Reading tasks were analyzed into small units and each unit of behavior was taught separately using reinforcement procedures. Eleven children were taught individual sounds, blending of sounds into words, naming, and, in some cases, reading phrases. Reinforcement consisted of tokens and verbal and social approval. Initially, close approximations to reading were reinforced, but as learning of each unit progressed, closer approximations were required for reinforcement. Results indicated that some progress had been made by all children, with five being able to read by the end of the program.

These studies demonstrate the efficacy of behavioral procedures in teaching beginning reading skills to mentally retarded children. The literature is not extensive and the methodology of these studies has not been particularly robust, but their results suggest that a closer examination of the behavioral procedures be made. A number of questions, particularly those pertaining to maintenance, generalization, and follow-up, remain unanswered.

4. SYMBOL ACCENTUATION

Symbol accentuation involves making a printed word topographically similar to the object it represents. Thus, the word *WALK* would be written with its letters appearing to walk. The assumption behind this technique is that if written words are accentuated visually to closely resemble the objects they represent, it will be easier for the child to acquire their meaning or symbolic function. Once meaning is attached to the written word, the accentuation is faded out and the child is able to read the word in conventional (orthographic) form.

In two related experiments, A. Miller and Miller (1968, 1971) found that EMR/TMR children learned to read a list of words more rapidly when presented in an accentuated form than in the conventional printed form. However, the subjects showed no difference in their ability to identify the words in sentences; words taught with the accentuated procedure were identified in their conventional form as well as, but not better than, words taught under the conventional form. More recently, Jeffree (1981) used a modified version of this approach to teach four TMR children a number of sight words. In a study which used a method closely resembling the symbol accentuation technique, Worrall and Singh (1983) taught a group of TMR children to read using a picture-cueing procedure. They found this procedure to be superior to the rebus system which uses symbols only.

Although the symbol accentuation procedure appears to be relatively easy to use in the classroom, there are no data to show that it is superior to any of the other more traditional methods (e.g., phonics). Moreover, a large number of basic sight words cannot be easily accentuated to enhance their meaning. A related problem is that it does not teach the beginning reader a technique by which new words can be read or decoded.

5. PHONOLOGICAL PAIRING

B. B. Miller (1975) has suggested that the pairing of new words which are phonologically similar (identical in sound except for the first phoneme in the words) to words already in the child's reading vocabulary may be a viable way of rapidly increasing the reading of mentally retarded children. Thirty-seven EMR children were randomly divided into three groups and presented with a list of five content (e.g., floor) and five function words (e.g., more). One group was presented words phonologically paired in a content–function order. The word order was reversed (i.e., function–content) for the second group, and the third group was presented words in a random order. The first two groups, which had phonological pairing, learned their words much faster than the other group, which had a randomly chosen list of words, Moreover, those that had content–function word order learned faster than the function–content group. The results suggest that new function words could be paired with already learned content words to increase the rate of learning to read new words. If these results are reliable and can be replicated with other groups of children and new sets of words, then this method may be useful for those children who already have a modest sight-word vocabulary.

6. TACTILE-KINESTHETIC PROCEDURES

Following the early work of Fernald with reading-disabled normal children (Fernald & Keller, 1921) and the mentally retarded (Fernald, 1943), Kirk (1933) investigated the effects of manual tracing of words on the reading ability of mentally retarded children. Six TMR boys were taught 150 commonly used three-letter words through the conventional "look-and-say" or sight method and by the tactile-kinesthetic method. In the conventional method, the child is shown a flash card on which a word is printed, the teacher verbally labels the word, and then the child repeats it. In the tactile-kinesthetic method the child, in addition, traces the word with a dull pencil or finger, saying each part of the word as it is being traced. Although there was great variability in the data, it was clear that, while there was no overall difference between the two techniques in terms of initial learning, the tactile-kinesthetic procedure was superior in terms of retention.

Although no other data-based studies are available to support the utility of this procedure with mentally retarded children, variations of this technique have been used with children with severe reading problems (Johnson, 1966; Cawley, Goldstein, & Burrow, 1972). It has been suggested that the technique works not so much as a result of the manual training but because it directs the attention of the reader to the word and word parts, its individualized instruction, and the novelty of the approach (McCarthy & Oliver, 1965). Teachers of the mentally retarded should be cautious in the use of this technique in the absence of firm data on its efficacy. Moreover, data comparing the effects of this procedure against that of other well-established procedures are needed before its use can be advocated.

B.   Phonics Approaches

Although the phonics method was the prevailing method of teaching reading to beginning readers from 1900 to 1920, thereafter it lost ground to the look-and-say, whole-word approaches. It was not until the mid-1950s that phonics crept back into the teaching system, causing the great debate between the protagonists for these two procedures (Chall, 1983). Research reviews suggest that with normal children the phonics approach may be superior to the look-and-say approach, both in terms of word recognition and spelling (Bliesmer & Yarborough, 1965; Chall, 1983; Gurren & Hughes, 1965).

Although only limited research data are available regarding the mentally retarded, the findings seem to be similar to those with normal children as far as the slow learner is concerned (Chall, 1983). The few studies carried out with EMR children suggest that phonics can be successfully used with them as well (French, 1950; Hegge, 1934).

1. PHONICS

There are few published studies which have evaluated the effects of phonics instruction on the reading ability of EMR and TMR students, although there is a small literature on the slow learner. The basic principles and strategies used have been described in several publications (Carnine, 1979; Carnine & Silbert, 1979; Englemann, 1967; Weisberg, Packer, & Weisberg, 1981), and a number of reading programs use this as their major approach (e.g., Distar, SRA linguistic readers).

Richardson, Winsberg, and Bialer (1973) tested the efficacy of two phonic instruction programs with a mixed group of 18 mentally retarded children. One group (IQs 46 to 97) received phonics instruction on the PAT-1 program (Richardson & Collier, 1971), and the other group (IQs 58 to 93), on the BRL-Sullivan program (Sullivan, 1968). Pre- and posttest measures showed that both groups had acquired phonic skills after only 6 hours of tutoring. However, only those on the PAT program were able to generalize their phonic skills. These results suggested that phonics instruction was useful with the mentally retarded and could be used to teach reading skills. Further, these findings were replicated with another mixed group of 19 mentally retarded children (IQs 38 to 80) by Richardson, Oestereicher, Bialer, and Winsberg (1975) using a revised version of the PAT-1.

The *Distar Reading Program* (Engelmann & Bruner, 1969), designed initially for teaching reading to slow learners and culturally deprived children, is a reading program based on the phonics approach. However, the program has been advocated for use with the mentally retarded as well (Engelmann, 1967), but almost no evaluative data are available. In perhaps the only experimental study using Distar with retarded children, Bracey, Maggs, and Morath (1975) used the Distar Reading Level I program to teach a group of six TMR children initial reading skills. The children received group instruction for 41 hours. There was a significant difference in the pre- and posttest results on 14 out of 19 tests of mastery in blending and reading sounds. This study showed that the Distar Reading Program was useful in teaching basic word-attack skills to TMR children.

2. PHONICS VERSUS WHOLE-WORD APPROACHES

Only two studies have compared the effects of teaching sight words through phonics and whole-word approaches. In one study Neville and Vandever (1973) taught 60 mentally normal and EMR children two lists of high-frequency words using the phonics and whole-word approaches. The children were divided into four matched groups of 15 subjects each: phonics (retarded), whole-word (retarded), phonics (nonretarded), and whole-word (nonretarded). Results showed that both retarded and nonretarded children learned more words using the phonics approach than the whole-word approach. Furthermore, those using the phonics approach scored higher on transfer tasks (i.e., reading new words) than the children who used the whole-word approach. Neville and Vandever (1973) suggested that the phonics method was more successful since it taught the children word-attack skills which generalized to the decoding of unfamiliar words. These results were replicated in a later study by the same authors (Vandever & Neville, 1976).

C. Modified Alphabet Approaches

A number of programs for teaching initial sight words to children use modified alphabets. These include the single-sound UNIFON (Malone, 1963), the Diacritical Marking System (Fry, 1963), the Simplified Spelling Society's system (Dewey, 1960), and the Initial Teaching Alphabet (ITA). Only the ITA has been used with the mentally retarded.

The ITA presents an alternative medium to traditional orthography for the teaching of reading to slow learners who have made little progress in reading. It consists of an augmented alphabet of 44 characters consisting of 24 letters from the Roman alphabet (with q and x being omitted) and 20 new ones for phonemes which do not have a single letter of their own in traditional orthography. Thus, each English sound is associated with only one letter. It has regularized spelling phonologically (e.g., "one" is written as "wun" to correspond with "bun," and "sun," etc.) and uses lower-case letters only. It is seen only as a transitional writing system, with the change to traditional orthography occurring usually at the end of the first grade.

The data supporting the efficacy of the ITA in enhancing the reading rate of beginning readers are mixed, derived mostly from anecdotal and case reports. The few experimental studies available provide inconclusive data (Dawson,

1969). The ITA has been used with EMR and TMR children, with some reports suggesting that the ITA enhances their reading ability (Downing, 1967a, b, 1968, 1969, 1979; Mazurkiewicz, 1966; Orman, 1966; Ward & Beauchamp, 1966), but no hard data have been published to substantiate any claims for its efficacy with the mentally retarded. Perhaps the efficacy of the ITA should be experimentally verified before it becomes firmly entrenched in the school system.

D. Programmed Instruction and Automated Approaches

Several attempts have been made to use programmed instruction for the teaching of reading to mentally retarded persons (see Greene, 1966; Malpass, 1967, for early reviews). The general finding has been that some mentally retarded children, particularly those with higher IQs, can be taught to read by means of programmed instruction. However, comparative studies have indicated that traditional classroom techniques are equally as good as programmed instruction (Hofmeister, 1971; Malpass, Hardy, Gilmore, & Williams, 1964).

A number of commercial programmed readers are available which have been used with slow learners and mentally retarded children. These include the *Sullivan Programmed Readers* (Buchannon & Sullivan Associates, 1963), the *Progressive Choice Reading Program* (Woolman, 1962), the *Peabody Rebus Reading Program* (Woodcock & Clark, 1969), the *Edmark Reading Program* (Bijou, 1972), and the *Fitzhugh Plus Program* (Fitzhugh & Fitzhugh, 1966). The evaluative literature on the effectiveness of these programs with the EMR/TMR populations is extremely limited, and no general conclusions on their usefulness can be drawn at present. What literature there is has been reviewed by Gillespie and Johnson (1974), Greene (1966), and Malpass (1967).

Teaching machines have also been used in the same manner as programmed readers (Greene, 1966; Roberts, 1976). Several papers have reported the use of teaching machines with varying degrees of sophistication to teach sight words to beginning readers. For example, Peach and Lewis (1969) used *Tach-X* and the *Controlled Reader,* Cleary and Packham (1968) used a touch-detecting teaching machine, and Malpass *et al.* (1964) used *Teachall* and *Wyckoff's Film Tutor.* As with programmed texts, the data are limited on the efficacy of teaching machines in the teaching of reading to mentally retarded persons. The few studies that are available suggest that teaching machines are only as good as the programs they use and produce results no better than those obtained with the traditional teaching methods (Blackman & Capobianco, 1965).

Finally, computer-assisted instruction (CAI) has also been used to teach reading to the mentally retarded (Atkinson & Fletcher, 1972; Brebner, Hallworth, & Brown, 1977; Hallworth & Brebner, 1979; Lally, 1981). However, the data on the utility of CAI for reading with the mentally retarded are very scarce, and the system is still being developed.

E. Summary

The bulk of the literature on teaching reading to the mentally retarded deals with ways in which word recognition skills can be taught. Researchers and teachers have relied heavily on whole-word approaches in teaching these skills, although the data on their efficacy with the mentally retarded are mixed. Six of these techniques were reviewed. The literature on phonics is meager and little experimental evidence is available on its efficacy with the mentally retarded. A similar situation was noted with respect to the other two approaches, modified alphabets and programmed instruction and automated approaches.

Most of the studies on word recognition used TMR students, with only a few using EMR and the severely mentally retarded. Why this bias exists in the literature is not immediately apparent, but it is likely that EMR children are taught word recognition skills using techniques similar to those used for teaching normal children. Few evaluative studies are available on these well-established techniques. As for the severely mentally retarded, the assumption in the literature has been that they are not capable of learning to read, and thus few attempts have been made to test the veracity of this assumption.

IV. COMPREHENSION

The ultimate aim of reading instruction is that the child be able to obtain information or meaning from what is read. The level of information acquired increases in complexity as the child progresses from learning individual words to combining them to form phrases and sentences. Finally, the child should be able to comprehend stories.

A. Testing for Comprehension

For beginning readers, comprehension is initially tested at the level of individual words. One simple way of doing this is to require the reader to point, touch, or perform what the word refers to. For example, given the word "orange," the reader may point to or touch the color orange or the object orange from a group of other objects. If the word is "sit," the reader may sit down to demonstrate comprehension. During later stages of reading acquisition the reader may provide synonyms or a definition of the word. The comprehension of phrases and sentences can be tested by having the reader perform what the written version refers to (e.g., sing a song). At a more advanced level, comprehension can be tested via question asking, cloze tests, or by asking the reader to retell the story in his own words. Other more sophisticated techniques such as an analysis of the reader's thoughts after reading a story have been advocated, but these have not been used with mentally retarded children.

Sidman (1971) taught a 17-year-old severely retarded microcephalic boy a series of auditory–visual equivalences which led to reading comprehension. The boy was initially unable to read printed words orally or with comprehension but could match spoken words to pictures and could name pictures. He was taught to match spoken words to visual (printed) words using discrimination learning techniques and then tested for oral reading (naming the printed words aloud) and comprehension (matching the printed words to pictures). Results showed that he had acquired both these skills to a high degree of proficiency. Sidman and Cresson (1973) successfully replicated these findings, using additional controls, with two Down's syndrome subjects who were more severely retarded than the subject in the previous study.

Comprehension was also tested in a series of studies conducted by Brown and his colleagues (see L. Brown, 1973). L. Brown et al. (1974) tested for reading comprehension at the word level. They trained three TMR children to read and understand the meaning of unconjugated action verbs and then tested them for comprehension by requiring them to perform the action indicated by the verbs. In another study, after teaching two TMR children to read and understand the meaning of adjective–noun phrases, L. Brown et al. (1972) tested their comprehension by requiring them to point to the objects referred to by the phrases (e.g., point to the *blue truck*). L. Brown and Perlmutter (1971), Domnie and Bellamy (1972), and Folk and Campbell (1978) used a similar methodology to test for comprehension at the sentence level with TMR children. And, finally, Domnie and Brown (1977) tested for comprehension at the questions level by requiring TMR children to print the answers to them. All these studies reported positive results suggesting that mentally retarded children can be taught to read with meaning. However, as noted previously, most of these studies are not methodologically rigorous enough to enable firm generalizations to be made.

A small number of studies have used the cloze technique to assess comprehension or the use of contextual information by mentally retarded children. Because of Streib's (1976–1977) excellent review of this area, only a brief summary and an update will be provided here. The cloze technique (Taylor, 1953) requires the reader to fill in the blanks with appropriate words while reading a passage in which every *n*th word has been deleted. The reader's responses which are acceptable are classified as either (1) exact, or (2) not exact but synonymous, grammatically correct. While this technique has been commonly used to assess general comprehension skills, it is perhaps more a test of a reader's ability to use contextual information to predict the deleted words than a test of the reader's critical and inferential comprehension skills (Hansen, 1979).

Streib's (1976–1977) analysis of the cloze literature suggested that some EMR children are capable of using contextual information beyond the sentence level. Although the data were not always clear, it was found that some children could give exact cloze responses provided the text material was not too difficult. Furthermore, with increasing text difficulty, retarded children were less likely than the nonretarded to produce appropriate word substitutions. However, the main conclusion that can be drawn from Streib's (1976–1977) review is that only incomplete information, often from methodologically weak studies, is available regarding the ability of EMR children to use contextual information.

Unfortunately, only limited new data are available. In one study, Allington (1980a) investigated the effects of manipulating the contextual richness on word identification by a group of 35 EMR children. All subjects were tested on 12 test sentences, with four sentences from each of three levels of contextual richness: rich, moderate, low. A contextually rich sentence was defined as a sentence which contained a deletion for which normal adults had little difficulty in supplying the cloze response. The contextually low sentence was one which contained a deletion that could generate a large number of different responses. Two target words which could fit the deletion were selected for each sentence—a high-frequency word and a low-frequency synonym. Each sentence required only one cloze response. It was found that contextually rich sentences facilitated correct cloze response by the subjects. However, while contextually rich sentences provided a strong effect for high-frequency words, the same contextual information had minimal influence when the cloze response involved a low-frequency word. Allington suggested that initial reading materials for the EMR should contain few low-frequency words and that reading instruction should attempt to increase oral vocabulary before exposing the child to the printed word.

In the other study, Crossland (1981) used the cloze procedure to compare the ability of 15 EMR children and a matched group (MA) of 15 nonretarded children. Both groups were required to read a single 200-word passage in which every fifth word was deleted. There was a significant difference between the cloze scores of the two groups, with the retarded children exhibiting a significant deficiency in their ability to use context. They performed poorly in supplying both exact and synonymous, grammatically correct words.

This study confirmed earlier comparative studies (Hargis, 1972) that found retarded children less able to use context than their nonretarded peers. It is well established that in the development of reading proficiency context is useful in deriving the meaning of both familiar and unfamiliar words. Undoubtedly, the inability of mentally retarded children to fully utilize contextual information is due in part to their language deficiencies. Thus, it is important that instruction in reading for the mentally retarded emphasize contextual information as a source of meaning for unfamiliar words.

B. Increasing Comprehension Skills

Two studies have examined ways by which the comprehension skills of mentally retarded readers can be enhanced. L. Brown, Huppler, VanDeventer, and Sontag (1973) reported a study in which the silent reading comprehension of 16 EMR children was increased by systematically manipulating two performance variables. One involved dividing the class into two teams, modeled after the television program "College Bowl," which could compete against each other. The assumption was that motivation for increasing the children's silent comprehension skills could be increased through competitiveness, peer pressure, team prize, etc. The other involved the contingent use of a powerful reinforcer, money. Reinforcement was provided to the *team* who won the "College Bowl" and to *individuals* whose comprehension scores increased or remained at 100%. Dramatic increases in the children's comprehension scores were reported. However, since only correlational data were obtained and a robust experimental methodology was lacking, these data must await replication. As noted by the authors, this technique only maximizes the children's performance by increasing their motivational levels but may not be as effective when more complex comprehension skills are needed.

In the other study, Belch (1978) examined the effects of selective teacher questioning on the comprehension scores of 75 EMR children. The children, who were divided into three matched groups of 24 students each, were required to read especially prepared reading selections and then answer some questions. The first group answered 10–15 written "higher order" questions which required the students to evaluate, synthesize, and read for the main idea of the passage. The second group answered 10–15 written "low-order" questions which emphasized factual recall and memorization, and students in the third group were simply asked whether they liked the story or not. Students read one story each day and answered the questions which followed. Mastery criterion was 100%. After 25 days the children were tested for changes in their comprehension ability. The data showed that those children who were exposed to "higher order" questioning had significantly higher scores than the other two groups. Belch (1978) suggested that higher order questioning is a useful strategy for increasing comprehension skills and that EMR children are capable of increasing their comprehension through this procedure.

C. Summary

The literature on comprehension is meager and the evidence for comprehension in EMR children is sparse. However, if the results from these studies are reliable and replicable, they suggest that EMR children can be taught to read with comprehension and that their level of comprehension can be improved by direct training and by increasing their motivational level for reading. No studies have been reported in the literature which attempted to assess the comprehension level of TMR children using the cloze procedure. Nor were there any studies which attempted to increase their comprehension levels through training. However, the studies by Brown did indicate that TMR children can be taught a range of reading and comprehension skills. Finally, the studies by Sidman demonstrated that severely retarded persons can be taught some basic functional reading skills.

V.   REMEDIATION OF ORAL READING ERRORS

Although there is at present some controversy about the role of oral reading in functional reading (Jenkins, 1979), it is useful for several reasons: (1) it is an important instructional medium; (2) it serves as an excellent indicator of reading achievement; (3) it serves as a diagnostic tool for reading problems; and (4) it is the best medium for remediating reading problems. Although oral reading is not important for adult reading, beginning, less proficient readers do need this skill so that appropriate instruction and/or remediation can be provided for reading problems. Moreover, oral reading ability is highly correlated with comprehension, with studies showing a clear relationship between fluency in oral reading and comprehension scores (Doehring, 1977; Perfetti & Hogoboam, 1975). Our own position is that oral reading is a very important skill for mentally retarded children and, as noted by Jenkins (1979, p. 69), it "can be considered one legitimate measure of reading ability, both because of the demonstrated interrelatedness of various reading skills and because oral reading miscues can reflect comprehension."

A.   Oral Reading Errors

There are several ways of assessing word recognition errors. One of the most useful is the "miscue analysis" technique developed by Goodman from his psycholinguistic theory of reading (K. S. Goodman, 1969). The analysis technique was further developed by Y. M. Goodman and Burke (1972) and categorizes the child's errors during oral reading as substitutions, omissions (words, word endings, punctuation), mispronunciations, hesitations, additions, repetitions, and aided pronunciations. The miscue or error analysis of oral reading assists the teacher in detecting the child's reading problems and in providing appropriate remediation.

A few studies have compared the oral reading errors of mentally retarded children with those of their normal peers, but the findings are unclear. In some studies it was found that normal children were better at using contextual cues than their EMR peers (Dunn, 1954; Shepherd, 1967). However, in other studies (Levitt, 1970) EMR children performed as well as normal children. Further, comparative research is necessary to determine the nature of oral reading errors made by normal children and their mentally retarded peers.

B. Remediation

Only a few studies have looked at the remediation of oral reading errors in mentally retarded children, all using different remediation techniques.

1. REPEATED READING

The earliest attempt to correct the oral reading errors of mentally retarded children was reported as a case study by Samuels (1979) with a procedure called repeated reading (see Moyer, 1982, for a review of this procedure). Basically, this method involves having the child read a short meaningful passage of about 50–200 words several times (usually 3–7 times) until an acceptable level of reading fluency is reached. The whole procedure is then repeated with a new passage. Repeated reading is useful in that it increases the motivation of the poor reader to read because each reading of a passage makes increasingly more sense through increased fluency (i.e., his reading speed and word recognition accuracy). In addition, subsequent passages are read faster, with fewer oral reading errors.

Samuels (1979) reported the case of a mentally retarded student who repeatedly read five passages in succession over 27 sessions, with new passages being introduced at sessions 1, 8, 15, 21, and 25. The criterion for introducing a new passage was a reading rate of 85 words per minute. The results showed that the student took 7, 7, 6, 5, and 3 sessions to read the five passages, respectively. It was evident that word recognition errors decreased as the reading speed increased and that the initial reading speed for each new passage was greater than the initial speed of the previously read passages.

While Samuel's (1979) case report presented strong correlational data to support the efficacy of repeated reading in increasing the fluency and comprehension of one reader, replication studies with robust experimental designs are needed before general conclusions can be drawn. Certainly, the method may prove to be useful with the mentally retarded as much as it has been shown to be useful with other populations such as the brain damaged (Moyer, 1979), backward readers (Chomsky, 1978; O'Neil, 1980), and even proficient readers (Gonzales & Elijah, 1975).

2. OVERCORRECTION

Overcorrection procedures have been used in a variety of ways to treat psychopathological disorders, especially in mentally retarded children. Recently, these procedures have been employed to teach academic skills to children (see Singh, 1985). For example, spelling has been taught to elementary and junior high school students (Foxx & Jones, 1978), young normal children (Ollendick, Matson, Esveldt-Dawson, & Shapiro, 1980), and the mentally retarded (Matson, Esveldt-Dawson, & Kazdin, 1982; Stewart & Singh, 1986). In addition, sign language has been taught using overcorrection procedures (Linton & Singh, 1984).

Three recent studies have demonstrated the efficacy of overcorrection procedures in reading remediation. In the first study, the effects of overcorrection alone and in combination with positive reinforcement were tested with a no-training control condition on the number of oral reading errors and self-corrections of four TMR children (Singh, Singh, & Winton, 1984). During the overcorrection condition, each word read incorrectly had to be repeated five times and the sentence in which the word occurred, correctly repeated once. During the overcorrection plus positive reinforcement condition, the reinforcement of each self-corrected error was added to the procedure. No assistance was provided during the no-treatment control condition. Using an alternating-treatments design analysis, it was shown that both remediation procedures reduced oral reading errors and increased self-correction of errors but the combined procedure was superior to the overcorrection alone condition. No changes were observed in the no-treatment control condition.

The second study showed that the overcorrection procedure was equally effective in individual and group training formats with TMR children (Singh, 1986). Finally, Singh and Singh (1986) found overcorrection to be more effective than drill in increasing the oral reading proficiency of TMR children.

3. ANTECEDENT CONTROL PROCEDURES

Antecedent stimulus events have been emphasized in some theoretical models of reading. For example, contextual cues are considered an important variable for proficient reading according to adherents of psycholinguistic models. In terms of remediation, one implication of this model is that increasing the reader's use of contextual cues should result in more proficient reading. Indeed, there are limited data to show that manipulating a poor- or low-progress reader's attention to contextual cues during remedial reading can improve reading fluency (Wong & McNaughton, 1980).

N. N. Singh and Singh (1984) examined the effects of manipulating contextual cues (as a class of antecedent stimulus events) on the reading proficiency of four TMR children. Using an alternating-treatments design, the effects of previewing the target text were compared with previewing an unrelated text and no previewing. Previewing involved the teacher discussing the target text with the subject before it was read orally by the subject with no teacher assistance. The same procedure was used in the other previewing condition but with the exception that an unrelated text was previewed, i.e., during testing, the subject read a non-previewed text matched for level of reading difficulty. This condition was used to equate for time spent by the teacher with the child in the first condition. In the third condition, the subjects spent no additional time with the teacher and did not preview the text.

The results were very clear. Oral reading errors decreased substantially and self-corrections increased when the subjects previewed the target text with their teacher before reading it orally. Moreover, total reading errors (errors plus self-corrections) declined during this condition. No changes were observed as a result of implementing the other two procedures. The results were replicated across four children, suggesting that the reading proficiency of TMR children can be increased by manipulating antecedent stimulus events prior to oral reading.

4. ATTENTION TO READING ERRORS

Descriptive and observational studies of teacher behavior during oral reading by children show that teachers attend to the oral reading errors of beginning readers much more often than to their correct reading (Allington, 1980b; Weinstein, 1976). Similar findings have recently been reported for a small sample of teachers of the mentally retarded (J. Singh & Singh, 1983). Recent research has shown that immediate teacher attention to errors can increase the accuracy of oral reading, although greater increases can be achieved if the attention is delayed by a few seconds (McNaughton & Glynn, 1981).

Only one study has analyzed the effects of immediate versus delayed attention to oral reading errors of mentally retarded children. N. N. Singh, Winton, and Singh (1985) compared the effects of two variations of teacher attention to oral reading errors and a no-attention control condition in an alternating-treatments design. During the immediate attention condition, the teacher corrected each error word immediately, and during the delayed condition, the error word was corrected at the end of the sentence in which it occurred or within 10 to 15 seconds if the subject paused following an error. No teacher attention was provided in the control condition. The results, which were replicated across four TMR children, showed that both immediate and delayed teacher attention were effective in reducing the number of oral reading errors and in increasing the number of self-corrections of errors when compared to the control condition. However, delayed attention was more effective than immediate attention on both measures. This study showed that mentally retarded children tend to improve their performance if their opportunities for self-correcting an error are not pre-empted by the teacher.

5. WORD SUPPLY VERSUS WORD ANALYSIS

Word supply is perhaps one of the most frequently used methods of remedial instruction during oral reading. Word supply involves the teacher supplying or telling the reader the correct word following an oral reading error. This technique is frequently employed by those teachers who use the whole-word method of teaching sight words and by those who place greater emphasis initially on word identification than on meaning. Word analysis requires the teacher to direct the child's attention to various phonetic elements of the error word which enable the word to be pronounced. The word-analysis method teaches the beginning reader a technique for working out the correct verbal equivalent of written words (see Section II,A,2,b). Unlike the word-supply method, which requires the teacher to label each new word the child encounters, this technique relies on the child learning a number of letter sounds which are later combined to pronounce new words. However, there are a number of words which are phonically irregular (e.g., two, the, said, some, their, were) and have to be taught using the whole-word method (see Section II,A,2,a).

Recently, J. Singh and Singh (1985) compared the effects of word-supply and word-analysis procedures along with a no-training control condition on the oral reading errors and self-corrections of four TMR children. An alternating-treatments design analysis showed that both the word-supply and word-analysis procedures greatly reduced the number of oral reading errors of all subjects when compared to the baseline and no-training control conditions. However, the word-analysis method was significantly more effective than word supply. Both procedures appeared to be equally effective in terms of self-correction of errors for two subjects, but word analysis was superior with the other two. This study indicated that those mentally retarded children who do not already possess word-analysis skills can be taught to improve their oral reading abilities through this technique.

C. Summary

Few studies have examined the efficacy of various remediation techniques in improving the oral reading proficiency of mentally retarded children. Of the five studies discussed, one (S. J. Samuels, 1979) was simply an illustrative case example of repeated reading. This procedure needs to be experimentally evaluated with both normal and mentally retarded children. The other four studies used an alternating-treatments design to evaluate the comparative efficacy of a number of procedures. Positive practice for errors plus positive reinforcement for self-corrections, delayed attention to error words, antecedent control through previewing, and word analysis procedures have been found to be effective. However, the experimental data are limited, come from only one group of investigators, and need to be replicated. In addition, there are a number of other procedures which need to be investigated with the mentally retarded. These include sentence repeat, end-of-page review, word meaning, and drill. Some of these procedures have been found to be useful with learning-disabled children (Jenkins & Larson, 1979) and may well prove useful with the mentally retarded. Furthermore, since all the experimental studies involved TMR children, the efficacy of all these remediation techniques with the EMR remains to be investigated.

VI. CONCLUSIONS AND FUTURE PERSPECTIVES

Taken in their best light, the studies on word recognition and comprehension suggest that EMR, TMR, and, to a limited extent, severely mentally retarded children can be taught to read. However, it is clear from the present review that research on teaching reading skills to the mentally retarded is still in the embryonic stage and much additional research needs to be undertaken before we have an effective and efficient technology of instruction. This section summarizes the current status of reading research and identifies areas in need of further research.

A. Reading Research and Teaching

Although well over 1000 papers on reading research are published yearly, less than 1% deal with the mentally retarded. Furthermore, only about 10% of these papers are data based. Our search of the reading literature revealed that more "authorities" had published papers providing hints and advice to teachers on how to teach reading than in any other academic area. Most of these papers were not based on any research data at all and relied heavily on the personal experiences of the authors with small groups of retarded children. Others extrapolated from the reading research literature on slow learners and learning-disabled children. Often, subsequent research has shown that the abilities of mentally retarded children have been grossly underestimated in these reports and have led some teachers to believe that these children cannot be taught to read beyond a few simple words. Our advice to teachers is to ignore such well-intentioned but misleading advice and to rely only on data-based evaluations.

B. What Does Reading Research Show?

The research findings can be best summarized in terms of the retardation level of the children. The bulk of the research literature on EMR children deals with reading comprehension rather than word recognition skills. It is probable that EMR children are taught word recognition skills by methods similar to that employed to teach slow learners and average readers and that word recognition presents few problems to this population. Consequently, the focus of the research has been on their ability to comprehend the reading material.

Although the literature is limited, it does appear that EMR children read below their mental age level (Dunn, 1954; Quay, 1963) and that their class placement (i.e., special class or mainstreamed) has little effect on reading achievement (Carter, 1975). Teacher attitude, emphasis on learning to read, and the child's IQ appear to correlate significantly with reading achievement (Carter, 1975; Kirk, 1964). The EMR do not appear to have problems with word recognition (Pope & Haklay, 1970), but their comprehension skills are limited usually to the lowest levels of understanding, literal and interpretive (see Section II,B). The cloze studies indicate that they have some difficulty in using contextual cues to enhance their comprehension. However, there is some suggestion in the literature that comprehension can be enhanced through direct training and by increasing the motivation levels of the children. The literature is sparse in this area and further research should investigate ways in which comprehension can be increased in EMR children.

Although the TMR have been neglected in the past as far as reading has been concerned, a large number of studies with this population have been published within the last two decades. Most of these deal with basic word recognition skills. The best evidence for their ability to recognize words comes from studies using stimulus fading and behavioral techniques. However, data are limited on the delay procedure and, while current research suggests that this method may be effective, further research is needed to validate this. Moreover, the behavioral studies need to be replicated and extended using more rigorous experimental methodology than that employed in past studies.

The evidence for comprehension in TMR children comes from only a handful of studies. These studies dealt with simple literal comprehension, assessing only the reader's ability to perform the actions indicated in the material that is read. Interpretive and other forms of comprehension by the TMR have yet to be assessed.

Only one series of studies investigated the possibility of teaching initial reading skills to severely mentally retarded persons (Sidman, 1977). The experiments in this series were exemplary in terms of methodological sophistication and provide the best evidence that basic reading skills can be taught to this population as well. However, further research is needed to extend Sidman's findings, possibly to the meaningful reading of phrases and sentences.

In terms of remediation, a small number of studies assessed the effectiveness of various procedures on the oral reading errors of TMR children. These studies suggested that a number of methods are useful in increasing the reading proficiency of TMR readers. If these findings are reliable and can be replicated with other populations, such as the EMR, then we do seem to have the beginnings of a technology for remediation.

C. Training and Remediation Techniques

While comparative evaluations of the effectiveness of various procedures are necessary so that the strengths and weaknesses of each procedure can be identified, it would be a serious mistake for teachers and researchers to seek the *best* training or remediation strategy. There is no one best strategy. Training and remediation methods will vary depending on the reading level of the child, the problem being remediated, the past learning history of the child, the context of instruction (e.g., group or individual), and a number of other variables. More research is needed to assist teachers in choosing the most appropriate technique to use with particular problems that children may encounter at different levels of reading.

A case in point is the teaching of word recognition skills to mentally retarded children. At present there appears to be some controversy about the place of whole-word and phonic approaches in the teaching of sight words. Proponents of the phonics approach cite the conclusions of Chall (1983), who found phonics to be superior to the whole-word approach. Nevertheless, most basal readers used in about 75% of American schools use the whole-word approach. Moreover, almost all the data-based studies with the mentally retarded have analyzed the effects of the whole-word method, with few studies using the phonics method. Thus, classroom teachers will need to have some guidance in choosing one of these techniques for classroom use. In this particular case, as Sulzbacher and Kidder (1979) have suggested, the efficacy of these methods may be related to the retardation level of the readers, with phonics working best at higher IQ levels and the whole-word approaches working best with the more severely retarded. Furthermore, future research may show that a combination of these two methods may be more effective than either being used alone.

D. Factors Affecting Reading Performance

A number of factors have been identified which may contribute to reading failure in normal children and it is likely that some of these may also affect the performance of those who are mentally retarded. These include physiological (e.g., brain damage, maturational lag, genetic inheritance, cerebral dominance, ocular factors) and nonphysiological factors (e.g., environmental). Research on the effects of such factors has been restricted to a few studies with slow learners, and almost no methodologically rigorous studies are available on the EMR or TMR. As noted by Aman and Singh (1983), with reference to specific reading disorders, etiological considerations have serious implications for research design and future research must assess the effects of these variables on the reading performance of mentally retarded children.

E. Limitations of Current Research

With the exception of the work by a few groups of investigators, the research in this area is fragmentary and without a conceptual focus. Few investigators have pursued a programmed series of research in any one area of reading. The notable exceptions are the studies by Dorry and Zeaman on stimulus fading techniques, Sidman's studies on auditory–visual equivalence, Brown's studies using behavioral techniques, and the recent group of studies on oral reading errors. Systematic, programmed research of this sort is long overdue in this area. In addition, replication and follow-up studies are needed. For example, in the Brown studies, selected reading skills were taught but no follow-up data were available to show whether the children used, maintained, and generalized their newly acquired reading skills. In the Dorry and Zeaman studies, no follow-up data are available to indicate whether those children actually progressed beyond simple word recognition skills. Future investigations should be directed at long-term reading instruction of mentally retarded persons if we are to extend our research findings from the laboratory to the regular classroom.

F. Summary

This review briefly summarized the current status of reading research with mentally retarded children, particularly the EMR and TMR. While the research literature is at present severely limited, the outcome of this research shows that the mentally retarded can indeed be taught to read. Moreover, indications are that the field is ripe for a rapid growth, both in terms of evaluative research and instructional technology. It is hoped that this article will act to stimulate such a growth.

ACKNOWLEDGMENTS

We would like to thank Professor Ken Strongman for his comments on an earlier draft of this chapter and Lyonne Dalley for her meticulous typing of the manuscript. Preparation of this chapter was supported in part by Grant #82/3/54 from the University of Canterbury.

REFERENCES

Allington, R. L. (1980a). Word frequency and contextual richness effects of word identification of educable mentally retarded children. *Education and Training of the Mentally Retarded,* **15,** 118–121.

Allington, R. L. (1980b). Teacher interruption behaviors during primary-grade oral reading. *Journal of Educational Psychology,* **72,** 371–377.

Aman, M. G., & Singh, N. N. (1983). Specific reading disorders: Concepts of etiology reconsidered. In K. D. Gadow & I. Bialer (Eds.), *Advances in learning and behavioral disabilities* (Vol. 2). Greenwich, CT: JAI Press.

Atkinson, R. C., & Fletcher, J. D. (1972). Teaching children to read with a computer. *Reading Teacher, 25,* 319–327.

Belch, P. J. (1978). Improving the reading comprehension scores of secondary level educable mentally handicapped students through selective teacher questioning. *Education and Training of the Mentally Retarded, 13,* 385–389.

Bennett, A. (1929). Reading ability in special classes. *Journal of Educational Research, 20,* 236–238.

Bijou, S. W. (1972). *The Edmark reading program.* Seattle: Edmark Associates.

Blackman, L. S., & Capobianco, R. J. (1965). An evaluation of programmed instruction with the mentally retarded utilizing teaching machines. *American Journal of Mental Deficiency, 70,* 262–269.

Blackman, L. S., & Holden, E. A., Jr. (1963). Support vs non-support in an autoinstructional word program for educable retardates. *American Journal of Mental Deficiency, 67,* 592–600.

Bliesmer, E. P. (1954). Reading abilities of bright and dull children of comparable mental ages. *Journal of Educational Psychology, 45,* 321–329.

Bliesmer, E. P., & Yarborough, B. H. (1965). A comparison of ten different beginning reading programs in first grade. *Phi Delta Kappan, 56,* 500–504.

Borreca, F., Burger, R., Goldstein, I., & Simches, R. A. (1953). A functional core vocabulary for slow learners. *American Journal of Mental Deficiency, 58,* 273–300.

Bracey, S., Maggs, A., & Morath, P. (1975). The effects of a direct phonic approach in teaching reading with six moderately retarded children: Acquisition and mastery learning stages 1, 2. *Slow Learning Child, 22,* 83–90.

Brebner, A., Hallworth, H. J., & Brown, R. I. (1977). Computer instruction programs and terminals for the mentally retarded. In P. Mittler (Ed.), *Research to practice in mental retardation: Education and training* (Vol. 2). Baltimore: University Park Press.

Brown, D. A. (1982). *Reading diagnosis and remediation.* Englewood Cliffs, NJ: Prentice-Hall.

Brown, L. (1973). Instructional programs for trainable level retarded students. In L. Mann & D. A. Sabatino (Eds.), *The first review of special education.* Philadelphia, PA: JSE Press.

Brown, L., Fenrick, N., & Klemme, H. (1971). Trainable pupils learn to teach each other. *Teaching Exceptional Children, 4,* 18–24.

Brown, L., Hermanson, J., Klemme, H., Haubrick, P., & Ora, J. P. (1970). Using behavior modification principles to teach sight vocabulary. *Teaching Exceptional Children, 2,* 120–128.

Brown, L., Huppler, B., Pierce, L., York, B., & Sontag, E. (1974). Teaching trainable-level students to read unconjugated action verbs. *Journal of Special Education, 8,* 51–56.

Brown, L., Huppler, B., VanDeventer, P., & Sontag, E. (1973). Use of the ''College Bowl'' format to increase silent reading comprehension. *Child Study Journal, 3,* 181–193.

Brown, L., Jones, S., Troccolo, E., Heiser, C., Bellamy, T., & Sontag, E. (1972). Teaching functional reading to young trainable students: Toward longitudinal objectives. *Journal of Special Education, 6,* 237–246.

Brown, L., & Perlmutter, L. (1971). Teaching functional reading to trainable level retarded students. *Education and Training of the Mentally Retarded, 6,* 74–84.

Buchannon, C. D., & Sullivan Associates. (1963). *Sullivan programmed readers.* New York: McGraw-Hill.

Burton, T. A. (1974). Education for trainables: An impossible dream? *Mental Retardation, 12*(1), 45–46.

Carnine, D. W. (1979). Research on designing and implementing procedures for teaching sounds. In J. E. Button, T. C. Lovitt, & T. D. Rowland (Eds.), *Communications research in learning disabilities and mental retardation.* Baltimore: University Park Press. 1979.

Carnine, D. W., & Silbert, J. (1979). *Direct instruction reading.* Columbus, OH: Merrill.

Carter, J. L. (1975). Intelligence and reading achievement of EMR children in three educational settings. *Mental Retardation,* **13,** 26–27.

Cawley, J., & Pappanikou, A. J. (1967). The educable mentally retarded. In N. G. Haring & R. L. Schiefelbusch (Eds.), *Methods in special education.* New York: McGraw-Hill.

Cawley, J. F., Goldstein, H. A., & Burrow, W. H. (1972). *The slow learner and the reading problem.* Springfield, IL: Charles C. Thomas.

Chall, J. S. (1983). *Learning to read: The great debate* (updated ed.). New York: McGraw-Hill.

Chomsky, C. (1978). When you still can't read in third grade: After decoding, what? In S. J. Samuels (Ed.), *What research has to say about reading instruction.* Newark, DE: International Reading Association.

Cleary, A., & Puckham, D. A. (1968). A touch-detecting teaching machine with auditory reinforcement. *Journal of Applied Behavior Analysis,* **1,** 341–345.

Corey, J. R., & Shamow, J. (1972). The effects of fading on the acquisition and retention of oral reading. *Journal of Applied Behavior Analysis,* **5,** 311–315.

Crossland, C. L. (1981). A comparison of retarded and non-retarded on the ability to use context in reading. *Journal of Special Educators,* **17,** 234–241.

D'Amelio, D. (1971). *Severely retarded children: Wider horizons.* Columbus, OH: Charles E. Merrill.

Davy, R. A. (1962). Adaptation of progressive-choice method for teaching reading to retarded children. *American Journal of Mental Deficiency,* **67,** 274–280.

Dawson, M. A. (1969). How effective is i.t.a. in reading instruction? In N. B. Smith (Ed.), *Current issues in reading.* Newark, DE: International Reading Association.

Dewey, G. (1960). *Experimental investigation of use of a phonemic notation for the first teaching of reading and writing.* New York: Lake Placid Club.

Doehring, D. G. (1977). Comprehension of printed sentences by children with reading disability. *Bulletin of the Psychonomic Society,* **10,** 350–352.

Dolch, E. W. (1936). A basic sight vocabulary. *Elementary School Journal,* **36,** 456–460.

Domnie, M., & Bellamy, T. (1972). A sequential procedure for teaching reading skills to trainable retarded students. In L. Brown & E. Sontag (Eds.), *Toward the development and implementation of an empirically based public school program for trainable mentally retarded and severely emotionally disturbed students* (Pt. 2). Madison, WI: Madison Public Schools.

Domnie, M., & Brown, L. (1977). Teaching severely handicapped students reading skills requiring printed answers to who, what, and where questions. *Education and Training of the Mentally Retarded,* **12,** 324–331.

Dorry, G. W. (1976). Attentional model for the effectiveness of fading in training reading vocabulary with retarded persons. *American Journal of Mental Deficiency,* **81,** 271–279.

Dorry, G. W., & Zeaman, D. (1973). The use of a fading technique in paired-associate teaching of a reading vocabulary with retardates. *Mental Retardation,* **11**(6), 3–6.

Dorry, G. W., & Zeaman, D. (1975). Teaching a simple reading vocabulary to retarded children: Effectiveness of fading and non-fading procedures. *American Journal of Mental Deficiency,* **79,** 711–716.

Downing, J. (1967a). The effects of the initial teaching alphabet on educationally subnormal pupils: A survey of teacher reports. *Slow Learning Child,* **13,** 164–175.

Downing, J. (1967b). E.S.N. school teachers assess i.t.a. *Special Education,* **56,** 12–16.

Downing, J. (1968). The initial teaching alphabet and educationally subnormal children. *Developmental Medicine and Child Neurology,* **10,** 200–205.

Downing, J. (1969). How effective is i.t.a.? In N. B. Smith (Ed), *Current issues in reading.* Newark, DE: International Reading Association.

Downing, J. (1979). Results of teaching reading in i.t.a. to children with cognitive defects. *Reading World,* **18,** 290–299.

Duffy, G. G., & Sherman, G. B. (1977). *Systematic reading instruction* (2nd ed.). New York: Harper & Row.

Duffy, G. G., Sherman, G. B., & Roehler, L. R. (1977). *How to teach reading systematically* (2nd ed.). New York: Harper & Row.

Dunn, L. M. (1954). A comparison of the reading processes of mentally retarded boys of the same mental age. In L. M. Dunn & R. J. Capobianco (Eds.), *Studies of reading and arithmetic in mentally retarded boys. Child Development Monographs,* **19,** 2–99.

Engelmann, S. (1967). Teaching reading to children with low mental ages. *Education and Training of the Mentally Retarded,* **2,** 193–201.

Engelmann, S., & Bruner, E. C. (1969). *Distar Reading: An instructional system.* Chicago: Science Research Associate.

Fernald, G. M. (1943). *Remedial techniques in basic school subjects.* New York: McGraw-Hill.

Fernald, G. M., & Keller, H. (1921). The effect of kinaesthetic factors in the development of word recognition in the case of non-readers. *Journal of Educational Research,* **4,** 355–377.

Fitzhugh, K., & Fitzhugh, L. (1966). *The Fitzhugh plus program.* Galen, MI: Allied Educational Council.

Folk, M. C., & Campbell, J. C. (1978). Teaching functional reading to the TMR. *Education and Training of the Mentally Retarded,* **13,** 322–326.

Foxx, R. M., & Jones, J. R. (1978). A remediation program for increasing the spelling achievement of elementary and junior high school students. *Behavior Modification,* **2,** 211–230.

French, E. L. (1950). Reading disability and mental deficiency: A preliminary report. *Training School Bulletin,* **47,** 47–57.

Fry, E. (1963). *A diacritical marking system for beginning reading instruction.* Paper presented at the Conference on Perceptual and Linguistic Aspects of Reading. Center for Advanced Study in the Behavioral Sciences, Stanford, CA.

Gearhart, B. R., & Litton, F. W. (1975). *The trainable retarded: A foundations approach.* St. Louis: Mosby.

Gillespie, P. H., & Johnson, L. E. (1974). *Teaching reading to the mildly retarded child.* Columbus, OH: Merrill.

Gonzales, P. C., & Elijah, D. V. (1975). Rereading: Effect on error patterns and performance levels on the IRI. *Reading Teacher,* **28,** 647–654.

Goodman, K. S. (1969). Analysis of oral reading miscues: Applied psycholinguistics. *Reading Research Quarterly,* **5,** 9–30.

Goodman, Y. M., & Burke, C. (1972). *Reading miscue inventory.* New York: Macmillan.

Greene, F. M. (1966). Programmed instruction techniques for the mentally retarded. In N. R. Ellis (Ed.), *International review of research in mental retardation* (Vol. 2). New York: Academic Press.

Grossman, H. (1973). *Manual on terminology and classification in mental retardation* (rev. ed.). Washington, DC: American Association on Mental Deficiency.

Gurren, L., & Hughes, A. (1965). Intensive phonics vs gradual phonics in beginning reading: A review. *Journal of Educational Research,* **58,** 339–346.

Hallworth, H. J., & Brebner, A. (1979). Development of computer-assisted instruction at V.R.R.I. In R. I. Brown & M. B. Bayer (Eds.), *Research, demonstration and practice: 10 years of progress.* Calgary: Vocational and Rehabilitation Research Institute.

Hansen, G. L. (1979). Chicken soup and other forms of comprehension. In J. E. Button, T. C. Lovitt, & J. D. Rowland (Eds.), *Communications research in learning disabilities and mental retardation.* Baltimore: University Park Press.

Hargis, C. H. (1972). A comparison of retarded and non-retarded children on the ability to use context in reading. *American Journal of Mental Deficiency,* **76,** 726–728.

Hargis, C. H. (1982). *Teaching reading to the handicapped.* Denver: Love.

Hawker, J. R. (1968). A further investigation of prompting and confirmation in sight vocabulary learning by retardates. *American Journal of Mental Deficiency, 72,* 594–498.

Hawker, J. R., Geertz, U. W., & Shrago, M. (1964). Prompting and confirmation in sight vocabulary learning by retardates. *American Journal of Mental Deficiency, 68,* 751–756.

Hegge, T. G. (1934). Special reading disability with particular reference to the mentally deficient. *Journal of Psycho-Asthenics, 39,* 297–343.

Hofmeister, A. (1971). Programmed instruction revisited: Implications for educating the retarded. *Education and Training of the Mentally Retarded, 6,* 172–176.

Ingram, C. (1953). *Education of the slow learning child.* New York: World.

Jeffree, D. (1981). A bridge between pictures and print. *Special Education: Forward Trends, 8,* 28–31.

Jenkins, J. R. (1979). Oral reading: Considerations for special and remedial education teachers. In J. E. Button, T. C. Lovitt, & R. D. Rowland (Eds.), *Communications research in learning disabilities and mental retardation.* Baltimore: University Park Press.

Jenkins, J. R., & Larson, K. (1979). Evaluating error-correction procedures for oral reading. *Journal of Special Education, 13,* 145–156.

Johnson, M. S. (1966). Tracing and kinesthetic techniques. In J. Money & G. Schiffman (Eds.), *The disabled reader.* Baltimore: Johns Hopkins Press.

Kirk, S. A. (1933). The influence of manual tracing on the learning of simple words in the case of subnormal boys. *Journal of Educational Psychology, 24,* 525–535.

Kirk, S. A. (1964). Research in education. In H. A. Stevens & R. F. Heber (Eds.), *Mental retardation: A review of research.* Chicago: University of Chicago Press.

Kirk, S. A. (1972). *Educating exceptional children* (2nd ed.). Boston: Houghton Mifflin.

Kirk, S. A., & Johnson, G. O. (1951). *Educating the retarded child.* Boston: Houghton Mifflin.

Kirk, S. A., Kleibhan, Sister J. M., & Lerner, J. W. (1978). *Teaching reading to slow and disabled learners.* Boston: Houghton Mifflin.

Lally, M. (1981). Computer-assisted teaching of sight-word recognition for mentally retarded school children. *American Journal of Mental Deficiency, 85,* 383–388.

Lambert, J. L. (1975). Extinction by retarded children following discrimination learning with and without errors. *American Journal of Mental Deficiency, 80,* 286–291.

Levitt, E. (1970). The effect of context on the reading of retarded and normal children at the first-grade levels. *Journal of Special Education, 4,* 425–429.

Linton, J. M., & Singh, N. N. (1984). Acquisition of sign language using positive practice overcorrection. *Behavior Modification, 8,* 553–556.

MacAulay, B. D. (1968). A program for teaching speech and beginning reading to nonverbal retardates. In H. N. Sloane & B. D. MacAulay (Eds.), *Operant procedures in remedial speech and language training.* New York: Houghton Mifflin.

MacIntyre, E. M. (1937). Teaching of reading to mentally defective children. *Journal of Psycho-Asthenics, 42,* 59–67.

Malone, J. R. (1963). *Single-sound UNIFON: Does it fill the need for a compatible and consistent auxilary orthography for teaching English and other european languages?* Paper presented at the Conference on Perceptual and Linguistic Aspects of Reading. Center for Advanced Study in the Behavioral Sciences, Stanford, CA.

Malpass, L. F. (1967). Programmed instruction for retarded children. In A. A. Baumeister (Ed.), *Mental retardation: Appraisal, education and rehabilitation.* Chicago: Aldine.

Malpass, L. F., Hardy, M. W., Gilmore, A. S., & Williams, C. F. (1964). Automated instruction for retarded children. *American Journal of Mental Deficiency, 69,* 405–421.

Matson, J. L., Esveldt-Dawson, K., & Kazdin, A. E. (1982). Treatment of spelling deficits in mentally retarded children. *Mental Retardation, 20,* 76–81.

Mazurkiewicz, A. J. (1966). The initial teaching alphabet. In J. Money & G. Schiffman (Eds.), *The disabled reader: Education of the dyslexic child.* Baltimore: Johns Hopkins Press.

McCarthy, W., & Oliver, J. (1965). Some tactile–kinesthetic procedures for teaching reading to slow learning children. *Exceptional Children, 31,* 419–421.

McGee, G. M., & McCoy, J. F. (1981). Training procedures for acquisition and retention of reading in retarded youth. *Applied Research in Mental Retardation, 2,* 263–276.

McNaughton, S., & Glynn, T. (1981). Delayed versus immediate attention to oral reading errors: Effects on accuracy and self-correction. *Educational Psychology, 1,* 57–65.

Merrill, M. A. (1924). On the relation of intelligence to achievement in the case of mentally retarded children. *Comparative Psychological Monographs, 51,* 1–100.

Miller, A., & Miller, E. E. (1968). Symbol accentuation: The perceptual transfer of meaning from spoken to printed words. *American Journal of Mental Deficiency, 73,* 200–208.

Miller, A., & Miller, E. E. (1971). Symbol accentuation, single-track functioning and early reading. *American Journal of Mental Deficiency, 76,* 110–117.

Miller, B. B. (1975). Phonological pairing as a reading aid for retarded children. *Journal of Reading Behavior, 7,* 181–186.

Moyer, S. B. (1979). Rehabilitation of alexia: A case study. *Cortex, 15,* 139–144.

Moyer, S. B. (1982). Repeated reading. *Journal of Learning Disabilities, 15,* 619–623.

Neville, D., & Vandever, T. R. (1973). Decoding as a result of synthetic and analytic presentation for retarded and nonretarded children. *American Journal of Mental Deficiency, 77,* 533–537.

Nietupski, J., Williams, W., York, R., Johnson, R., & Brown, L. (1976). A review of instructional programs designed to teach selected reading and spelling skills to severely handicapped students. In W. Blanton (Eds.), *Reading and mental retardation.* Newark, DE: International Reading Association.

Ollendick, T. H., Matson, J. L., Esveldt-Dawson, K., & Shapiro, E. (1980). Increasing spelling achievement: An analysis of treatment procedures utilizing an alternating treatments design. *Journal of Applied Behavior Analysis, 13,* 645–654.

O'Neill, K. (1980). Turn kids on with repeated readings. *Teaching Exceptional Children, 12,* 63–64.

Orman, J. (1966). Introduction to reading through the initial teaching alphabet. *Teaching and Training, 4,* 189–213.

Peach, W. J., & Lewis, B. (1969). Automated reading instruction for educable mentally retarded adolescents. *Slow Learning Child, 16,* 15–19.

Perfetti, C., & Hogoboam, T. (1975). Relationship between single word decoding and reading comprehension skill. *Journal of Educational Psychology, 67,* 461–469.

Perry, N. (1960). *Teaching the mentally retarded child.* New York: Columbia University Press.

Pope, L., & Haklay, A. (1970). Reading disability. In J. Wortis (Ed.), *Mental retardation: An annual review* (Vol. 2). New York: Grune & Stratton.

Quay, L. C. (1963). Academic skills. In N. R. Ellis (Ed.), *Handbook of mental deficiency.* New York: McGraw-Hill.

Richardson, E., & Collier, L. (1971). Programmed tutoring of decoding skills with third- and fifth-grade nonreaders. *Journal of Experimental Education, 39,* 57–64.

Richardson, E., Oestereicher, M. H., Bialer, I., & Winsberg, B. G. (1975). Teaching beginning reading skills to retarded children in community classrooms: A programmatic case study. *Mental Retardation, 13*(1), 11–15.

Richardson, E., Winsberg, B. G., & Bialer, I. (1973). Assessment of two methods of teaching phonic skills to neuropsychiatrically impaired children. *Journal of Learning Disabilities, 6,* 628–635.

Riese, H. (1956). Academic work with an eleven year old girl with an IQ of 41. *American Journal of Mental Deficiency, 60,* 545–551.

Roberts, B. (1976). Instructional materials for severely/profoundly retarded learners. *Mental Retardation*, **14**, 39–42.

Samuels, S. J. (1970). Effects of pictures on learning to read comprehension and attitudes. *Review of Educational Research*, **40**, 397–407.

Samuels, S. J. (1979). The method of repeated readings. *Reading Teacher*, **32**, 403–408.

Shepherd, G. (1967). Selected factors in the reading ability of educably mentally retarded boys. *American Journal of Mental Deficiency*, **71**, 563–570.

Sidman, M. (1971). Reading and auditory–visual equivalences. *Journal of Speech and Hearing Research*, **14**, 5–13.

Sidman, M. (1977). Teaching some basic prerequisites for reading. In P. Mittler (Ed.), *Research to practice in mental retardation: Education and Training* (Vol. 2). Baltimore: University Park Press.

Sidman, M., & Cresson, Jr., O. (1973). Reading and cross modal transfer of stimulus equivalences in severe retardation. *American Journal of Mental Deficiency*, **3**, 181–193.

Singh, J., & Singh, N. N. (1983). *Analysis of teacher behavior during oral reading by mentally retarded children*. Unpublished manuscript. University of Canterbury, Christchurch, New Zealand.

Singh, J., & Singh, N. N. (1985). A comparison of word supply and word analysis error correction procedures on oral reading by mentally retarded children. *American Journal of Mental Deficiency*, **90**, 64–70.

Singh, N. N. (1985). Overcorrection of academic behavior. In C. Sharpley, A. Hudson, E. C. Lee (Eds.), *Proceedings of the eighth annual conference of the Australian Behavior Modification Association*. (Pp. 382–391). Melbourne, Australia: ABMA.

Singh, N. N. (1986). Overcorrection of oral reading errors: A comparison of individual and group training formats. *Behavior Modification*, in press.

Singh, N. N., & Singh, J. (1984). Antecedent control of oral reading errors and self-corrections by mentally retarded children. *Journal of Applied Behavior Analysis*, **17**, 111–119.

Singh, N. N., Singh, J., & Winton, A. S. W. (1984). Positive practice overcorrection of oral reading errors. *Behavior Modification*, **8**, 23–37.

Singh, N. N. & Singh, J. (1985). Increasing oral reading proficiency: A comparative analysis of drill and positive practice overcorrection procedures. *Behavior Modification*, **10**, 115–130.

Singh, N. N., & Singh, J. (1986). A behavioral remediation program for oral reading: Effects on errors and comprehension. *Educational Psychology*, **6**, 105–114.

Singh, N. N., Winton, A. S. W., & Singh, J. (1985). Effects of delayed versus immediate attention to oral reading errors on the reading proficiency of mentally retarded children. *Applied Research in Mental Retardation*, **6**, 295–305.

Smith, N. B. (1969). The many faces of reading comprehension. *Reading Teacher*, **23**, 249–259, 291.

Snell, M. E. (1978). Functional reading. In M. E. Snell (Ed.), *Systematic instruction of the moderately and severely handicapped*. Columbus, OH: Charles E. Merrill.

Stewart, C. A. & Singh, N. N. (1986). Overcorrection of spelling deficits in mentally retarded children. *Behavior Modification*, in press.

Stolurow, L. M. (1961). *Teaching by machine* (Cooperative Research Monograph No. 6). Washington, DC: U.S. Office of Education.

Streib, R. (1976–1977). Context utilization in reading by educable mentally retarded children. *Reading Research Quarterly*, **12**, 32–54.

Sullivan, M. W. (1968). *Sullivan reading program*. Palo Alto, CA: Behavioral Research Laboratories.

Sulzbacher, S. I., & Kidder, J. D. (1979). Teaching sight words to severely retarded children and adolescents. In J. E. Button, T. C. Lovitt, & T. D. Rowland (Eds.), *Communications research in learning disabilities and mental retardation.* Baltimore: University Park Press.

Taylor, W. L. (1953). Cloze procedure: A new tool for measuring readability. *Journalism Quarterly,* **30,** 415–433.

Terrace, H. S. (1963a). Discrimination learning with and without "errors". *Journal of the Experimental Analysis of Behavior,* **6,** 1–27.

Terrace, H. S. (1963b). Errorless transfer of a discrimination across two continua. *Journal of the Experimental Analysis of Behavior,* **6,** 223–232.

Touchette, P. E. (1968). The effects of graduated stimulus change on the acquisition of a simple discrimination in severely retarded boys. *Journal of the Experimental Analysis of Behavior,* **11,** 39–48.

Touchette, P. E. (1971). Transfer of stimulus control: Measuring the moment of transfer. *Journal of the Experimental Analysis of Behavior,* **15,** 347–354.

Vandever, T. R., & Neville, D. D. (1976). Transfer as a result of synthetic and analytic reading instruction. *American Journal of Mental Deficiency,* **80,** 498–503.

Wallin, W. (1924). *The education of handicapped children.* Boston: Houghton Mifflin.

Walsh, B. F., & Lamberts, F. (1979). Errorless discrimination and picture fading as techniques for teaching sight words to TMR students. *American Journal of Mental Deficiency,* **83,** 473–479.

Ward, B. J., & Beauchamp, J. (1966). i.t.a. and teaching techniques for the mentally retarded. In J. Downing (Ed.), *The First International Reading Symposium.* London: Cassell.

Weinstein, R. (1976). Reading group membership in first grade: Teacher behaviors and pupil experience over time. *Journal of Educational Psychology,* **68,** 103–116.

Weisberg, P., Packer, R. A., & Weisberg, R. S. (1981). Academic training. In J. L. Matson & J. R. McCartney (Eds.), *Handbook of behavior modification with the mentally retarded.* New York: Plenum.

Williams, J. (1979). Reading instruction today. *American Psychologist,* **34,** 917–922.

Wong, P., & McNaughton, S. (1980). The effects of prior provision of context on the oral reading proficiency of a low progress reader. *New Zealand Journal of Educational Studies,* **15,** 169–175.

Woodcock, R., & Clark, C. L. (1969). *Peabody Rebus reading program.* Circle Pines, MN: American Guidance Service.

Woolman, M. (1962). *The progressive choice reading program.* Washington, DC: Institute of Educational Research.

Worrall, N., & Singh, Y. (1983). Teaching TMR children to read using integrated picture cueing. *American Journal of Mental Deficiency,* **87,** 422–429.

Families with a Mentally Retarded Child

BERNARD FARBER

DEPARTMENT OF SOCIOLOGY
ARIZONA STATE UNIVERSITY
TEMPE, ARIZONA 85287

LOUIS ROWITZ

SCHOOL OF PUBLIC HEALTH
UNIVERSITY OF ILLINOIS AT CHICAGO
CHICAGO, ILLINOIS 60680

I. INTRODUCTION

This chapter will focus upon research dealing with families with severely and profoundly mentally retarded children rather than with those families whose children have been designated as "mildly retarded." Individuals with mild mental retardation form a separate population, and they ordinarily present a different set of problems for their parents and siblings (Farber, 1968). Most family research on children classified as having mild mental retardation has centered upon family factors in the etiology of the disability and not upon the effects of the child on family relationships.

Three strands of research on families with children who are mentally retarded will be discussed. The first consists of studies that focus on the impact of the birth and/or presence of a child with mental retardation on the internal dynamics of the family; this strand will be described as a medical or clinical model of family relationships (Schutz & Morris, 1984). The second strand consists of studies that focus on the means families use to maintain community ties while coping with the child with mental retardation; this strand will be described as applying a perspective based on labeling theory (Rowitz, 1981c; Scheff, 1984) and a dramaturgical model (Brisset & Edgley, 1975). The third strand consists of

INTERNATIONAL REVIEW OF RESEARCH IN
MENTAL RETARDATION, Vol. 14

studies that focus on the interaction between internal stresses and community ties and commitments; this strand will be described as utilizing a family organization perspective (Farber, 1968).

Each strand appears to be useful for certain kinds of applications. The clinical model strand uncovers the kinds of problems that yield to remedial action. Some of these studies have contributed to the development and operation of such programs as parent support groups, supplemental home assistance, and counseling and respite services (Bruininks & Krantz, 1979). The labeling–dramaturgical strand has been useful in promoting advocacy legislation and in assisting families in their dealings with social agencies and the public (Begab & Richardson, 1975). Last, the family organization strand serves to integrate the other two (Crnic *et al.*, 1983). Together, these strands permit the identification of different concerns and methodologies in research on families with retarded children.

II. THE CLINICAL MODEL

Early research on family problems generated by the presence of a mentally retarded child was guided by the clinical model. Much of this research was undertaken shortly after World War II, when the demand for services for people with mental retardation expanded. This expansion stimulated the development of research programs to define and justify areas of need and to provide new techniques of remediation. The early programs of research dealt with areas of special concern to policy makers and to parents—institutional placement versus family residence, the efficacy of special classes for the trainable, the extent of stress in family life, mental health and economic difficulties, and so on (Farber, 1959, 1960a; Fotheringham, Skelton, & Hoddinott, 1971; Roghmann, Hecht, & Haggerty, 1973).

Research focusing on the need for remedial services presupposes the existence of a norm of a "healthy" family life. Consequently, the clinical model focuses on variables that pertain to departures from this norm—degree of family disintegration, role tension, conflict, personality disorders, psychosomatic illness, inhibition of school or occupational success of parents and siblings, and so on. As remedial services are implemented on a large scale, a second set of variables evolves. This second set focuses on the evaluation of remedial services—extent of utilization, barriers to effective utilization, and alternative paths to obtaining these services. The clinical model aims at the study of departures from "healthy" family life and the use of remedial services.

As formulated by Reuben Hill (1949), the clinical model defines the familial response to a stressful situation in terms of four elements: an event, family resources, interpretation of the event, and the crisis. The inability of families to handle an enduring crisis generated by the child with mental retardation required remedial action for the planning and provision of services in all areas—health, education, income maintenance, employment and manpower, housing, and the personal social services adapted to the particular needs of the mentally retarded and their families (Zimmerman, 1979). Hence, this approach led to questions about effects of a mentally retarded child on parents, siblings, and service utilization.

A. Effects on Parents

Although parents report some anxiety when they suspect that their child is not progressing according to an acceptable developmental timetable, the impact of a child with mental retardation on family relationships generally achieves critical proportions when the parents "realize" that the child is mentally retarded. A physician's definitive statement that the child is mentally retarded typically produces a tremendous turmoil in the parents (Farber, 1959, 1960b; MacKeith, 1973; Waisbren, 1980; Rowitz, 1981c; Blacher, 1984a).

The amount of turmoil is related to a variety of factors, but perhaps the most notable one is socioeconomic status. In American society, the combinations and permutations of socioeconomic and other labels are probably more significant in determining life chances for persons than is the stigma of having a retarded child. Viewing the label of mental retardation as only one in a series suggests that this label has different consequences for family relationships to the extent that it represents a contrast to other labels. At high socioeconomic levels, there is a large discrepancy between the mental retardation label and other labels ascribed to the family. However, in low socioeconomic status families, the label of mental retardation is not greatly divergent from other labels associated with low status; there is in fact a multiplicity of stigma. In line with these differences by socioeconomic level, one finds that, while high-status parents tend to have a strong emotional reaction to the diagnosis, low status parents are often not so severely shaken by the diagnosis.

As this discussion suggests, the nature of the label is tied intimately to the kinds of problems faced by the families. An early study by Korkes (1956) indicated that a child who was uncontrollable was seen by the parents as "unhuman," but a child whose disability was considered as a care problem became the family invalid. In her investigation of families who have institutionalized their child, Mercer (1973) made a somewhat similar differentiation between the burden of care and interpersonal stress as precipitators of family crisis.

The connection between the stress induced by the diagnosis and problems of behavior management has led some investigators to develop techniques of guided management for parents of children with mental retardation (R. I. Brown, 1976; Travormina, Henggeler, & Gayton, 1976; Weiss & Weiss, 1976). For example, Weiss and Weiss applied a guided approach to labeling on the assumption that parents who were realistic in their assessment of the child's limitations could develop appropriate techniques in child management.

Still, investigation of parental stress extended beyond problems surrounding labeling or child care. Several studies have focused on factors responsible for the continued impact of the child with mental retardation on the family (Beckman, 1983). Researchers have studied the extent to which family stress depends upon age and sex (of both child and parent), the nature of the disability, extrafamily relationships, and the social, economic, and religious background of the parents. The findings reported in this section suggest that these factors interacted in a complex way to affect parents' reactions to their mentally retarded children (Crnic, Friedrich, & Greenberg, 1983; Intagliata & Doyle, 1984).

Type of handicap appears to affect family relationships differentially. Mentally retarded children seem to have a more severe effect on mothers than do children with other disabilities. Cummings, Bayley, and Rie (1966) reported that middle-class mothers of retarded children showed more signs of stress than did mothers of chronically ill children. In a study using the Minnesota Multiphasic Personality Inventory (MMPI), parents of mentally retarded children were found to have significantly elevated profiles in comparison to normative groups. These parents tended to resemble parents of emotionally disturbed children even though the total score elevations appeared to be less marked (W. H. Miller & Keirn (1978).

The complex interaction of factors affecting parental perceptions is revealed further in findings on fathers. Generally, women are more accepting of handicapped children than are men (Fletcher, 1974). The effects on the fathers, however, depend in a large part on the sex of the child and the diagnostic classification. Tallman (1963) found that fathers tended to be more highly motivated in coping with problems of retarded boys than those of retarded girls. Similarly, fathers seemed better able to cope with nonmongoloid children. Tallman's findings also indicated that, in contrast to the importance of the child's sex and diagnosis for the father, the mother's ability to cope with the child was associated with factors intrinsic to the parent–child relationship (such as child's IQ and social competence) (see also S. T. Cummings, 1976). The results suggested to Tallman that the fathers' expectations for their retarded children were highly influenced by nonfamily social factors.

Farber, Jenne, and Toigo (1960) found that the initial stress on parents seemed to be somewhat sex linked, with the mother indicating a slightly greater impact if the retarded child was a girl and the father a markedly greater impact (regardless of social status) if the retarded child was a boy. In low social status families, where there was much sex differentiation in family roles, mothers suffered a much greater impact (than in middle-class families) when the retarded child was a girl (see also Bristol, 1979). With time, however, the nature of the impact on the low-status mothers shifted; eventually the mothers of retarded boys were confronted with greater problems than were the mothers of retarded girls. Beckman (1983) pointed out that the number of parents in the home was associated with the amount of stress reported. Single mothers reported more stress than mothers in intact homes.

As for the issue as to whether the increasing age of the retarded child increases or decreases stress on the family, several studies have examined the impact of the child at various stages in the family life cycle (Turnbull & Turnbull, 1985). L. G. Miller (1969), in reviewing seven stages in the life cycle of the family with a retarded child, has argued that with time situations become increasingly stressful. These stresses manifested themselves in several ways: (1) threats to the husband–wife relationship, (2) inhibition of father–child relationships, and (3) adverse effects on sibling ties. When the normal children left home, unlike other families, the family with a retarded child moved toward increased stress. When parents could no longer deal with the stress, they sought institutionalization either in public or private residential settings. In spite of the deinstitutionalization movement, the child's level of mental retardation and adaptive behavior skills were the best predictor for out-of-home placements (Eyman, O'Connor, Tarjan, & Justice, 1972). Sherman and Cocozza (1984) argued that a number of situational factors including family characteristics, stress on family, and factors such as social support and community service were critical factors in out-of-home placements. When children were released from institutions, they often did not return to their natural homes (Seltzer & Krauss, 1984; Meyer, 1980).

Suelzle and Keenan (1981) reported that the utilization of personal and professional support networks by parents varies over the life cycle of their retarded children. Using data of 330 parents in a mail survey, the authors examined four stages in the life cycle: preschool (birth to 5 years of age), elementary (6–12 years), teenage (13–18 years), and young adult (19–21 years). They found that parents of younger children utilized more community services and support networks, and they were more in favor of mainstreaming. Parents of older retarded children were less supportive of services and community networks, more isolated, and more in need of expanded services.

A more profound influence of the child with mental retardation on the family involves the restriction of fertility. Early studies reported that families with a child with mental retardation tended to avoid having additional children (Carver & Carver, 1972). Recent literature does not deal with this issue.

Much of the tragic impact of the retarded child on the parents apparently involves a sense of guilt (Featherstone, 1981). Some early research examined the relationship between feelings of guilt and religious background. For example, Zuk (1959, 1962; Zuk, Miller, Bertram, & Kling, 1961) reported that Catholic mothers were more acceptant than non-Catholic mothers. The role of Catholicism has been studied by several investigators. Using a predominantly Catholic sample, Bernard (1974) compared 50 families with a severely mentally retarded child (aged 5–17) with 50 families with nonhandicapped children in the same age range. The samples were similar in degree of marital integration, amount of siblings' role tension, extent of neighborliness, and amount of religious participation. More than Protestants, Catholic mothers tended to deny responsibility for the child's condition, believing instead that God had given them a handicapped child for some purpose (Featherstone, 1981).

Taken together, research based on the clinical model points to the deleterious effects of a retarded child on the parents. To be sure, in some ways the retarded individual may have a salutory influence on the rest of the family (Featherstone, 1981). Yet, the bulk of the evidence points to the sometimes overwhelming stress and hardship.

B. Effects on Siblings

The structure of family roles is a significant factor in the impact of a retarded child on siblings of normal intelligence. The effect of the role structure of the family depends in large measure on socioeconomic characteristics as well as on age and sex composition of the household. Hence, most investigations showed these interactions between family structure and socioeconomic variables to be important in determining the kinds of adjustment made to the presence of a retarded sibling (see review in Rowitz, 1982).

In family life, birth order provides a basis for the allocation of roles in the domestic division of labor. Two children about the same age are generally accorded equal rights and responsibilities; chronological similarity in age is thereby translated into similarity in birth-order roles. But for the family with a retarded child, siblings may not retain the same birth-order roles, particularly if they are younger than the retarded child. Instead, the retarded child eventually is assigned the social role of the youngest child in the family (Farber, 1959; Birenbaum, 1971). This shift in birth-order roles seems to evoke difficulties in adjustment.

The Farber (1959) study of 240 Chicago area families with severely retarded children investigated characteristics of those normal siblings who were closest in age to the retarded child. When the retarded child required much care, the relationship between the normal siblings and their mother was adversely affected. When the children were young, interaction between the normal and retarded brothers and sisters tended to be on a equalitarian basis (playmates). However, as they grew older, the normal siblings generally assumed a superordinate (caretaker) position in the relationship. Moreover, the amount of interaction was related to the effect of the retarded child on the siblings. Those siblings who did not interact frequently with their retarded brother or sister were usually less affected in emotional ways or in outlook than were those who interacted frequently. The long-term effects of having a sibling with severe mental retardation are being examined in a 25-year follow-up study to Farber's work presently underway by the authors.

F. K. Grossman (1972) reported various effects consistent with the earlier investigations. Her research indicated how socioeconomic factors influence interaction with retarded siblings. Grossman examined the family styles of university students who had siblings with mental retardation or cerebral palsy. She compared students at Ivy League universities (from "upper sociocultural status" families) with those at "noncompetitive community colleges" (from "lower-middle socioeconomic status" homes). She found that siblings at the community colleges had spent more time with their siblings with mental retardation than had those at the private universities (both as playmates and as caretakers). Community-college students more often saw their retarded siblings as similar to themselves than did students at the private universities. Among private-university students (but not the others) the retarded sibling was seen as "human" when the students "saw their parents liking and accepting" the child; for community-college students, however, personal interaction with the retarded child was a more important determinant in seeing the child as human. There was a greater tendency for families of private-university students to institutionalize the retarded sibling than was the case for community-college families. Finally, since community-college women had spent the most time with their retarded siblings, they were most affected by the physical impairment of the sibling (see also Sagers, 1974). Moreover, community-college women from larger families (where there would be more caretakers) coped with their sibling better than did those women from small families.

The above findings were consistent with those of other investigations. For example, Cleveland and Miller (1977) found that female siblings reported a closer relationship to their handicapped siblings than did male respondents. As for activities associated with the caretaker role, S. G. Miller (1974) indicated that persons engaged in more instrumental activities with their mentally retarded sibling than with their normal siblings (and more expressive activities with their normal siblings than with their retarded sibling).

These findings show a shifting relationship between normal and retarded siblings as they grow up, a strong tendency to assign a daughter the caretaker role, and the greater ability (and perhaps motivation) for higher socioeconomic status families—than is true for families at lower socioeconomic levels—to isolate their intellectually normal children from contact with their retarded children.

C. Relation of Family to Treatment Services

The pattern of service usage in the community appears to have a strong relationship to family adaptation skills (Rowitz, 1974). It is within the family system that decision making occurs regarding the choice and continued use of treatment services. Coping strategies of the family are dependent upon a multidimensional configuration of social, psychological, economic, demographic, and medical considerations. In addition to internal family dynamics, a community network of social institutions impinges upon the ability of the family to handle its retarded member effectively. These include other families, neighborhood groups, schools, churches, businesses, public and private agencies, and so on. Because of the interrelationships among the numerous elements of a community social system, pressures and sanctions may be applied to a family to make particular choices concerning the treatment of its deviant member.

In addition to the family dynamics and community networks, the severity of the child's retardation itself influences the path of treatment services followed by the family. The severely or profoundly retarded child will probably be labeled early in life by a medical service provider, usually a physician, and the family will be forced to make a decision about treatment when the child is very young (Rowitz, 1974; Adams, 1982). This decision will usually be made in association with a medical or paramedical practitioner (McDonald, Carson, Palmer, & Slay, 1982; Rowitz, 1980). One of the first decisions would be whether to keep the child at home or to place him or her in one of a variety of private or public residential institutions.

In contrast to the severely and profoundly retarded child, the child with a milder handicap is ordinarily labeled later, often in a nonmedical setting, such as the school. The factors involved in labeling the less retarded child may be highly complex. The likelihood of being labeled as moderately retarded is relatively high at low socioeconomic levels and in particular ethnic groups (for example, blacks and hispanics) (Mercer, 1973; Rowitz & Gunn, 1984).

Once the child is labeled, the families become consumers seeking appropriate services (Rowitz, 1974). Over the past two decades, there has been a proliferation of nonresidential as well as residential alternatives to serve the mentally retarded population and their families (Bruininks, Meyers, Sigford, & Lakin, 1981). Several administrative considerations affect the use of treatment facilities, whether residential or nonresidential (H. J. Grossman & Rowitz, 1973). First, it is the service facility that defines the population it is willing to serve (Rowitz, 1973). This definition is the result of the negotiation of policies involving a central administration, a board of directors, financial considerations, and, in the case of public facilities, government decision-making processes. Second, the service personnel of an agency might also define a target population to be served, and their definitions might differ from official ones of the agency. Finally, service utilization patterns are affected by interagency relationships within the community (Rowitz & Lei, 1975).

Over time families generally use many different community services, and their pattern of service use might undergo numerous modifications. Part of this modification results from the establishment of new kinds of services. Researchers have identified several different models of service patterns. These include the work of Rowitz (1973, 1980, 1981a) on clinic utilization in Chicago, Gollay, Freedman, Wyngaarden, and Kurtz (1978) on the community experiences of deinstitutionalized mentally retarded people, O'Connor (1976) on the characteristics of people who use group homes, and Sheerenberger (1976) on the changes in residential institutions for the mentally retarded. Since the mentally retarded and their families use different kinds of services simultaneously, an adequate model should account for the several dimensions of the continuum of care.

One systematic approach to the study of the continuum of care is to analyze the service paths of families. Service-path analysis is a highly complex procedure requiring multiple levels of statistical analysis with both qualitative and quantitative data. Rowitz (1981b) has developed a methodology for the analysis of the continuum of care cycle. This cycle was defined as a longitudinal series of service contacts, and it extended from an initial contact for a specific problem (or set of problems) to a final disposition and/or resolution of the problem.

Rowitz analyzed service paths of families by asking a sample of parents to first reconstruct a history of all service contacts prior to admission of the child to a mental retardation clinic. The accuracy of the service histories by the parents was checked by an examination of case records of agencies. Service paths were delineated by determining the sequence of services or contacts with different agencies (interagency tracking). Length of contact with any particular agency was ignored. Instead, a service path was defined as a continuous series of service contacts with a referral from one source to the next source in the chain. Each time a parent or parent-surrogate initiated a contact with another agency, a new path was started. If one agency referred a parent to several different agencies, each referral became the beginning of a new service path. At any given time, a parent might be in more than one service path. Dates of contact with any particular agency were important in determining whether paths were overlapping. A path terminated when no new service agencies were added to that path.

In the Rowitz (1981b) service path study, all agency contacts were sorted into six categories: (1) physician contacts, (2) medically related public health or mental retardation agencies, (3) medically related private health or mental retardation agencies, (4) nonmedical service providers (social, educational, etc.), (5) medical combinations (physician, public, and private health-related combinations), and (6) combination of medical and nonmedical service providers.

After undertaking a case-history analysis of all clinic cases, Rowitz analyzed the demographic characteristics of parents by the service paths they followed. Using the six categories of service paths, Rowitz was able to determine whether, for example, initial paths consisting of a chain of physician contacts were longer than initial paths consisting of a chain of medically related public health and mental retardation agencies.

The service-path methodology suggests an approach to research on the relationship between the family and the continuum of care. First, an exploration of sequences in residential placement can be undertaken by applying the service-path methodology to various residential placement alternatives. The procedure permits an extensive time-series analysis. Second, since people with mental retardation use various community services, one can use this technique to investigate how people in different kinds of living arrangements follow particular types of service paths. Finally, the service-path technique permits an analysis of the relationship between paths followed and family adaptation patterns.

III. LABELING–DRAMATURGICAL MODEL

The labeling–dramaturgical model explains the actions of parents as efforts to present themselves and their domestic life to outsiders as "normal appearing." The parents either carry on a "normal" round of activities or explain away the peculiarities of their daily lives (Birenbaum, 1970, 1971; Voysey, 1972, 1975). This approach emerged in the late 1960s, when policy makers began to use "normalization" as a criterion for planning and evaluating service programs.

In this perspective, the destiny of deviant individuals is less a product of their own actions than it is a result of treatment by others on the basis of the deviance label. Proponents of the labeling perspective criticized the use of the clinical model in research because it placed the onus of deviance upon the handicapped person, who then required some sort of remediation. Deviance was thereby seen as a personal defect in the clinical model rather than as the result of a social definition and its consequences.

The labeling–dramaturgical viewpoint is based in large measure on the model developed by Erving Goffman (1959). Taking the metaphor that "all the world's a stage" literally, Goffman saw the primary motivation of people to be that of swaying those with whom they interact to accept their point of view regarding whatever matters are at hand. This aim is accomplished by giving a believable performance, by acting as political entrepreneurs (Darling, 1979), and by enlisting enlightened, powerful people to act as their advocates (Hewett, 1970).

In most social relationships, people act in ways that validate (or conform to) the roles in which others cast them. (Brissett & Edgeley, 1975). However, for the person who bears a stigma as a deviant or a "courtesy stigma" as a retarded child's parent (Birenbaum, 1970), it is usually against the individual's interests to validate that persona. Rather, the individual is motivated to hide or to disavow the stigma, to transform the stigmatized status into an elevated one, to account for the stigma in a rational way, or otherwise to disassociate it from one's self. Hence, in deviance, the task of impression management is that of convincing an "audience" that what it observes at first sight is not the true situation.

The attempt to make the stigma either irrelevant to a relationship or to make it a "natural" part of the relationship requires an individual to perform in ways that give interaction a "true" ring of normality. How this is done constitutes the core of interest of studies using the labeling–dramaturgical model.

A. The Labeling Process

In the analysis of the labeling process, researchers using the labeling–dramaturgical model focused on the causes and social meanings attributed to mental subnormality (Booth, 1978). They sought to determine the ways that violations of norms and their interpretation which affected social behavior served to designate the mentally handicapped as deviant (Booth, 1978).

Booth (1978) undertook the investigation of the critical stages in a drama which lay the foundation for the creation of mental subnormality as a social type. He found that the unfolding of the labeling generally proceeded from (1) arousal of parental suspicion that something is amiss to (2) assignment by a physician or psychologist of an ambiguous health status whereby the child is left not healthy and not sick (Booth, 1978) to (3) a reinforcement of earlier parental suspicions, and finally to (4) a degradation of the child by a diagnostic label.

But beyond the diagnosis, the parents are given little information about the way they will handle the child in daily life (Booth, 1978). In this they differ from parents with normal children. With a child who is tagged as normal, parents can anticipate a set of developmental rules and expectations. However, the social meaning of retardation entails an uncertainty in trends of family interaction. The social scientist using the labeling–dramaturgical model regards the task of the parents to be one of transforming this anomalous situation into a set of meanings that could be understood by everyone as falling within the realm of "normality" in social relations.

A study of Svarstad and Lipton (1977) reinforced Booth's conclusions. Svarstad and Lipton examined the nature and outcomes of professional communication with parents. They reviewed data from a multidisciplinary diagnostic clinic for developmentally disabled children. Parents were interviewed both before and after they were given a report of diagnostic findings. Professionals discussed the diagnosis of mental retardation with varying degrees of frankness. There was a significant relationship between the nature of the professional communication and the parents' willingness to accept the diagnosis of mental retardation. Moreover, parents were more likely to accept the diagnosis when they received a specific and clear communication from the professionals. Parental acceptance was not significantly related to the characteristics of the child, the parents, or the professionals who informed them.

One aspect of labeling is the necessity for parents to transmit an explanatory label to others. This transmission is necessary because the others, in turn, must integrate or establish rules for conduct with the handicapped person in the context of their more general rules governing interaction.

B. Normalization of Social Relations

Research based on the labeling–dramaturgical model consists of variations on the theme that families try to minimize the consequences of deviant labels on social relationships. Birenbaum (1970) suggested that the success of this effort depended in part on the age of the child. He reported that, when children are young, mothers can readily simulate a normal-appearing round of activities; at that time, there is only a small discrepancy between the retarded child and the other children with whom the family interacts. However, as the children grow older, the discrepancy becomes more pronounced, and it is increasingly difficult to maintain the appearance of a normal family life.

Voysey (1975) investigated parental management of interaction with others concerning a disabled child. She concluded that parents displayed their normality by accounting for differences in ways that others can perceive as reasonable or typical in the circumstances in question. In presenting their reactions as reasonable, parents tried to give an appearance that was congruent with normal parenthood and family life. Parents accomplished this legitimation of actions by applying acceptable ideologies. These ideologies were conventional justifications that served to persuade others that the apparent deviance in family activity was actually within the realm of normality.

The ideologies described by Voysey as those used by parents of disabled children to dispel the stigma of deviance were: "acceptance of the inevitable" by an individual as due to fate, loss of taken-for-granted attitudes about life, belief that there are people worse off, belief that phenomena were attributed to the nature of God or Being rather than to individuals, belief that suffering has positive value because it may produce deeper and closer family ties, greater tolerance, and family members may learn special things from coping with the disabled child.

People invoked these ideologies in organizing their family life to deal with structural characteristics over which they have no control. The ideologies provided a means for claiming (or disclaiming) responsibility in and/or control over handling potentially uneasy situations. By applying these constructions, parents could manage or account for the character of interaction vis-à-vis other people. In that way, the parents sustained the prevalent definition of what is normal and, at the same time, made it possible to survive in their familial and community relationships.

C. Methodological Difficulties

One concern about the labeling–dramaturgical model is the danger of overgeneralization of conclusions. Without exception, the studies based on this model were carried out on relatively small convenience samples whose parameters were undefined. Moreover, often the data were gathered only from the mother or her substitute rather than from the entire family unit. However, the very field techniques which yielded the rich data used in the analysis of the model operate to restrict sample size and to bias the sample away from persons who are unwilling to invest the time and effort needed to produce the information required.

The possible overgeneralization on interaction management to normalize relationships is suggested by the findings on kinds of problems that parents report in relation to their handicapped children. Dunlap and Hollinsworth (1977) indicated, that, in rural northern Alabama, few parents reported problems with social stigma (7%); instead, most family problems derived from time demands (45%), money (23%), and physical demands of caring for the child (23%). Similarly, in an English city, Michael Bayley (1973) stressed the crucial importance of "structures for coping" for the ability of families to handle their retarded child effectively. He found that it is primarily the reliable, frequent, and regular help and respite that were effective in alleviating pressure on the family. Such assistance is most often provided by informal social networks—kin, neighbors, and close friends. The absence of such assistance contributed to the necessity of institutionalization (Frolich, 1975).

Nevertheless, Bayley also indicated that the outsiders' help goes hand in hand with congenial social ties. He wrote that the support and acceptance of the neighborhood is more directly relevant to the lives of families than the general tolerance and understanding, or lack of it, of society at large (Bayley, 1973). In addition, it was important to the parents to belong to organizations, societies, and churches because these contacts were part of the normal part of everyday life. Thus, Bayley's work showed the intertwining between external ties and internal arrangements to handle the combination of pressures both within and outside the household.

IV. FAMILY ORGANIZATION MODEL

Many studies treat the family with a retarded child as if the presence of the child were the only problematic element in its existence. But families with retarded children also consist of parents and siblings who must face the same predicaments and dilemmas faced by other people. The retarded child is just one of several potentially problematic elements in a family (Farber, 1968, 1975). The parents must still make a living, maintain a home, and show a sensitivity to the needs of all family members. In most ways, the family seeks to provide a normal existence for all of its members.

The family organization perspective focuses upon the extent to which the presence of a retarded child affects the rules that govern the family. This perspective presupposes that rules governing the more immediate demands and the life course of a mentally retarded person are at odds with those rules pertaining to other family members. (Bubolz & Whiren, 1984). The continued presence of a handicapped child in the home represents a set of dynamic problems rather than a static problem which the term ''stigma'' implies. Even in so-called normal families, relationships are under continual pressure to change. This inherent instability derives, in part, from the fact that age–sex roles vary with the family life cycle. As both children and their parents age, role expectations and rules governing conduct are modified.

The presence of a handicapped child in the family can be regarded as a factor in the arrest of the family cycle, which is based on certain assumptions (Farber, 1959), discussed as follows.

First, in interaction with their children, parents tend to assign a status to each child commensurate with the capabilities they impute to him or her. The roles embodied in the status are classified on the basis of age grading. By definition, capability age is approximately equal to chronological age.

Second, as the child proceeds in his or her life career, the parents ordinarily revise their self-concepts and roles. With regard to their normal children, ideally, parents continually redefine relevant roles, obligations, and values to adjust to the changing role of the child in family, school, and community. With regard to their retarded child, the parental role is fairly constant. Regardless of his or her birth order in the family, the child with severe or profound mental retardation eventually becomes the youngest child socially. This child in the home is fated for a lifetime of circumscribed activities, typically dependent on parents and siblings for guidance, supervision, and personal management, even in maturity. In the progressive movement to the youngest-child status, the child would not merely slow the family cycle, but he or she would also generally prevent the development of the later stages in the cycle (for example, ''the empty nest'').

With family life-cycle arrest, two kinds of contradictions occur. First, parents are faced with two categories of children: the normal child, who shows a continual mastery in controlling the various levels of bodily and social processes, and the retarded child, who gives evidence of painfully slow progress. Second, in relation to people outside the family, the above discrepancy between normal and retarded is even more of a threat to expectations of decorum (Birenbaum, 1971). Only a minority of parents believe that developmentally disabled persons should be awarded full rights as adults (Suelzle & Keenan, 1981).

The central problems dealt with in the family organization perspective are (1) the extent to which contradictions in expectations occur, (2) the degree to which rules formulated in the retarded child's interests achieve priority over those rules governing the rest of the family, and (3) the ways by which the family rules are modified to resolve contradictions. Consequently, some research has focused upon organizational strategies used to cope with urgent demands and needs of the retarded person; other research has pertained to the overall patterning of rules as they balance demands of the retarded person with those of other family members; still other research has been concerned with the resolution of contradictions in rules governing different family members (Farber, 1979; Blacher, 1984b).

The central theme of family-organization studies is the extent to which family life revolves around the retarded child as compared with other foci. Parents are generally faced with the dilemma as to whether to overplay or underplay their child's handicap (Hewett, 1970). Some families turn in on themselves to cope with the child, while others are able to accommodate the variety of kinship and community activities of interest to individual family members.

Bayley (1973) made a distinction between "structure of coping" and "structure of living." The structure of coping pertains to the techniques that families develop to handle the often inordinate needs and demands of the retarded child. Even routines that are typically simple may become gargantuan challenges to families with a severely handicapped member, and the parents may require help from kith and kin in order to survive physically and mentally. The supplemental assistance seems to contribute most effectively to coping when it is readily available and reliable.

Whereas the structure of coping deals primarily with the demands of caretaking, the structure of living pertains to the needs of the parents and siblings of the retarded individual. The quality of life of the other family members depends in part upon their freedom from such caretaking. For many parents, the restrictions imposed by caretaking demands and limited financial and social resources curtail their participation in the social and organizational life of the community. But the opportunity to participate is different from the propensity to do so. Bayley (1973) suggested that the parents' interpretation of community attitudes toward them and to their subnormal child is tied to their attitude toward social activities in general.

One concern of parents is the difficulty of teaching the retarded child to bring the wide range of bodily processes under control—from toileting to inappropriate sounds and movements. Douglas (1975) proposed that in all societies there is a gradation in the valuation of the need for controlling bodily processes, with the shedding of used products ranking meanest (for example, excretions, spitting), processes not a part of discourse—noise—as next in rank (for example, sneezing, hiccups), and actions inappropriate to the situation as least offensive (for example, giggling, yawning). Douglas (1975) made the further points that (1) the greater the importance of the social event, the greater the demand for bodily control and the lower the threshold of tolerance of such inappropriate bodily processes, and (2) the more complex the social system, the stronger the control demanded.

Douglas implies that the expected decorum of the home and community defines the extent to which behavior of the mentally retarded child is seen as problematic and offensive. Generally, one would anticipate that upper-middle-class families would be especially troubled by the lack of control over bodily processes. The prospect of housing a retarded individual, who will never fully achieve social adulthood, seems to grate on middle-class mothers in particular (Farber, 1979). As a result, the middle-class family seems particularly vulnerable in attempting to balance the demands of the retarded child against those of other family members.

A. Family Types

The matter of priorities among family members is of special concern to families with retarded children. Farber (1968) noted different modes of resolving the contradictory pulls and pressures of caretaking as opposed to interests outside the family. Drawing upon data from parents with severely retarded children, Farber described three pure (or theoretical) types of family organization and one residual type.

The first type, parent-oriented families, are often upwardly mobile. They focus upon the father's and mother's occupational and social careers, and they assign to the retarded child a secondary position in determining the life chances and activities of the family members; husband and wife consider themselves to be colleagues in a family enterprise.

In child-oriented families, the parents subordinate their own ambitions in order to maximize the life chances of their normal children. The division of labor is ordinarily for the husband to specialize in work activities (often to the exclusion of other activities), while the wife cares for home and family. As in parent-oriented families, the couple expends a great deal of time and energy on their activities in order to compensate for the depressing effect of the retarded child on the family's life chances.

In the home-oriented type of family organization, the parents subordinate their occupational ambitions in order to maintain family unity. The focus of activities in this type is upon the mental well-being of all family members. Family cohesiveness, rather than achievement, becomes a central value.

In addition, there is a fourth type—families who do not show a consistent orientation—a residual type. The parents may disagree as to orientation or, perhaps most often, there is no crystallized orientation. Families in the residual category seem to focus their activities upon the retarded child and seem most affected in their cohesiveness and life chances by his or her presence.

An empirical typology of the way families with a severely retarded child organize their relationships was also developed by Mink, Nihira, and Meyers (1983). Using a cluster-analysis technique, the investigators derived five family types: cohesive, harmonious families (Type 1), control-oriented, somewhat nonharmonious families (Type 2), low-disclosure, nonharmonious families (Type 3), child-oriented, expressive families (Type 4), and disadvantaged, low-morale families (Type 5). Mink *et al.* did not attempt to indicate the relationships among these types. However, the family types appear to be related to one another in several important ways.

For instance, Type 1 families seem to represent the epitome of desirable family organization; there is openness, achievement orientation, concord on methods of child care, moral-religious emphasis, the presence of control, cohesion, and organization, an intellectual-cultural and an active-recreational orientation, and a spacious domicile. Of the positive features included in this typology, Type 1 lacks only the expressiveness characteristic of Type 2 and Type 4 families.

In general, the family types are clustered in two groupings, with Type 1 common to both groups. Types 1, 4, and 5 have openness and are achievement oriented; Types 1, 2, and 3 are characterized by concord on caretaking. In addition, Types 1 and 4 share the features of harmony and cohesiveness and Types 1 and 2 have the presence of control and a large domicile in common.

The organization of the types appears to be related to the frequency of stressful life events for the parents (Holmes & Rahe, 1967) and ratings of the negative influence of the retarded child on family relationship. Family Types 3 and 5, which were low in community and/or family solidarity, experienced the highest frequency of stressful life events. However, Type 4, in which only 67% of the homes have a father figure present—as compared with 88% for the other family types—experienced about the same frequency of stressful life events as Type 5. Family Types 1 and 2, which were both high in variables describing the importance of control in the structuring of family relationships, were lowest in the frequency of stressful life events.

A similar pattern of findings emerged with regard to interviewer ratings of the negative influence of the retarded child on the family. In Family Types 3 and 5 the impact of the retarded child was seen most often as negative (29 and 18% respectively). In this analysis, however, unlike that presented for frequency of stressful life events, the impact of the retarded child was seen as minimal in Types 1 and 4 (0 and 6%, respectively). For type 2, the impact was intermediate (13%).

The Mink *et al.* typology suggests that the same patterns of relationships developed by families to handle the exigencies of household and community existence were extended to accommodate the predicaments that families faced with regard to their retarded child. Those families which seem most affected by the retarded children were also those that encountered a variety of other stressful life events having little to do with the child.

B. Principle of Successive Minimal Adaptations

All parents of retarded children are faced with the strain and unpleasantness that accompany the presence of a severely or profoundly handicapped child. Yet, not all families find living with a severely or profoundly retarded child equally difficult. There are broad variations in the sense of stigma, in the amount of time and energy demanded, in the amount of family resources, and in prior loyalties and commitments. Some of these characteristics require more extreme adaptations on the part of the family than do others. The existence of a wide range of circumstances evokes the question: How do families decide on how much they must change their mode of living in order to sustain an acceptable quality of life? (Farber, 1975, 1976).

The principle of minimum successive adaptations suggests an answer. This principle implies that families will make as minimal an adaptation as possible in order to solve their problems (or at least to create a situation making it possible to live with these problems). A family problem is regarded here as any event or chronic situation which the family members collectively perceive as interfering with the successful attainment of their goals in family life. An adaptation is taken to be any sustained change in roles, norms, or family interaction patterns that family members make (individually or collectively) with the intention of effectively handling (by either solving or living with) an offensive situation. The minimal successive adaptation principle implies a temporal progression of adaptations from the simple to the complex, from the least disruptive to the potentially fully disruptive modifications. Because these adaptations represent a means for counteracting a threat to the integrity of the family, members are not likely to resort to extreme measures until those less risky have been tried. Anticipation of possible problems, however, may lead to skipping various phases. Especially as adaptations become extreme, conflict among family members as to the appropriateness of adaptations may itself generate additional family problems. Thus, in response to critical events, changes in family interaction may inch along, intruding upon different domains of interaction (possibly imperceptibly), until a profound revision occurs eventually in the organization of family life.

The principle of successive minimal adaptations involves a series of renegotiations of family relationships. If one assumes that at any given time partners in a social relationship have negotiated a set of understandings, then any potential new allocation of time, funds, or hierarchy of loyalties must be pitted against old ones in revising the structure of relationships. A reluctance to renegotiate an existing pattern of allocation of time, resources, or personal commitments inhibits the speed and amount of negotiation that occurs.

Ordinarily, problematic situations influence one family member's area of responsibility more than another's, or they strike at different roles in different ways. A consequence of the differential effect on roles is that the cost of a crisis is greater for one family member than for another. This person must then "purchase" a far larger allocation of time, loyalty, or other resource than he or she currently has "bought" from other family members. The process thus hinges upon the willingness of the lesser affected persons to renegotiate roles. These persons are thereby in a strong position to define the major value orientations of the family. For example, the position of the husband in families with retarded children is generally enhanced vis-à-vis the wife's status.

If the amount of interaction with the mentally retarded child was the same among all family members, one might anticipate that the family would progress as a unit through successive adaptations. However, because of variations in intensity of interaction, these phases refer more to family dyads: husband–wife, parent–normal child, parent–retarded child, and sibling–sibling. The necessity of living with a retarded child or sibling may evoke a series of secondary offenses in these family relationships. As secondary issues arise within these dyads, subordinate progressions of successive adaptations may be generated. Whereas the initial series of adaptations may refer to the retarded child as a problem, in later phases the focus may be on difficulties between parents or on a sibling's deviance.

The characterization of a family's reaction to problematic situations in terms of a series of minimal adaptations suggests the need to identify the various phases in the process, from the most minimal to the most extensive adaptations. Assuming the principle of successive minimal adaptations, one can outline a series of phases. The conditions which may affect this process were discussed by Farber (1975). At any stage, if the family believes that the kind of adaptation it has made has been effective in handling its predicament, it presumably would cease seeking further adaptations to its problem and would stabilize its organization (or structures of coping and of living; see Bayley, 1973). The putative successive adaptations include six phases.

1. *Labeling phase,* in which the bases for the existing role arrangements are removed, and there is a realization that major understandings underpinning family relationships may have to be renegotiated. The emotional impact and the uncertainties undercut what the parents had previously taken for granted in maping out their own lives.

2. *Normalization phase,* in which the family makes a pretense of maintaining its normal set of roles, while being considerate of each other for role lapses as the parents attempt to keep family life as normal as possible. In managing its interaction with outsiders, the family presents a face of normality and seeks to maintain liaisons with the world of normal families.

3. *Mobilization phase,* in which the family members intensify internal control, time, and effort given to coping with the retarded child's demands, without, however, giving up their claim to normality as a family. In this phase, the family works hard at maintaining a balance in priorities of its normal and retarded members; it becomes more intensely parent oriented, child oriented, or home oriented in establishing priorities.

4. *Revisionist phase,* in which the family, in isolating itself from community

involvements, can no longer maintain an identity of normality as it revises role expectations based on age and sex of family members. This revision represents an attempt to maintain cohesiveness in an uncaring and misunderstanding world. Heavy demands may be made upon the siblings in child care, as the mother in particular may find herself mentally or physically unable to cope with the demands of the household.

5. *Polarization phase,* in which the family, finding itself unable to maintain its coherence, turns its attention inward to seek the sources of its problems among the family members themselves. It suffers a breakdown in organization of priorities; it can no longer mobilize its resources; there is a loss of trust. The family becomes readily susceptible to stressful life events having little to do with the retarded child.

6. *Elimination phase,* in which the polarization eventuates in arrangements to preclude contact with the offending person (for example, the individual with mental retardation, an offending sibling, or an unaccepting spouse). In this phase, the family seeks to renegotiate its role structure (with whatever resources remain) to regain a semblance of "normality."

Recent studies suggest that, with the expansion of health, welfare, and educational services for people with mental retardation, relatively few families reach the more extreme stages of the adaptational process. However, with each stage in the process, the kinds of services and the pathways to those services differ (Rowitz, 1981a,b; Suelzle & Keenan, 1981).

V. CONCLUSIONS

Future research on families with children with severe mental retardation will undoubtedly involve all three strands—the clinical model, the labeling–dramaturgical model, and the family organization perspective. Within each strand, however, the focus of the research will likely shift. Our expectations are that social scientists applying the clinical model will increasingly evaluate services to the retarded and their families; those using the dramaturgical model will give more attention to the conditions under which specific kinds of impression management work in maintaining a believable aura of normality; and researchers utilizing the family organization perspective will undertake longitudinal analyses of the modifications in family adaptations which accompany changing circumstances.

REFERENCES

Adams, G. L. (1982). Referral advice given by physicians. *Mental Retardation, 20,* 16–20.

Bayley, M. (1973). *Mental handicap and community care: A study of mentally handicapped people in Sheffield.* Boston: Routledge & Kegan Paul.

Beckman, P. J. (1983). Influence of selected child characteristics on stress in families of handicapped infants. *American Journal of Mental Deficiency, 88,* 150–156.

Begab, M. J., & Richardson, S. A. (Eds.). (1975). *The mentally retarded and society: A social science perspective.* Baltimore: University Park Press.

Bernard, A. W. (1974). A comparative study of marital integration and sibling role tension differences between families who have a severely retarded child and families of non-handicapped children. *Dissertation Abstracts International, 35,* 2800B–2801B.

Birenbaum, A. (1970). On managing a courtesy stigma. *Journal of Health and Social Behavior, 11,* 196–206.

Birenbaum, A. (1971). The mentally retarded in the home and the family cycle. *Journal of Health and Social Behavior, 12,* 55–56.

Blacher, J. (1984a). Sequential stages of parental adjustment to the birth of a child with handicaps: fact or artifact? *Mental Retardation, 22,* 55–68.

Blacher, J. (Ed.). (1984b). *Severely handicapped young children and their families: Research in review.* Orlando, FL: Academic Press.

Booth, T. A. (1978). From normal baby to handicapped child: Unravelling the idea of subnormality in families of mentally handicapped children. *Sociology, 12,* 203–221.

Brissett, D., & Edgley, C. (Eds.). (1975). *Life as theater.* Chicago: Aldine.

Bristol, M. M. (1979). *Maternal coping with autistic children: Adequacy of interpersonal support and effects of child's characteristics.* Unpublished doctoral dissertation, University of North Carolina, Chapel Hill.

Brown, L., Wilcox, B., Sontag, E., Vincent, B., Dodd, N., & Grunewald, L. (1980). Toward the realization of the least restrictive educational environments for severely handicapped students. In R. S. Flynn & K. E. Nitsch (Eds.), *Normalization, social integration, and community service.* Baltimore: University Park Press.

Brown, R. I. (1976). *Psychology and education of slow learners.* Boston: Routledge & Kegan Paul.

Bruininks, R. H., & Krantz, G. C. (Eds.). (1979). *Family care of developmentally disabled members.* Minneapolis: University of Minnesota.

Bruininks, R. H., Meyers, C. E., Sigford, B. B., & Lakin, K. C. (Eds.). (1981). *Deinstitutionalization and community adjustment of mentally retarded people* (Monograph Series No. 4). Washington, DC: American Association on Mental Deficiency.

Bubolz, M. M., & Whiren, P. (1984). The family of the handicapped: an ecological model for policy and practice. *Family Relations, 33,* 5–24.

Carver, J. N., & Carver, N. E. (1972). *The family of the retarded child.* Syracuse, NY: Syracuse University Press.

Cleveland, D. W., & Miller, N. (1977). Attitudes and life commitments of older siblings of mentally retarded adults: An exploratory study. *Mental Retardation, 15,* 38–41.

Crnic, K. A., Friedrich, W. N., & Greenberg, M. (1983). Adaptation of families with mentally retarded children: A model of stress, coping and family ecology. *American Journal of Mental Deficiency, 88,* 125–138.

Cummings, S. T. (1976). The impact of the child's deficiency on the father: A study of fathers of mentally retarded and or chronically ill children. *American Journal of Orthopsychiatry, 46,* 246–255.

Cummings, T., Bayley, H. C., & Rie, H. E. (1966). Effects of the child's deficiency on the mother: A study of mothers of mentally retarded, chronically ill, and neurotic children. *American Journal of Orthopsychiatry,* **36,** 595–605.

Darling, R. B. (1979). *Families against society: A study of reactions to children with birth defects.* Beverly Hills, CA: Sage.

Douglas, M. (1975). *Implicit meanings, essays in anthropology.* Boston: Routledge & Kegan Paul.

Dunlap, W. R., & Hollinsworth, J. S. (1977). How does a handicapped child affect the family? Implications for practitioners. *Family Coordinator,* **26,** 286–293.

DuRand, J., & Neufeldt, A. H. (1980). Comprehensive vocational services. In R. S. Flynn & K. E. Nitsch (Eds.), *Normalization, social integration, and community service.* Baltimore: University Park Press.

Eyman, R. K., O'Connor, C., Tarjan, G., & Justice, R. S. (1972). Factors determining residential placement of mentally retarded children. *American Journal of Mental Deficiency,* **76,** 692–698.

Farber, B. (1959). Effects of a severely mentally retarded child on family integration. *Monographs of the Society for Research in Child Development,* No. 71.

Farber, B. (1960a). Family organization and crisis: Maintenance of integration in families with a severely mentally retarded child. *Monographs of the Society for Research in Child Development,* No. 75.

Farber, B. (1960b). Perceptions of crisis and related variables in the impact of a retarded child on the mother. *Journal of Health and Human Behavior,* **1,** 108–118.

Farber, B. (1968). *Mental retardation: Its social context and social consequences.* Boston: Houghton Mifflin.

Farber, B. (1975). Family adaptations to severely mentally retarded children. In M. J. Begab & S. A. Richardson (Eds.), *The mentally retarded and society.* Baltimore: University Park Press.

Farber, B. (1976). Family process. In W. M. Cruickshank (Ed.), *Cerebral palsy: A developmental disability.* Syracuse, NY: Syracuse University Press.

Farber, B. (1979). Developmental disability and sociological ambivalence. In R. H. Bruininks & G. C. Krantz (Eds.), *Family care of developmentally disabled members.* Minneapolis: University of Minnesota.

Farber, B., Jenne, W. C., & Toigo, R. (1960). *Family crisis and the decision to institutionalize the retarded child* (NEA Monograph Series No. A-1). Reston, VA: Council of Exceptional Children.

Featherstone, H. (1981). *A difference in the family.* New York: Penguin Books.

Fletcher, J. (1974). Attitudes toward defective newborns. *Hastings Center Study,* **2,** 21–32.

Fotheringham, J. B., Skelton, M., & Hoddinott, B. A. (1971). *The retarded child and his family.* Toronto: Ontario Institute for Studies in Education.

Frolich, P. (1975). *The 1967 national survey of institutionalized adults: Residents of long term medical care institutions* (DHEW Publication No. SSA 75-11803). Washington, DC: U.S. Department of Health, Education, and Welfare.

Goffman, E. (1959). *Presentation of self in everyday life.* New York: Doubleday.

Gollay, E., Freedman, R., Wyngaarden, M., & Kurtz, N. (1978). *Coming back.* Cambridge, MA: Abt Books.

Grossman, F. K. (1972). *Brothers and sisters of retarded children.* Syracuse, NY: Syracuse University Press.

Grossman, H. J., & Rowitz, L. (1973). A community approach to services for the retarded. In R. K. Eyman, C. E. Meyers, & G. Tarjan (Eds.), *Sociobehavioral studies in mental retardation* (Monograph Series). Washington, DC: American Association on Mental Deficiency.

Heal, L. W., Novak, A. R., Sigelman, C. K., & Switsky, H. W. (1980). Characteristics of community residential institutions. In A. R. Novak & L. W. Neal (Eds.), *Integration of developmentally disabled individuals into the community*. Baltimore: Paul H. Brooks.

Hewett, S. (1970). *The family and the handicapped child*. London: Allen & Unwin.

Hill, R. (1949). *Families under stress*. New York: Harper.

Holmes, T. H., & Rahe, R. H. (1967). The social readjustment rating scale. *Journal of Psychosomatic Research, 11*, 213–218.

Intagliata, J., & Doyle, N. (1984). Enhancing social support for parents of developmentally disabled children: Training in interpersonal problem solving skills. *Mental Retardation, 22*, 4–11.

Korkes, L. (1956). *A study of the impact of mentally ill children on their families*. Trenton, NJ: Department of Institutions and Agencies.

MacKeith, R. (1973). The feelings and behavior of parents and handicapped children. *Developmental Medicine and Child Neurology, 15*, 524–527.

McDonald, A. C., Carson, K. L., Palmer, D. J., & Slay, T. (1982). Physicians diagnostic information on parents of handicapped neonates. *Mental Retardation, 20*, 12–14.

Mercer, J. R. (1973). *Labeling the mentally retarded*. Berkeley: University of California Press.

Meyer, R. J. (1980). Attitudes of parents of institutionalized mentally retarded individuals toward deinstitutionalization. *American Journal of Mental Deficiency, 85*, 184–187.

Miller, L. G. (1969). *The seven stages in the life cycle of a family with a mentally retarded child* (Research Report No. 2). Olympia, WA: Washington Institutions Department.

Miller, S. G. (1974). An exploratory study of sibling relationships in families with retarded children. *Dissertation Abstracts International, 35*, 2994B–2995B.

Miller, W. H., & Keirn, W. C. (1978). Personality measurement in parents of retarded and emotionally disturbed children: A replication. *Journal of Clinical Psychology, 34*, 686–690.

Mink, I. T., Nihira, K., & Meyers, C. E. (1983). Taxonomy of family life styles: I. Homes with TMR children. *American Journal of Mental Deficiency, 87*, 484–497.

O'Connor, G. (1976). *Home is a good place* (Monograph Series). Washington, DC: American Association on Mental Deficiency.

Regier, D. A., Goldberg, I. D., & Taube, C. A. (1978). The de facto mental health service system. *Archives of General Psychiatry, 35*, 685–693.

Roghmann, K. J., Hecht, P. K., & Haggerty, R. J. (1973). Family coping with everyday illness: Self reports from a household survey. *Journal of Comparative Family Studies, 4*, 49–62.

Rowitz, L. (1973). A socioepidemiological analysis of admissions to a state operated outpatient clinic for retarded children. *American Journal of Mental Deficiency, 78*, 300–307.

Rowitz, L. (1974). Social factors in mental retardation. *Social Science and Medicine, 8*, 405–412.

Rowitz, L. (1980). Original identifiers of mental retardation in a clinic population. *American Journal of Mental Deficiency, 85*, 82–86.

Rowitz, L. (1981a, May). *Relationship between family type and the use of a clinic for mentally retarded individuals*. Paper presented at the annual meeting of the American Academy on Mental Retardation, Detroit.

Rowitz, L. (1981b). Service paths prior to clinic use by mentally retarded people: A retrospective study. In R. H. Bruininks, G. C. Meyers, B. B. Sigford, & K. C. Lakin (Eds.), *Deinstitutionalization and community adjustment of mentally retarded people* (Monograph No. 4). Washington, DC: American Association on Mental Deficiency.

Rowitz, L. (1981c). A sociological perspective on labeling in mental retardation. *Mental Retardation, 19*, 47–51.

Rowitz, L. (1982). *Family research in mental retardation: A state of the art*. Paper presented at the annual meeting of the American Association on Mental Retardation, Boston.

Rowitz, L., & Gunn, J. E. (1984). Epidemiological factors in the labeling of educable mentally retarded children. In L. Barton & S. Tomlinson (Eds.), *Special education and social interests*. London: Croom Helm.

Rowitz, L., & Lei, T. (1975). Differentials in characteristics between city and suburban admissions to a state clinic for retarded children. *American Journal of Mental Deficiency,* **80,** 165–171.

Sagers, P. S. (1974). A comparison of personality traits of siblings of mentally retarded institutionalized persons, siblings of mentally retarded persons, and persons without a retarded sibling. *Dissertation Abstracts International,* **34** 4045A.

Scheff, T. J. (1984). *Being mentally ill.* New York: Aldine.

Schutz, C. E., & Morris, N. M. (1984). The highest attainable standard: Common goals of MCH and MR/DD professionals. *Mental Retardation,* **22,** 209–211.

Seltzer, M. M., & Krauss, M. W. (1984). Family, community, residence and institutional placements of a sample of mentally retarded children. *American Journal of Mental Deficiency,* **89,** 257–266.

Sheerenberger, R. C. (1976). *Deinstitutionalization and institutional reform.* Springfield, IL: Charles C. Thomas.

Sherman, B. R., & Cocozza, J. J. (1984). Stress in families of the developmentally disabled: A literature review of factors affecting the decision to seek out-of-home placements. *Family Relations,* **33,** 95–103.

Suelzle, M., & Keenan, V. (1981). Changes in family support networks over the life cycle of mentally retarded persons. *American Journal of Mental Deficiency,* **86,** 267–274.

Svarstad, B. L., & Lipton, H. L. (1977). Informing parents about mental retardation: A study of professional communication and parent acceptance. *Social Science and Medicine,* **11,** 645–651.

Tallman, I. (1965). Spousal role differentiation and socialization of severely retarded children. *Journal of Marriage and the Family,* **27**(1), 37–42.

Travormina, J. B., Henggeler, S. W., & Gayton, W. F. (1976). Age trends in parental assessment of the behavior problems of their retarded children. *Mental Retardation,* **14,** 38–39.

Turnbull, H. R., III, & Turnbull, A. P. (1985). *Parents speak out: Then & now* (2nd ed.). Columbus, OH: Charles E. Merrill.

Voysey, M. (1972). Impression management by parents with disabled children. *Journal of Health and Social Behavior,* **13,** 80–89.

Voysey, M. (1975). *A constant burden: The reconstitution of family life.* Boston: Routledge & Kegan Paul.

Waisbren, S. E. (1980). Parents' reactions after the birth of a developmentally disabled child. *American Journal of Mental Deficiency,* **84,** 345–351.

Weiss, H. G., & Weiss, M. S. (1976). *Home is a learning place: A parents' guide to learning disabilities.* Boston: Little, Brown.

Zimmerman, Z. L. (1979). Families of the mentally disabled. In R. H. Bruininks & G. C. Krantz (Eds.), *Family care of developmentally disabled members.* Minneapolis: University of Minnesota.

Zuk, G. H. (1959). The religious factor and role of guilt in parental acceptance of the retarded child. *American Journal of Mental Deficiency,* **63,** 139–147.

Zuk, G. H. (1962). The cultural dilemma and spiritual crisis of the family with a handicapped child. *Exceptional Children,* **28,** 405–408.

Zuk, G. H., Miller, R. L., Bertram, J. B., & Kling, F. (1961). Maternal acceptance of retarded children: a questionnaire study of attitudes and religious background. *Child Development,* **32,** 525–540.

Social Competence and Employment of Retarded Persons

CHARLES L. SALZBERG, MARILYN LIKINS,
E. KATHRYN McCONAUGHY, AND
BENJAMIN LIGNUGARIS/KRAFT

DEPARTMENT OF SPECIAL EDUCATION
UTAH STATE UNIVERSITY
LOGAN, UTAH 84322

I. INTRODUCTION

The deinstitutionalization movement of the 1960s and 1970s has resulted in the large-scale transfer of mentally retarded people from state hospitals to community residential facilities (Conroy, 1977; Scheerenberger, 1977, 1982). However, placement in a community residence does not automatically lead to normative living patterns. One basic aspect of normal adult living is employment. People with jobs enjoy the self-respect that is derived from being economically self sufficient. Conversely, people who are chronically unemployed are dependent upon the welfare of others for their basic subsistence and often are not held in high esteem (Wolfensberger, 1972).

Chronic unemployment has been a bane to handicapped people. According to a study by the U.S. Commission on Civil Rights (1983), the percentage of handicapped people who are unemployed is between 50 and 75%. Similar results have been reported in other investigations (Hasazi, Preskill, Gordon, & Collins, 1982; Wehman, 1981). Moreover, underemployment and low wages further exacerbate the employment problems experienced by mentally retarded individuals (Mithaug, Horiuchi, & Fanning, 1985).

Although employment problems have plagued mentally retarded persons, the recent development of sophisticated competitive employment training and placement models (Brickey & Campbell, 1981; Krauss & MacEachron, 1982; Sowers, Thompson, & Connis, 1979; Walls, Sienicki, & Crist, 1981; Wehman

INTERNATIONAL REVIEW OF RESEARCH IN
MENTAL RETARDATION, Vol. 14

& Hill, 1981) is demonstrating that, with systematic support, some mentally retarded persons can succeed at work. While the number of participants is limited, the results from model programs suggest that mentally retarded persons could occupy a more substantial place in the labor force. For example, Wehman and his colleagues (Wehman, 1981; Wehman, Hill, Goodall, Cleveland, Brooke, & Pentecost, Jr., 1982; Wehman, Hill, & Koehler, 1979) monitored moderately mentally retarded workers placed in competitive jobs who were previously considered unemployable by professionals and parents. The results of a 3-year follow-up study indicated that, of 63 clients who were placed, 42 were currently employed. The collective earnings of these workers was $265,000. The state and federal taxes paid by them were in excess of $26,000. Brickey and Campbell (1981) examined the outcomes for mildly and moderately mentally retarded workers in a model program sponsored, in part, by the McDonald's Corporation. A retention rate of 59% was reported in the first year of this project. In the second year the retention rate increased to 100%. This result of the McDonald's project markedly contrasts with the high turnover rate typical in fast-food restaurants.

Certainly, there are numerous factors that influence employment of retarded persons: the general economic climate, the attitudes of employers toward mentally retarded workers, the attitudes of employment training and placement agency staff (e.g., vocational rehabilitation counselors) toward mentally retarded individuals, and the effectiveness of these agencies in job placement and training. However, employability of the mentally retarded is most directly impacted by how vocationally competent the worker is. The more vocationally competent people are, the more likely they will be successful if and when job opportunities arise.

Vocational competence may be viewed as the product of three interacting factors: (1) job responsibility, (2) task–production competence, and (3) social–vocational competence. Job responsibility refers to behaviors that suggest a commitment to the job, such as being punctual, low absenteeism, and working continuously at job tasks (Rusch & Mithaug, 1980; Sowers, Rusch, Connis, & Cummings, 1980; Wehman, 1981). The second factor, task–production competence, refers to the production of work tasks to company standards for accuracy and for expected rates. Social–vocational competence, a third factor that contributes to vocational competence (Schutz & Rusch, 1982), refers to the adequacy of an individual's interactions with co-workers or supervisors. These interactions may be directly related to an individual's ability to get along with other workers. This review will address research that has attempted to identify and describe social factors related to the employment success (i.e., social–vocational factors) of mentally retarded individuals.

II. SOCIAL–VOCATIONAL COMPETENCE

To examine how social competence relates to vocational competence, it is necessary to understand the parameters that define "social" as well as the dimensions that determine "competence." Generally, social behaviors have been regarded as those behaviors that directly influence the behavior of others (Combs & Slabey, 1977; Foote & Cottrell, 1955; Weinstein, 1969) or as behaviors by two or more individuals with respect to a common environment (Skinner, 1953). Early research examined social behavior in terms of empathy, individual autonomy, intelligence, role-taking ability, and development of self-identity (Foote & Cottrell, 1955; Weinstein, 1969). Recent examinations have characterized social behavior in terms of a distinct set of learned skills (Combs & Slabey, 1977; Rinn & Markle, 1979; Van Hasselt, Hersen, Whitehill, & Bellack, 1979). That is, social behaviors such as smiling, acknowledging, questioning, or any number of gestures might be combined to produce social skills or social repertoires. Social skills in the workplace may include offering assistance to others, clarifying instructions, or working cooperatively. Individual social skills are important if they contribute to co-worker or employer judgments of overall vocational competence (McFall, 1982). Competence is an evaluative term that reflects a judgment about the adequacy of a person's behavior (Farber, 1968; McFall, 1982). Thus, one way to identify the parameters of social skills would be to examine factors that influence those judgments.

Judgments of social competence may be in relation to an individual social skill or to combinations of social skills. Several factors may influence judgments of competence. First there is social context. That is, the adequacy of a social response may be judged differently at work than during break. Similarly, workers may be viewed as socially competent in a workshop context but as socially incompetent in a competitive employment setting. Second, the basis for judgments of competence may vary. Judgments may be made against a performance standard that reflects expected social-skill proficiency, or workers' social skills may be evaluated relative to one another. Third, judgments may vary with the person making them and when they were made. In field testing a social–vocational assessment instrument, 20 pairs of staff from vocational rehabilitation facilities evaluated the social skills of the handicapped clients under their supervision (Likins, Stowitscheck, Salzberg, McConaughy, Agran, & Lignugaris/Kraft, 1984). High interrater agreement ocurred only for behaviors of clients who were identified as either the most or the least competent workers. In the vocational literature there is little data comparing co-worker, supervisor, and employer judgments of workers' social competence. However, discrepancies among co-workers', supervisors', and employers' estimations of nonsocial work performance have generally been the rule (Rusch, 1983; Rusch & Mithaug, 1980; Smith, 1976).

Discrepant judgments by co-workers, supervisors, and employers warrant further investigation, particularly in regard to social competence. Two factors that might contribute to differences in judgments of social–vocational competence are the frequency and the context of the interactions between the rater and the worker being evaluated. That is, a co-worker who interacts with a worker throughout the work day might judge that individual's social–vocational competence differently than a supervisor who interacts with that individual only in reference to specific jobs. Judgments of social competence may also differ depending on whether they are based on a single behavior in isolation or on a range of behaviors in context. Rusch, Weithers, Menchetti, and Schutz (1980) examined the frequency of topic repetitions of a moderately retarded adult during break and lunchtime in a food-service setting. Co-workers indicated that, following intervention, the subject continued to repeat himself too often. In contrast, objective observations suggested that topics had not been repeated for a 3-week period. There are at least two possible explanations for the discrepancy between co-worker judgments and the observations. First, co-worker judgments might have been based on the worker's conversational behavior throughout the day rather than just during lunch or break. Thus, social behavior in one context might have influenced judgments made in another context. Second, the operational definition used by the experimental observers to measure topic repetitions might have been different from that used by co-workers in making judgments. For example, co-worker judgments might have been influenced by the content of the worker's conversation or by his general task performance. It is probable that judgments of competence of a specific social skill are influenced by judgments about other related social skills.

In contrast to the Rusch (1983) study, correspondence between supervisors' judgments of social competence and changes in observed worker behavior were found by Agran, Salzberg, and Stowitschek (1985). Two behaviors were targeted for training: (1) contacting the supervisor for more materials, and (2) requesting supervisory assistance to complete a task. Supervisors rated the frequency with which workers performed two targeted behaviors as well as five other social behaviors not targeted for training. In addition, supervisors evaluated workers' general social competence. Significant differences were found between the baseline and the postintervention ratings of the targeted behaviors. Differences in ratings of the other behaviors were not significant except for working continuously, a behavior that may have been related to the targeted behaviors. Moreover, general social competence ratings were higher after training than prior to training. However, since supervisors had assisted in executing the behavior assessments during training, inferences from these results must be guarded. That is, supervisors' higher postintervention ratings may have resulted from a knowledge of which behaviors were targeted for training.

In summary, social–vocational competence refers to judgments about behaviors by which workers influence others (Schutz & Rusch, 1982). There are various dimensions that might influence co-workers', supervisors', or employers' evaluation of social competence. First, the presence or absence of critical social repertoires is likely to influence judgments of social competence at work. For example, individuals who do not follow instructions might be viewed as insubordinate in the workplace. Second, competence might be influenced by the general context in which interaction occurs (e.g., sheltered workshops or competitive employment) as well as specific situations in which social responses are expected (i.e., breaks or work) (Brody & Stoneman, 1977). Third, an individual's proficiency might influence judgments of competence. For example, individuals who follow instructions inconsistently or inadequately (i.e., not acknowledging or inadequately completing) might be judged incompetent. Clearly, understanding the dimensions that influence judgments of social competence are important to the vocational habilitation of mentally retarded individuals. In the following sections, survey and observational research that has attempted either to identify important social–vocational behaviors or to describe parameters that might influence judgments of social–vocational competence will be reviewed.

III. SURVEY RESEARCH

Survey research uses a variety of methods to procure individuals' opinions or perceptions about a particular area of interest (Borg & Gall, 1979). The studies reviewed in this section have attempted to identify behaviors relevant to job success. Two survey methodologies that have been used to study social–vocational factors in employment are examination of termination records and questionnaires or interviews with work supervisors or vocational training staff. In the examination of termination records, behaviors that led to employee termination are drawn from supervisory or institutional records. In the questionnaire/interview method, respondents rate the importance or frequency of behaviors that are selected from literature reviews, assessment instruments, or by expert appraisal.

A. Studies of Job Termination

Job termination provides a point of departure from which to examine social factors related to successful employment. At first, it would seem that behaviors resulting in termination may be the mirror image of factors related to employment success. That is, lack of vocational competence contributes to termination. Conversely, highly developed skills bring success. However, termination and successful employment are not as obviously related as they first appear unless success is defined narrowly as not being fired. Whereas termination precludes the opportunity to succeed, not getting fired does not guarantee vocational success. For example, a marginal worker (O'Reilly & Weitz, 1980) may continue to be employed but not necessarily be regarded as successful. It is likely that multiple factors contribute to successful employment. In contrast, the reasons that people get fired may often be singular (e.g., stealing) or, at least, less complex. This section of the review will analyze research that has addressed social–vocational factors relating to job loss.

The subjects in these studies were mildly mentally retarded unless otherwise noted. There have been few examinations of the reasons for job loss among moderately or severely mentally retarded workers (Brickey, Browning, & Campbell, 1982; Wehman et al., 1982). Restaurant jobs such as dishwashers, kitchen helpers, and food-service workers were, by far, the most common type of employment of the individuals studied. Other common occupations included janitors and maintenance men, housekeepers and motel maids, factory workers, grounds or lawn-care workers, laundry workers, car washers, and farm hands. In general, the type of jobs procured for mentally retarded workers appears to have remained relatively unchanged over the past 30 years.

1. STATISTICAL INFORMATION ON JOB LOSS

Job loss in low-wage occupations has been studied with the general population as well as with mentally retarded individuals. Wanous, Stumpf, and Bedrosian (1979) collected information about 1736 nonhandicapped employees who were newly placed in low-wage, blue-collar jobs. Of these, 575 worked 1 week or less and only 497, or 27%, were still employed 7 months after they began employment. Of the 1239 workers no longer employed, 42% quit of their own accord, 28% were laid off when job demand slackened or when their companies went out of business, and 30% were discharged for job responsibility, social behavior, or productivity problems.

Job retention data available for a limited sample of mentally retarded workers compares favorably with that for nonhandicapped entry-level workers. Wehman et al. (1982) followed-up 63 moderately and mildly mentally retarded individuals that had been placed in entry-level jobs. After 1 year, 67% of the mentally retarded subjects had retained their jobs, whereas 27% of the nonhandicapped workers were reported to have retained jobs by Wanous et al. (1979). Likewise, Brickey et al. (1982) reported on 73 former sheltered workshop employees (mean age of 26.9 years) who were placed in competitive jobs. The majority of these workers were mildly or moderately retarded. Only two had IQs exceeding 70. At follow-up, 60% of these workers were still employed. The comparison between follow-up data for retarded and nonretarded workers must be interpreted with caution, however. Many of the mentally retarded workers investigated in the termination studies were participants in highly intensive and systematic job training and placement programs (Brickey et al., 1982; Ford, Dineen, & Hall, 1984; Wehman et al., 1982). Retention of the nonhandicapped participants in the Wanous et al. (1979) study might have been better if they had also been beneficiaries of similar programs.

2. REPORTED REASONS FOR TERMINATION

The types of reasons reported for job termination vary, from subjective impressions that might indicate inadequate social behavior at work, such as bad attitude toward work and temperament problems, to analyses of quantified variables, such as the number of people fired for attendance problems or stealing. The sources of data were open-ended interviews of job supervisors, social workers, or employment training staff, post hoc structured interviews with clients or employers, and examination of existing records kept by training programs, employers, or institutions. Finally, these studies span 34 years (1951–1985), rural and urban locales, and two industrial nations (U.S.A. and England).

Factors related to termination of entry-level employees will be described within three categories: (1) job responsibility, (2) task–production competence, and (3) social behavior. Social behavior will be further divided into two subcategories: (1) behaviors that directly relate to performance of job tasks (e.g., following instructions, responding to criticism, cooperating with other employees), and (2) personal–social behaviors (e.g., language deficits, bizarre and emotional behavior). Since this review focuses on social competence related to employment, the first two categories, job responsibility and task–production competence, will be only briefly summarized. The social behavior factors related to employment will be treated more fully.

3. BEHAVIORAL PROBLEMS RELATED
TO JOB RESPONSIBILITY

The phrase "job responsibility" is commonly used by employers during interviews, but it has not been rigorously or consensually defined. In this review, "lack of job responsibility" will be used as a summary term for behaviors from which one might infer that a worker is not committed to his job. The absence of detailed reporting precludes determining precisely how many workers were terminated for reasons relating to job responsibility. However, of seven studies that identified causes for termination of mentally retarded employees (Brickey et al., 1982; Cohen, 1960; Collman & Newlyn, 1956; Ford et al., 1984; Greenspan & Shoultz, 1981; Peckham, 1951–1952; Wehman et al., 1982), six cite one or more behaviors related to job responsibility. Most common were attendance and punctuality problems. Some individuals lost jobs, in part, because they failed to telephone their supervisors when they were going to be late or absent (Peckham, 1951–1952). After poor attendance and punctuality, stealing was a frequently noted job responsibility problem. In addition, some employees failed to consistently attend to required tasks.

Lack of motivation has been related to job responsibility deficits leading to job loss for mentally retarded workers (Cohen, 1960; Ford *et al.*, 1984). As evidence of lack of job commitment, several studies point to the number of workers who quit jobs precipitously even though they had no other job or alternative activity (Brickey *et al.*, 1982; Cohen, 1960; Ford *et al.*, 1984; Peckham, 1951–1952).

While many interrelated variables contribute to undermining workers' motivation to maintain their jobs, economic factors may be among the most pervasive. Ford *et al.* (1984) note that newly hired mentally retarded adults often do not experience any increase in spending money after they are employed because their salaries are earmarked for housing and living costs previously borne by the state or their parents. In fact, some clients simply turn their paychecks over to their parents without opening the pay envelope (Ford *et al.*, 1984). In another study, Brickey and Campbell (1981) noted that, while employment produced a financial benefit to society, it resulted in an average financial net loss for the mentally retarded worker of $1015 per year compared to prior income in the sheltered workshop.

4. TASK–PRODUCTION COMPETENCE

Most studies reported that specific or general abilities or subject characteristics such as IQ, sex, age, residence, sexual preference, or education were not significantly related to employment loss (Brickey *et al.*, 1982; Fulton, 1975; Madison, 1964). However, these observations may be misleading. Subjects who lack the ability to learn the necessary tasks may never gain competitive employment. Thus, these deficits may not show up in termination studies because people with basic skill deficits are not placed in jobs. In contrast, Kolstoe (1966) found that assembly skills, sorting skills, wrapping skills, use of hand tools, and good performance on janitorial and laundry skill evaluations were significant predictors of employment success. Basic abilities may also have been deemphasized in termination studies because the skills needed in unskilled jobs are considered elementary. It is probable that as mentally retarded individuals are placed in more sophisticated jobs, the ability to do increasingly complex job tasks will become a more salient consideration.

5. SOCIAL BEHAVIORS RELATED TO TERMINATION

The termination studies do not provide data necessary to calculate the percentage of workers fired for social reasons compared to those fired for productivity or job responsibility reasons. However, it is clear that many mentally retarded workers encounter serious problems as a function of inadequate or inappropriate social behavior. For purposes of description, social behaviors are subcategorized into task-related social behaviors and personal social behaviors. Task-related social behaviors refer to social interactions that are directly related to accomplishing job tasks (e.g., giving assistance to others). Personal social behaviors refer to social interactions that are not necessarily or directly related to the performance of specific tasks, although they may indirectly affect work production or job responsibility (e.g., inappropriate conversation).

Some studies (Brickey et al., 1982; Ford et al., 1984; Peckham, 1951–1952; Wehman et al., 1982) have noted that problems interacting with co-workers and/or supervisors contributed to job termination. General task-related social behavior problems frequently cited included not following directions (sometimes referred to as noncompliance), not listening to others, back-talk to supervisors, blaming others (Greenspan & Shoultz, 1981), responding inappropriately to criticism (Cohen, 1960), not requesting information or assistance when needed (Peckham, 1951–1952), and failure to cooperate (Kolstoe, 1966; O'Reilly & Weitz, 1980).

Many unsuccessful mentally retarded workers also had critical personal social behavior problems. Among these, many related to conversational problems (e.g., inappropriate conversation, inappropriate language, obscene language, incessantly talking, and interrupting other people when they were talking). In addition, unseemly or aberrant behavior (sometimes referred to as bizarre or emotional behavior or as a temperament problem) has often been noted (Collman & Newlyn, 1956; Greenspan & Shoultz, 1981; Wehman et al., 1982). Sexual misconduct was also frequently cited (Cohen, 1960; Collman & Newlyn, 1956), as were hygiene problems (Collman & Newlyn, 1956; Ford et al., 1984), general discourtesy (Cohen, 1960), personal appearance problems (Brickey et al., 1982; O'Reilly & Weitz, 1980; Peckham, 1951–1952), being nosy (Greenspan & Shoultz, 1981), general health (Collman & Newlyn, 1956; Ford et al., 1984), being immature (Cohen, 1960), being unruly (Collman & Newlyn, 1956), and general unspecified inappropriate behavior (Brickey et al., 1982). Most important is the consistently replicated finding that a large proportion (greater than 40%) of mentally retarded workers who had failed to retain jobs did so for reasons related to social and life skills rather than for reasons directly related to performance of job tasks (Cohen, 1960; Collman & Newlyn, 1956; Ford et al., 1984; Greenspan & Shoultz, 1981; Peckham, 1951–1952).

6. SUMMARY OF FACTORS RELATED TO TERMINATION

Several factors that contribute to employability emerge from the job-termination literature. First, to be successful, a new employee needs to be motivated to retain his job. A worker's lack of motivation may be implied by absenteeism, by a lack of punctuality, by overly long breaks, by not working diligently, and by precipitously quitting a job without warning or reason (Cohen, 1960; Ford *et al.*, 1984).

Second, to hold a job, a worker must have the ability to do the tasks required by the job, although lack of ability to perform job tasks seems to be an infrequent problem according to this literature. However, a few cases were noted in which a mentally retarded worker had difficulty learning to do a job fast enough or had difficulty learning to handle the variety of required tasks. Further, in the McDonald's project (Brickey & Campbell, 1981), jobs were often restricted or adapted for mentally retarded workers. It is possible that job adaptations went unnoticed in many other studies and, therefore, were unreported.

Third, workers must be viewed as productive by their work supervisors. Lack of productivity is a commonly stated reason for termination of mentally retarded workers as well as nonhandicapped workers (O'Reilly & Weitz, 1980; Wanous *et al.*, 1979). Production problems may related to a lack of motivation, inadequate training, an inability to work independently, or an inability to do required tasks with sufficient speed. Further, productivity problems may result from deficits in social skills associated with obtaining necessary information, requesting help, or cooperating with others.

Finally, successful entry-level workers must interact effectively and appropriately with supervisors, co-workers, and, in some cases, with customers. Although termination studies rarely identified specific skills, it is clear that a large number of mentally retarded workers who were fired had serious deficits in both task-related and personal social skills. Sometimes, the social (e.g., following instructions or directions, responding appropriately to criticism or feedback, requesting assistance or obtaining information as needed) deficits interfered with the worker's ability to learn on the job (Cohen, 1960; Greenspan & Shoultz, 1981; Peckham, 1951–1952; Wehman *et al.*, 1982). In other cases, problems were related to the inability or refusal to cooperate with co-workers or blaming others for work-related problems (Brickey *et al.*, 1982; Ford *et al.*, 1984; Greenspan & Shoultz, 1981). There were frequently reported deficits in general social demeanor. Sometimes, the complaint regarded conversational behavior that was inappropriate, bizarre, or obscene (Cohen, 1960; Greenspan & Shoultz, 1981; Wehman *et al.*, 1982). In other cases, emotional behavior was the focus of attention (Collman & Newlyn, 1956; Greenspan & Shoultz, 1981). In a few cases, hygiene, health problems, and sexual misconduct were sources of job loss (Cohen, 1960; Collman & Newlyn, 1956; Ford *et al.*, 1984). In at least one case, the inability to handle teasing and ridicule from co-workers was a serious issue (Peckham, 1951–1952). Personal appearance also was cited as a significant factor in some studies (Brickey *et al.*, 1982; Kolstoe, 1966; O'Reilly & Weitz, 1980; Peckham, 1951–1952).

Inferences from this literature must be treated cautiously because of methodological flaws in the research or omissions in the reports. Procedures for collecting data were often not reported or were reported only in very general terms. For example, interview studies did not report interview protocols, procedures, forms, or formats; neither did they report how long the interviews were or how the respondents were prompted to answer questions. Further, the information was often based on questionably reliable recollections that took place months and, sometimes, even years after the critical events occurred. Similarly, studies that gathered data from existing records did not report how that information was selected or quality controlled. The only exception was Greenspan and Shoultz (1981), who assessed how reliably reasons for termination were coded into six categories. However, even here, there was no assurance that the raw data (existing records or interviews with case workers, training staff, and employers) were accurate reflections of employee behavior or that they validly represented the reasons why mentally retarded workers were fired.

Taken together, these termination studies do make a persuasive case that social skills deficits and the occurrence of social behavior problems with mentally retarded workers are frequently associated with involuntary termination. Some studies make inferences about general constructs such as affiliation or sociability (Melstrom, 1982), bad attitude (O'Reilly & Weitz, 1980), and unruliness and laziness (Collman & Newlyn, 1956) that suggest that social behavior was an important factor in job termination with mentally retarded workers. Other studies used somewhat more specific categories (such as inappropriate conversation, bizarre behavior, problem interacting with co-workers). However, neither the general constructs nor the categories of social behavior that have been identified are sufficiently specific to guide development of employment training or research programs. For example, "inappropriate conversation" can refer to countless maladaptive behaviors and can occur in many different contexts.

Questionnaire/interview studies in which employers are asked to identify social behaviors that relate to employment success provide a useful expansion of information from termination studies. Questionnaire/interview studies should be less subject to errors that may result from faulty memory or inaccurate institutional records. Further, respondents may be prompted to provide more detailed accounts of social behavior that might relate to vocational competence.

B. Studies on Experts' Opinions of Factors Related to Employability

Questionnaire/interview surveys have been conducted in sheltered workshops, competitive employment sites, and institutions. The sheltered workshops have varied in programs, in geographic location, and in the number of clients served. For example, Foss and Peterson (1981) surveyed 93 workshops, each employing 50 or more clients, throughout the western United States. In contrast, Johnson and Mithaug (1978) examined 15 supervisors in a work-activity center in Kansas. Other surveys have been conducted in institutions (Michal-Smith, 1950) and in competitive employment sites (Gruenhagen, 1982; McConaughy, Stow-itschek, Salzberg, & Peatross, 1985). Given the diversity of settings included in these studies, one would expect to find a similarly diverse array of social behaviors included in the questionnaires and interviews.

The types of behaviors assessed in questionnaires/interviews can be categorized into four skill areas: basic social skills (e.g., eye contact, correct tone of voice), task-related social skills (e.g., following instructions, seeking assistance), productivity-related nonsocial skills (e.g., keeps sales area tidy, completes work on time), and social learning ability (e.g., learns new job tasks by watching co-workers/supervisors perform task). Studies differ with respect to the specificity of descriptions provided for the behaviors. Some questionnaires/interviews provide general descriptions of social skills that are difficult to interpret (Foss & Bostwick, 1981; Foss & Peterson, 1981; LaGreca, Stone, & Bell, 1982; Gruenhagen, 1982). For example, in Foss and Bostwick's study (1981), one highly rated item was "getting along with the boss." The category, "getting along with the boss," may encompass any number of behaviors: acknowledging comments made by the boss, smiling when the boss passes your work station, following the boss's instructions, and getting to work on time. When rating "getting along with the boss," each respondent may have had a completely different set of skills in mind. For this reason, general categories such as those identified by Foss and Bostwick (1981) cannot easily be translated into trainable behaviors.

Other studies have examined more specifically defined behaviors such as "follows one-step instructions" (LaGreca *et al.,* 1982; Mithaug & Hagmeier, 1978; Rusch, Schutz, & Agran, 1982). In these studies, the questionnaire items were presented to respondents either as titles for discrete behaviors (e.g., interrupts others) or as behavioral descriptions (e.g., when given an instruction, the client follows the instruction within 6 to 8 seconds). Logically, the more specific the description, the more applicable it would be to training. Therefore, questionnaires that provide concrete descriptions of social skills should be more useful for guiding curriculum development and research.

There were several uncontrolled variables that qualify the interpretations of these studies. These variables include the type of respondents, the assumptions the respondents made about questionnaire/interview items, and the dimensions used to rate the items.

1. RESPONDENTS

The type of respondents selected for questionnaires/interviews may be critical. Individuals were usually selected who were considered to be "vocational experts." Typically, respondents have been work or work-training supervisors

(Foss & Bostwick, 1981; Johnson & Mithaug, 1978; LaGreca *et al.*, 1982). However, this title has encompassed a broad array of individuals, including program directors (Michal-Smith, 1950), sheltered workshop staff members (Foss & Bostwick, 1981), counselors (LaGreca *et al.*, 1982), job placement personnel (Foss & Peterson, 1981), and competitive employment supervisors (Gruenhagen, 1982).

A wide range of respondents may result in contradictory data sets and lead to erroneous conclusions about job-related social skills. For example, in most surveys, sheltered workshop supervisors (LaGreca *et al.*, 1982) or vocational rehabilitation personnel (Foss & Bostwick, 1981) served as respondents, not competitive employment personnel. These respondents may have misjudged the skills necessary for competitive job success. A few studies have questioned competitive employment supervisors about the skills necessary for success at work. Gruenhagen (1982) asked managers of fast-food chains to generate a list of worker characteristics that they would look for in hiring their next employee. McConaughy *et al.* (1985) surveyed supervisors in three types of businesses: manufacturers, restaurants, and community service businesses. These supervisors were asked about the types of social skills they judged to be most relevant for new employees. In another study (Salzberg, Agran, & Lignugaris/Kraft, 1985), work supervisors rated social skills pertinent to five entry-level jobs commonly obtained by mentally retarded workers.

The studies by Gruenhagen (1982), McConaughy *et al.* (1985), and Salzberg, Agran, and Lignugaris/Kraft (1985) allow judgments by competitive employment supervisors to be compared to those of sheltered workshop employers. When the skills are considered in broad categories, there was general correspondence of opinion between types of respondents regarding relevant social skills. For example, following instructions, being of help to co-workers, and responding to supervisory criticism have been consistently identified in the questionnaire/interview literature as necessary for successful employment (Foss & Peterson, 1981; Johnson & Mithaug, 1978; McConaughy *et al.*, 1985; Mithaug, Hagmeier, & Haring, 1977; Salzberg, Agran, & Lignugaris/Kraft, 1985). A study by Rusch *et al.* (1982) provides a direct comparison of the correspondence between sheltered workshop personnel and competitive employers. They asked competitive employers to complete the same instrument that Mithaug and Hagmeier (1978) had administered to sheltered workshop and work-activity center personnel. Not surprisingly, there were some differences between the two groups. For example, workshop personnel identified "working at a job in a continuous fashion" as one of the ten most important behaviors, whereas "working continuously" was not rated as one of the top behaviors by employment supervisors. However, certain behavioral categories such as maintaining appearance, basic communication skills, attention to job tasks, and following instructions were highly rated by both types of respondents.

In another study, mildly mentally retarded adults served as respondents along with vocational rehabilitation personnel (Foss & Bostwick, 1981). The inclusion of mentally retarded workers as respondents makes it possible to examine the correspondence between their perceptions and those of supervisors. In the Foss and Bostwick (1981) study, the mentally retarded respondents differed from their nonhandicapped counterparts on priorities assigned to employment behaviors. As the authors indicated, these differences have important implications for training since it may be difficult to train a behavior that a person views as being of little relevance. Clearly, systematic replications of this research across jobs, types of businesses, levels of supervision, and severity of handicapped subjects are needed.

2. ASSUMPTIONS ABOUT PROFICIENCY LEVELS

A second variable that may affect the interpretation of the studies is the variability in the levels of proficiency that respondents assume when they rate a specific skill. For example, two supervisors, one from an institution and one from a competitive employment site, may both identify "follows instructions" as important. But, what level of proficiency is each respondent suggesting is required by a worker? What proportion of the time must a successful worker follow instructions? What degree of accuracy is required? Must instructions be followed under all conditions? Some instructions call for immediate action, others for a delayed response. Are they equally important for success? Some instructions may be very simple, others terribly complex. When a supervisor says that "following instructions" is important, what level of difficulty is the referent for his judgment? In the final analysis, answers to these proficiency questions, largely ignored to date, may provide the most useful information for research and training. Future survey research might replace questions of the form "How important is following instructions for job success?" with "What kind of instructions do successful workers in your business have to follow? How often? How proficiently?"

Proficiency levels of selected behaviors important for entry into sheltered workshops were examined by Mithaug et al. (1977). Supervisors from four sheltered workshops responded to questions such as:

> Follows: a) 1–2 word instructions; b) 3–5 word instructions;
> c) 6–8 word instructions; d) more than 8 words. [p. 97]

Respondents were to select the criterion that they considered necessary for entry into their workshop. Workshop supervisors agreed on less than half (42%) of these questions. The results of this study suggest that, even when supervisors agree that a particular skill is important (e.g., responsiveness to instructions) for successful sheltered employment, expected levels of proficiency may vary from workshop to workshop. Were this study to be replicated with competitive employers, proficiency expectations might vary across different jobs to an even greater extent than they did across sheltered workshops.

3. DIMENSIONS USED TO RATE SOCIAL BEHAVIORS

A third variable, the different dimensions used to rate behaviors, also makes comparisons across results of studies difficult. Most studies examined skills with a Likert-type scale applied to a single dimension or criterion. These dimensions have included how often the behavior occurs (LaGreca *et al.*, 1982; Mc-Conaughy *et al.*, 1985; Salzberg, Agran, & Lignugaris/Kraft, 1985), the importance of the behavior (Johnson & Mithaug, 1978; McConaughy *et al.*, 1985; Michal-Smith, 1950; Mithaug & Hagmeier, 1978; Mithaug *et al.*, 1977; Rusch *et al.*, 1982; Salzberg, Agran, & Lignugaris/Kraft, 1985), the respondents' satisfaction with the workers' performance of the behavior (McConaughy *et al.*, 1985), the criticalness/relevance of the skill to job success (Foss & Peterson, 1981), and the seriousness of the behavior (LaGreca *et al.*, 1982). Other studies have asked respondents to generate lists of behaviors that are problematic (Foss & Bostwick, 1981) or that are given consideration when hiring employees (Gruehagen, 1982).

Another problem in interpreting the results of questionnaire/interview studies is that a response based on one dimension may be misinterpreted depending on whether employment is enhanced or jeopardized by the behavior's presence or absence. For example, "using obscene language" and "working cooperatively" may both be rated as important to work success. However, it is the occurrence of obscene language but the absence of working cooperatively that leads to difficulties on the job. Further, the behavior's presence may be important in one context, but its absence important in another context. For example, it may be important to interact with co-workers during breaks, but it may be equally important not to interact with them on a production line.

To account for the occurrence or nonoccurrence of a skill, a few studies have added a frequency dimension to one or more other rating dimensions. Mc-Conaughy and her colleagues (1985) examined social behaviors along four dimensions. In this study, 60 direct supervisors of employees in unskilled jobs rated social behaviors according to (1) frequency of occurrence, (2) importance to successful job performance, (3) satisfaction of the supervisor with the performance of entry-level employees in regard to each behavior, and (4) concern about the behavior in the supervisor's decisions to hire, to retain, and to promote employees. Most behaviors were rated as being at least moderately important and supervisors were at least moderately satisfied with the performance of these behaviors. However, a wider spread of ratings was noted on the frequency dimension. That is, some behaviors occur frequently while others occur rarely. The results also suggest that no single rating dimension is sufficient to determine the relevance of a skill to successful employment.

In two studies (Salzberg, Agran, and Lignugaris/Kraft, 1985; Rusch *et al.*,

1982), supervisors of different entry-level jobs (i.e., janitorial, maid, dish-washers, etc.) were surveyed about the importance and frequency of 23 behaviors. In both studies, supervisors agreed about the general types of skills that were important, but the ratings for specific behaviors varied across jobs. This may indicate that, to some extent, behaviors relevant to employment success may be specific to a particular job type.

4. SUMMARY OF OPINIONS OF SKILLS
RELATED TO EMPLOYMENT

A number of skills have been identified through the use of questionnaires/interviews as relevant to successful employment. The general consensus is that mentally retarded workers, like their nonretarded counterparts, must possess a set of basic skills to be employed. Workers must demonstrate proper grooming and personal appearance (Gruenhagen, 1982; Mithaug & Hagmeier, 1978; Michal-Smith, 1950; Rusch et al., 1982), have basic communication skills (Mithaug & Hagmeier, 1978; Rusch et al., 1982), be able to work quickly as well as attend to their work for extended periods of time (Foss & Bostwick, 1981; Gruenhagen, 1982; LaGreca et al., 1982; Mithaug & Hagmeier, 1978; Mithaug et al., 1977; Rusch et al., 1982), and be at their work stations on time (Foss & Bostwick, 1981; Gruenhagen, 1982; LaGreca et al., 1982; Mithaug & Hagmeier 1978). While demonstration of certain basic skills may be sufficient for a handicapped person to obtain a job, performance of work-related social skills may assure that the handicapped employee is viewed more favorably by supervisors and co-workers.

One frequently cited skill area related to successful employment is instruction following. Behaviors in this category include following instructions (Foss & Peterson, 1981; McConaughy et al., 1985; Mithaug & Hagmeier, 1978; Mithaug et al., 1977; Rusch et al., 1982; Salzberg, Agran, & Lignugaris/Kraft, 1985), asking for clarification (Johnson & Mithaug, 1978; McConaughy et al., 1985; Mithaug et al., 1977; Salzberg, Agran, & Lignugaris/Kraft, 1985), and getting information when necessary (McConaughy et al., 1985; Salzberg, Agran, & Lignugaris/Kraft, 1985). In addition, successful workers must be able to provide job-related information when necessary and to offer assistance to others (McConaughy et al., 1985; Salzberg, Agran, & Lignugaris/Kraft, 1985).

Conversation skills have also been identified as relevant for employment success. Behaviors such as interacting appropriately with co-workers and supervisors (Foss & Peterson, 1981; Johnson & Mithaug, 1978; Mithaug et al., 1977), being pleasant (Gruenhagen, 1982), using social amenities, showing appreciation (McConaughy et al., 1985), and responding appropriately to criticism (Foss & Peterson, 1981; Johnson & Mithaug, 1978; McConaughy et al., 1985; Salzberg, Agran, & Lignugaris/Kraft, 1985) were rated by many respondents as necessary skills for employment. Other conversational behaviors were inversely related to employment success. Some were interrupting the supervisor, discussing nonwork-related topics with the supervisor (LaGreca *et al.*, 1982), conversing in small talk, and using weak excuses for absenteeism and/or incomplete work (McConaughy *et al.*, 1985; Salzberg, Agran, & Lignugaris/Kraft, 1985).

Finally, to be successfully employed, mentally retarded workers must refrain from exhibiting unusual and/or bizarre behaviors, from being aggressive (Foss & Peterson, 1981), from distracting co-workers by "clowning around," and from teasing their co-workers (LaGreca *et al.*, 1982). This has been summarized by noting that mentally retarded workers must adhere to shop behavior standards (Mithaug *et al.*, 1977) and must be even-tempered (Michal-Smith, 1950).

In summary, numerous work-related social skills have been identified in survey research as relevant to job success. Table I provides a list of social factors commonly cited in termination, questionnaire/interview studies as related to employment success. Where there are differences between termination and questionnaire/interview studies in the priorities assigned to specific behavior, these may be attributable to the methodology used, to the respondents, and to the specificity of the behavioral descriptions. Disagreement may also be attributable to the fact that this research has not related behaviors to the specific contexts that define their appropriateness. This problem is due, in part, to the survey methodology, since it is difficult ask respondents to make detailed, conditional judgments about contextual parameters. A better methodology for this purpose might be observational research conducted across a variety of work settings. Observational research on work-related social behaviors is reviewed in the following section.

IV. OBSERVATIONAL RESEARCH

Survey research has attempted to quantify judgments of social–vocational competence by co-workers, supervisors, and employers according to one or more dimensions of social behavior. Observational research, on the other hand, is characterized by descriptions of one or more dimensions of actual behavior (Cairns & Green, 1979). Observational research has provided information on what social behaviors occur in work settings and on the contexts in which those behaviors are embedded. However, it is not clear which social behaviors in what contexts are important for work success.

A. Research on Types of Social Behavior at Work

Social–vocational behavior has been examined using behavior checklists (Lignugaris/Kraft, Rule, Salzberg, & Stowitschek, 1986; Mathews, Whang, &

TABLE I
SOCIAL/VOCATIONAL SKILLS COMMONLY CITED IN THE SURVEY LITERATURE

Social/vocational skills	References
Basic communication skills	Mithaug & Hagmeier (1978); Rusch, Schutz, & Agran (1982)
Interacts appropriately	Brickey, Browning, & Cambell (1982); Ford, Dineen, & Hall (1984); Foss & Bostwick (1981); Foss & Peterson (1981); Gruenhagen (1982); LaGreca, Stone & Bell (1982); Mithaug, Hagmeier, & Haring (1977); Peckham (1951–1952)
Appropriate conversational skills	Collman & Newlyn (1956); Greenspan & Shoultz (1981); Johnson & Mithaug (1978); LaGreca *et al.* (1982); McConaughy, Stowitschek, Salzberg, & Peatross (1985); Mithaug *et al.* (1977); Salzberg, Agran, & Lignugaris/Kraft (1985); Wehman, Hill, Goodall, Cleveland, Brooke, & Pentecoste, Jr. (1982)
Follows instructions	Foss & Peterson (1981); Greenspan & Shoultz (1981); Johnson & Mithaug (1978); McConaughy *et al.* (1985); Mithaug & Hagmeier (1978); Mithaug *et al.* (1977); O'Reilly & Weitz (1980); Rusch *et al.* (1982); Salzberg *et al.* (1985) Wehman *et al.* (1982)
Responds appropriately to criticism	Cohen (1960); Foss & Peterson (1981); Greenspan & Shoultz (1981); Johnson & Mithaug (1978); McConaughy *et al.* (1985); Mithuag *et al.* (1977); Peckham (1951–1952); Salzberg *et al.* (1985)
Requests or provides information or assistance	Foss & Peterson (1981); Johnson & Mithaug (1978); McConaughy *et al.* (1985); Mithaug *et al.* (1977); Peckham (1951–1952); Salzberg *et al.* (1985)
Cooperates with others	Kolstoe (1966); O'Reilly & Weitz (1980)
Courteous to co-workers or customers	Collman & Newlyn (1956); Greenspan & Shoultz (1981); McConaughy *et al.* (1985)
Proper grooming/personal appearance	Brickey *et al.* (1982); Collman & Newlyn (1956); Ford *et al.* (1984); Foss & Peterson (1981); Gruenhagen (1982); Michal-Smith (1950; Mithaug & Hagmeier (1978); O'Reilly & Weitz (1980); Peckham (1951–1952); Rusch *et al.* (1982)
Refrains from exhibiting bizarre or aggressive behavior	Cohen (1960); Collman & Newlyn (1956); Foss & Peterson (1981); Greenspan & Shoultz (1981); Wehman *et al.* (1982)

Fawcett, 1981, 1982; Romer & Berkson, 1981) and participant observation techniques (Cheney & Foss, 1984; Salzberg, Lignugaris/Kraft, Likins, & Curl, 1985) in sheltered and nonsheltered work settings. Each approach has contributed information to an emerging data base about social–vocational behavior.

1. RESEARCH WITH CHECKLISTS

Social behavior in the workplace has been recorded most often using behavioral checklists. Lignugaris/Kraft *et al.* (1986) used a 35-item checklist to record the behavior of mildly mentally retarded workers and nonhandicapped workers during work in two nonprofit businesses. The mean age of the mentally retarded workers was 36 years. These workers either lived independently in apartments or with their families. The mean age of the nonhandicapped workers was 61 years and these individuals either lived independently or with their families. Information was gathered on the general content of interactions (i.e., work-related or nonwork-related) and the extent to which individuals worked cooperatively, criticized each other, exhibited inappropriate behaviors, and were socially isolated. In this study, workers were observed to cooperate and offer assistance to each other. Few incidences of criticism or inappropriate physical or verbal behaviors were recorded. In general, conversations among workers addressed work-related topics.

A more detailed checklist that contained 100 behavior categories was used by Berkson and his colleagues (Berkson & Romer, 1980; Romer & Berkson, 1981; Romer & Heller, 1983) to record observations of mentally retarded and mentally ill workers in four sheltered workshops during break and lunch times. There were more males than females and more mentally retarded than mentally ill individuals in the sample. The subjects' mean age was 41.4 years and most lived in sheltered-care residences. There were 28 categories of interactive behavior, each of which was subdivided into an active or receptive category. For example, verbal communication was divided into an active verbalization category and a receptive verbalization category. Other interactive categories included sign language, affection, disapproval, approval, aggression, offering, and helping. Another 22 categories were used to code noninteractive behavior. Each noninteractive category was subdivided into solitary behavior and aggregate behavior (i.e., conducted in the presence of others). Behaviors in the noninteractive category included listening to music, viewing TV, sleeping, eating and drinking, and stereotypy. Approximately 100 5-second observations spanning a period of 3 to 5 months were obtained for each of 304 workers. The data suggest that there is considerable stability in the type of behaviors observed for facilities, despite some variability in the percentage of occurrence for different behaviors across settings. The 12 most frequently observed behavior categories and their mean percentage of occurrence across work settings were aggregate nonsocial (75), active verbalization (26), aggregate eating (17.3), receptive verbalization (4.3), inactive communication (3), active unclear verbalization (3.3), solitary nonsocial (1.5), active affection (1.5), active gesture (1.3), solitary stereotypic behavior (1), solitary sleep (.8), and aggregate TV (.3). It appears that the workplace might generally be characterized by a socially active and cooperative ecology in which aggressive or bizarre behavior is seldom observed. Berkson and Romer (1980) suggest that aggressive behavior in sheltered facilities may be regarded as problematic because of the intensity rather than the frequency of incidence. Teaching individuals to be responsive to a socially active and cooperative environment is likely to promote interactions that would contribute to social adjustment and to judgments of social–vocational competence (Romer & Heller, 1983).

Recent research has begun to shed light on specific social skills that might contribute to successful social adjustment at work. In two studies, Mathews *et al.* (1981, 1982) examined selected social–vocational skills of unemployed and employed adults and learning-disabled and normal adolescents. The unemployed subjects in the first study were volunteers who responded to newspaper advertisements. The mean age of these individuals was 45 years and their previous work experience ranged from none to 50 full-time jobs. The employed adults (mean age 45 years) were university employees or volunteers from businesses identified through the local Chamber of Commerce and had been employed in their current job for a minimum of 1 year. These individuals had held from 2 to 50 full-time jobs. In a second study (Mathews *et al.*, 1982), selected social–vocational skills were examined with learning-disabled and normal adolescents. The participants, selected from a high school with approximately 1800 students, ranged in age from 15 to 19 years and in work experience from none to six part-time jobs.

The skills examined in both studies were derived from previous research (Mathews, Whang, & Fawcett, 1980) and included "accepting a suggestion from an employer," "accepting criticism from an employer," "criticizing a co-worker," "explaining a problem to a supervisor," "complimenting a co-worker," and "accepting a compliment." Each skill was subdivided into two to nine component behaviors. For example, accepting a compliment included thanking the person and commenting about the content of the compliment. Role-play situations were used to assess skill performance. Participants were provided descriptions of employment situations and the materials required to perform job tasks. Subjects were also instructed to perform each job task and respond to a confederate supervisor "as if" in the actual employment situation. The mean percentage of behaviors performed correctly by employed and normal adolescents in "accepting criticism from an employer" and "explaining a problem to a supervisor" was significantly higher than the mean percentage of behaviors performed correctly by unemployed and learning-disabled adolescents. The employed individuals also performed significantly more correct behaviors than the unemployed individuals in "complimenting a co-worker" and "accepting a compliment." However, these data must be interpreted cautiously. Responses in role-play situations may not be representative of responses in the natural environment, even when subjects are instructed to respond "as if" they were actually in the situations being portrayed (Bellack, 1979; McFall, 1977). Role-play assessments of the social behavior of mentally retarded adults have repeatedly suggested positive training effects that have not been confirmed in the natural environment (Bates, 1980; Perry & Cerreto, 1977; Whang, Fawcett, & Mathews, 1984).

A pervasive problem in observational research is that the presence of observers in some work settings might change existing behavior patterns (Rusch *et al.*, 1984). For example, few studies have reported situations involving supervisory criticism (Lignugaris/Kraft *et al.*, 1986; Romer & Berkson, 1981). It is possible that the presence of observers deterred supervisory criticism of workers. In the future, low-frequency, potentially important social behaviors such as "responding to criticism" may best be examined through the use of participant observation.

2. OBSERVATIONAL RESEARCH
   WITH PARTICIPANT OBSERVERS

In participant-observer research, an observer enters, as naturally as possible, into the lives of the persons being studied. The participant observer listens, observes, asks questions, and participates in the normal flow of activities (Edgerton, 1984). Investigators in mental retardation have rarely made use of participant observation because it is costly and often results in massive, complex, and often contradictory data. Moreover, bias and subjectivity are difficult to control when interactions between the investigated and the investigator might change the stimulus conditions that normally control the behaviors under study. It is too often assumed that participant observers have a clear idea of which events to record and that they record that information consistently and accurately (Cairns & Green, 1979). For example, Cheney and Foss (1984) used participant observers to identify social problems of mentally retarded clients in transitional training programs. Supervisors in nine workshops were provided with a notepad on which to record the social problems of workers for a 1-week period. A listing of eight social areas identified in earlier research (Foss & Peterson, 1981) was attached to the notepad. When supervisors observed a problematic social situation, they noted who was involved, where the problem occurred, and what was said or done to resolve the situation. Problems most often noted were accepting criticism or correction, requesting assistance, and following instructions. Unfortunately, neither the consistency nor the accuracy of supervisors' information were reported.

The continued development of a participant observation methodology might provide a way to gain information about behavior in a broad range of competitive work settings. The study by Cheney and Foss (1984) illustrates how low-frequency social behavior in work settings might be observed and, thus, better understood. However, the use of participant observers introduces the possibility of introducing systematic bias in the data-recording process. For that reason, procedures are needed that will ensure the reliability of participant observers' recordings.

A methodology for assessing reliability of participant observers was developed in a study by Salzberg, Lignugaris/Kraft, Likins, and Curl (1985). New employees were used as participant observers to describe the job acclimation process in occupations often held by mentally retarded workers (i.e., kitchen helpers, dishwashers, and housekeepers). Conversations with supervisors and coworkers were recorded on tape recorders worn by the participant observers. In addition, the newly employed participant observers recorded when they began and completed tasks and when problematic situations occurred that required them to initiate interactions. For example, in one situation, a participant observer was refilling dressing containers on a salad bar. There was not enough ranch dressing. Therefore, the participant observer needed to ask a co-worker or the supervisor where the dressing was stored. The new employee narrated the problem situation (i.e., "not enough ranch dressing"; "don't know where it is kept") into the recorder and then asked a co-worker for the necessary information to complete the task. The participant observers in the Salzberg, Lignugaris/Kraft, Likins, and Curl (1985) study were initially trained in the use of the data-collection procedures in a competitive business. Reliability was assessed during training by presenting verbal and nonverbal problem situations to participant observers. These situations were natural to that business and were presented as part of the normal flow of events. Moreover, the participant observers were naive to the preplanned situations. For example, a situation for "asking for assistance" was arranged by having the work supervisor tell the employee to clean a table that had a heavy coffee grinder on it. In most cases, workers asked for assistance when they attempted to clean beneath the coffee grinder. The narrative descriptions on the transcripts from the tape recording were compared to the preplanned events. The proportion of prearranged situations that matched the transcript provided an estimate of recording reliability. Preliminary data have suggested that a high degree of reliability is achievable.

The participant-observer data being collected might also provide detailed information about repertoires that contribute to social adjustment in specific occupations. For example, prior research has noted that workers occasionally need to clarify ambiguous instructions. However, this study is describing the specific application of that skill to kitchen-worker jobs. Additional information is also being gained on how response requirements change as employees acclimate to new jobs. Over the first 4 to 8 hours on the job, instructions given to the worker generally decline. Conversely, there is an increase in the number of problem situations to which workers need to respond. These data suggest that it would be beneficial to teach mentally retarded workers how to seek information at work and how to discriminate the stimulus conditions under which this skill is needed.

Participant observation can provide information in work sites where overt observation would be intrusive. Moreover, it can provide a means to examine what people do and why they respond in particular ways.

B. Context of Social Interactions

Social behavior cannot be understood independent of the context in which it is embedded (Cairns, 1979). However, there are few examinations of social context in the workplace.

Most available research has been conducted in sheltered work settings (Berkson & Romer, 1980; Lignugaris/Kraft, Salzberg, Stowitschek, & Mc-Conaughy, 1985). Employing a time-sampling observation procedure, Berkson and Romer (1980) described the extent to which workers interacted and the character of their interactions during break and lunch in five sheltered workshops. The workers interacted about one-third of the time and spent most of their break in dyadic interaction with one or more peers. Individuals were observed to be alone about 10% of the time, suggesting that, in general, workers were socially active. Moreover, a high correlation (.77) between subjects' interaction level during the first and third months of observations suggested that interaction levels were stable over time. However, there was variation in the frequency of interaction across workshops. Other researchers (Levy & Glascoe, 1984) have suggested that differences in interaction levels across work sites might be a function of environmental factors. For example, Levy and Glascoe (1984) reported that moderately mentally retarded employees who performed collating and packaging tasks and nonhandicapped assembly-line workers interacted more often than mildly mentally retarded workers who were refurbishing clothing or nonhandicapped factory workers. Workers in closer proximity interacted more often.

In another study, Lignugaris/Kraft et al. (1985) observed the social behavior of mentally retarded adults in two sheltered workshops during break and work. The mean level of interaction during break was slightly higher in these settings than in those reported by Berkson and Romer (1981). In addition, workers were often observed to interact in groups during breaks. In contrast to break, work time was characterized by short interactions that occurred about 25% of the time. Moreover, group interactions during work occurred about half as often as dyadic interactions. These studies suggest that the amount and character of interactions in an employment setting may be influenced by the proximity between workers and whether it is a work or a break period.

In a second investigation, Lignugaris/Kraft *et al.* (1985) examined interactions of mildly mentally retarded workers and nohandicapped employees in a semisheltered work setting during breaks and work. Statistically significant differences were reported between break and work in the total amount of interaction, the occurrence of dyadic interaction, and the occurrence of larger group interactions. These settings were characterized by more frequent interaction and more group interaction during break than during work. In contrast, dyadic interactions were shorter during break than during work. These data support the suggestion that, in general, the social ecology during work times is different than during break or lunch times.

In addition, Lignugaris/Kraft *et al.* (1985) noted that there were no statistically significant differences between the interaction levels or the character of the interactions of the mentally retarded or nonhandicapped employees. This finding may be related to the fact that the mentally retarded workers were selected for the study because they had achieved long-term employment success. In addition, many of their demographic and personal characteristics (other than IQ) closely matched those of the nonhandicapped subjects. However, differences in interaction levels across settings have been reported in other studies (Berkson & Romer, 1980; Levy & Glascoe, 1984).

A critical parameter of job success might be the extent to which individuals adapt to the prevailing interaction level in a given environment. In one study (Heller, Berkson, & Romer, 1981), 34 mentally retarded individuals in a training and evaluation center were placed in two sheltered workshops, each characterized by a different level of interaction. Observations of each worker were conducted in the evaluation center and in the workshops. In general, the individuals who were able to adapt to the prevailing level of interaction of the workshop in which they were placed were the ones who maintained their placements. Additional observation of handicapped and nonhandicapped workers in competitive employment sites is needed to determine if adaptability to the prevailing interaction levels is also a critical factor in competitive jobs.

Observational research has provided considerable information about frequently occurring social behaviors (e.g., seeking work-related information). There is much less information available about social behaviors that occur infrequently (e.g., responding to criticism) or about the relationship between social responses and the conditions under which they are required in competitive job sites. Moreover, there is a paucity of information about the interactions between the various dimensions of social behavior in work sites (i.e., type of social behavior, amount of social interaction, the specific context and form of social–vocational interaction) and the judgments of social competence at work.

V. CONCLUSIONS AND SUGGESTIONS
FOR FUTURE RESEARCH

This review has attempted to identify social–vocational factors related to the vocational competence of the employment success of mentally retarded individuals. Survey and observational research with mentally retarded workers were critically reviewed.

In the survey literature, numerous skills were cited as relevant to job success. Unfortunately, many were described so generally that they are of questionable value to employment training or research programs. Moreover, sheltered workshop rather than competitive employment supervisors most often were the respondents who identified the social skills important for employment success. In the future, researchers might focus on the judgments of competitive employers. Surveys currently available in the literature have collapsed data across different types of jobs. However, since social skill demands may vary from job to job, surveys that address one job at a time might be more useful. Replications of single job surveys would produce a data base that could be readily translated into job-specific training curricula.

Observational methodology has been used to examine various dimensions of social behavior. To date, the majority of observational research has focused on frequently occurring social behaviors; little information is available about infrequently occurring social behaviors or about the conditions under which social–vocational repertoires are required. Participant observation methodology may be one promising approach to gain this potentially important information.

A. Employment Success: What Is the Standard?

The research reviewed in this chapter has been guided by the question, what social factors are related to employment success? However, there is little consensus about the criteria for success. When employers, work training staff, or employment counselors identified behaviors important for job success, they may not have been responding to the same standards. In termination studies, the measure of job success was holding a job for a minimum period of time. However, keeping a job need not be the sole indicator of employment success. Some people lost jobs for economic reasons; others left jobs to seek better ones. In one study (Key, 1972), 40% of the entry-level, mentally retarded workers quit their jobs voluntarily. Of that number, half said they were leaving to seek another job.

Another measure of job success might be how much an immediate supervisor values a worker. Certainly, pleasing the boss could be one indicator of successful employment. In addition, this sort of measure might be a more sensitive indicator of success than whether a worker was fired. If pleasing the boss is relevant for evaluating employment success, what about pleasing oneself? To what extent should job satisfaction be a measure of successful employment (Seltzer, 1984)? Who is more successful, a 45-year-old executive with ulcers and heart disease or the janitor who cleans his office building and leads a healthy, happy life?

It seems that employment success is a highly subjective and variable concept. Perhaps a combination of measures would provide a more operational yardstick of employment success. These might include job tenure, pay increases, promotions, employer and co-worker judgments of vocational competence, and observed increases in job skills.

B.   Which Is More Important: Productivity or Social Skills?

The role of social competence in employment has been controversial. Chaffin (1969) suggested that production rate was of primary importance in the job success of mentally retarded adolescents. Greenspan and Shoultz (1981) found that mentally retarded workers lost jobs for social reasons about as often as for reasons related to productivity. In a recent survey of competitive employers, Salzberg, Agran, and Lignugaris/Kraft (1986) noted that some social behaviors were rated as important as production behaviors. More important, they observed that social behavior and productivity were intertwined. For example, the completion of job tasks might depend on the extent to which workers clarify instructions, follow instructions, cooperate with other workers, request information, and ask for assistance. There are few jobs in which workers with serious deficits in social–vocational skills could be normatively productive. Conversely, productivity deficits could affect social relationships. For example, if a worker fails to meet productivity standards, other workers who have to pick up the load might be resentful. This, in turn, may affect the worker's social interactions with his peers.

In summary, productivity and social–vocational competence are intertwined. Attempts to compare their relative importance are based on the questionable premise that social behavior and productivity are independent or may be evaluated independently. Mentally retarded workers must be able to do required job tasks *and* to interact effectively with co-workers, supervisors, and, in some cases, customers. Some jobs may require more sophisticated task skills; others may require more refined social skills. In the final analysis, teaching social skills in the context of productivity will probably enhance mentally retarded workers' employability.

C.   A System for Conceptualizing Important Social–Vocational Skills

Survey research has examined co-workers', supervisors', and employers' judgments about a large array of social behaviors. However, it is not clear how these judgments relate to the situations that workers have to respond to or to what they actually do on the job. In contrast, observational research has described what workers do, but these descriptions have not been related to judgments of vocational competence. Unfortunately, survey research, from which values are assigned to social skills, and observational research, which describes what people do at work, do not intersect. Judgments of a social skill may not necessarily reflect how an individual performs that skill. Similarly, how workers perform a social skill may not influence judgments of social competence.

In a recent study, Stowitschek, McConaughy, and Michielsen (1984) examined the relationship between workers' relative standing among their peers and employers' judgments of each workers' social behavior. First, competitive employment supervisors were asked, "If you were starting your own business and needed workers, which of your current entry-level workers would you want to hire first? Who would you hire next?" Using this procedure, supervisors rankordered their entry-level workers. The rank order provided a measure of each worker's vocational competence relative to his peers. Next, supervisors rated 36 behaviors in regard to how much each contributed to the employee's ranking. Social behaviors that separated top-ranked employees from bottom-ranked employees included seeking clarification, finding necessary information, notifying the supervisor when assistance is needed, following simple instructions, and arriving at work on time. Future observational research can determine the specific dimensions of social behaviors that distinguish top- from bottom-ranked workers as well as the situations in which those behaviors occur.

Given the variety of occupations, it is not surprising that a wide array of behavioral repertoires has been identified that contributes to job success. However, this ever-enlarging list of behaviors needs to be conceptualized in a way that has practical applicability for employment preparation of mentally retarded people. One such conceptualization is illustrated in Table II. The first part presents examples of core social–vocational skills required of entry-level workers. Some of the core skills in Table II were identified in survey research (e.g., following instructions and asking for assistance). The second part of Table II presents examples of social learning abilities that may facilitate vocationally adaptive behavior. Several of these social learning abilities were identified in survey studies (e.g., learning from verbal instruction, clarifying instructions, requesting information).

Successful workers must acclimate to a dynamic work environment in which job tasks change as do co-workers, supervisors, and operating procedures. Accommodation to these changes depends on an individual's ability to acquire new repertoires in a normative way at the employment site. It seems clear that an important social repertoire is the ability to qualitatively adjust one's social behavior to different situations and environmental settings (Brody & Stoneman, 1977).

Social skills and social learning abilities are constructed from basic skill constituents that can be assembled in various combinations. For example, the behav-

TABLE II
An Analytical Model for Relating Social–Vocational Repertoires to Their Basic Skill Constituents

A. Examples of Core Social–Vocational Skills

Basic skill constituents	Following instructions	Cooperating with co-worker	Providing information	Requesting & offering assistance	Responding to criticism	Responding to feedback
Acknowledge	X		X	X	X	X
Maintain eye contact	X		X	X	X	X
Proper tone of voice	X		X	X	X	X
Maintain appropriate distance	X		X			
Verbal initiation			X	X		
Making social amenities		X		X	X	

B. Examples of Social Learning Abilities

Basic skill constituents	Obs. learn. from co-workers	Requesting information	Learning from verbal instructions	Clarifying instructions	Learning from criticism	Learning from feedback
Auditory/visual attending	X	X	X	X	X	X
Sensitive to normal on-the-job consequences	X		X		X	X
Imitation	X					

ioral building blocks for "following instructions" might include acknowledging the instruction, maintaining eye contact, using appropriate tone of voice, and maintaining proper distance, as well as the task skills necessary to comply with the instruction. Similarly, the ability to learn by responding to supervisory criticism would require auditory attending skills, visual attending skills, and sensitivity to the normal consequences in work situations. The key issue is not whether mentally retarded individuals can learn a particular social skill, but whether the skill will persevere over time and whether the individual will be able to build an increasingly complex repertoire from that skill (McCuller & Salzberg, 1982).

Sophisticated social–vocational repertoires might develop as core social–vocational skills interact in the workplace with an individual's social learning abilities. For example, consider the core social–vocational skill of requesting new tasks from the supervisor. A worker who has completed packaging raisins might say, "What should I do next?" After several days, the same worker might again be packaging dried fruit. When the task is completed, the worker might anticipate the supervisor's response with a question such as, "Do you want these put in the cooler?" In the first case, the worker responded to the condition of completing a task with a simple request for a new task. In the second case, the worker anticipated likely tasks, selected the one that seemed to fit the present situation, and then requested confirmation. It is the dynamic development of core social–vocational skills as workers acclimate to the job that may contribute to positive supervisory judgments of social competence.

The conceptual system provided in Table II is intended as an illustration, not as a comprehensive analysis. Nevertheless, it directs future researchers to expand and refine knowledge about the interaction between basic skill constituents, social–vocational skills, and social learning abilities. Research on social learning abilities at the workplace may become more important as greater numbers of mentally retarded workers are placed in competitive jobs. Workers with well-developed repertoires of social–vocational skills and social learning abilities may become gradually more competent and secure in their positions, while workers who lack those skills may deteriorate and, perhaps, lose their jobs.

REFERENCES

Agran, M., Salzberg, C. L., & Stowitschek, J. J. (1985). *An analysis of the effects of a self-instructional training program on the acquisition and generalization of social behaviors in a work setting.* Unpublished manuscript, Utah State University, Department of Special Education, Logan.

Bates, P. (1980). The effectiveness of interpersonal skills training on the social skills acquisition of moderately and mildly retarded adults. *Journal of Applied Behavior Analysis, 13*, 237–248.

Bellack, A. S. (1979). Behavioral assessment of social skills. In A. S. Bellack & M. Hersen (Eds.), *Research and practice in social skills training.* New York: Plenum.

Berkson, G., & Romer, D. (1980). Social ecology of supervised communal facilities for mentally disabled adults: I. Introduction. *American Journal of Mental Deficiency*, **85**, 219–228.

Borg, W. R., & Gall, M. D. (1979). *Educational research* (3rd ed.). New York: Longman.

Brickey, M., Browning, L., & Campbell, K. (1982). Vocational histories of sheltered workshop employees placed in projects with industry and competitive jobs. *Mental Retardation*, **20**(2), 52–57.

Brickey, M., & Campbell, K. (1981). Fast food employment for moderately and mildly mentally retarded adults: The McDonald's Project. *Mental Retardation*, **19**(3), 113–116.

Brody, G. H., & Stoneman, Z. (1977). Social competencies in the developmentally disabled: Some suggestions for research and training. *Mental Retardation*, **15**(1), 41–43.

Cairns, R. B. (1979). Social interactional methods: An introduction. In R. B. Cairns (Ed.), *The analysis of social interactions: Methods, issues, and illustrations*. Hillsdale, NJ: Erlbaum.

Cairns, R. B., & Green, J. A. (1979). How to assess personality and social patterns: Observation or ratings? In R. B. Cairns (Ed.), *The analysis of social interactions: Methods, issues, and illustrations*. Hillsdale, NJ: Erlbaum.

Chaffin, J. (1969). Production rate as a variable in the job success or failure of educable mentally retarded adolescents. *Exceptional Children*, **35**, 533–538.

Cheney, D., & Foss, G. (1984). An examination of the social behavior of mentally retarded workers. *Education and Training of the Mentally Retarded*, **19**, 216–221.

Cohen, J. S. (1960). An analysis of vocational failures of mental retardates placed in the community after a period of institutionalization. *American Journal of Mental Deficiency*, **65**, 371–375.

Collman, R. D., & Newlyn, D. (1956). Employment success of educationally subnormal expupils in England. *American Journal of Mental Deficiency*, **60**, 733–749.

Combs, M. L., & Slabey, D. A. (1977). Social skills training with children. In B. B. Lahey & A. E. Kazdin (Eds.), *Advances in clinical child psychology* (Vol. 1, pp. 161–201). New York: Plenum.

Conroy, J. W. (1977). Trends in deinstitutionalization. *Mental Retardation*, **15**(4), 44–46.

DeFazio, N. D., & Flexer, R. W. (1983). Organizational barriers to productivity, meaningful wages, and normalized work opportunity for mentally retarded persons. *Mental Retardation*, **21**(4), 157–163.

Edgerton, R. B. (1984). The participant–observer approach to research in mental retardation. *American Journal of Mental Deficiency*, **88**, 498–505.

Farber, B. (1968). *Mental retardation: Its social concept and social consequences*. New York: Houghton Mifflin.

Foote, N. M., & Cottrell, L. S. (1955). *Identity and interpersonal competence*. Chicago: University of Chicago Press.

Ford, L., Dineen, J., & Hall, J. (1984). Is there life after placement? *Education and Training of the Mentally Retarded*, **19**, 291–296.

Foss, G., & Bostwick, D. (1981). Problems of mentally retarded adults: A study of rehabilitation service consumers and providers. *Rehabilitation Counseling Bulletin*, **25**(2), 66–73.

Foss, G., & Peterson, S. L. (1981). Social–interpersonal skills relevant to job tenure for mentally retarded adults. *Mental Retardation*, **19**(3), 103–106.

Fulton, R. W. (1975). Job retention of the mentally retarded. *Mental Retardation*, **13**(2), 26.

Greenspan, S., & Shoultz, B. (1981). Why mentally retarded adults lose their jobs: Social competence as a factor in work adjustment. *Applied Research in Mental Retardation*, **2**, 23–38.

Gruenhagen, K. A. (1982). Attitudes of fast food restaurant managers towards hiring the mentally retarded. *Career Development for Exceptional Individuals*, Fall, pp. 98–105.

Hasazi, S., Preskill, H., Gordon, L., & Collins, C. (1982). *Factors associated with the employment status of handicapped youth*. Paper presented at the American Educational Research Association, New York.

Heller, T., Berkson, G., & Romer, D. (1981). Social ecology of supervised communal facilities for mentally disabled adults: VI. Initial social adaptation. *American Journal of Mental Deficiency,* **86,** 43–49.

Johnson, J. L., & Mithaug, D. E. (1978). A replication of sheltered workshop entry requirements. *AAESPH Review,* **3,** 115–122.

Key, L. C. (1972). *A survey of the reasons leading to work termination of mentally handicapped workers.* Unpublished master's thesis, Utah State University, Logan.

Kolstoe, O. P. (1966). An examination of some characteristics which discriminate between employed and non-employed retarded males. *American Journal of Mental Deficiency,* **66,** 472–482.

Konczak, L. J., & Johnson, C. M. (1983). Reducing inappropriate verbalizations in a sheltered workshop through differential reinforcement of other behavior. *Education and Training for the Mentally Retarded,* **1,** 120–124.

Krauss, M. W., & MacEachron, A. E. (1982). Competitive employment training for mentally retarded adults: The supported work model. *American Journal of Mental Deficiency,* **86,** 650–653.

LaGreca, A. M., Stone, W. L., & Bell, C. R., III. (1982). Assessing the problematic interpersonal skills of mentally retarded individuals in a vocational setting. *Applied Research in Mental Retardation,* **3,** 37–53.

Levy, S. M., & Glascoe, F. P. (1984, April). *An evaluation of work-related social skills in handicapped and nonhandicapped employees.* Paper presented at the annual meeting of the Council for Exceptional Children, Washington, DC.

Lignugaris/Kraft, B., Rule, S., Salzberg, C. L., & Stowitschek, J. J. (1986). A descriptive analysis of social–interpersonal skills among handicapped and nonhandicapped adults in an employment setting, *Journal of Employment Counseling,* in press.

Lignugaris/Kraft, B., Salzberg, C. L., Stowitschek, J. J., & McConaughy, E. K. (1985). *Social interaction patterns among employees in sheltered and non-profit business settings.* Unpublished manuscript, Utah State University, Department of Special Education, Logan.

Likins, M., Stowitschek, J. J., Salzberg, C., McConaughy, K., Agran, M., & Lignugaris/Kraft, B. (1984, May). *Using social rating and ranking procedures to identify trainees and training targets.* Paper presented at the annual conference of the Association for Behavior Analysis, Nashville, TN.

Madison, H. (1964). Work placement success for the mentally retarded. *American Journal of Mental Deficiency,* **69,** 50–53.

Mathews, R. M., Whang, P. L., & Fawcett, S. B. (1980). Development and validation of an occupational skills assessment instrument. *Behavioral Assessment,* **2,** 71–85.

Mathews, R. M., Whang, P. L., & Fawcett, S. B. (1981). Behavioral assessment of job-related skills. *Journal of Employment Counseling,* **18,** 3–11.

Mathews, R. M., Whang, P. L., & Fawcett, S. B. (1982). Behavioral assessment of occupational skills in learning disabled adolescents. *Journal of Learning Disabilities,* **15,** 38–41.

McConaughy, E. K., Stowitschek, J. J., Salzberg, C. L., & Peatross, D. K. (1985). *Ratings of employees' social behavior by work supervisors.* Unpublished manuscript, Utah State University, Department of Special Education, Logan.

McCuller, W. R., & Salzberg, C. L. (1982). The functional analysis of imitation. In N. R. Ellis (Ed.), *International review of research in mental retardation* (Vol. 11). New York: Academic Press.

McFall, R. M. (1977). Analogue methods in behavioral assessment: Issues and prospects. In J. D. Cone & R. P. Hawkin (Eds.), *Behavioral assessment.* New York: Bruner/Mazel.

McFall, R. M. (1982). A review and reformulation of the concept of social skills. *Behavioral Assessment,* **4,** 1–33.

Melstrom, M. A. (1982). Social ecology of supervised communal facilities for mentally disabled adults: VII. Productivity and turnover rate in sheltered workshops. *American Journal of Mental Deficiency*, **87**, 40–47.

Michal-Smith, H. (1950). A study of the personal characteristics desirable for the vocational success of the mentally deficient. *American Journal of Mental Deficiencies*, **55**, 139–143.

Mithaug, D. E., & Hagmeier, L. D. (1978). The development of procedures to assess prevocational competencies of severely handicapped young adults. *AAESPH Review*, **3**, 94–115.

Mithaug, D. E., Hagmeier, L. D., & Haring, N. G. (1977). The relationship between training activities and job placement in vocational education of the severely and profoundly handicapped. *AAESPH Review*, **2**, 89–109.

Mithaug, D. E., Horiuchi, C. N., & Fanning, P. N. (1985). A report on the Colorado statewide follow-up survey of special education students. *Exceptional Children*, **51**, 397–404.

O'Reilly, C. A., III, & Weitz, B. A. (1980). Managing marginal employees: The use of warnings and dismissals. *Administrative Science Quarterly*, **25**, 467–484.

Peckham, R. A. (1951–1952). Problems in job adjustment of the mentally retarded. *American Journal of Mental Deficiency*, **56**, 448–453.

Perry, M. A., & Cerreto, M. C. (1977). Structured learning training of social skills for the retarded. *Mental Retardation*, **15**(1), 31–33.

Rinn, R. C., & Markle, A. (1979). Modification of skill deficits in children. In A. S. Bellack & M. Hersen (Eds.), *Research and practice in social skills training*. New York: Plenum.

Romer, D., & Berkson, G. (1981). Social ecology of supervised communal facilities for mentally disabled adults: IV. Characteristics of social behavior. *American Journal of Mental Deficiency*, **86**, 28–38.

Romer, D., & Heller, T. (1983). Social adaptation of mentally retarded adults in community settings: A social–ecological approach. *Applied Research in Mental Retardation*, **4**, 303–314.

Rusch, F. R. (1983). Evaluating the degree of concordance between employers' evaluations of work behavior. *Applied Research in Mental Retardation*, **4**, 95–103.

Rusch, F. R., Menchetti, B. M., Crouch, K., Riva, M., Morgan, T. K., & Agran, M. (1984). Competitive employment: Assessing employee reactivity to naturalistic observation. *Applied Research in Mental Retardation*, **5**, 339–351.

Rusch, F. R., & Mithaug, D. E. (1980). *Vocational training for mentally retarded adults: A behavior analytic approach*. Champaign, IL: Research Press.

Rusch, F. R., Schutz, R. P., & Agran, M. (1982). Validating entry-level survival skills for service occupations: Implications for curriculum development. *Journal of the Association of the Severely Handicapped*, **8**, 32–41.

Rusch, F. R., Weithers, J. A., Menchetti, B. M., & Schutz, R. P. (1980). Social validation of a program to reduce topic repetition in a nonsheltered setting. *Education and Training of the Mentally Retarded*, **15**, 208–215.

Salzberg, C. L., Agran, M., & Lignugaris/Kraft, B. (1986). Behaviors that contribute to entry-level employment: A profile of five jobs. *Applied Research in Mental Retardation*, in press.

Salzberg, C. L., Lignugaris/Kraft, B., Likins, M., & Curl, R. M. (1985, May). *Learning a new job: Empirically observing the task and job acclimation process*. Poster presented at the eleventh annual convention of the Association for Behavior Analysis, Columbus, OH.

Scheerenberger, R. (1977). Deinstitutionalization in perspective. In J. L. Paul, D. J. Stedman, & G. R. Neufeld (Eds.), *Deinstitutionalization: Program and policy development*. Syracuse, NY: Syracuse University Press.

Scheerenberger, R. (1982). Public residential services for the mentally retarded. *Mental Retardation*, **20**(4), 210–215.

Schutz, R. P., & Rusch, F. R. (1982). Competitive employment: Toward employment integration for mentally retarded persons. In K. P. Lynch, W. E. Kiernan, & J. A. Stark (Eds.), *Prevocational and vocational education for special needs youth* (pp. 133–159). Baltimore: Paul H. Brookes.

Seltzer, M. M. (1984). Patterns of job satisfaction among mentally retarded adults. *Applied Research in Mental Retardation, 5, 147–159.*

Skinner, B. F. (1953). *Science and human behavior.* New York: Macmillan.

Smith, P. C. (1976). Behaviors, results, and organizational effectiveness: The problem of criteria. In M. D. Dunnette (Ed.), *Handbook of industrial and organizational psychology.* Chicago: Rand McNally.

Sowers, J., Rusch, F. R., Connis, R., & Cummings, L. (1980). Teaching mentally retarded adults to time manage in a vocational setting. *Journal of Applied Behavior Analysis, 13, 119–128.*

Sowers, J., Thompson, L., & Connis, R. (1979). The food service vocational training program. In T. Bellamy, G. O'Connor, & O. Karan (Eds.), *Vocational rehabilitation of severely handicapped persons: Contemporary service strategies.* Baltimore: University Park Press.

Stowitschek, J. J., McConaughy, E. K., & Michielsen, H. (1984, May). *Work supervisor verification of social situations related to job acquisition and retention.* Paper presented at the tenth annual convention of the Association for Behavior Analysis, Nashville, TN.

U.S. Commission on Civil Rights. (1983). *Accommodating the spectrum of individual abilities.* Washington, DC: Author.

Van Hasselt, V. B., Hersen, M., Whitehill, M. B., & Bellack, A. S. (1979). Social skill assessment and training for children: On evaluative review. *Behaviour Research and Therapy, 17, 413–437.*

Walls, R. T., Sienicki, D. H., & Crist, K. (1981). Operation training in vocational skills. *American Journal of Mental Deficiency, 85, 357–367.*

Wanous, J. P., Stumpf, S. A., & Bedrosian, H. (1979). Job survival of new employees. *Personnel Psychology, 32, 651–662.*

Wehman, P. (1981). *Competitive employment: New horizons for severely disabled individuals.* Baltimore: Paul H. Brookes.

Wehman, P. (1984). Transition for handicapped youth from school to work. *Interchange,* October, 1–6.

Wehman, P., & Hill, J. W. (1981). Competitive employment for moderately and severely handicapped individuals. *Exceptional Children, 47, 338–345.*

Wehman, P., Hill, M., Goodall, P., Cleveland, P., Brooke, V., & Pentecoste, J. H., Jr. (1982). Job placement and follow-up of moderately and severely handicapped individuals after three years. *Journal of the Association for the Severely Handicapped, 7, 5–16.*

Wehman, P., Hill, J., & Koehler, F. (1979). Helping severely handicapped persons enter competitive employment. *Journal of the Association for the Severely Handicapped, 4, 274–290.*

Weinstein, E. A. (1969). The development of interpersonal competence. In D. A. Goslin (Ed.), *Handbook of socialization theory and research.* Chicago: Rand McNally.

Whang, P. L., Fawcett, S. B., & Mathews, R. M. (1984). Teaching job-related social skills to learning disabled adolescents. *Analysis and Intervention in Developmental Disabilities, 4, 29–39.*

Wolfensberger, W. (1972). *The principle of normalization in human services.* Toronto: National Institute of Mental Retardation.

Toward a Taxonomy
of Home Environments

SHARON LANDESMAN

DEPARTMENT OF PSYCHIATRY AND BEHAVIORAL SCIENCES
CHILD DEVELOPMENT AND MENTAL RETARDATION CENTER
UNIVERSITY OF WASHINGTON
SEATTLE, WASHINGTON 98195

I. INTRODUCTION

Taxonomy is the branch of science devoted to the study of classification and the discovery of basic principles that govern the grouping of individual elements (e.g., organisms, objects, experiences, environments) into meaningful sets. There is no taxonomy of home environments, despite the increased research on the effects of residential settings (Bruininks, Meyers, Sigford, & Lakin, 1981; Butterfield, 1967, 1985; Heal, Sigelman, & Switzky, 1978; Janicki, 1981; Landesman-Dwyer, 1981; Landesman & Vietze, 1986; Windle, 1962) and the expanded array of residential alternatives available (Apolloni, Cappuccilli, & Cooke, 1980; Baker, Seltzer, & Seltzer, 1977; Landesman-Dwyer & Butterfield, 1983). Taxonomy provides an opportunity to organize existing knowledge and to develop theory-based guidelines for categorizing residential settings and experiences. As George Gaylord Simpson (1961), the founder of modern animal taxonomy, observed, "The necessity for aggregating things (or what is operationally equivalent, the sensations from them) into classes is a completely general characteristic of living things" (p. 3).

In this chapter, the reasons for a formal taxonomy and a standard terminology of environments are examined. A set of basic principles to guide the conceptualization, description, categorization, and evaluation of residential environments is proposed. To demonstrate how such principles could be used to classify home environments and to test hypotheses about the influence of different types of homes on individuals, a classification scheme is proposed and implications for research discussed. Before addressing these major tasks, the terms taxonomy, classification, and environment will be defined.

259

INTERNATIONAL REVIEW OF RESEARCH IN
MENTAL RETARDATION, Vol. 14

II. DEFINITIONS

A. Taxonomy Versus Classification

Formally, *taxonomy* refers to "the theoretical study of classification, including its bases, principles, procedures, and rules" (Simpson, 1961, p. 11). Often scientists lament the lack of a "taxonomy" in their field. Contextual analysis indicates they mean a method for classifying or a comprehensive inventory (catalog) of the phenomena they study, rather than formal taxonomy. For example, Magnusson (1981a) has written about "the problem of taxonomy of situations," using taxonomy as a synonym for a classification scheme. Similarly, when Rosenblum (1978) discusses how to create "behavioral taxonomies," taxonomy refers to "a descriptive list" of "segments of ongoing behavior that are ultimately quantifiable and pertinent to the research problem at hand" (p. 15).

In this chapter, taxonomy proper is distinguished from the actual activity and products (e.g., categorization schemes, keys, typologies) of classifying. Classification involves the ordering of elements into groups, based on rules such as contiguity and similarity. As such, the subject of classification consists of the individual elements (e.g., environments, behavioral acts) and what is known about them. In contrast, the subject of taxonomy proper is classification, including its processes, its products, and its implications for scientific study within a given field. Taxonomy provides alternatives for arranging complex data into forms that may serve theory, aesthetics, or practice.

For a scholarly and fascinating discourse on taxonomy and its history related to systematics, categorization, and nomenclature, consult Simpson's (1961) classic work on the *Principles of Animal Taxonomy*. Without a doubt, his thoughtful and detailed reflections on his own life's work provided the inspiration for this chapter.

B. The Concept of Environment

Any exploration of the concept of "environment" leads to several sweeping conclusions.

First, human environments do not exist apart from human beings. This means that assessing directional influences or causality is very difficult. If a certain environment is associated with a particular pattern of human behavior, we cannot discern whether the environment fostered the behavior or whether the people who created or entered that kind of environment were predisposed to behave that way, or at least to structure their environment in ways that would support particular kinds of behavior. Fundamentally, the line that separates environments from the people who design, use, and evaluate them is arbitrary and conventional, not absolute.

Second, human environments may be described and analyzed at many levels. Bronfenbrenner (1977) described the "ecological environment" as one "conceived topologically as a nested arrangement of structures, each contained within the next" (p. 514). Within this broad environment, the levels for study range from immediate settings (microsystem) to the interrelations among the major settings in an individual's life at a particular time (mesosystem) to the external social structures (exosystem), both formal and informal, that influence particular settings. Given this multilevel nature of environments, any discussion or classification of environments needs to begin with an explicit delineation of the scope of "environment."

Third, environments include many diverse features and elements. Environments are at least as complex and problematic to delineate and to measure as are individuals. Deductively, environments ought to be even more complex than individuals, because environments contain both animate and inanimate components and all the relationships among these components.

Fourth, environments are dynamic, not static. This necessitates monitoring the key features or variables over time. Theoretically, this dynamic nature of an environment, including changes associated with internal and external factors, is an important dimension of the environment. Single or static assessment of environments thus ignores a central quality of environments and yields, by definition, an incomplete picture.

Fifth, environments may be evaluated in both objective and subjective terms. Many environmental and developmental psychologists (Lewin, 1935; Magnusson, 1981b; Pervin & Lewis, 1978; Russell & Ward, 1982; Stokols, 1982) discuss the distinctions between external, geographical, objectively observed, or "actual" environments on the one hand and behavioral, immediate, subjective, or "perceived" environments on the other. These different perspectives can yield markedly different conclusions about the relative significance of particular environmental variables. Individuals vary in how they perceive and respond to the multitude of sensory opportunities that collectively represent an environment (Gibson, 1979; Ittelson, 1978). Indeed, expectations and "cognitive environmental sets" (Leff & Gordon, 1980) significantly alter what features individuals notice in their environments and the importance they attach to the presence of various elements.

Sixth, and finally, environments are responded to as a whole. That is, the total impression (gestalt) of environments is more than a collection of many separate and diverse characteristics, resources, relationships, etc. This conclusion is not at odds with the fact that some features of environments are more important than are others; neither does this imply that individuals fail to dimensionalize their own environments or to perceive some elements as distinctive within the total environment. Rather, this characteristic of being whole (i.e., a single entity) implies a psychological dimension that cannot be derived by merely summing the parts. This underscores the need to study environmental variables in their natural context, interrelated to other variables (Stokols, 1978), rather than in isolated situations.

Dictionary definitions of environment tend to be highly inclusive: e.g., "all the conditions, circumstances, and influences surrounding, and affecting, the development of an organism or group of organisms" (*Webster's New World Dictionary*) or "the aggregate of surrounding things, conditions, or influences, esp. as affecting the existence or development of someone or something" (*The Random House Dictionary of the English Language*). For the present purposes, environment is defined more narrowly. Specifically, *environments* are identified in terms of four dimensions: (1) geographical boundaries, (2) distinguishing physical and social resources within these boundaries, (3) a recognized purpose or role in society, and (4) a set of relationships to the larger community. Accordingly, environments are more than momentary settings [see, e.g., Barker's, (1968) "behavior settings"] and yet less than all the external influences on an individual. This definition focuses on objectively measured features of environments, but does *not* assume that the distinctive elements that identify a particular environment are necessarily the most important ones for the occupants of that environment.

Stokols (1982) described the field of environmental psychology as "coming of age" in exploring the long recognized *social* and *biological* significance of situations and environments [see Cronbach's (1975) plea for a study of environments]. Russell and Ward (1982) reviewed the research in this field and concluded with the admonition that "time spent thinking rather than data-gathering would not be wasted" (p. 680). Contrary to the familiar call for more research on the same topic, they encourage diversification in research efforts without lowering standards for empirical rigor simply because a field is "young." Such conclusions apply equally well to environmental research about homes. These views are not new: Windle (1962) and Butterfield (1967) carefully reviewed the effects of residential environments on mentally retarded individuals. Their analyses remain valid today (Butterfield, 1985); most studies are flawed by poor design and lack of a strong conceptual framework to guide the selection of subjects and measures.

III. WHY CLASSIFY ENVIRONMENTS?

Beyond the general need living organisms may have to classify experiences and knowledge, there are compelling reasons to develop systematic strategies for categorizing home environments. At the most fundamental level, communication needs to be improved, both within the scientific community and between researchers and families, service providers, and policy makers. Classification helps achieve this goal by requiring a definition for each "type" of environment. Because membership criteria must be explicit, the use of standard descriptive terms is encouraged, even when the actual categories, or their definitions, differ across alternative classification schemes. Categories also provide a shorthand means for conveying lots of information about complex and naturally correlated variables. A categorical label can substitute efficiently for a long list of characteristics that distinguish a particular kind of environment from others. More importantly, classification schemes offer an opportunity to summarize existing knowledge, e.g., via elegant grouping of particular environments on the basis of findings about the effects of certain variables on behavioral development. Finally, and most importantly, classification can facilitate the formulation of cohesive and comprehensive theories about human adaptation to various environmental conditions. This is most likely when categories are based on explicit assumptions about which environmental features are salient and important. The validity of such categories can be tested directly, as well as hypotheses about the internal cohesiveness of categories, their relationship to one another, and their contribution to differential developmental outcomes for individuals, groups, or society. Historically, classification has proven heuristic in many scientific areas of inquiry.

A. Communication Via Standard Nomenclature

All scientific fields rely on a core set of precisely defined terms, concepts, subjects, and procedures. Similarly, practitioners in any area need a uniform language to identify their functional activities and the objects (including people) of their practice. The manual on *Classification in Mental Retardation* (Grossman, 1983) is an example of a reference used by practitioners and researchers to establish uniformity in diagnosis, description, and classification of mentally retarded individuals. Such manuals seldom are considered definitive; they require constant revision to reflect changes in the field, to correct past mistakes, to clarify ambiguities, and to incorporate new findings (e.g., the discovery of new etiological factors or the identification of new syndromes in mental retardation). Although a primary reference source cannot guarantee actual practices will conform with its recommendations, it can foster better communication by minimizing problems associated with inconsistent or ambiguous use of terms.

Concerning residential environments, current classification and nomenclature is confusing and potentially dangerous. I illustrate this via several examples. In the first, the same words refer to markedly different environments; in the second, different terms are used for similar environments. The third and fourth examples highlight problems typical of user-specific categories not grounded in theory or widespread practice. Such categories obscure comparing results across studies or service delivery systems or extracting generalizable principles about person–environment interactions. Because there is little recognition of the seriousness of these problems in studying residential environments, considerable detail is provided.

Poor delineation of *types* of residential environments is one reason for the limited knowledge base about the effects of alternative residential settings on mentally retarded people. Apparently, discrepant reports about the "success" of a particular form of residence may reflect inconsistent labeling rather than real differences. Conversely, relevant findings may be overlooked when investigators use unfamiliar or idiosyncratic terms to label the environments studied.

Example 1: The meaning of "foster care." The largest study of foster care for retarded individuals has been conducted in southern California. This longitudinal investigation was designed to answer questions about what characteristics of foster parents and home environments promote positive development for foster children.

The form of "foster care" selected for study deviates in many ways from its common connotation. Specifically, many of the California "foster homes" were managed by a nonwhite woman over 50 years old, who assumed caretaking responsibility for four or five unrelated mentally retarded adults. Reimbursement for providing care often represented the sole source of income for the home (Eyman, Borthwick, & Sheehy, 1986; Lei, Nihira, Sheehy, & Meyers, 1981). Such a profile of foster care differs markedly from that in states where foster care usually means a two-parent family that chooses to have one or two mentally retarded children enter the preexisting family situation. For these families, remuneration seldom constitutes the primary family income, often not covering actual expenses incurred by the family in caring for a handicapped foster child. Most of these foster families have nonretarded children (usually biological offspring) living at home; some may have their own handicapped children as well. Many states require special licensing for such foster homes, offer formal training and preparation for foster parents, and set a limit of two or three foster children per family. In fact, there is much variation in the character of foster homes described in the literature (Intagliata, Crosby, & Neider, 1981), and the California families themselves are quite heterogeneous in their social composition, parental characteristics, and motivational factors (Lei *et al.*, 1981).

The problem is *not* that foster families show wide natural variation, but rather that the identification of foster homes relies on administrative criteria that are inconsistent across states. Using a common label is misleading, for instance, when one state labels a single-parent home for five retarded adults as foster care, while another considers this a group home, because foster families may serve only two school-aged children. Such categorical terms convey little or no information about the structure, function, or goals of the residential programs. When client eligibility and facility licensing criteria differ markedly across service-delivery systems, then gathering descriptive data about service providers and residents mostly checks on the rigor of enforcing regulations. That is, the data do not provide valid information about what types of individuals are willing to provide care for handicapped individuals. *If* the concept of family foster care has social and psychological implications that warrant scientific study, then local definitions of foster homes cannot be the sole basis for selecting families to be investigated. The danger in the present situation is that results from the California study will be used, *without adequate recognition of such major differences,* to shape public policy about foster care, based on how "successful" it has been in southern California. The taxonomic issue is whether there are sound reasons to group this diverse set of environments into a single category. Even when investigators try to evaluate the effects of identified environmental variables, such as parental characteristics, no statistical procedures can compensate for the constraints or confounding associated with the initial reliance on administrative categories to sample environments.

Example 2: Renaming public institutions. Ten years ago, most large state-owned and operated residential facilities were called institutions, hospitals, colonies, or state schools. Today, few retain the same categorical labels. The new terms include "developmental centers," "central core facilities," and "residential habilitation centers." This renaming is an effort to free these particular environments from their widespread negative connotations (Center on Human Policy, 1979; Ferleger & Boyd, 1979). What complicates matters is that some state institutions and state hospitals have made dramatic changes in their size, their location, the populations they serve, their structural and functional organization, and the services they provide, while others have not (Landesman-Dwyer, 1985; Landesman 1986)—yet whether a facility has been renamed is *not* reliably associated with such changes. The names have been changed for social and political reasons. Little information can be gleaned from any of the current terms. Worse yet, the new labels in one state often are the same as those used elsewhere to describe completely different kinds of programs. For instance, in some states, "developmental centers" refer to daytime training programs for mentally retarded adults who are not eligible for formal vocational training, while in other states, "developmental centers" identify the newly titled, traditional state institutions.

Example 3: A national survey of residential facilities. Bruininks and colleagues (1983) at the Center for Residential and Community Services in Minnesota analyzed data from a national survey of residential facilities. They divided all facilities into seven types, based on administrator's self-categorization:

1. A residence with with one or more retarded people living as family members (e.g., foster home).
2. A residence with supervising staff for one or more mentally retarded people (e.g., group residence).
3. A residence with staff living in a separate unit in the same building (e.g., supervised apartments).
4. A residence with staff who may visit, but without day-to-day supervision.
5. A residence with no regular care or supervision of residents (e.g., boarding homes).
6. A residence with no formal training of residents (e.g., personal care home).
7. A nursing home.

In contrast, Borthwick, Meyers, and Eyman (1981) classified residential environments (that collectively served more than 6000 developmentally disabled people in a three-state region) into five types:

1. *Institutions* providing comprehensive care primarily to severely mentally retarded residents.
2. *Convalescent hospitals* with nursing facilities for nonambulatory severely and profoundly retarded persons.
3. *Board and care homes* including group homes and residential schools.
4. *Family care homes* providing care for six or fewer developmentally disabled persons of all ages and levels of retardation.
5. *Clients who reside with their own parents.*

The above studies rely on administratively determined or user-specific classification schemes. Although the investigators clearly define the types of facilities, the distinctions among the categories tend to be unique to the study or to a particular region's administrative labels. More importantly, because considerably heterogeneous facilities are combined into a few broad categories, meaningful comparisons across these studies cannot be made. For instance, in the first study, boarding homes have no regular care or supervision, whereas supervised group homes are included in the category "board and care." Similarly, family care homes from the second study would be considered foster homes or group homes in the first. Even more problematic for comparison's sake is that the first study excluded facilities *not* specially licensed to serve mentally retarded clients, while the second study included generically licensed facilities.

Interestingly, both studies were designed to provide large data sets suitable for describing mental retardation service-delivery systems, the relationship of differential client outcomes to particular types of residences, and the comparative cost of alternative forms of residential services. Given the significantly different ways the investigators grouped these facilities—without gathering sufficient data to permit reanalysis or regrouping according to alternative typologies or definitions—it is difficult to estimate the scientific or practical utility of the data gathered. As mentioned earlier, many potential users of these findings will not recognize the vast differences in how the residential services initially were defined. Instead, readers are likely to assume comparability across studies or similarity to their own service-delivery system, based on the use of the categorical terms themselves.

Example 4: A repeated assessment of a state's service-delivery system. In 1974–1975 and in 1980, my colleagues and I conducted statewide surveys of the developmentally disabled clients receiving publicly supported residential care in Washington state (Landesman-Dwyer & Brown, 1976; Landesman-Dwyer & Mai-Dalton, 1981). We gathered detailed data on the adjustment of more than 8000 representatively sampled clients and conducted independent studies on the reliability and validity of interview and case-record data. We, unfortunately, neglected to document the precise nature of the clients' residential environments and relied on the administrative categories to describe residential services. During this 5-year period, the licensing and standards regulating several kinds of residences (e.g., congregate care facilities, nursing homes, adult foster homes, group homes) changed significantly, while a number of new types of residences emerged (e.g., specialized group homes, community-based Title XIX Intermediate Care Facilities for the Mentally Retarded (ICF/MR), core cluster homes, and tenant support). The differences in the array of environments, coupled with shifts in ideology and placement practices, were so great that we cannot make valid inferences about the relationship of particular types of residences to outcomes such as client adjustment, community integration, cost, quality of day-to-day care, etc. Although the surveys provided descriptive facts needed by state planners for each time period, we could have generated far more useful findings *if* we had recognized the need for collecting a standard set of descriptive environmental variables *independent of existing administrative labels.*

Although data from the above four surveys were gathered for similar analytic purposes, comparing their findings is problematic. Because Bruininks *et al.* (1983) reported data on all states, an interesting profile for Washington state emerged from their categorization scheme. As shown in Table I, the Landesman-Dwyer *et al.* study generated a markedly different picture than did the Bruininks *et al.* (1983) data set. The significant differences include the apparent diversity of the residential options, the total number of clients served, and the presence of special foster care. The only similar estimate for number of clients served occurred in the category labeled "special nursing" or community-based ICF/MR—which was identified by formal federal licensing standards.

Communication is not only a problem *within* the field of mental retardation, but one that extends to interaction with the broader scientific and service-delivery

TABLE I
PROFILE OF WASHINGTON STATE'S RESIDENTIAL PROGRAMS ACCORDING TO
TWO DIFFERENT SURVEYS

Bruininks, Meyers, Sigford, & Lakin (1981)[a]		Landesman-Dwyer, Stein, & Sackett (1976)[b]	
Special foster care	0	Licensed foster care for developmentally disabled (DD):	
Personal care	119	Children	414
Group residence	3896	Adults	159
Semi-independent	32	Group care:	
Board and room	153	State institutions	2226
Special nursing	381	Licensed group homes for DD	666
		Congregate care facilities	825
		Semi-independent	101
		Boarding home	83
		Community ICF/MR	377
		Skilled nursing facilities	743[c]
		Intermediate care facilities	377[c]
Estimated total	*4581*	*Estimated total*	*5971*

[a]Based on data provided by administrators in response to questionnaires mailed in 1980.

[b]Based on in-person interview data from case managers in 1980, except for estimate of institutional population obtained from state records.

[c]These clients were receiving community services and training programs for developmentally disabled persons. Note: Bruininks *et al.* excluded generic facilities on the basis that they were not providing "special" services for this population.

communities. Isolationism is reflected in the fact that investigators in mental retardation rarely cite relevant findings about nursing and retirement homes, institutions for mentally ill persons, foster and adoptive homes for nonretarded children, or treatment facilities for juvenile populations. At the same time, important principles derived from study of retarded individuals in various residential settings seldom are noticed by researchers or clinicians interested in other populations. Even investigators interested in families and homes for mentally retarded children seem to have segregated themselves from those who study out-of-home placement or group care. Further divisions occur based on the population studied—typically, mildly and moderately retarded versus severely and profoundly retarded subjects and children versus adults. A common and standard language to describe key aspects of environments could provide a sound start to unite the field and improve communication, even without a widely accepted or theory-based classification scheme.

B. Categories as Data-Reduction Devices

Given the fundamentally rich and complex nature of environments, comprehensive description and assessment is an exceedingly challenging task. So far, our information-gathering skills seem more advanced and energetic than do our abilities to analyze and present such multivariate data sets. Especially important is the need to convey a *unitary*, rather than merely a compartmentalized, impression of environments. When environmental variables are considered singly or only in small related sets (e.g., two-way interactions or factor scores), the "wholeness" that is a fundamental quality of environments is neglected. Categories thus provide a convenient and conceptually powerful means of capturing many diverse environmental features in their naturally intertwined patterns. In this sense, categories are tools that function as effective data reducers.

There are many statistical techniques commonly used to group or reduce data sets. Experienced users appreciate that these procedures do not represent simple or straightforward solutions (Bakeman, 1978; Everitt, 1980; Gottman, 1981). Their proper use involves the same kind of aesthetic sense and good judgment needed to develop any sound classification scheme. Being based on empirically gathered descriptive data, such statistically generated categories may not yield category systems that are exhaustive of all possibilities. Neither are these statistically derived products likely to detect the most salient criteria used to recognize places (i.e., to distinguish them as similar to or different from other environments). There are appropriate uses of such statistical groupings, but factors or clusters are not any less biased, more natural, or empirically valid than are other ways of organizing and reducing data. Simple categories that reflect everyday distinctions can be as useful and as elegant as those derived from computing algebraic and geometrical relationships among highly correlated, transformed observations of environments.

C. Organization of Existing Knowledge

Classification can serve to arrange scientific findings in ways that foster understanding of the phenomena they describe. For example, the evolutionary relationships among various groups of mammals have been incorporated into modern mammalian classification. Once an organism is correctly identified, one immediately knows a great deal more about that animal, including its genetic and present relationships to other organisms as well as its primary structural, functional, and developmental characteristics. As Simpson (1961) appreciated, there is a delicate balance to maintain so that classification schemes remain up-to-date with scientific knowledge, yet are stable enough to serve their vital role in fostering communication and facilitating comparison of findings across studies and over time. Simpson's rule favors "consistency": "*A published classification in cur-*

rent use should be changed when it is definitely inconsistent with known facts and accepted principles, but only as far as necessary to bring it into consistency" (p. 112).

D. Theory Testing and Theory Building

If categories were used only to improve communication, reduce complex data sets, and organize existing findings, then they would be viewed primarily as technical or academic aids. Yet historically, formal classification schemes have served theory as much as (or more than) practice. In the basic sciences, the ways in which the phenomena of interest are grouped have provided the basic framework for presenting fundamental assumptions. From such classification schemes, direct tests could be made of these basic assumptions and more complex hypotheses could be derived by extending either the content or the contexts to which the classification had been applied. Elegant examples of the theoretical significance of classification can be found in chemistry, physics, astronomy, biology, geology, and zoology. The potential theoretical value of classifying residential environments, however, cannot be proven by these examples. An example of a theory-based classification scheme of home environments may be more appropriate and to the point. To be convincing, such an example should generate interesting, testable hypotheses and should be suitable for modification in accord with empirical findings. Even without an all-encompassing theory of environments, a classification scheme organized on explicit assumptions about how environments function can be heuristic. But before offering such an example, a brief review of existing classification schemes is warranted.

IV. EXISTING CLASSIFICATION SCHEMES

To date, three types of classification schemes have been used to group residential environments for retarded individuals: typological, evaluative, and administratively determined.

The best example of a *typological classification scheme* is that proposed by Baker *et al.* (1977). They conducted a national survey of 314 community-based group care settings. Based on responses to their initial survey instrument, they identified 10 major "types" or frequently occurring profiles of facilities. This typology then served to organize their subsequent data collection efforts in which they visited 17 facilities that represented a sampling of these 10 different types. Their effort was commendable in that they were the first to describe systematically what day-to-day life was like in a wide range of community-based residential options. Their typology, shown in Table II, was based on a few straightfor-

TABLE II
Example of a Typological Classification Scheme[a]

Category	Description
1. Small group home	Serves 10 or fewer retarded adults
2. Medium group home	Serves 11–20 retarded adults
3. Large group home	Serves 21–40 retarded adults
4. Mini-institution	Serves 41–80 retarded adults
5. Mixed group home	Serves both retarded adults and other types of clients, usually former mental hospital patients or ex-offenders
6. Group homes for older adults	Often serves retarded and other elderly individuals
7. Foster family care	Serves 5 or fewer retarded adults in a family's own home
8. Sheltered village	Involves a segregated and self-contained community, usually in a rural setting, for retarded adults and has live-in staff
9. Workshop dormitory	Has a vocational program linked administratively and usually physically to the residential program
10. Semi-independent unit	Provides less than 24-hour supervision for retarded adults

[a]From Baker, Seltzer, & Seltzer (1977).

ward, objective characteristics. The typology was not generated by uniformly assessing the same descriptive features, but rather involved naturally occurring combinations of variables—size, age group of clients, autonomy of facility, staffing pattern, and purpose. This typology, in fact, does not permit categorizing all community residences (e.g., congregate care facilities that serve more than 80 residents) and the categories are not strictly exclusive (e.g., some sheltered villages or workshop dormitories could qualify also as mixed-group homes). Their typology served to highlight two important conclusions: first, that there were many diverse kinds of community group homes that varied initially in their clients, their philosophy, and their size; and second, sweeping generalizations could not be made about "quality of life" or about differential effects on residents attributable to type of home. Such typological classifications may serve to characterize existing environments, but they are especially vulnerable to changes in the service-delivery system and readily become outdated. Such schemes also are not ideally suited to analysis of the contribution of particular environmental variables to clients' development.

Evaluative classification schemes involve a set of a priori assumptions about quality of life. Individual facilities then are grouped on this basis. For example, Butler and Bjaanes (1977) classified facilities into three types: therapeutic, maintaining, or custodial. They assumed that four key variables differentiated residential environments into the above categories: (1) presence of habilitation programs, (2) degree of community contact, (3) activity level within the facility, and (4) intensity of caretaker involvement with residents. In this typology, places are judged to be therapeutic *if* they have vigorous training programs, frequent community contact, high activity levels, and very committed caretakers. In contrast, custodial programs are low in all four areas, providing no habilitiation programs, no community contact, extremely low activity levels, and minimal caretaker involvement. Butler and Bjaanes' central theorem is that client outcome is directly related to these variables. Although the explicitness of the model is admirable, it contains two major flaws. The first is that most residential facilities will not fit neatly into one of the three categories. That is, residential programs typically have an uneven distribution of strengths and weaknesses. Their model assumes an integrated program that does very well, average, or poorly in all four areas, and the areas are not differentially weighted for guiding decisions about classifying a particular residence. Moreover, one or more of these four variables easily can change (e.g., staff turnover can alter the degree of staff–resident involvement, changes in funding could affect the provision of active habilitation services). Would such a change mean that the facility would have to be classified as a different "type?" Another problem is that the standards for judging whether a habilitation program is "intensive," "minimal," or nonexistent are subject to constant revision and dispute. Accordingly, a facility judged to be therapeutic by one set of standards may qualify only as "maintaining" by another set. In fact, today's institutions judged "custodial" would have appeared quite active, stimulating, and habilitative by the standards of the mid-1950s (Berkson & Landesman-Dwyer, 1977). The second, perhaps more serious, flaw is that this typology relies on a directional premise that the more intensive each of these four variables is, the better the program will be for the residents. This premise is testable, of course, but an a priori evaluative labeling creates a situation in which "therapeutic" homes may *not* be "therapeutic" by independent (outcome) criteria.

The use of administratively defined categories is by far the most common, and examples of the problems associated with these were provided earlier. This classification method requires only that residential settings be sorted according to some criteria used by the current service-delivery system. Even if the actual procedures used by the service system result in incorrect or inconsistent labeling of environments, the user of such an administratively determined system need not care. The objective is simply to describe or compare places that have different labels, regardless of the source of such labeling. A quick review of the residential categories used by different states reveals tremendous differences in how facilities are labeled, licensed, funded, and monitored. Even more striking is the evidence that, within a given state, the criteria used to identify residential settings may not be consistent, but instead represent a diverse set of historically differentiated programs, federally funded programs, and new or innovative state and local programs. To understand why the various residential categories came into existence, who these facilities serve, and what the distinguishing structural or functional features of such programs are, extensive investigation is required. Few states have a succinct, up-to-date listing and description of all their residential environments.

These three types of classification strategies each serve different purposes and undoubtedly will continue to exist in various forms. Each is atheoretical and in some ways constrains opportunities for scientifically studying the impact environments have on individuals, groups, or society. Another kind of classification—based on explicit theoretical assumptions about the structural and functional features of environments and how they are perceived—is proposed below.

V. A CONCEPTUAL FRAMEWORK FOR STUDYING AND CLASSIFYING HOME ENVIRONMENTS

As an alternative to existing classification approaches, a conceptually based strategy for classifying environments is proposed. Because the model is new and presented for the first time in this chapter, many details and precise relationships are yet to be specified. The typology is presented to illustrate a theoretically guided typology of home environments and to encourage other investigators to consider systematic inquiry using this typology. The assumptions and hypotheses of the typology may be tested formally and subsequent modifications and elaboration of the model may occur.

In creating this typology, there were four major tasks. The first was to consider the types of taxonomic principles to be incorporated in the model. In what ways would the choice about the categorization scheme serve to influence the range and kind of person–environment principles to be explored? How much detail should be included in the initial categorization of homes? Second, all basic assumptions considered relevant and important for classifying home environments needed to be specified. Even the concept "home" needed defining. Third, pragmatic issues and procedures available to classify homes had to be reviewed. The categorical system originally envisioned could not be applied easily because a few key variables could not be measured in a straightforward, valid, or reliable way. In developing this classification approach, I repeatedly questioned "Is this typology practically useful?" A theoretically elegant scheme that demands too much of users is likely to remain an academic exercise. Fourth, the preliminary answers and available data had to be organized in a single, cohesive, and explicated framework. These steps will now be reviewed task by task. Here it is—task by task.

A. Task 1: Preliminary Decisions about Taxonomic Principles and Format

Classification clearly involves a number of levels, starting with the first non-technical recognition that an element potentially belongs to a broader class, which in turn may be subsumed by higher order (subordinated) groupings or may be keyed by an array of descriptive characteristics. *Hierarchical schemes* are the most familiar to us and there is much interest in "hierarchy theory" as a means of understanding complex systems (Pattee, 1973) in their own right. A truly hierarchical system incorporates decisions about which dimensions assume priority over others. The principles governing hierarchical systems should be theoretical (external to the system), sometimes presuming to reflect natural arrangements. In contrast, a *taxonomic key* is a systematic framework made up of a sequence of classes at each level, which may be combined (overlapped) to create more restricted classes at the next higher level. A key does not involve the same theoretical assumptions about priorities among the classes or descriptive features. Keys thus lend themselves to alternative forms of diagramming, to underscore variables of interest for specified levels of analysis. In fact, keys can be arranged to look remarkably similar to formal hierarchies. Taxonomic approaches need not be pure—that is, a classification scheme can be mixed, containing some hierarchical features and other arbitrarily arrayed dimensions judged important for identifying or distinguishing individual elements.

In the home classification system proposed, a *mixed model* is used that assigns primary significance to four variables—etiology (how the home came into existence), major purpose or goals, anticipated duration (short- versus long-term home), and the nature of the relationships among home members/participants. Some of these variables are suitable for hierarchical arrangement, while others are easier to conceptualize as descriptor variables of equal importance for classification. The categories can be further subdivided if and when more detailed structural and functional data are available about the homes. The ideal is that any given home could be correctly and stably classified (i.e., named), even though a considerable range of expression will exist within a given home type.

A general taxonomic issue concerns how much and what types of data to include in classifying, consistent with the rationale for developing a given classification scheme. Concerning the classification of home environments, especially those serving special needs populations, a primary objective is to facilitate understanding the effects of different environments on different types of individuals. Given this objective, it is extremely important that the consequences of a home environment (i.e., the outcome data) *not* be included in the initial classification. Similarly, the developmental and psychological status of the individuals within a home should *not* be included in classifying the home for two reasons. First, this would constrain scientific inquiry about person–environment interaction since the initial classification of environments would include person-specific characteristics and thus not permit comparing how different types of individuals respond to similar types of homes. Although in practice there will be some types of homes that tend to serve only certain kinds of persons, this should not be elevated to a taxonomically prescribed category. Second, many individual characteristics theoretically may change as a function of environmental conditions; accordingly, to use such changeable variables as a basis for classifying a home would mean that homes would be subject to frequent reclassification *because* of the effects they have on home members. In such a situation, longitudinal evaluation of outcomes would be aborted or confounded hopelessly.

B.   Task 2: Set Delineation and Formulation of Basic Assumptions about Elements

What is "home"? Home represents a broad category or class of environments. O'Connor (1976) titled her report of a national survey of community residential facilities *Home is a Good Place*. This captures two essential features of homes. First, homes are places, circumscribed in space. Second, homes inherently are charged with emotional and social significance—the kind that leads us to say "a house does not make a home" and "home is where the heart is." This important personal connotation of homes is reflected in O'Connor's choice of the adjective "good" to convey her conclusion that most of the new, community-based living arrangements offered something positive for many mentally retarded individuals who were leaving large public institutions. In addition to these two characteristics, homes may be distinguished from other types of environments by their intended purpose: to be the primary source for an individual's board and care, often coupled with providing protection and security (both physical and psychological). Ironically, home simultaneously represents a place away from the rest of the world and yet is an inseparable part of our everyday worlds.

Although homes vary in their stability and the nature of the relationships among their occupants, they theoretically represent the most person-specific environments within a society. That is, the characteristics, needs, preferences, and behavior of the person(s) within a home are hypothesized to contribute relatively more influence on the home environment than they do on other places. Clearly, places such as schools, work settings, temporary domiciles (e.g., hotels, hospitals), recreational sites, and retail shops also make accommodations for and are altered in significant ways by their users. Nonetheless, homes are perceived by society's members to be the places that are "their very own," even though the actual distribution of control or decision-making within particular homes may be far from democratic and persons even can be "trapped" within their own homes.

At first glance, a definition of "home" may seem unnecessary or rather academic. Typically, investigators accept without question the premise that wherever someone lives is their home and simply do not discuss the concept of "home." The empirical literature in mental retardation represents a compilation of studies about residential facilities per se, regardless of the role of these environments in the actual lives of their occupants. In fact, the majority of people live in their homes most of the time, so that the distinction may appear trivial. Mentally retarded individuals, however, are more likely to be residing in exceptional or atypical situations. For instance, mentally retarded children in foster homes or even in group homes frequently continue to think of their parents' home, where they previously resided, as their "real" home, and the new care-providers often share this view (Landesman-Dwyer & Mai-Dalton, 1981; Landesman-Dwyer, Stein, & Sackett, 1976). Also, mentally retarded individuals often receive temporary respite care in established group care facilities, sometimes leading to longer term or permanent residence in those facilities. Furthermore, many residential programs require prospective residents to have a trial visit before making a placement decision. Accordingly, not all facilities that provide a bed and food can be considered equivalent "homes" for all occupants. This fact needs to be recognized when evaluating the impact of a facility on individuals.

If homes are more than houses, and not all houses are homes, then a number of related questions arise. For example: Where are the boundaries of "home?" Does everyone have a home at all times (since basic care needs have to be met somewhere), or can people be "homeless?" When home environments are described, should everyone and everything in contact with that home be considered part of the environment? Given the affective and personal nature of homes, does this mean that objective measurement of environmental variables will have little predictive validity for the adaptation and developmental outcome of residents? Can one house provide more than one kind of home for its residents? Can a person have more than one home (e.g., if a person's needs are met equally or distributively in two different places)? Can a particular home cease to be a home—and if so, what criteria determine this functional change in the primary nature of the environment? I do not intend to answer all these quetions definitively; rather, I hope to elucidate the centrality of such issues to the scientific study of home environments.

Although home is rarely defined operationally, the literature is replete with references to "homelike" environments. This phrase is used to convey the notion that a residence looks or functions like a "normal" single-family home— the conceptual prototype within our society. Although this subjective judgment may be important for some purposes, investigators rarely have comparative data regarding natural family habitats. Moreover, there is substantial evidence that the nuclear family model—a stable arrangement involving mother, father, and their biological children residing in their own domicile—is less prevalent than in the past, with an increasing diversity of social groupings and physical arrangements representing "homes" for the general population (*Household and Family Characteristics,* 1982). The important point is that there is neither widespread agreement about nor systematic basis for estimating how "homelike" a real home is. The problem is that standards for such judgments vary over time and across cultures. Without careful description of the qualities contributing to such global impressions, the term "homelike" remains elusive.

The current depiction of a residential facility as "homelike" seems to connote that it fosters all the good things that good family homes do. There is a pervasive belief (Flynn, 1980; Wolfensberger, Nirje, Olshansky, Perske, & Roos, 1972) that what is typical for and/or appealing to most citizens will be what is best for mentally retarded citizens. This belief is reflected, for instance, in a chapter advising attorneys who represent institutionalized mentally retarded persons: "The lawyer can safely and profitably start from the rebuttable presumption that things that he or she would find disagreeable or unpleasant will have the same effect on the client" (Luckasson & Ellis, 1983, p. 51). This premise has *not* been verified scientifically; to the contrary, there is evidence that individual response differences and preferences are substantial (Baker *et al.,* 1977; Gunzburg & Gunzburg, 1973; Landesman-Dwyer, 1981). In fact, Suedfeld (1980) demonstrated that even some extremely restricted conditions (e.g., sensory deprivation) did not elicit universal affective responses: some people reported pleasurable sensations in settings that others described in extremely negative terms.

The concept of "home," as used here, is not associated with a priori notions of positive or negative value. The potential variety of homes—all of which are "homelike" in an absolute sense of the word—is vast. In particular, homes for mentally retarded children and adults continue to increase in number and diversity, representing a wide range of structural, organizational, social, emotional, and functional conditions. The correlates and consequences of these different kinds of homes warrant careful investigation. To achieve an understanding of person–environment interactions that transcends the description of individual cases, there must be meaningful ways to measure, identify, and classify residential facilities.

The formal delineation of the set "homes" starts with the following definition:

> A home is a physical place that constitutes a major residence for an individual, as perceived by that individual and by significant others who know the individual and as evidenced by patterns of daily behavior. The purpose of a primary residence is to provide a central place intended to offer personal, physical, and psychological support to the individual who lives there.

A number of important axioms derive from this definition, including the following: (1) it is possible for a person to have more than one home at a given time; (2) a person may reside at a place other than his/her home (usually for relatively brief periods of time); (3) some individuals may be truly "homeless," even if they sleep in the same physical environment over a period of time. *To delineate whether a place qualifies for inclusion in the set of "homes," a person-specific evaluation is critical.* That is, a particular physical place may be home to some but not all of the people who sleep or eat there. In fact, a place may be the "home" to someone who at the moment does not actually sleep or eat on the premises. Alternatively, just saying or feeling that a place is one's home does not make it so. The proposed definition requires *both* objective evidence and subjective confirmation to establish that a place is actually a person's home. Objective evidence can include signs of primary residency and commitment such as location of physical possessions, the amount of time and type of resources an individual invests in a given physical environment, and the behavioral activities engaged in by those who reside in or enter a particular environment. Subjective data may be obtained directly from an individual and/or significant others in his/her life. Finally, it is important to note that a home is *not* required to succeed in its mission of providing primary nurturance, protection, and assistance—but rather must have this as its major functional goal or reason for existence.

ADDITIONAL ASSUMPTIONS
ABOUT HOME ENVIRONMENTS

The most fundamental assumptions about all human environments, discussed earlier, include the interdependence and inseparability between people and places, their multidimensionality—as reflected in analysis of diverse features and multiple levels, their dynamic nature, the potential differences between objective features and perceived (subjective) dimensions, and the fact that environments have a holistic quality that is more than the sum of their components.

The proposed model incorporates many other assumptions relevant to home environments per se. In this section, only assumptions central to the classification system (*after* a place has qualified as a home) are enumerated.

Assumption 1, Point of Origin: All homes have a specific beginning date when home members first established residency there and/or initiated functional activities consistent with the mission of the home.

Assumption 2, Path of Origin: Prior to origination, there are activities relevant to the type of home that will be created. This is referred to as path of origin or etiology of the home.

Assumption 3, Mission Identification: All homes will have identifiable missions, that is, a set of goals, purposes, or demands related to their existence. The ease of identifying a home's mission is expected to differ significantly across individual homes and does not have to be formulated clearly by all home members.

Assumption 4, Within-Home Mission Variation: Within a given home, variation in mission (goals) can exist in the following forms: (1) shifts over time as a function of changes in home members and their characteristics, (2) changes in amount and type of physical and social resources available to the home, and (3) differences in how members of the home perceive their mission.

Assumption 5, Anticipated Duration: All homes can be characterized in terms of their expected duration of association among home members. This feature is not assumed to be isomorphic with actual longevity.

Assumption 6, Structural Social Arrangement: All homes have a structural arrangement of home members. Although there are many important descriptive features of the structural social arrangement of a home, the minimal elements needed for correct classification are (1) the number of individuals who are part of the home unit, and (2) the number of individuals assuming primary responsibility in achieving the home's mission—which may include home members, those involved in home management day-to-day activities who may not live there (referred to as participants), or both home members and participants.

An example of another social structural feature hypothesized to influence the functioning of a home, but not used for initial classification, is the heterogeneity of the home members in terms of age, sex ratio, developmental competencies, supervisory needs, and prior residential experiences. A variable such as this concerns the comparative arrangement of collected individual characteristics rather than a mere listing of personal variables.

Assumption 7, Primacy of Functional Style: Each home has a distinctive functional style, which by its nature is complex and multidimensional. Because functional style is hypothesized to reflect direct influences of individual home members, home mission, and resources available to the home, as well as many indirect effects from outside the home, functional style changes considerably over time, settings, or individuals. Despite inherent complexity, homes are assumed to have a highly salient and dominant functional style—i.e., primacy of functional style—that transcends these expected variations. To determine the primary functional style, data from three sources are useful: (1) direct observation of activities in the home, (2) direct questioning of home members or home participants, and (3) independent confirmation from objective evidence of implementation of functional style in the home environment. Because this variable may be conceptualized and analyzed at so many levels (refer to the substantial psychological and sociological literature related to families and parenting styles, group behavior and leadership, and management of organizations), this will not be discussed in detail here. Rather, this assumption underscores the fact that some explicit conceptualization of functional style is necessary for more refined classification. A preliminary differentiation is proposed based on degree of authoritarianism and location of functional control, because this serves to distinguish many existing types of homes for mentally retarded individuals. This does not imply, however, that these functional style variables are the most salient or influential ones within a given home.

Assumption 8, Significance of Assumptions 1–7: The above assumptions concern all homes. The variables identified are hypothesized to affect everyday behavior and activities within the home, the relationship of the home to the outside, the perceptions and attitudes of home members and participants, and the developmental progress or behavioral changes of home members and participants over time. Collectively, these home variables represent the minimal data set needed to categorize a particular home.

C. Task 3: How to Use Assumptions in Developing Grouping and Identification Procedures

Because the variables identified above are hypothesized to exert a significant influence on the functioning of a home, they were assigned a central role in the development of the present classification system. Many other variables, however, are potentially as important as these in affecting the functioning of a home. The typology has been designed so that additional descriptive features and further subdivisions within the general types of homes can occur. A primary consideration in creating this typology was to have a system that was simple and could be applied to individual homes prior to conducting an in-depth evaluation or studying differential outcomes on those who live in a home. The typology also was intended to generate some recognizable classes of homes (e.g., adoptive homes, nuclear families, group homes with shifts of staff, institutions) based on a common core of dimensions, while not necessarily being limited to only those types of homes that have been studied or currently exist. More importantly, the proposed categories relate to a conceptual model of human adaptation to environments.

CONCEPTUAL MODEL

The conceptual model guiding the proposed categorization is adapted from a general ecological theory that views behavior as an adaptive response shaped by the demands of the environment, the resources available within the environment, and the behavioral repertoire and personal response tendencies of the individual. An individual's behavioral repertoire (adaptive behavior skills) and personal response tendencies are considered the product of both learning and maturation, given the initial and ongoing presence of significant individual biobehavioral differences (attributable to genetic, prenatal, disease and trauma, medical treatment, and individual variables). This model of individual behavior has been expanded here to home environments, such that the home becomes the single unit of analysis, analogous to the individual, and the term "functioning" is used interchangeably with "behavior."

The functioning of a home can be assessed from multiple perspectives and includes both observable activities (objective behavioral data) and subjective experiences (e.g., perceptions, thoughts, emotions, satisfaction) of home members and participants. In addition to the actual activities and experiences that occur in particular homes (i.e., functional content), homes may be characterized in terms of metafunctional characteristics, such as their complexity (e.g., range and diversity of activities of individuals and the group, similarity of behavior and experiences among home members), sensitivity to environmental change (e.g., as evidenced by changes in patterns of activity and/or experiences), and consistency over time and situations. The relative significance of functional content versus metafunctional characteristics is not known, but findings from systematic inquiry about this issue may inform later modifications in the classification scheme. Theoretically, certain types of homes could be inextricably linked with certain functional patterns, but this has yet to be explored systematically.

Homes are hypothesized to differ significantly as a function of how they were created (origin), their projected permanency (anticipated duration), the reasons for their existence (home mission), and their social composition (social structure). As discussed earlier, simple causal directionality cannot be inferred from such variation because of the fundamental interdependency between people and the environments in which they live. Longitudinal and comparative studies, however, permit assessing the relative contribution of these environmental variables to different functional patterns.

In the proposed conceptual model, the *origin of a home* is hypothesized to matter largely because society has markedly different expectations (demands) and provides different patterns of support (resources) depending on how a home originated. Homes are distinguished first by whether the decision to create the home was made by the members (natural or internal origin) or by nonmembers (external origin). Within natural homes, there are families and nonfamilies. A *family* is the natural social unit in which at least one member assumes primary responsibility for providing an environment conducive to development of children and/or individuals whose functional status is childlike or dependent. In families, the relationship of an individual to the other home members may be biological, adoptive, or mixed (e.g., living with a biological parent, a step-parent, and step-siblings). A *naturally originating nonfamily* includes peer groups as well as mutual helping arrangements (e.g., home members who exchange services and/or resources to their mutual, though not necessarily equal, benefit). *Externally originated homes* include almost all public and private residential facilities that are sponsored by societal agencies, regardless of source of funding or monitoring responsibility. An extremely important feature of the origin of these homes is whether home members and participants have control over who lives and participates in their home. The original decision is considered theoretically important because it directly influences the home members and participants by altering their ability to control the home's social composition, demands, and resources in ways that they expect to maximize achieving their goals. To the extent that initial control is exerted by those responsible for the home's functioning versus outsiders, variation might be expected in adaptive responses.

A home's *anticipated duration* is hypothesized to affect the behavior of home members and participants by altering motivation, expectations, and the actual demands to resolve certain problems or to establish particular kinds of emotional ties among home members. Homes sometimes are acknowledged to be time limited, such as a home associated with schooling in a particular locale or a home that provides highly specialized treatment or training. Because there is no theoretical basis as yet for grouping units of time, nor a method to estimate the exact number of years most individuals expect to live in their homes, a somewhat loose distinction is proposed between long- and short-term. Usually, a short-term home ends when an individual achieves certain developmental milestones (e.g., reaching adult or independent status within a few years, graduating from a school) or when alternative residential options become available (e.g., the opening of new buildings or programs for which home members will be eligible). A long-term home is one where residents may expect to live for many years, whether in fact this happens or not. Note that a long-term home does not imply in any way that home members have less ambitious expectations regarding the amount or timing of their own personal development, compared to those in short-term homes. A tentative guideline is that a place anticipated to be someone's home for 5 or more years is considered long term.

Determining a home's *mission emphasis* is not easy, especially because there may not be a clear consensus of goals or an explicit recognition of goals by home members. For the present purposes, only broad missions have been identified. These are presumed to capture global aspects of a home's mission, focusing on the areas *most* valued by the majority of those who live or participate in the home. It is well recognized that homes with a similar global mission may differ vastly in their zeal and strategies to realize their goals. Nonetheless, even these broad purposes are expected to influence many daily choices and behavioral patterns within the home, as well as the allocation of physical resources. The four primary mission emphases included here are (1) basic care provision, (2) emotional and social support, (3) educational (i.e., developmental training or active habilitation,) and (4) combined social and educational. The latter three missions do not imply that basic care needs are not valued, but rather that the other goals receive relatively more attention within the home.

Finally, the *social structure* of a home is hypothesized to exert a direct effect on the demands within the home and the social resources available to meet those demands. The key features of social structure traditionally include the number of individuals and their relational roles to one another. In the present typology, the number and ratio of independent and dependent home members and participants (i.e., those who are involved in a home's regular activities but do not consider the place to be their own home) are considered. Independent status is assigned to individuals (usually adults) who assume an active role in fulfilling the home's mission, while dependent status is reserved for children and for adults who actively require assistance in many areas of daily functioning. Although determining the exact degree of dependency (or developmental status) for each home member and/or participant requires current assessment of each individual, generally a dichotomous categorization—independent versus dependent (e.g., parents versus children, staff versus clients who need supervision/habilitation)—can be made in advance. In this preliminary typology, this variable remains a descriptive or qualifier variable to help further identify the type of home, such as indicating the home has two parents and one child or has four staff members and six residents. Table III summarizes the major definitions and assumptions discussed thus far.

TABLE III
Summary of Definitions and Assumptions about Home Environments Relevant to Proposed Classification

A. Basic assumptions about human environments
  1. Human environments do not exist apart from human beings; thus, many environmental and individual variables are fundamentally confounded.
  2. Environments may be described and analyzed at many different levels.
  3. Environments include many diverse features and elements, which may exert independent and interactive effects.
  4. Environments are dynamic, not static.
  5. Environments may be evaluated in both objective and subjective terms.
  6. Environments are responded to as a whole (as well as to their many separate features).
B. Criteria for identifying an individual's home
  1. A physical place that is identified as the person's major residence
    a. By the individual (or his/her representative)
    b. By significant others in the individual's life
    c. By behavioral and/or physical signs of activity
  2. A place that is intended to provide personal, physical, and psychological support to the individual(s) living there
C. Initial assumptions about home environments
  1. Homes have a point of origin
  2. Homes have identifiable paths of origin (etiology)
  3. Homes are distinguished by their primary mission (most valued goals)
  4. Aspects of a home's mission may vary with time, conditions, people
  5. Homes have an anticipated duration (expected end)
  6. Homes are identifiable by the structural social arrangement of members
  7. Homes have distinctive functional styles, inherently complex and related to environmental and individual variables operating within and outside the home

(continued)

TABLE III *(continued)*

8. All of the above features exert a significant effect on functioning within a home
D. Definitions of keyed variables and terms in classification scheme
   1. Home member: someone residing in a place that meets the criteria for his or her home
   2. Home participant: someone who is actively involved in regular activities of a place that meets home criteria for others but not for him or her (e.g., live-in or live-out staff member, volunteer, nonresident parent of home member)
   3. Terms related to types of home origins
      a. Natural (internal) origin: one or more home members decided to establish home
      b. External origin: nonhome individual(s) or agency decided to establish home
      c. Family home: a home for a naturally originating social unit where at least one home member is designated to have major responsibility for achieving home's mission as related to at least one child or dependent member who is related (either biologically or adoptively)
      d. Foster family: social unit (internal or external origin) with a target person(s) who is *not* related to the other(s) for whom the place qualifies as a type of family home
   4. Anticipated home durations
      a. Short-term: end expected based on changes in the person(s), the external environment, or a combination, usually in less than a 5-year period
      b. Long-term: end not planned in near future (usually more than 5-year period). Note that the major change attributable to making the transition from childhood to adulthood does not preclude a home from being long term.
   5. Types of home mission emphasis (may vary in amount and expressed form even within each type)
      a. Care providing: major focus is on the physical health, safety, well-being of home members (i.e., meeting room, board, and everyday self-care needs)
      b. Social and emotional support: primary goals center on providing social opportunities and emotional support (e.g., love, affection, encouragement) to home members
      c. Educational support: the most valued mission is that of teaching skills to home members that will increase their potential for independent functioning both within and outside the home. A developmental training or habilitation model often characterizes homes with this mission.
      d. Combined social–educational: an equal commitment is displayed to social/emotional goals and to developmental/habilitative ones

D. Task 4: Proposed Layout of Classification Scheme

The definition of a home delineates the scope of the set. A somewhat unusual feature of this classification scheme is that the *determination of home type is always done on an individual basis*. This means that a given physical place cannot be assumed to provide exactly the same type of home for everyone who lives there. Obvious examples include a place that is a foster home to one child, but a biological family home to another; a place that is a respite (short-term) training home for a person recovering from a traumatic injury, but a long-term board-and-care home for others who live there; and a public institutional setting that seeks to provide active social and educational support for some residents, but not for others. Recognition of this fundamental aspect in the classification of home environments is critical to its appropriate theoretical use. An environment that does not qualify as a "home" for an individual is not hypothesized to exert comparable effects to an objectively identical environment that is a "home."

Table IV illustrates, in part, the way in which these proposed dimensions of home environments could be arranged to generate distinctive categories of homes. The categories presented do not even begin to represent the universe of possible combinations of the variables selected. Many existing homes, however, where mentally retarded individuals live fit unambiguously into the categories singled out. Some traditional terms, such as institutions and community-based group homes, are avoided, largely because of their historical connotations and their failure to emphasize environmental variables that are hypothesized to be important on the basis of available research findings, theory, or both.

Note again that the actual ability of individuals residing in homes and their ages and their medical needs are not considered in the initial classification, unlike most other administratively determined or user-specific systems available. This is because there appears to be no sound theoretical basis for such groupings. Moreover, such typologies necessitate relabeling simply when residents become older or alter their developmental competencies or change health status. Certainly, this does not happen for natural families. Including the primary mission of facilities, however, as an initial sorting variable does help differentiate which aspects of the home environment have assumed a central role in a given place— leading to distinctions among nursing-type or room-and-board facilities that focus mostly on caretaking functions, more active habilitation-oriented homes, and homes that emphasize providing a warm and supportive environment more than the mastery of new skills toward independence, etc.

At this stage, I propose that other investigators consider using these environmental variables uniformly to describe and to categorize the homes they study. A few words of caution: this categorization focuses on homes as defined earlier. Presently, there are residential facilities where mentally retarded individuals live that do *not* qualify as homes for all mentally retarded individuals who sleep and eat there. Presently, I am applying this classification scheme to data gathered from several independent studies of mentally retarded individuals in a wide variety of residential settings, comparing the conclusions to those derived when using the administratively determined categories (that is, the state's labels for these facilities). One comparison indicated that nearly 30% of the facilities *within* an administratively determined category could be classified quite differently when considering the actual mission and locus of control for the individual homes. Also, this classification leads to a situation in which a traditional institution is divided into subunits that may represent different types of homes and some subunits that may not qualify as homes at all. Such an empirically based

TABLE IV
ILLUSTRATED (PARTIAL) APPLICATION OF HOME CATEGORIZATION
ACCORDING TO PROPOSED CONCEPTUAL MODEL[a]

1. NATURAL (INTERNAL) ORIGIN HOMES
11. NATURAL ORIGIN FAMILY HOMES
  111. Biological family homes
    111.1. Long-term (stable) biological family homes
      111.1.1. with caretaking emphasis
      111.1.2. with social–emotional support emphasis
      111.1.3. with educational emphasis
      111.1.4. with combined social and educational emphasis
    111.2. Short-term (transitional) biological family homes
      111.2.1. Same as above
      111.2.2. Same as above
      111.2.3. Same as above
      111.2.4. Same as above
  112. Adoptive family homes
    (All further subtypes same as above)
  113. Mixed-relation family homes (mix must be specified, may include foster home)
    (Same as above)

Note: Family homes are *not* further divided here by locus of control, because it is rare that a natural origin family home does not control the primary functional activities to achieve its mission. There are exceptions, however, including natural-origin families convicted of child neglect or abuse and under court-mandated compliance with outside agency and natural-origin families living in a communal society where responsible adults do not make independent decisions about daily home functioning

12. NATURAL ORIGIN NONFAMILY HOMES
  121. Peer group homes, internal locus of control (mutual support)
    (Same as above)
  122. Peer group homes, external locus of control (outside support)
    (Same as above)
  123. Supervised group (i.e., a priori differentiation of independent versus dependent status of home members), internal control
    (Same as above)
  124. Supervised group, external control
    (Same as above)

2. EXTERNAL ORIGIN HOMES
21. EXTERNAL ORIGIN FOSTER FAMILY HOMES
  211. Formal foster family homes, external control (refers to control over placement, standards, and monitoring of home, as in foster placements arranged by external agencies)
    (Same as above)
  212. Informal foster family homes, internal control (ie., not sponsored by external agency)
    (Same as above)

(continued)

TABLE IV (*continued*)

---

22. EXTERNAL ORIGIN NONFAMILY HOMES

    221. Peer group homes, internal control
        (Same as above)
    222. Peer group homes, external control
        (same as above)
    223. Supervised homes, internal control
        (Same as above)
    224. Supervised homes, external control
        (Same as above)

Note: External-origin family homes are not identified here, because of rarity. Even an unusual possibility such as that of a surrogate mother who carried and delivered a baby for others, but who at a later time lives with her biological child in a family home could not be considered "external origin," because the subsequent decision to mother the child would have been an internal (self-chosen) one

---

[a]To conserve space, shorthand references are used to identify subtypes previously listed.

---

classification system may help unravel which environmental variables within traditionally established public institutions lead to negative outcome and which may serve to buffer such effects or to promote positive outcomes. Additional study of the day-to-day patterns of activity and their distinctiveness as a function of the various home types is needed.

VI. SUMMARY

A preliminary approach to classifying home environments has been presented to illustrate the issues that must be addressed in creating a theory-based method for identifying and studying home environments. Assumptions about the nature of person–environment interactions and universal characteristics of homes were listed and incorporated in the typology. Because this has not been tested empirically or used to make predictions about outcomes for mentally retarded individuals, the scientific and practical utility of the typology cannot yet be evaluated. There are a number of important topics relevant to the use of this ecological model in conducting prospective studies, which are discussed by Landesman-Dwyer and Knowles (1986) elsewhere. These include formulation within the model of three broad categories of "effects" that can be measured in studying home environments: (1) direct versus indirect effects, (2) immediate versus long-term effects, and (3) qualitative versus quantitative effects.

The potential value of systematic description, relying on a common and operationally defined set of terms to describe features of residential environments, and standard classification of the homes for mentally retarded individuals were discussed. The conclusion was straightforward: without an increase in the use of objective and standardized means for selecting, categorizing, describing, and evaluating residential environments, our scientific knowledge base for understanding the ways in which home environments influence the development of individuals and the behavior of groups will remain extremely limited. The challenge is not a trivial one, and the disorder in the research literature and the service-delivery system is considerable. The most positive note I could find to keep me struggling with this challenge, and to encourage other investigators to think seriously about taxonomy (the science of classifying), comes from the man whose own dedication to taxonomy contributed immensely to zoology:

It is not a real contradiction that the most creative scientists are frequently just those not only willing to accept the existence of disorder but also positively attracted to it. The evident reason is that the recognition of disorder is an opportunity and in fact a necessary preliminary for the creative act of ordering. [Simpson, 1961, p. 5]

REFERENCES

Apolloni, T., Cappuccilli, J., & Cooke, T. P. (Eds.). (1980). *Achievements in residential services for persons with disabilities: Toward excellence.* Baltimore: University Park Press.

Bakeman, R. (1978). Untangling streams of behavior: A sequential analysis of observation data. In G. P. Sackett (Ed.), *Observing behavior: Vol. 2. Data collection and analysis methods.* Baltimore: University Park Press.

Baker, B. L., Seltzer, G. B., & Seltzer, M. M. (1977). *As close as possible: Community residences for retarded adults.* Boston: Little, Brown.

Barker, R. G. (1968). *Ecological psychology.* Stanford, CA: Stanford University Press.

Berkson, G., & Landesman-Dwyer, S. (1977). Behavioral research on severe and profound mental retardation (1955–1974). *American Journal of Mental Deficiency,* **81,** 428–454.

Borthwick, S. A., Meyers, C. E., & Eyman, R. K. (1981). Comparative adaptive and maladaptive behavior of mentally retarded clients of five residential settings in three Western states. In R. H. Bruininks, C. E. Meyers, B. B. Sigford, & K. C. Lakin (Eds.), *Deinstitutionalization and community adjustment of mentally retarded people* (Monograph No. 4, pp. 351–359). Washington, DC: American Association on Mental Deficiency.

Bronfenbrenner, U. (1977). Toward an experimental ecology of human development. *American Psychologist,* **32,** 513–531.

Bruininks, R. H., Lakin, K. C., Mauber, F. A., Rotegard, L., Hill, B. K., & White, C. (1983). *Tables summarizing key data elements by type of facility in each state.* Unpublished correspondence, University of Minnesota, Center for Residential and Community Services, Minneapolis.

Bruininks, R. H., Meyers, C. E., Sigford, B. B., & Lakin, K. C. (Eds.). (1981). *Deinstitutionalization and community adjustment of mentally retarded people* (Monograph No. 4). Washington, DC: American Association on Mental Deficiency.

Butler, E. W., & Bjaanes, A. T. (1977). A typology of community care facilities and differential normalization outcomes. In P. Mittler (Eds.), *Research to practice in mental retardation: Vol. 1. Care and intervention* (pp. 337–347). Baltimore: University Park Press.

Butterfield, E. C. (1967). The role of environmental factors in the treatment of institutionalized mental retardates. In A. A. Baumeister (Ed.), *Mental retardation: Appraisal, education, and rehabilitation* (pp. 120–137). Chicago: Aldine.

Butterfield, E. C. (1985). The consequences of bias in studies of living arrangements for the mentally retarded. In D. Bricker & J. Filler (Eds.), *The severely mentally retarded: From research to practice.* Reston, VA: Council for Exceptional Children.

Center on Human Policy. (1979). *The community imperative: A refutation of all arguments in support of institutionalizing anybody because of mental retardation.* Syracuse, NY: Syracuse University.

Cronbach, L. J. (1975). Beyond the two disciplines of scientific psychology. *American Psychologist,* **30,** 116–127.

Everitt, B. (1980). *Cluster analysis* (2nd ed.). New York: Halsted.

Eyman, R. K., Borthwick, S. A., & Sheehy, N. (1986). A longitudinal study of foster care placement. In S. Landesman & P. Vietze (Eds.), *Living environments and mental retardation.* Washington, DC: American Association on Mental Deficiency. In press.

Ferleger, D., & Boyd, P. A. (1979). Anti-institutionalization: The promise of the Pennhurst Case. *Stanford Law Review,* **31,** 100–135.

Flynn, R. J. (1980). Normalization, PASS, and service quality assessment: How normalizing are current human services? In R. J. Flynn & K. E. Nitsch (Eds.), *Normalization, social integration, and community services* (pp. 323–359). Baltimore: University Park Press.

Gibson, J. J. (1979). *An ecological approach to visual perception.* Boston: Houghton Mifflin.

Gottman, J. M. (1981). *Time-series analysis: A comprehensive introduction for social scientists.* London: Cambridge University Press.

Grossman, H. J. (Ed.). (1983). *Classification in mental retardation.* Washington, DC: American Association on Mental Deficiency.

Gunzburg, H. C., & Gunzburg, A. L. (1973). *Mental handicap and physical environment: The application of an operational philosophy to planning.* London: Baillière.

Heal, L. W., Sigelman, C. K., & Switzky, H. N. (1978). Research on community residential alternatives for the mentally retarded. In N. R. Ellis (Ed.), *International review of research in mental retardation* (Vol. 9, pp. 209–249). New York: Academic Press.

Household and family characteristics. (1982). (Current Population Report: Population Characteristics Series P-20, No. 381). Washington, DC: U.S. Department of Commerce, Bureau of the Census.

Intagliata, J., Crosby, N., & Neider, L. (1981). Foster family care for mentally retarded people: A qualitative review. In R. H. Bruininks, C. E. Meyers, B. B. Sigford, & K. C. Lakin (Eds.), *Deinstitutionalization and community adjustment of mentally retarded people* (Monograph No. 4, pp. 233–259). Washington, DC: American Association on Mental Deficiency.

Ittelson, W. H. (1978). Environmental perception and urban experience. *Environment and Behavior,* **10,** 193–213.

Janicki, M. P. (1981). Personal growth and community residence environments: A review. In H. C. Haywood & J. R. Newbrough (Eds.), *Living environments for developmentally retarded persons.* Baltimore: University Park Press.

Landesman-Dwyer, S. (1981). Living in the community. *American Journal of Mental Deficiency,* **86,** 223–234.

Landesman-Dwyer, S. (1985). Describing and evaluating residential environments. In R. H. Bruininks & K. C. Lakin (Eds.), *Living and learning in the least restrictive environment* (pp. 185–196). Baltimore: Paul H. Brookes.

Landesman, S. (1986). The changing structure and function of institutions: A search for optimal group care environments. In S. Landesman & P. Vietze (Eds.), *Living environments and mental retardation.* Washington, DC: American Association on Mental Deficiency. In press.

Landesman-Dwyer, S., & Brown, T. R. (1976). *A method for subgrouping mentally retarded citizens on the basis of services needs.* Olympia, WA: Department of Social and Health Services.

Landesman-Dwyer, S., & Butterfield, G. (1983). *Specialized group homes: Evaluation of a new residential program.* Olympia, WA: Department of Social and Health Services.

Landesman-Dwyer, S., & Knowles, M. (1986). Ecological analysis of staff training in residential settings. In J. Hogg & P. J. Mittler (Eds.), *Issues in staff training in mental handicap.* London: Croom Helm. In press.

Landesman-Dwyer, S., & Mai-Dalton, R. (1981). *A statewide survey of individuals receiving Case Management Services for the Division of Developmental Disabilities.* Olympia, WA: Department of Social and Health Services.

Landesman-Dwyer, S., Stein, J. G., & Sackett, G. P. (1976). *Group homes for the mentally retarded: An ecological and behavioral study.* Olympia, WA: Department of Social and Health Services.

Landesman, S., & Vietze P. (Eds.). *Living environments and mental retardation.* Washington, D.C.: American Association on Mental Retardation. In press.

Leff, H. L., & Gordon, L. R. (1980). Environmental cognitive sets: A longitudinal study. *Environment and Behavior,* **12,** 291–328.

Lei, T., Nihira, L., Sheehy, N., & Meyers, C. E. (1981). A study of small family care for mentally retarded people. In R. H. Bruininks, C. E. Meyers, B. B. Sigford, & K. C. Lakin (Eds.), *Deinstitutionalization and community adjustment of mentally retarded people* (Monograph No. 4, pp. 265–281). Washington, DC: American Association on Mental Deficiency.

Lewin, K. (1935). *A dynamic theory of personality.* New York: McGraw-Hill.

Luckasson, R. A., & Ellis, J. W. (1983). Representing institutionalized mentally retarded persons. *Mental Disability Law Reporter,* **7.**

Magnusson, D. (1981a). Wanted: A psychology of situations. In D. Magnusson (Ed.), *Toward a psychology of situations: An interactional perspective* (pp. 9–32). Hillsdale, NJ: Erlbaum.

Magnusson, D. (1981b). *Toward a psychology of situations: An interactional perspective* (D. Magnusson, Ed.). Hillsdale, NJ: Erlbaum.

Mischel, W. (1977). The interaction of person and situation. In D. Magnusson & N. S. Endler (Eds.), *Personality at the crossroads: Current issues in interactional psychology* (pp. 333–352). Hillsdale, NJ: Erlbaum.

O'Connor, G. (1976). *Home is a good place: A national perspective of community residential facilities for developmentally disabled persons* (Monograph No. 2). Washington, DC: American Association on Mental Deficiency.

Pattee, H. H. (Ed.). (1973). *Hierarchy theory: The challenge of complex systems.* New York: Braziller.

Pervin, L. A., & Lewis, M. (Eds.). (1978). *Perspectives in interactional psychology.* New York: Plenum.

Rosenblum, L. A. (1978). The creation of a behavioral taxonomy. In G. P. Sackett (Ed.), *Observing behavior: Vol. 2. Data collection and analysis methods* (pp. 15–24). Baltimore: University Park Press.

Russell, J. A., & Ward, W. (1982). Environmental psychology. *Annual Review of Psychology,* **33,** 651–688.

Simpson, G. G. (1961). *Principles of animal taxonomy.* New York: Columbia University Press.

Stokols, D. (1978). Environmental psychology. *Annual Review of Psychology,* **29,** 253–295.

Stokols, D. (1982). Environmental psychology: A coming of age. In A. Kraut (Ed.), *G. Stanley Hall Lecture Series* (Vol. 2). Washington, DC: American Psychological Association.

Suedfeld, P. (1980). *Restricted environmental stimulation.* New York: Wiley.

Windle, C. (1962). Prognosis of mental subnormals. *American Journal of Mental Deficiency, Monograph Supplement,* **66,** 1–180.

Wolfensberger, W., Nirje, B., Olshansky, S., Perske, R., & Roos, P. (Eds.). (1972). *The principle of normalization in human services.* Toronto: National Institute on Mental Retardation.

Behavioral Treatment of the Sexually Deviant Behavior of Mentally Retarded Individuals

R. M. FOXX, R. G. BITTLE, D. R. BECHTEL, AND J. R. LIVESAY

ANNA MENTAL HEALTH AND DEVELOPMENTAL CENTER
ANNA, ILLINOIS 62906

I. INTRODUCTION

Despite the proliferation of behavioral treatments for mentally retarded individuals during the past two decades, their maladaptive sexual behavior has received little attention. Indeed, most of the research on the sexual behavior of mentally retarded individuals has been devoted to discovering how much they know and do sexually (Edmondson, McCombs, & Wish, 1979; Edmondson & Wish, 1975; Hall, Morris, & Barker, 1973; Timmers, DuCharme, & Jacob, 1981) rather than developing methods of treating aberrant sexual behaviors. In an effort to call attention to this problem, this article will critically review the existing behavioral literature on the treatment of maladaptive sexual behavior. Our review is limited to behavioral treatment since the results of traditional psychotherapy with mentally retarded individuals have been particularly poor (Kolvin, 1967).

The paper's first section deals with the various aberrant behaviors and their treatment. The behaviors include exhibitionism, fetishism, pedophilia, public masturbation, promiscuity, and trichophobia. Each study will be examined in terms of (1) the target behavior(s), (2) subject characteristics, (3) the treatment setting(s), (4) treatment duration and session length, (5) initial and long-term treatment effectiveness, and (6) the generalization of treatment effects. The second section evaluates the studies in terms of (1) independent variables, (2) dependent measures, (3) the experimental design, (4) subject/client descriptions, (5) follow-up and maintenance of effects, and (6) generalization effects. The final section offers some conclusions and recommendations for future research and practice.

INTERNATIONAL REVIEW OF RESEARCH IN
MENTAL RETARDATION, Vol. 14

II. BEHAVIORS TREATED

A. Exhibitionism

Exhibitionism is a condition in which a male exposes his genitals to involuntary female observers in socially unacceptable situations (Frazier, Campbell, Marshall, & Werner, 1975; Katchadourian & Lunde, 1975). Often the exhibitionist's source of gratification results from observing his victim's reaction, which is predictably surprise, fear, or disgust. The type of gratification varies: some exhibitionists experience ejaculation at the scene of exposure; others merely experience "psychic release"; and others become highly aroused and masturbate immediately afterward (Katchadourian & Lunde, 1975).

The first behavioral treatment of exhibitionism by "mentally retarded" individuals was reported by Fookes (1960; see also Table I). Although Fookes treated seven individuals in a series of case studies, only six were identified as possessing "below average intelligence." Unfortunately, not enough detail was provided to differentiate the results on the basis of diagnosis. Hence, all seven clients have been included in this review. All but one of the seven were habitual offenders and three had served prison sentences for exhibiting themselves. Five of the seven were described as being inhibited in normal sexual relationships. All seven were treated as hospital inpatients.

The treatment consisted of pairing "painful" faradic shock with the imagined and/or actual act of exhibitionism. The first two clients treated were required to attempt to visualize exposing themselves. The client then signaled to the therapist, who delivered a shock to the client's forearm. The other five clients were required to visualize and expose themselves and received shock for both. Daily 1-hour treatment sessions were conducted for the first 2 weeks. Thereafter, treatment sessions were conducted twice per week, then once per week, and finally once per month. As many as 500 shocks were delivered per session. Six of the seven cases were reported to be successes after an average treatment period of 5 months. Treatment success was defined as the unrefuted claim by the client that he had lost his desire to expose himself. The weakest effects were obtained for the two clients who were only required to imagine exposing themselves. One represented the only reported failure and the other's exhibitionism fluctuated over the next 2 years so that additional intensive treatment was required. The failure of these two individuals might be explained by the fact that the shock presentation was contingent on their imagining exposing themselves rather than on the actual act of exposure. Thus, their exhibitionism had never been paired with the delivery of shock.

Lutzker (1974) treated the "exhibitionism" of a 52-year-old institutionalized profoundly retarded man. The man was frequently observed to have his pants unzipped which allowed his penis to be exposed. On some occasions, his exposed penis was observed to be erect.

TABLE I
Behavioral Treatment of the Deviant Sexual Behavior of Mentally Retarded Individuals

Study	N	Clients' diagnosis and treatment setting	Target behavior and type of measurement	Experimental design	Type of treatment	Frequency and duration of treatment	Effectiveness (behavioral reduction)		Generalization
							Initial	Follow-up	
Fookes (1960)	7	"Below normal intelligence" (adults; inpatient)	Exhibitionism [self-report (R = N.R.)[a]]	Case study (B)	B = Contingent faradic shock	1/day for 2 wk 2/wk for 2 wk 1/wk for 1 mo 1/mo Average length: 5 mo	86% (A)[a]	71% Average length: 39.5 mo (A)	
Lutzker (1974)	1	Profoundly mentally retarded (52-yr-old male; ward)	Exhibitionism [frequency count (R = D)[a]]	ABCB	A = Baseline B = DRO[a] C = Extinction	4 hours/day 7 days/wk 46 days total	100% reduction after day 43 (D)	Maintained at 3 mo (D)	
Kolvin (1967)	1	"Intellectually dull" (14-yr-old male; outpatient)	Fetishism—women's clothes [self-report (R = N.R.)]	Case study (B)	B = Aversive imagery	2/day 7 in 3 wk	100% after 3 wk (A)	100% at 13 and 17 mo (A)	+ Increased prosocial behavior and maturity (A) + Absence of response generalization (A)
Shaw & Walker (1979)	1	Mildly mentally retarded (8-yr-old male; hospital and home)	Fetishism/foot fetish [latency (R = N.R.)]	AB	A = Baseline B = Relaxation training, reinforced relaxation	1/day for 3 days relaxation training 2/day for 3 days reinforced relaxation	100% after 1 wk (D)	Maintained at 18 mo (A)	+ Increased appropriate behavior (A) + Effects generalized to novel settings (A)
Rosenthal (1973)	1	Mildly mentally retarded [31-yr-old male; clinic outpatient (during period of incarceration)]	Pedophilia [self-report (R = N.R.)]	ABC	A = Baseline B = Fixed duration presentation of electric shock C = Variable duration presentation of electric shock	2 days/wk 4 months total 2 booster sessions 5 mo after treatment	Self-reported decrease in urges and imagery during phase 2 (A)	Maintained at 32 mo (A)	

(continued)

TABLE I (continued)

Study	N	Clients' diagnosis and treatment setting	Target behavior and type of measurement	Experimental design	Type of treatment	Frequency and duration of treatment	Effectiveness (behavioral reduction) Initial	Effectiveness (behavioral reduction) Follow-up	Generalization
Wong, Gaydos, & Fuqua (1982)	1	Mildly mentally retarded (31-yr-old male; group home)	Pedophilia—physical approaches to children [time sample (R = D)]	Multiple baseline across responses (AB)	A = Baseline B = Instruction and contingent confinement	2–3/wk 10 mo total	100% after third confinement (D)	Maintained at 3 mo (D)	+ Effects generalized (A)
Luiselli, Helfen, Pemberton, & Reisman (1977)	1	Mentally retarded (8-yr-old male; classroom)	Public masturbation [Frequency count (R = D)]	AB	A = Reinforcement B = Reinforcement and overcorrection procedure	36 min/school day 33 days total	100% after 9 days (D)	Maintained at 12 mo (D)	
Cook, Altman, Shaw, & Blaylock (1978)	1	Severely mentally retarded (7-yr-old male; classroom and home)	Public masturbation [Frequency count (R = D)]	Additive (ABC) and multiple baseline across settings	A = Slap hand B = Ignore C = Contingent squirt of lemon juice	7 days/wk (across home and school) 75 days total	Near 100% after 16 days (school) and 13 days (home) (D)	Maintained at 6 mo (D)	
Polvinale & Lutzker (1980)	1	Severely mentally retarded (13-yr-old male; classroom)	Public masturbation and aggressive sexual behavior	Additive (ABC) and multiple baseline across settings	A = Baseline B = DRO C = DRO and	2/day 32 days total	100% in C phase in about	Maintained at 6 mo (D)	+ Effects generalized to novel trainers (D)

294

Study	N	Subjects	Target behavior (measure)	Design	Treatment	Sessions/Duration	Outcome	Follow-up	Comments
			[frequency count (R = D)]		apology				
Barmann & Murray (1981)	1	Severely mentally retarded (14-yr-old male; classroom, school bus, and home)	Public masturbation [frequency count (R = D)]	Multiple baseline across settings (AB)	A = Baseline B = Facial screening	3/day at school 2/day on bus 3/day at home 20 days total	20 days (D)	90% or better in all treatment settings	Maintained at 6 mo	+ Staff expressed preference for procedure (A)
Anant (1968)	1	Mildly mentally retarded (20-yr-old female; institution)	Promiscuity [self-reports (R = NR)]	Case study (B)	Relaxation training, aversive imagery, daily practice	5/wk 2 wk total		Maintained at 8 mo (A)		
Dial (1968)	51	Mentally retarded (x̄ I.Q. = 64) (adult women; institution)	Promiscuity	Additive (ABC)	A = Baseline (regular program) B = Social Adjustment Training (required) C = Therapy Group (voluntary)	B = 1/wk for 24 wk C = 1/wk	Clinically significant reduction in readmissions for sexual misconduct			
Rivenq (1974)	1	Mildly mentally retarded (13-yr-old male; institution)	Trichophobia	AB	A = Baseline B = Systematic desensitization	6 sessions	Phobia eliminated after 4 sessions		+ Increased positive peer interaction and better sexual identity (A)

[a]Abbreviations: R, reliability; N.R., not reported; A, anecdotal; D, data-based; DRO, differential reinforcement of other behavior.

An ABCB design was employed that consisted of baseline (A), differential reinforcement of other behavior (DRO) (B), and extinction (C) conditions. Recording and intervention occurred during 2-hour sessions that were conducted daily on both the morning and afternoon shifts by the regular ward staff. Data were recorded using a momentary time-sampling technique in which a staff member would observe and record whether the client's penis was exposed at the end of 10-minute intervals signaled by an automatic buzzer. Presence or absence of an erection was not monitored.

During a 9-day baseline, the staff were instructed to interact with the client in their regular manner, which consisted of occasional social interaction (i.e., attention and hugs) independent of whether or not his penis was exposed. This condition was followed by the DRO program for 12 days. During this condition, staff provided social praise and hugs at the end of each 10-minute interval in which the target behavior had not occurred. If the client's penis was exposed, the staff were instructed to ignore him. A 4-day extinction condition followed in which no staff interaction followed the behavior. In the final condition, the DRO procedure was reimplemented for 21 days. This DRO program was not conducted systematically thereafter due to staff shortages. However, the staff did provide social praise and hugs after about every other interval, i.e., 20 minutes, provided that the target behavior had not occurred.

The initial DRO procedure reduced the target behavior to near zero within 7 days. During the extinction condition, there was an immediate increase in the rate of exhibiting behavior to a level higher than during baseline. The reimplementation of the DRO procedure rapidly reduced exhibiting to relatively low levels. However, there was more variability in the target behavior and the reduction of the behavior to zero took longer (about 17 days) than in the first DRO condition. A 3-week follow-up indicated that exhibiting remained at a zero level despite the use of the attenuated schedule of reinforcement.

B. Fetishism

Fetishism is the attachment of sexual interest to an inanimate object that serves as a substitute for the original object or person of sexual interest (Frazier et al., 1975; Katchadourian & Lunde, 1975). This sexual deviation is almost exclusively displayed by males (American Psychiatric Association, 1980; Frazier et al., 1975).

Two case studies have described the treatment of fetishism. In the earliest one, Kolvin (1967) utilized an "aversive imagery" procedure with a 14-year-old male who was described as "educationally backward" and in the "lowest stream" academically. The client was described as having a fetish since he felt compelled to run after a young woman wearing a skirt and put his hand under her clothes. He would then run away trembling with excitement and fear. He had been charged with indecent assault on three women.

Because of the client's limited verbal abilities, a traditional psychotherapeutic approach was eschewed for one involving the use of aversive imagery supplemented by simple psychosexual instruction. Unfortunately, no description of the content or method of this latter training was provided.

The client was treated as an outpatient during seven 30-minute sessions over a 3-week period. Because he reported that images of falling or looking down from great heights were very unpleasant, these images were selected to be the aversive stimuli during treatment.

The aversive imagery conditioning was conducted in a darkened room with the client relaxing on a couch in order to facilitate the imagery process. The client was instructed to visualize a scene that corresponded to a description read by the therapist that contained material associated with an arousing or precipitative event (e.g., an attractively dressed woman walking down the street). The therapist inferred when the client "was just becoming affectively excited" from the boy's motor activity, breathing, and expression. At that point the therapist introduced the aversive images in "a suggestive and vividly descriptive manner" in order to interrupt the client's deviant imagery and associate it with the unpleasant stimuli. One month after the treatment was completed "some reinforcement was administered," although no specific information was given.

Evaluation of the success of this program is predicated solely on anecdotal information since it was reported that the client reacted "immediately" and with "distaste" to the presentation of the aversive images within sessions and that he denied experiencing any further compulsive urges after treatment. The boy's mother also reported that he was less difficult, less inclined to sulk, and more manageable. A probation officer familiar with the client indicated "there was some evidence for a growing maturity." Follow-up at 13 and 17 months suggested no reoccurrence of the fetish behavior and that the client was working and apparently doing well.

Shaw and Walker (1979) utilized a relaxation program to eliminate the foot fetish of an 8-year-old mildly retarded male. Initially, physiological arousal was to be measured by the use of a penile plethysmograph. However, due to an equipment malfunction, the dependent measure was changed to the time from the point the client noticed a female therapist/model's bare feet until he began to masturbate. Female therapist/models were used to conduct *in vivo* sessions because the presentation of pictures and/or slides of women's feet had evoked no response from the client.

Because the client lived in a rural community, he was admitted to a pediatric hospital for treatment. The relaxation training was conducted utilizing audio tapes of basic relaxation techniques. The initial training sessions were conducted at bedtime to take advantage of natural fatigue and thereby ensure the client's acquisition of the relaxation response. Three measures of relaxation were employed: (1) the length of time following the beginning instructions until the client was relaxed, (2) how long he remained relaxed following the completion of the instructions, and (3) self-reports. The relaxation training was conducted for 3 days.

After the client learned the relaxation responses, he was exposed to a barefoot female therapist during structured sessions conducted twice per day for 3 days. Whenever the client began to approach the therapist's feet, the relaxation instructions were given. His successful attempts to relax were reinforced with candy and social praise. The number of times he was instructed to relax decreased from 27 in the first 50-minute session to 4 in the last treatment session. During a pretreatment assessment, response latency was 4.5 minutes; the posttreatment session was terminated after no response was observed after 10 minutes.

Following treatment, the client's mother conducted the overall program at home since she had observed all treatment sessions through a one-way mirror and had received instruction and supervised practice in how to conduct training. The authors monitored treatment progress via weekly phone contacts. At 6-, 12-, and 18-month follow-ups, the boy's family reported no reoccurrence of the target behavior and improvement in his overall behavior in other settings, e.g., school.

C. Pedophilia

Pedophilia is defined as the act or fantasy of using children (typically prepubescent) for sexual gratification (Katchadourian & Lunde, 1975). Almost all pedophiles are adults who know the victim, e.g., a relative, family friend, or neighbor (American Psychiatric Association, 1980). As many as 20% of all pedophiles have been reported to be mentally retarded (Gebhard, Gagnon, Pomeroy, & Christenson, 1965).

Two studies have treated pedophilia. Rosenthal (1973) described the treatment of an incarcerated mildly retarded 21-year-old male. The client was referred for faradic aversion therapy following his third arrest. Prior to treatment, the painful nature of the therapy was explained to the client, who subsequently discussed it with his attorney and probation officer. Both recommended treatment as preferable to further incarceration. A physical examination revealed no medical contraindications to the proposed therapy. The man was confined to the county jail except when he was brought to the therapist's office for treatment.

Because the man was quite anxious, deep muscle relaxation training was provided to ensure that he would remain calm before and between shock presentations. The arousing stimuli consisted of pictures showing "pretty little girls, most often in demure frocks, undergarments, or revealing sun and bathing costumes" (Rosenthal, 1973, p. 441). The dependent measure was response latency (i.e., the time between the stimulus presentation and the client signaling by a finger movement the onset of sexual arousal or imagined erotic contact with the child). Sessions usually lasted 2 hours, with as many as 50 shocks delivered per session. Twenty-six training sessions were conducted, usually twice per week, over a 4-month period.

An additive design was employed that consisted of a baseline followed by two treatment phases. All baseline response latencies were reported to be 1 second or less. During the first six sessions of treatment phase 1, shock intensity values were varied unpredictably from the lowest to the highest levels (none of which were specified). Shock duration also was varied from 1 to 6 seconds. Since little success was achieved, an attempt was made to increase the aversiveness of treatment by simultaneously pairing an unpleasant high-frequency tone delivered through earphones with the shock during the next three sessions. Shock intensity also was varied. Because this modification failed to increase latency of responding, the tone was eliminated and the highest intensity shock level was applied for about 7 seconds from sessions 10 to 15. The results from this phase suggested no "deviant imagery" during the shock program, although little change in responding or difficulty in attaining deviant images was noted.

In treatment phase 2, the intensity of shock was kept at the highest level, while shock duration was varied as a function of response latency. Thus, shock duration was increased when latencies decreased or remained constant, and decreased when latencies increased. The duration of shock ranged from 1 to 120 seconds, although durations of more than 30 seconds were rarely used.

A rapid increase in response latency was reported, such that within ten sessions the client spontaneously began reporting an inability to attain deviant imagery or impulses in the presence of the stimulus items. Shortly thereafter treatment was discontinued and the client was discharged from prison and placed on a trial probationary period. Two booster sessions were conducted 5 months after treatment. The median response latency during these sessions was 115.5 seconds, or 17 times greater than those obtained during treatment phase 2. The client continued to state that he was unable to achieve deviant imagery or impulses. Periodic follow-ups over 32 months suggested the absence of both pedophilic images and behavior.

Wong, Gaydos, and Fuqua (1982) dealt with pedophilia much differently. Their subject was a 31-year-old mildly retarded male living in a group home. Although never incarcerated, the client had been placed in a state institution because of an alleged sexual molestation of a young girl. Shortly before he was referred for treatment, he had been repeatedly accused of molesting children near the group home. The group home staff had been informed by the police that any further complaints against this client could probably result in his permanent confinement to an institution.

A multiple baseline design across responses was employed to assess the effects of treatment on approaches to (1) females 18 years old or younger, (2) males 12 years old or younger, and (3) adults. The first two categories represented individuals who the client found to be sexually attractive. Approach was defined as facing and moving directly toward a person as well as speech or gestures directed at a person. Recordings were made when the client came within 25 feet of any person encountered during $\frac{1}{2}$ to $1\frac{1}{2}$ hour walks through the suburban neighborhood where the group home was located. The walks usually occurred two to three times per week. During these walks the client was free to go anywhere, although he typically walked to a nearby park and grocery store. Observations were conducted by having staff clandestinely follow the client at a distance and having unfamiliar observers await him at predetermined locations.

A 10-second partial-interval time-sampling technique (Powell, Martindale, & Kulp, 1975) was used to record approaches or no approaches during the client's encounters with persons (i.e., the client coming within 25 feet of a person). This procedure yielded a percentage of intervals in which an approach occurred given the availability of a "target."

During baseline, the client received periodic instructions from group home staff not to interact or play with any of the target populations. During his walks there were no consequences for approaching a target person, although the observers would intervene if he engaged in physical contact or moved out of sight with the person. If intervention was necessary, the client was confined to his room for the remainder of the day. The treatment phase began with an initial training session in which photographs were used to specify those individuals who were not to be approached. How to ignore a child encountered during a walk was modeled by a therapist. The client was told that if he approached a target person (groups 1 and 2 above), then an observer would immediately confront him, describe his inappropriate behavior, and escort him back to the group home. He would then be restricted to his bedroom for that evening and lose his parental visiting privileges for the subsequent weekend.

During baseline, approaches to girls (i.e., under age 18) and boys (i.e., under age 12) averaged 47.9% and 73.4%, respectively. No interventions by observers were necessary. During treatment, approaches to the two target groups were eliminated after the third confinement to his bedroom. These data were augmented by the group home staff's anecdotal reports that the client avoided children at times other than walks. Approaches to adults briefly decreased during the initial segment of treatment but subsequently returned to baseline levels. The successful treatment results were maintained during the 10 months of the study and at the 3-month data-based follow-up.

D. Public Masturbation

Public masturbation is probably the most common form of sexually deviant behavior displayed by mentally retarded persons, since 84% of 82 residential facilities surveyed by Mulhern (1975) indicated that they had clients who did so. Obviously, it is not masturbatory behavior per se that is troublesome, but rather the time or place in which the behavior occurs. Four studies (Barmann & Murray, 1981; Cook, Altman, Shaw, & Blaylock, 1978; Luiselli, Helfen, Pemberton, & Reisman, 1977; Polvinale & Lutzker, 1980) have treated public masturbation.

Luiselli *et al.* (1977) eliminated the persistent in-class masturbation of an 8-year-old mentally retarded boy. Masturbation was defined as the boy rubbing his hand on the zipper region of his pants in order to stimulate his penis. His teachers stated that his high rate of masturbatory behavior prevented him from engaging in educational activities. Persistent public masturbation was also reported to be a problem in the home, although it was not treated there.

All sessions were conducted during three daily preacademic instructional periods since informal pretreatment observations had revealed that the child confined his masturbation almost exclusively to these times. The child's regular teachers conducted the procedures and collected the data. Frequency of masturbation was measured by having a teacher indicate whether the response had occurred during a 4-minute period of task presentation. An average of nine 4-minute sessions were recorded each day.

An AB design was employed. During the 4 days of phase A, the child was provided with tokens, social praise, and positive feedback for on-task behavior (e.g., working puzzles, sorting shapes, matching colors) during each 4-minute period. After this procedure failed to reduce the behavior, an overcorrection-based procedure (Foxx & Azrin, 1973) was added (phase B). It consisted of instructing the child, following each instance of masturbation, to move his arms to one of four positions (i.e., arms overhead, extended laterally in front of the body, extended laterally from the sides, and wrapped across the chest). Each position was held for 3 seconds. Graduated guidance was used whenever the child failed to respond promptly to the instructions. Masturbation was completely suppressed after 9 days and this suppression was maintained throughout a 12-month data-based follow-up.

Polvinale and Lutzker (1980) also utilized overcorrection and reinforcement procedures to treat the genital self-stimulation of a 13-year-old Down's syndrome male. The boy was considered to be severely retarded (I.Q. = 36, MA = 42 months). Assaultive behavior and aggressive sexual behaviors (i.e., enticing or coercing other children into sexual interactions) also were targeted for treatment.

The treatment program was conducted at the boy's school. Treatment sessions lasting 25 minutes each were conducted outside during a late-morning exercise period and during early-afternoon recess period. A 30-second continuous-interval recording system was used in which an observer recorded the frequency of each target behavior during each interval.

A modified multiple baseline design across settings was used. After a 7-day baseline in both settings, a DRO procedure was used on a variable-interval (VI) schedule of reinforcement (i.e., social praise was delivered provided that none of the target behaviors had occurred during the interval). At the same time, a combination of the DRO procedure and an apology procedure based on the overcorrection rationale (Foxx & Azrin, 1972) was implemented in the afternoon setting. The apology procedure was specific to each type of target behavior and required that the boy apologize to six different peers/teachers. If the boy did not begin to apologize within 5 seconds of being instructed to do so, an additional person was added. The boy could thus minimize the procedural response requirements by complying with the initial instruction. The apology procedure typically lasted from 2 to 4 minutes. After 3 days, the combined DRO and apology program was implemented in both activity periods. In order to transfer control of the program from a professional trainer to the boy's teachers, the social reinforcement schedule was attenuated from VI 2 minutes to VI 20 minutes. The teachers also began conducting the apology training with the professional trainer fading out his involvement.

When used alone, the DRO procedure was ineffective; however, the combined program greatly reduced all three target behaviors within 1 week. No more than eight individuals were ever needed to complete the apology consequence during the 32-day study. An additional finding was that the control over the inappropriate behaviors generalized from the original trainer to teachers who were present during the intervention but who did not participate. Follow-up data indicated that the clinical gains were maintained at 6 months.

Cook *et al.* (1978) demonstrated the effectiveness of lemon juice as a punisher for the public masturbation of a 7-year-old severely retarded male. The boy's public masturbation at home and in public was a source of concern for his parents, who had considered readmitting him to an institution if the behavior could not be controlled. His parents expressed no concern about his private masturbation in a bedroom or bathroom. Since the behavior was problematic at home and school, a multiple baseline design was utilized to assess the effects of the treatment in both settings. The target behavior was defined as occurring when the boy placed either hand inside his pants and directed it toward his penis and ending when he removed his hand.

A 5-minute time-sampling procedure was implemented at home and school with six observation periods conducted at random times during the day in both locations. Two pretreatment conditions were implemented. In the beginning of the study, both the child's teachers and parents slapped his hand whenever masturbation occurred. The data indicated an increasing trend during this phase. Given the possibility that the child was masturbating to gain adult attention, the teachers and parents were then told to ignore the child whenever he masturbated. This manipulation produced no behavioral change at school but a dramatic increase in the variability of masturbation at home.

Consequently, a punishment procedure was implemented at school, while masturbation continued to be ignored at home. During the punishment procedure, a teacher (or aide) squirted 5–10 cc of unsweetened lemon juice into the boy's mouth whenever he attempted to masturbate. No additional positive reinforcement procedures were introduced. After 13 days of treatment in the classroom, the parents implemented the procedure at home.

Lemon juice appeared to serve as an effective punisher, since public masturbation decreased to zero after about 16 days of classroom treatment and after 13 days of home treatment. In both settings, most of the applications of lemon juice occurred during the first days of treatment. Follow-up data through 6 months indicated that treatment success had been maintained in both settings.

Barmann and Murray (1981) used a facial screening procedure to eliminate the public masturbation of a 14-year-old severely retarded male. The client had engaged in public masturbation for a period of 8 years. Previously unsuccessful procedures included DRO, verbal reprimands, overcorrection, extinction, and timeout. The target response was defined as the boy forcefully rubbing his crotch area for more than 5 seconds while in the presence of one or more individuals.

A multiple baseline design across settings was used to assess the effects of sequential treatment in the child's classroom, on the school bus, and at home. Three daily 30-minute observation periods were scheduled for the home and classroom settings. Two additional 30-minute sessions were conducted each day on the school bus. A 30-second continuous-interval system was used to record response frequency. There was no report of the use of any reinforcement programs.

During the baseline conditions, verbal reprimands were used following each occurrence of masturbation, e.g., "No, _____." The facial screening procedure consisted of (1) providing negative verbal feedback ("No touching in public"), and (2) loosely pulling a terrycloth bib over the client's face and holding it at the back of his head for at least 5 seconds or until he stopped masturbating. The bib measured 64 cm long by 58 cm wide, with a nonabrasive tie around its circumference. The first two treatment sessions in each setting were conducted by a behavior therapist, who modeled the proper method of implementing the procedure for the individuals who would be responsible for conducting it thereafter (i.e., teachers, bus aides, and parents).

Genital self-stimulation was reduced by 90% or more in all three settings after approximately 5 days of treatment. The longest procedural application lasted 14 seconds. Follow-up through 6 months indicated that the clinical benefits had been maintained. During the follow-up period the client was provided with a sex education program that stressed the appropriateness of private masturbation. The possible contribution of this program to the maintenance of the treatment effect was unknown.

E. Promiscuity

Two studies (Anant, 1968; Dial, 1968) reported treating promiscuity. Anant (1968) attempted to treat a mildly retarded 20-year-old female who had given birth to an illegitimate son 5 years previously. Although she had held a variety of jobs, her frequent attempts to seduce customers resulted in her being frequently fired and ultimately readmitted to a residential facility.

The treatment program featured the use of verbal aversion therapy. All treatment sessions lasted 1 hour. During the first session, the therapist described the treatment program and discussed the potential negative consequences for the woman's indiscriminate sexual behavior, i.e., an unwanted pregnancy, contracting syphilis or other venereal diseases, and murder at the hands of a "sex fiend." She also was taught relaxation via reciprocal inhibition (Wolpe, 1958) and breathing exercises. During subsequent sessions, the therapist described scenes that corresponded to the three negative consequences described above while the client attempted to imagine the scenes. After the client had relaxed following the termination of a description, she was asked to rate her "fear" of the scene on a percentile scale. The intensity of the scenes was increased until all reports were near a 100% "fear" level. The client was also instructed to practice imagining the scenes at least twice a day on her living unit. Treatment was terminated after ten sessions because the client had reached near a 100% level of "fear" on all scenes and because she was offered and accepted a job in the community.

The author anecdotally reported that the treatment was a success because the institutional superintendent reported in a phone conversation that the client continued to be employed at the same position 8 months after treatment.

A second "behavioral" study (Dial, 1968) also used recidivism as the measure of the effectiveness of social/sexual skills training for 51 women in a vocational rehabilitation program. The average I.Q. was 64 (range 50–96) and the average age 23 (range 17–37 yrs). The women had been readmitted to a residential facility primarily because of inappropriate sexual behavior.

Social skills training was divided into two programs: Social Adjustment Class and Therapy Group. The Social Adjustment Class was a structured program of information exchange and feedback supplemented with guest speakers and audio–visual presentations. The curriculum consisted of information concerning dating, venereal diseases, alcoholism, smoking, narcotics, marriage, and how to relate to others. The discussion session that followed each didactic presentation served to provide corrective and positive feedback. The Therapy Group was offered on a voluntary basis following an individual's completion of the Social Adjustment Class. Thirty-five of the fifty-one girls volunteered for the Therapy Group. The therapist utilized a client-centered counseling approach to encourage growth in self-esteem, increase verbal expression of feelings, and facilitate the resolution of individual problems. The Social Adjustment training lasted 24 weeks with the group meeting for an hour each week. The Therapy Group met for 90 minutes each week with the number of sessions attended by each client variable.

Because only two women were readmitted for sexual misconduct following the training, Dial (1968) stated that "since nine girls were returned to the institution during two years prior to the beginning of the five year group project, it is indicated that the project has been important to the vocational rehabilitation of females from an institution" (p. 13).

F. Trichophobia

It has been increasingly recognized in recent years that mentally retarded individuals can manifest psychiatric symptomatology since they can suffer the same types of emotional problems that nonretarded individuals develop (Szymanski & Grossman, 1984). These individuals typically carry a dual diagnosis of mental retardation and mental illness. Rivenq (1974) reported the treatment of such an individual. The client was a 13-year-old mildly retarded institutionalized male with slight gynecomastia (i.e., abnormal breast development) who suffered from trichophobia (i.e., fear of hair). The boy was experiencing severe adjustment problems with his peers as a result of his gynecomastia-induced gender identity problem and fear of body hair (especially pubic and facial hair). He also expressed fears that his male peers were trying to poison him or send him to another planet to make him an old man. His trichophobia was selected for treatment in the hope that its successful treatment might affect his other fears.

The treatment chosen was systematic desensitization (Wolpe, 1958). Because the client's poor verbal skills made the construction of an anxiety hierarchy difficult, the therapist had to infer anxiety level by observing the client's posture and facial expressions. Another difficulty was teaching the client to relax in order to pair a reduction in anxiety with the phobic stimulus. To overcome this problem, candy and French pastries were used to obtain an alternative physiological condition that was considered to be conceptually incompatible with anxiety. The therapist also used instructions and feedback to correct the boy's psychosexual misconceptions.

During the desensitization procedure, a picture of a man with a slight mustache was presented at a distance and gradually brought closer until the boy emitted an avoidance behavior. Over six sessions, pictures of increasingly hairy men were presented in the same graduated format. It was reported that the phobia was eliminated in four sessions and that the boy's sexual identity improved with a resultant increase in appropriate peer interaction. The author concluded that the boy had accepted a male identity as evidenced by his desire to build big muscles.

III. EVALUATION

Before critically evaluating these studies, two factors must be considered. One, the goal of all of the studies was to ameliorate clinically troublesome behavior rather than conduct a formal analysis of the variables controlling that behavior (Avery-Clark & Laws, 1984; Henson & Rubin, 1971). Two, the early case studies lacked the sophisticated single-subject experimental designs that are currently accepted practice (Hersen & Barlow, 1976). Although this renders their conclusions as tenuous, these studies do suggest that the deviant sexual behavior of mentally retarded individuals may be amenable to treatment. Given these factors, our methodological critique will focus primarily on the more recent studies in an attempt to establish some directions for future research and implications for clinical treatment. Our critique addresses the (1) independent variables, (2) types of dependent variables, (3) experimental design, (4) subject/client descriptions, (5) follow-up and maintenance of effects, and (6) generalization of effects.

A. Independent Variables

A variety of procedures or independent variables have been used in the treatment of deviant sexual behaviors: faradic shock (Fookes, 1960; Rosenthal, 1973), overcorrection (Luiselli et al., 1977; Polvinale & Lutzker, 1980), aversive imagery (Anant, 1968; Kolvin, 1967), facial screening (Barmann & Murray, 1981), contingent application of lemon juice (Cook et al., 1978), relaxation training (Anant, 1968; Rivenq, 1974; Shaw & Walker, 1979), DRO and extinction (Lutzker, 1974), contingent confinement or timeout (Wong et al., 1982), and didactic training (Dial, 1968). A close inspection of these procedures reveals that two basic treatment strategies were used.

One strategy did not treat the target behavior in the natural setting (Anant, 1968; Fookes, 1960; Rivenq, 1974; Rosenthal, 1973; Shaw & Walker, 1979). Rather, an analogue situation was created, i.e., a therapy room, in which eliciting or arousing stimuli were presented symbolically via pictures or stories. [The exception was Shaw and Walker (1979), who used a barefoot model in treating a foot fetish.] The treatment procedure was then made contingent on a response to the stimuli. The second strategy (Barmann & Murray, 1981; Cook et al., 1978; Fookes, 1960; Luiselli et al., 1977; Polvinale & Lutzker, 1980; Wong et al., 1982) treated the target behavior in the natural setting whenever it occurred.

The first strategy appears to have been based on a respondent/classical conditioning rationale, since the treatment thrust was to attempt to alter the power of an antecedent stimulus to elicit a deviant physiological response by providing counterconditioning for that stimulus. Consider for example, the pairing of an arousing stimulus, pictures of young girls, with a strong aversive stimulus, electric shock, in order to weaken a response, physiological arousal. If the shock is powerful enough, the power of the pictures to elicit physiological arousal should be eliminated after a number of trials. The second strategy appears to have been based on an operant conditioning rationale, since the treatment thrust was to attempt to alter the future probability of a response by providing consequences for that response, e.g., applying a facial screen to an individual who is masturbating publicly.

However, it would be a mistake to attempt to classify the above procedures solely on the basis of an operant versus respondent conditioning distinction since some procedures contained elements of both.

B.   Dependent Measures

The degree to which a procedure is effective is reflected, in part, by the dependent measures that are chosen. Measures used included institutional readmission (Anant, 1968; Dial, 1968), self-report (Anant, 1968; Fookes, 1960; Kolvin, 1967; Rosenthal, 1973), frequency of occurrence (Barmann & Murray, 1981; Cook et al., 1978; Luiselli et al., 1977; Lutzker, 1974; Polvinale & Lutzker, 1980; Wong et al., 1982), and response latency (Rivenq, 1974; Rosenthal, 1973; Shaw & Walker, 1979).

The selection of an appropriate dependent measure in treating sexual deviancies is obviously crucial and appears to be a function of a number of considerations. The first is the topography of the response and the setting events or environmental conditions in which the behavior occurs. For example, masturbation is an easily detectable response that is only problematic when it occurs in public. Hence, the studies that dealt with public masturbation used a direct behavioral observation system, i.e., time sampling or a frequency count in the target environment. However, when the target behavior or environment was less circumscribed, analogue situations were developed in order to assess responding (Anant, 1968; Fookes, 1960; Kolvin, 1967; Rosenthal, 1973). Interestingly, Shaw and Walker (1979) had to abandon their original plans to utilize plethysmographically transduced responding to slides/pictures because of equipment failure and the inability of analogue stimuli to elicit/evoke a response. As a result, they had to switch from an analogue format to a direct assessment model by measuring response latency in vivo.

A second consideration is the amount of environmental impact the behavior creates. For example, pedophilia simply cannot be allowed to occur. Thus, Wong et al. (1982) selected an early response in the pedophilia chain for treatment and utilized the duration of approach to potential victims as a dependent measure. This made sense conceptually, since punishment was programmed to occur early in the response chain, where the responses were weakest (Azrin & Holz, 1966).

A third consideration is the frequency of the behavior. Studies dealing with potentially low-frequency behavior tended to use analogue situations; thus, the dependent measure was behavior frequency in the presence of analogue stimuli rather than in the natural setting (Fookes, 1960; Kolvin, 1967). In such cases, corroborating anecdotal reports often were provided to augment the validity of the intrasession measures.

A fourth consideration is that many deviant sexual behaviors are a function of the opportunity to respond. For example, promiscuity requires a willing partner, whereas public masturbation can occur at any time. Clearly, frequency of promiscuous behavior would not be a very sensitive measure if a heterosexually "promiscuous" individual was confined to a sexually homogeneous living arrangement.

Once a dependent measure has been selected, the validity and reliability of that measure must be questioned. For example, if electric shock is made contingent on a client's report that he is fantasizing about fondling a young female, then the obvious question regarding validity is whether the probability that the client will fondle young girls in the natural environment has been changed or only his reporting during treatment sessions that he is thinking about doing so (Laws & Holmen, 1978).

Once validity has been established, the reliability of the measure must be evaluated. The studies that reported reliability assessments (Barmann & Murray, 1981; Cook *et al.,* 1978; Luiselli *et al.,* 1977; Lutzker, 1974; Polvinale & Lutzker, 1980; Wong *et al.,* 1982) were recent ones that dealt with easily detectable responses in a circumscribed setting. Studies that did not report reliability were generally published earlier, when the absence of reliability data was characteristic of single-case design at that time. Nevertheless, assessments of reliability must hereafter be conducted.

Overall, there appears to be a trend toward treating deviant sexual behavior in a natural rather than an artificial/analogue setting. This practice should enhance the validity of the dependent measures. Future research and clinical practice also should consider the social validity (Foxx & Jones, 1978; Wolf, 1978) of the measure by empirically assessing the reaction of both the client and significant persons in the environment (e.g., teachers, parents, peers, or parole officers) to the changes in the target behavior.

C. Experimental Design

The evaluation of the effectiveness of treatment also may be enhanced by the experimental design that is used. Thus, simple case studies (Anant, 1968; Fookes, 1960; Kolvin, 1967) and baseline/treatment or AB designs (Luiselli *et al.,* 1977; Rivenq, 1974; Shaw & Walker, 1979) can be faulted for not controlling variables that may threaten the internal validity of the results. Simply put, these designs suggest the possible benefits of a particular treatment but do not permit any conclusive statements to be made.

Although more rigorous control can be demonstrated with additive designs (Dial, 1968; Lutzker, 1974; Rosenthal, 1973), the use of ABC designs (i.e., baseline, treatment 1, treatment 2) (Dial, 1968; Rosenthal, 1973) raises the possibility of order effects and significantly dilutes a study's findings. For example, Lutzker (1974) employed an ABCB (i.e., baseline, treatment 1, treatment 2, treatment 1) design to assess the effects of DRO (B phase) and extinction (C phase) on an "exhibitionist." The alteration of treatments during the BCB phases allows the two procedures to be compared and increases confidence in conclusions regarding the effectiveness of the DRO procedure. Unfortunately, this is the only formal analysis that can be conducted since the A and C phases were different conditions and a comparison of the baseline (A) and DRO (B) conditions suffers from the same problems mentioned above for AB design (Hersen & Barlow, 1976).

The most rigorous experimental control was provided when multiple baseline designs were used (Barmann & Murray, 1981; Cook et al., 1978; Polvinale & Lutzker, 1980; Wong et al., 1982), since the target behavior was assessed in several settings with treatment introduced sequentially across settings. Hence, this design allowed the relatively strong conclusion that the treatment procedure was responsible for the decreases in the target behavior.

Modifications of the multiple baseline were used in two studies that treated public masturbation (Cook et al., 1978; Polvinale & Lutzker, 1980). Cook et al. (1978) utilized a multiple baseline (i.e., assessment in the child's classroom and home) in combination with an additive design (ABC). The A phase, or baseline, represented an active control condition (Foxx & Bechtel, 1982), since the child's hand was slapped by his teachers and parents whenever he engaged in public masturbation. In phase B, both the teachers and parents ignored the child's masturbation. During the C phase, the teachers squirted lemon juice into the child's mouth whenever he masturbated in class, while his parents continued to ignore the behavior. After success was achieved at school, the parents began using the lemon juice procedure at home. Unfortunately, the simultaneous manipulation of the independent variable in both settings during the first two phases makes a complete analysis of the treatment data difficult. Polvinale and Lutzker (1980) conducted observations in two different activity periods. After baseline, a DRO/apology procedure was implemented in an afternoon activity, while the DRO procedure alone was implemented in a morning activity. Unfortunately, this design did not permit the assessment of generalization given that the two treatments were implemented simultaneously. Thus, the decrease in responding during the DRO only condition could be attributed not only to that procedure but also to a punishment generalization effect.

Wong et al. (1982) employed a multiple baseline across responses rather than settings. Responses consisted of approaches to potential groups of "victims" by a pedophile. The three groups consisted of females 18 years or younger, boys 12 years or younger, and adults, i.e., all other individuals. However, the independence of the response can be questioned for several reasons. First, the selection of the groups' age ranges was arbitrary. Second, no information was given regarding any attempt to verify the age of an individual with whom the client had contact. Hence, the data for approaches to adults may be somewhat spurious given the difficulty of discriminating between a 12- and 13-year-old male. Third, several responses could occur simultaneously, i.e., the client could and did approach a mixed group of girls, boys, and adults. A second problem concerns clinical benefit versus scientific explanation. The decrease of the target behavior in all settings after treatment was implemented in only one setting (i.e., approaches to all age groups decreased, although it was not completely suppressed for the adults) is obviously clinically advantageous; however, such a spread of effect reduces the confidence by which the behavior change can be attributed to the independent variable.

To summarize, our review yielded the following conclusions: (1) there has been a lack of appropriate experimental control in many of the studies, especially those using case-study (Anant, 1968; Fookes, 1960; Kolvin, 1967), AB (Luiselli *et al.*, 1977; Rivenq, 1974; Shaw & Walker, 1979), and additive designs (Dial, 1968; Rosenthal, 1973); (2) the more recent studies (Barmann & Murray, 1981; Cook *et al.*, 1978; Lutzker, 1974; Polvinale & Lutzker, 1980; Wong *et al.*, 1982) have shown an increased concern for experimental control, especially in the use of multiple baseline designs; and (3) several studies that used variations of the multiple baseline design did not permit a complete analysis of the treatment effect because they violated the design strategy by the simultaneous manipulation of independent variables in all treatment settings (Cook *et al.*, 1978; Polvinale & Lutzker, 1980) or failed to provide for independence of the response (Wong *et al.*, 1982).

D.   Description of Subjects/Clients

Many of the subject/clients' descriptions were incomplete. For example, descriptions such as "below normal intelligence" (Fookes, 1960), "intellectually dull and verbally unforthcoming" (Kolvin, 1967), or simply "mildly retarded intelligence" (Rosenthal, 1973) did not provide adequate information about the subjects' skill levels. The paucity of assessment information from these early studies may well have reflected the state of art in assessment at that time in contrast to the more refined assessment techniques that are available today. A more complete subject description also is needed when instructional-based interventions are used, since the degree to which a subject can process information is crucial to the evaluation of a treatment procedure.

The use of labels for the client's clinical status also bears mention. For example, describing a profoundly retarded client as an "exhibitionist" (Lutzker, 1974) seems questionable. Low-functioning mentally retarded individuals who remove their clothing or will not remain dressed are common in institutional environments (Foxx, 1976). While "running around naked" is certainly exhibitionistic in one sense, the motivation for doing so does not appear to be the same as for the "flasher" at the bus depot. Thus one must question whether such clients fit the standard definition associated with exhibitionism.

E. Follow-Up and Maintenance of Effects

The duration of treatment effects is of considerable importance and perhaps no more so than in the treatment of sexual deviancies. The studies reviewed reported surprisingly long and generally favorable follow-ups, e.g., maintained success after more than 40 months (Fookes, 1960). However, an analysis of their follow-up assessment methods revealed the same problems that were inherent during treatment; namely, validity and reliable measurement of the target response. Thus, it was not surprising that studies utilizing empirical treatment assessments also provided data-based follow-ups indicating the maintenance of the clinical gains (Barmann & Murray, 1981; Cook et al., 1978; Luiselli et al., 1977; Lutzker, 1974; Polvinale & Lutzker, 1980; Wong et al., 1982), whereas those that did not either provided only anecdotal evidence (Anant, 1968; Fookes, 1960; Kolvin, 1967; Rosenthal, 1973) or no follow-up information (Dial, 1968; Rivenq, 1974). The exception was Shaw and Walker (1979), who conducted an empirically based treatment but presented an anecdotal follow-up.

In a 10-year follow-up of cases treated by overcorrection procedures, Foxx and Livesay (1984) stressed the need for programming for maintenance. While this recommendation usually refers to the application of behavioral techniques such as fading, attenuation of schedules of reinforcement, or increasing the use of more "natural" rather than "contrived" reinforcers, several studies (Barmann & Murray, 1981; Polvinale & Lutzker, 1980; Wong et al., 1982) approached the issue of maintenance from a different perspective by training appropriate social/sexual behavior following treatment. Although such training may lessen the degree to which follow-up results can be directly attributed to the treatment procedure, there appears to have been a good rationale for doing so. Consider that the behavior of many of the subjects created an "at risk" situation in the sense that they might physically harm another individual or were in danger themselves of receiving restrictive consequences, e.g., incarceration, institutional readmission. Thus, there was a clinical urgency to use a behavioral intervention before providing systematic instruction in correct responding.

Nevertheless, social/sexual skills education is clearly indicated for these individuals since their deviant sexual behavior may be a function of the lack of opportunity or ability to develop such skills. This appears to be the case, since sex education programs (Dial, 1968; Monat, 1982) often focus on providing basic sexual information (e.g., the human reproductive system, venereal disease, birth control methods) without training appropriate social/sexual skills. Yet, teaching these skills may serve both a preventative and a remedial function, since the opportunity for sexual expression is being increased as more mentally retarded persons move from institutions to less restrictive environments. Hence, individuals who have these skills should be less likely to incur negative social consequences since they will have learned appropriate ways of accessing sexual reinforcers. Fortunately, such training programs now exist. For example, Foxx, McMorrow, Storey, and Rogers (1984) recently developed a social/sexual skills training package that uses modeling, response-specific feedback, self-monitoring, positive reinforcement, and individualized performance criterion to teach a variety of skills in a number of different situations.

A final point concerns the ethical indefensibility of punishing a response without training an alternative, appropriate response. This is an especially crucial concern given that mentally retarded individuals often have limited outlets for sexual expression. For example, masturbation may well represent the only form of sexual gratification for more severely handicapped individuals. It follows then, that punishing public masturbation is not appropriate unless training is given regarding the appropriate time/place in which to masturbate.

F. Generalization Effects

Two types of generalization can result from the implementation of a procedure. One is stimulus generalization, which refers to changes in the target behavior under stimulus conditions different from the treatment setting. For example, if a procedure reduces masturbation in a classroom, what are the effects on masturbation in the home, where no treatment is provided? The other type is response generalization, which refers to changes in behavior other than the target behavior. For example, a client who has been treated for masturbating with his hand in his pants may begin masturbating by rubbing against furniture. The response generalization process typically accounts for the ''side effects'' of a procedure and these unprogrammed changes in collateral behavior may be either positive, i.e., increases in prosocial responding following suppression of a maladaptive behavior, or negative, i.e., the emergence of new topographies of maladaptive behavior (Foxx & Bechtel, 1982).

None of the studies reported negative response generalization. Reports of positive response generalization effects included improvements in overall level of appropriate behavior/daily living skills (Shaw & Walker, 1979), absence of any symptom substitution (Kolvin, 1967), and improved peer interaction and social/sexual development (Rivenq, 1974). Although these reports provide some corroborative evidence for treatment success, they must be interpreted very cautiously since they were anecdotal.

Positive stimulus generalization was reported following treatment when the target behavior no longer occurred in stimulus conditions that differed from the treatment setting (Polvinale & Lutzker, 1980; Shaw & Walker, 1979; Wong *et al.*, 1982). For example, Wong *et al.* (1982) anecdotally reported that a pedophile avoided contact with potential "victims" in untreated settings. These reports are encouraging given that punishment effects often are situation specific (Newsom, Favell, & Rincover, 1983), but they must be interpreted cautiously since they were anecdotal.

The data from studies using multiple baseline designs (Barmann & Murray, 1981; Cook *et al.*, 1978; Polvinale & Lutzker, 1980; Wong *et al.*, 1982) indicated little stimulus generalization to nontreated settings. This lack of stimulus generalization added methodological rigor by establishing the independence of response/setting and substantiated the need for cautious interpretation of the anecdotal reports of positive stimulus generalization. A potentially mediating variable that may explain these positive effects is the implicit generalization training that is inherent in the multiple baseline design.

IV. CONCLUSIONS AND RECOMMENDATIONS

A. Conclusions

Our review suggests several conclusions:

1. Mentally retarded individuals, like nonretarded persons, can display deviant sexual behaviors such as pedophilia, exhibitionism, and fetishes.

2. A variety of independent variables (i.e., treatments) have been employed using both operant and respondent conditioning rationales. The operant-based studies featured better experimental design and reliability assessments and usually treated the target behavior in the natural environment. The respondent-based studies were less rigorously controlled and used analogue arousing stimuli and self-report measures of questionable reliability. However, the operant-based studies generally dealt with more frequent and public behavior, e.g., public masturbation, while the respondent-based studies dealt with relatively less frequent and public responses, e.g., pedophilia. At a conceptual level, it is possible that the respondent conditioning studies that purported to be using countercondioning were actually using operant punishment procedures.

3. The majority of studies did not employ sufficiently rigorous experimental designs to permit an unequivocal evaluation of their findings. Thus, they should be viewed as promissory in nature and suggestive that a technology to treat the maladaptive sexual behavior of mentally retarded persons can be developed.

4. The empirically based studies suggest that a relatively efficient technology does exist for dealing with problem sexual behaviors in circumscribed settings, e.g., masturbation in the classroom.

5. The validity of self-report measures of deviant sexual behavior is tenuous. Increased emphasis should be placed on establishing valid and reliable measures. The use of behavioral observation systems in the natural setting is strongly encouraged. If analogue settings must be used, e.g., because of the target behavior's potential for harm, then behavioral referents for the changes in the target behavior must be provided.

6. Anecdotal reports indicate an absence of negative side effects following treatment and positive effects such as the spread of the treatment effect and an increase in general functioning. These reports, however, should be viewed extremely cautiously given a variety of methodological weaknesses that were inherent in the studies.

7. In general, follow-ups have been of sufficient duration to indicate a maintenance of the treatment effect. More confidence can be placed in those follow-up reports that were empirically based.

B. Recommendations

Our review suggests the following:

1. A clinician/researcher orientation is needed if the knowledge base regarding how to treat inappropriate sexual behavior is to be advanced. Many of the studies had as their goals the direct amelioration of clinically significant behavior problems, and these goals often overshadowed concerns for experimental design or the validity and reliability of the dependent measures. Thus, future studies should address both clinical and methodological issues. A number of experimental designs (Hersen & Barlow, 1976), observational systems (Powell *et al.*, 1975), and instrumentation aids (Laws & Osborn, 1983) are now available for these purposes.

2. Emphasis needs to be placed on better pretreatment assessment of the clients' social/sexual skill levels. Sexual behavior represents an area in which information often is acquired and disseminated in a rather ambiguous manner. Hence, determining the extent to which clients have faulty or erroneous knowledge may be a significant factor in developing procedures to modify their inappropriate sexual behavior.

3. Sex education for mentally retarded individuals needs to be expanded. Although information-based programs are essential (Monat, 1982), there needs to be more emphasis on developing a technology of direct instruction in social/sexual behavior (Foxx *et al.*, 1984). Because lack of support from parents and care givers may be hindering the process (Goodman, Budner, & Lesh, 1971; Hammar, Wright, & Jensen, 1967; Mitchell, Doctor, & Butler, 1978; Mulhern, 1975; Timmers *et al.*, 1981), gaining their support appears to be a necessary precursor to the successful implementation of sex education programs.

4. The opportunity for sexual expression by mentally retarded individuals has been increased by the availability of community living arrangements. This means, of course, that unusual sexual behavior (as a particular community defines it) may result in an individual's receiving restrictive consequences such as institutional readmission, legal charges, or incarceration (Hill & Bruininks, 1984). Thus, it seems imperative that sex education programs that emphasize the acquisition of information and social/sexual skills be routinely included in program/habilitation plans as both a preventative and a remedial measure.

5. It is clear that mentally retarded individuals are not immune from developing emotional disturbances, psychiatric complications (Alford & Locke, 1984; Reiss, Levitan, & McNally, 1982; Szymanski & Grossman, 1984; Tanguay & Szymanski, 1980), or deviant sexual behaviors. The paucity of literature on the behavioral treatment of their deviant sexual behavior seems curious and clearly does not reflect the incidence/prevalence of such behavior. Consider, for example, that sexual victimization, patterns of heterosexual and homosexual coercion, and inappropriate touching/fondling are common but unresearched problems. This gap in the literature may indicate our failure to acknowledge the maladaptive sexual behavior of mentally retarded persons rather than the absence of such behavior. It is hoped that this review will facilitate an awareness of the sexual behavior problems of mentally retarded persons and thereby provide a basis for future research and clinical practice.

ACKNOWLEDGMENTS

The authors wish to thank Martin J. McMorrow for his comments on an earlier version of the chapter and Sarah Fenlon for her overall assistance.

REFERENCES

Alford, J. D., & Locke, B. J. (1984). Clinical responses to psychopathology of mentally retarded persons. *American Journal of Mental Deficiency, 89,* 195–197.

American Psychiatric Association. (1980). *Diagnostic and statistical manual of mental disorders* (3rd ed.). Washington, DC: Author.

Anant, S. S. (1968). Verbal aversion therapy with a promiscuous girl: Case report. *Psychological Reports, 22,* 795–796.

Avery-Clark, C. A., & Laws, D. R. (1984). Differential erection response patterns of sexual child abusers to stimuli describing activities with children. *Behavior Therapy, 15,* 71–83.

Azrin, N. H., & Holz, W. C. (1966). Punishment. In W. K. Honig (Ed.), *Operant behavior: Areas of research and application* (pp. 380–447). New York: Appleton-Century-Crofts.

Barmann, B. C., & Murray, W. J. (1981). Suppression of inappropriate sexual behavior by facial screening. *Behavior Therapy, 12,* 730–735.

Cook, J. W., Altman, K., Shaw, J., & Blaylock, M. (1978). Use of contingent lemon juice to eliminate public masturbation by a severely retarded boy. *Behaviour Research and Therapy, 16,* 131–134.

Dial, K. B. (1968). A report of group work to increase social skills of females in a vocational rehabilitation program. *Mental Retardation,* **6,** 11–14.

Edmondson, B., McCombs, K., & Wish, J. (1979). What retarded adults believe about sex. *American Journal of Mental Deficiency,* **84,** 11–18.

Edmondson, B., & Wish, J. (1975). Sex knowledge and attitudes of moderately retarded males. *American Journal of Mental Deficiency,* **80,** 172–179.

Fookes, B. H. (1960). Some experiences in the use of aversion therapy in male homosexuality, exhibitionism, and fetishism–transvestism. *British Journal of Psychiatry,* **115,** 339–341.

Foxx, R. M. (1976). The use of overcorrection to eliminate the public disrobing (stripping) of retarded women. *Behaviour Research and Therapy,* **14,** 53–61.

Foxx, R. M., & Azrin, N. H. (1972). Restitution: A method of eliminating aggressive–disruptive behavior of retarded and brain damaged patients. *Behaviour Research and Therapy,* **10,** 15–27.

Foxx, R. M., & Azrin, N. H. (1973). The elimination of autistic self-stimulatory behavior by overcorrection. *Journal of Applied Behavior Analysis,* **6,** 1–14.

Foxx, R. M., & Bechtel, D. R. (1982). Overcorrection. In M. Hersen, R. M. Eisler, & P. M. Miller (Eds.), *Progress in behavior modification* (Vol. 13, pp. 227–288). New York: Academic Press.

Foxx, R. M., & Jones, J. R. (1978). A remediation program for increasing the spelling achievement of elementary and junior high school students. *Behavior Modification,* **2,** 211–230.

Foxx, R. M., & Livesay, J. (1984). Maintenance of response suppression following overcorrection: A ten year retrospective examination of eight cases. *Analysis and Intervention in Developmental Disabilities,* **4,** 65–80.

Foxx, R. M., McMorrow, M. J., Storey, K., & Rogers, B. M. (1984). Teaching social/sexual skills to mentally retarded adults. *American Journal of Mental Deficiency,* **89,** 9–15.

Frazier, S. H., Campbell, R. J., Marshall, M. H., & Werner, A. (1975). *A psychiatric glossary: The meaning of terms frequently used in psychiatry.* New York: Basic Books.

Gebhard, P. H., Gagnon, J. H., Pomeroy, W. B., & Christenson, C. V. (1965). *Sex offenders.* New York: Harper & Row.

Goodman, L., Budner, S., & Lesh, B. (1971). The parent's role in sex education for the retarded. *Mental Retardation,* **9,** 43–45.

Hall, J. E., Morris, H. L., & Barker, H. R. (1973). Sexual knowledge and attitudes of mentally retarded adolescents. *American Journal of Mental Deficiency,* **77,** 706–709.

Hammar, S. L., Wright, L. S., & Jensen, D. L. (1967). Sex education for the retarded adolescent: A survey of parental attitudes and methods of management in 50 adolescent retardates. *Clinical Pediatrics,* **6,** 621–627.

Henson, D. E., & Rubin, H. B. (1971). Voluntary control of eroticism. *Journal of Applied Behavior Analysis,* **4,** 37–44.

Hersen, M., & Barlow, D. H. (1976). *Single case experimental designs: Strategies for studying behavior change.* New York: Pergamon.

Hill, B. K., & Bruininks, R. H. (1984). Maladaptive behavior of mentally retarded individuals in residential facilities. *American Journal of Mental Deficiency,* **88,** 380–387.

Katchadourian, H. A., & Lunde, D. T. (1975). *Fundamentals of human sexuality.* New York: Holt, Rinehart & Winston.

Kazdin, A. E., & Hartmann, D. P. (1978). The simultaneous-treatment design. *Behavior Therapy,* **9,** 912–922.

Kolvin, I. (1967). "Aversive imagery" treatment in adolescents. *Behaviour Research and Therapy,* **5,** 245–248.

Laws, D. R., & Holmen, M. L. (1978). Sexual response fading by pedophiles. *Criminal Justice and Behavior,* **5,** 343–356.

Laws, D. R., & Osborn, C. A. (1983). How to build and operate a behavioral laboratory to evaluate and treat sexual deviance. In J. G. Greer & I. Stuart (Eds.), *The sexual aggressor: Current perspectives on treatment* (pp. 293–335). New York: Van Nostrand-Reinhold.

Luiselli, J. K., Helfen, C. S., Pemberton, B. W., & Reisman, J. (1977). The elimination of a child's in-class masturbation by overcorrection and reinforcement. *Journal of Behavior Therapy and Experimental Psychiatry*, **8**, 201–204.

Lutzker, J. R. (1974). Social reinforcement control of exhibitionism in a profoundly retarded adult. *Mental Retardation*, **12**, 46–47.

Mitchell, L., Doctor, R. M., & Butler, D. C. (1978). Attitudes of caretakers toward the sexual behavior of mentally retarded persons. *American Journal of Mental Deficiency*, **83**, 289–296.

Monat, R. K. (1982). *Sexuality and the mentally retarded*. San Diego: College Hill Press.

Mulhern, T. J. (1975). Survey of reported sexual behavior and policies characterizing residential facilities for retarded citizens. *American Journal of Mental Deficiency*, **79**, 670–673.

Newsom, C., Favell, J. E., & Rincover, A. (1983). The side effects of punishment. In S. Axelrod & J. Apsche (Eds.), *The effects of punishment on human behavior* (pp. 285–316). New York: Academic Press.

Polvinale, R. A., & Lutzker, J. R. (1980). Elimination of assaultive and inappropriate sexual behavior by reinforcement and social-restitution. *Mental Retardation*, **18**, 27–30.

Powell, J., Martindale, A., & Kulp, S. (1975). An evaluation of time-sample measures of behavior. *Journal of Applied Behavior Analysis*, **8**, 463–469.

Reiss, S., Levitan, G. W., & McNally, R. J. (1982). Emotionally disturbed mentally retarded people: An underserved population. *American Psychologist*, **37**, 361–367.

Rivenq, B. (1974). Behavioral therapy of phobias: A case with gynecomastia and mental retardation. *Mental Retardation*, **12**, 44–45.

Rosenthal, T. L. (1973). Response-contingent versus fixed punishment in aversion conditioning of pedophilia: A case study. *Journal of Nervous and Mental Disease*, **156**, 440–443.

Shaw, W. J., & Walker, C. E. (1979). Use of relaxation in the short-term treatment of fetishistic behavior: An exploratory case study. *Journal of Pediatric Psychology*, **4**, 403–407.

Szymanski, L. S., & Grossman, H. (1984). Dual implications of "dual diagnosis." *Mental Retardation*, **22**, 155–156.

Tanguay, P. E., & Szymanski, L. S. (1980). Training of mental health professionals in mental retardation. In L. S. Szymanski & P. E. Tanguay (Eds.), *Emotional disorders of mentally retarded persons: Assessment, treatment, and consultation*. Baltimore: University Park Press.

Timmers, R. L., DuCharme, P., & Jacob, G. (1981). Sexual knowledge, attitudes and behaviors of developmentally disabled adults living in a normalized apartment setting. *Sexuality and Disabilities*, **4**, 27–39.

Wolf, M. M. (1978). Social validity: The case for subjective measurement or how applied behavior analysis is finding its heart. *Journal of Applied Behavior Analysis*, **11**, 203–214.

Wolpe, J. (1958). *Psychotherapy by reciprocal inhibition*. Stanford, CA: Stanford University Press.

Wong, S. E., Gaydos, G. R., & Fuqua, R. W. (1982). Operant control of pedophilia: Reducing approaches to children. *Behavior Modification*, **6**, 73–84.

Behavioral Approaches to Toilet Training for Retarded Persons

S. BETTISON[1]

HORNSBY AND KU-RING-GAI AREA HEALTH
SERVICE FOR THE DEVELOPMENTALLY DISABLED
SYDNEY, NEW SOUTH WALES, AUSTRALIA

I. INTRODUCTION

Until the 1950s, incontinence, together with the many other functional impairments which retarded persons might have, was widely regarded as due to genetic or disease factors and was therefore considered to be largely unmodifiable (Kugel & Wolfensberger, 1969; Tizard, 1974; Tredgold & Soddy, 1956). As a result, research into toilet training methods for retarded persons was virtually nonexistent. However, this view has gradually been replaced by one which sees such impairments as resulting, at least in part, from a reduced capacity to learn (Clarke & Clarke, 1974). At the same time, many aspects of human development were being reexamined from a learning rather than a maturational perspective as a result of laboratory research into the control of operant behavior (Bijou & Baer, 1961, 1965). These developments have informed the efforts to devise toilet training procedures for retarded persons over the past two decades, with daytime wetting and soiling in institutions attracting the most research attention.

The view that incontinence in the absence of associated organic pathology is primarily due to faulty learning is partially supported by evidence that it can be reduced by toilet training. Evidence of this kind has been reported for both nonhandicapped children and retarded persons. However, this evidence is not straightforward and its interpretation will be greatly helped if we first briefly consider the nature of bladder and bowel control and its normal development.

[1]Present Address: Department of Health, Sydney, New South Wales 2000, Australia.

INTERNATIONAL REVIEW OF RESEARCH IN
MENTAL RETARDATION, Vol. 14

II. THE NATURE AND DEVELOPMENT OF BLADDER
AND BOWEL CONTROL

The mechanisms involved in the voiding of urine and feces and the voluntary control of these processes are not fully understood. However, what is known has been summarized by a number of authors (Bettison, 1982b; Caldwell, 1975; Hjalmos, 1976; Kolvin, MacKeith, & Meadow, 1973; Schaefer, 1979; Schuster, 1968; Young, 1973). The available evidence suggests that voluntary bladder and bowel control is a complex skill, gradually acquired in the early years of life and involving some degree of neurological and physiological maturation (Muellner, 1960a,b; Yates, 1970). As such, its acquisition takes some time, with occasional failures during acquisition but with an increasing success rate as the child becomes older.

The voluntary inhibition of voiding is achieved by contracting muscle groups in the perineum. The acquisition of this skill probably assists in the increase in bladder capacity and the lengthening time between urinations which occur during early childhood (MacKeith, Meadow, & Turner, 1973; Muellner, 1958, 1960a,b, 1965). To voluntarily induce voiding, several muscle groups must be coordinated, including the thoracic diaphragm, the lower abdominal muscles, and the perineal muscles. Skilled coordination of these muscle groups can eventually be used to bring about urination voluntarily at low bladder volumes before the urge to void occurs. Both the induction and inhibition of voiding depend on the ability to discriminate the minimal cues arising from changing pressure levels in the bladder and bowel. Voluntary control also involves a number of additional skills. The individual must be able to locate and approach the toilet, manipulate clothing, direct voiding into the toilet, and recognize when voiding has finished. These skills, together with those involved in bladder and bowel control, make up the complex behavior known as toileting.

According to this analysis, mastery of toileting requires the acquisition of a number of fine discriminations and responses which must be performed in a fixed sequence or chain. This sequence is represented in Fig. 1 as an operant chain of responses linked by discriminative stimuli which also act as reinforcers for the responses preceding them. However, this conception of toileting is complicated by the fact that some elements in the sequence are not readily observable. For example, contraction and relaxation of the perineal muscles to inhibit or bring about voiding cannot be directly observed, although they can sometimes be inferred from the presence or absence of voiding. In addition, discrimination of bladder or bowel pressure cannot be detected except indirectly. Moreover, some responses in the sequence must be performed concurrently. For example, the contraction of the perineal muscles to hold back voiding when the bladder or bowel is full (R7A in Fig. 1) must be maintained while the individual locates the toilet (R7), manipulates clothing (R6), and takes up an appropriate position at the

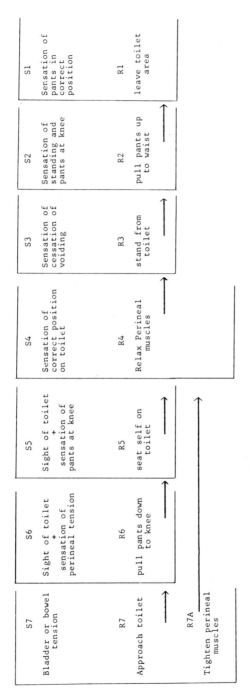

FIG. 1. Representation of the sequence of self-toileting tasks.

toilet (R5). A further complication arises from the reflexive nature of uncontrolled voiding. The process of bringing voiding under voluntary control inserts a number of voluntary responses between the initial eliciting stimuli of bladder or bowel distention and the reflex voiding response. It also imposes environmental control over the reflexes themselves so that they can be delayed or induced at will (Muellner, 1960a,b). Because of the initial reflexive nature of voiding, it is possible that classical conditioning is at least partly involved in the development of bladder and bowel control, although most approaches to toilet training have been primarily based on an operant model.

III. ACQUISITION OF TOILETING SKILLS WITH TRAINING

Since 1960, there have been over 90 studies of training to establish daytime toileting. Most have applied techniques based on the principles of operant conditioning. The majority have been with retarded children or adults, although there have been a number reporting procedures for nonhandicapped children. The studies range from anecdotal accounts and individual or group case studies to controlled experiments. In many cases the experimental studies have lacked methodological sophistication or provided inadequate information from which to interpret their findings.

The present article concentrates on the studies with retarded persons which incorporated some form of experimental or statistical control. These fall into four major categories. The first consists of demonstration studies which compare the effects of systematic training with the traditional approaches to the management of incontinence. The second covers those studies which investigated methods directed at toileting as a single unit of behavior. The third considers complex training procedures which have been designed to establish the entire toileting sequence. The fourth group of studies examines the effects of a number of factors on the acquisition of toileting skills during training, including some of the specific principles and procedures commonly used in toilet-training programs.

A. The General Efficacy of Systematic Training Programs

There is some evidence that systematic training of various kinds can alleviate incontinence in institutionalized retarded persons. This evidence is drawn from studies which were concerned with changes in several abilities, including toileting, over a period of several months or years. The independent variable in each study was the provision of some kind of systematic training, with the control condition being the absence of training. The focus was on whether training made a difference rather than on what kinds of training had an effect or how those effects were achieved.

Two studies were directly concerned with the likelihood of improvement in bladder and bowel control under several training and nontraining conditions (Eyman, Silverstein, & McLain, 1975; Eyman, Tarjan, & Cassady, 1970). They were part of an ongoing program of research at Pacific State Hospital into the role of institutional patterns of care in the habilitation of moderately, severely, and profoundly retarded persons. Each study followed a group of new admissions for a 3-year period to assess any changes which occurred in a number of basic skills and characteristics. Four assessments were carried out at approximately yearly intervals. The assessment scales were developed so that they could be completed by attendants with a high degree of reliability and validity (O'Connor, Crawford, & Gunn, 1964; Lohmann, Eyman, & Lask, 1967).

The first of the two studies (Eyman et al., 1970) found some improvement in toileting skill over the three years without any systematic training (67, or 31% of 215). A much higher rate of improvement occurred among those who attended special programs (27, or 71% of 38). However, it cannot be concluded that special training made the difference, since the two groups may have differed in other important respects besides the provision or nonprovision of training.

The second study (Eyman et al., 1975) overcame this problem by matching groups for age, IQ, diagnosis, and initial toileting skill. These variables had previously been shown to be related to the acquisition of toileting skills in the absence of training. In addition, the matching variables were used as covariates in the statistical analysis of toileting status at the 3-year follow-up. Three groups attended one of three special educational and training programs, one remained in standard care, and those in the fifth group were placed in foster homes.

The results indicated that, although about 20% in standard care improved in toileting, significantly more of those attending special programs improved. There were differences in the number who improved in the three programs (33 to 45%), but insufficient information was provided to allow any conclusions as to their relative merits. The most interesting finding concerned the group in foster care, among whom 50% improved. This was a greater improvement than occurred when special training was provided.

This finding raises two issues which are central, not only to the evaluation of toilet-training procedures, but to program evaluation generally. One issue concerns the role of consistent individualized attention and personal commitment from care givers in the acquisition and performance of basic skills. The other concerns the function of different environments in facilitating or impeding that acquisition. Few researchers have controlled for these two factors when examining the efficacy of training programs.

The difficulty of separating these variables is highlighted in a study by Gray and Kasteler (1969). They divided 140 institutionalized children into two groups

using similar matching variables and statistical controls to those used by Eyman
et al. (1975). Children in one group were each assigned a foster grandparent who
provided love, attention, and training in a number of skills, including toileting,
for 4 hours a day during the year of the program. The control group remained in
standard care. General changes in scores on the Vineland Social Maturity Scale
(VSMS) were assessed. This scale included a category on toileting, although
toileting skills were not analyzed separately. Both groups showed significant
increments in VSMS scores, with the experimental group making the greatest
gains. However, how much of this effect can be attributed to training and how
much to individualized attention is open to question.

Following Ellis' (1963) theoretical analysis of toileting behavior using an S-R
reinforcement paradigm, a number of authors reported toilet-training programs
which were partially inspired by the analysis, although few followed his suggestions in all respects. Three such studies suggested that training using behavior-shaping techniques could improve a range of skills, including toileting
(Bensberg, Colwell, & Cassell, 1965; Kimbrell, Luckey, Barbuto, & Love,
1967; Roos & Oliver, 1969). In each case a number of severely and profoundly
retarded institutionalized children were placed in a special environment and
trained throughout each day for a number of months and compared with one or
more groups matched for VSMS scores and either remaining in standard care or
receiving a short period of sensory motor training each day. All found significantly greater improvement in VSMS scores in the experimental groups. The
former two studies also noted specific improvement in the VSMS toileting
scores. Furthermore, follow-up scores for the trainees from the Kimbrell *et al.*
study 3 years later indicated that they had maintained that improvement after
training had been withdrawn (Leath & Flournoy, 1970). This is one of the rare
attempts to assess whether toilet training has any long-term effect on the everyday lives of retarded persons.

The seven studies reviewed in this section together suggest that some form of
systematic intervention may increase the ability of institutionalized severely
retarded children to control at least some aspects of their bladder and bowel
functions. They do not indicate what kinds of intervention are effective, nor what
aspects of toileting are influenced by training. The attempts to answer these
questions will be considered in the following sections.

B. Training Directed at Toileting as a Single Unit

It has been assumed by many researchers that the muscle control required to
voluntarily hold back and start voiding is not only operant in nature, and therefore susceptible to control by positive reinforcement, but can also be strengthened as a single unit in isolation from the rest of the toileting sequence. These
studies usually provided minimal information about the pretraining toileting

abilities of their subjects, and few attempted to control for nontraining variables. In addition, evidence for the suggested improvements in toileting skill was often insufficient to establish the efficacy of positive reinforcement. However, five studies did use experimental controls in an attempt to identify at least some of the treatment effects.

One of the earliest of these reports was by Blackwood (1963). He divided 45 institutionalized, severely and profoundly retarded children into three groups, matched for mean age, I.Q., and years spent in the institution. One group of 15 acted as a no-reinforcement control and remained in their usual ward under custodial conditions. This ward contained 30 children in all, with a staff–child ratio of 1:20. The other two groups were transferred together into a ward in which the staff–child ratio was doubled, 1:10, thus providing more individual attention. The toilet voiding of one of these groups was rewarded with praise and food. The toileting of the other group was handled in the conventional institutional manner without programmed reinforcement.

No evidence as to actual performance was provided. However, the accident rate was reduced to the same degree in both the attention and reinforcement groups, while remaining unchanged in the control group. Blackwood attributed this to increased attention, which quite simply may have involved more trips to the toilet for the two experimental groups than for the control group because more staff were available. If that were the case, the improvement may have reflected increased staff opportunity to catch more voidings in the toilet rather than an increase in the children's voluntary toilet voidings.

This may also have been the case in Dayan's (1964) study, in which training consisted of toileting every 2 hours with reinforcement for every toilet voiding. Dayan's evidence for improvement consisted of a reduction in hand laundry for the experimental group in comparison with the rest of the institution, a measure even further removed from the actual perfomance of toileting skills than the occurrence of voiding accidents.

A study by Hundziak, Maurer, and Watson (1971) supports this interpretation of the Blackwood and Dayan findings. They compared the same three conditions considered by Blackwood, using both accident and toilet voiding rates, this last being a direct measure of toileting behavior. In addition, the reinforcement and attention groups were both toileted every 2 hours. Accident rate did not change significantly for any group. Toilet voiding increased significantly with reinforcement, but there was no similar increase in either the attention or control groups.

Suggestive as these studies are, they indicate little more than that voiding rates can be brought under the control of environmental consequences to at least some extent. They certainly give no indication that new toilcting skills can be acquired with the application of either reinforcement or extra attention, although Hundziak et al. did report that one child in their reinforcement group began to toilet himself spontaneously during training. However, as in most of the toilet-training literature, they give no information about pretraining toileting ability apart from the measures of voiding frequencies.

An earlier review of toilet-training procedures for both retarded persons and nonhandicapped children (Bettison, 1980) suggested that the few trainees who do begin to perform the entire toileting sequence when reinforcement is provided for only one or two elements in the chain already possess most of the required skills. In such cases, the entire toileting sequence as a unit probably comes under reinforcement control. There is some evidence for this view in the reversal and multiple baseline studies by Ando (1977) and Wolf, Risley, Johnston, Harris, and Allen (1967). Both established independent toileting by rewarding toilet use and, in Ando's study, also by punishing accidents. The child in the Wolf study could perform all the nonvoiding tasks and hold back voiding for long periods before training, and quickly established virtually accident-free toilet use which was maintained after training. The child in Ando's study possessed fewer skills and, although accidents reduced and he began toileting himself, continued to have frequent voiding accidents throughout training.

In cases where even fewer of the skills exist it is doubtful whether selecting one or two elements to be strengthened in this way can establish fully independent bladder and bowel control, since the responses in the toileting sequence are interdependent. For example, in order to inhibit voiding accidents, the individual needs to recognize bladder or bowel tension, be able to find a toilet, deal with clothing, sit, and bring about the onset of voiding once on the toilet. If the individual instead has to rely on others to do most of these things for him, failure to gain assistance with any of these tasks may result in accidents, which clearly can interfere with any systematic attempt to strengthen bladder or bowel control. For these reasons, more recent research has concentrated on procedures directed at establishing some or all of the component skills in the toileting sequence. This research is discussed in the next section.

C. Training Directed at Toileting as a Complex Skill

The conception of toileting as a complex behavioral sequence has resulted in a variety of procedural combinations in toilet training. Several such programs have been described in detail and illustrated with case studies (Giles & Wolf, 1966; Hamilton, 1971; Fielding, 1972; Grabowski & Thompson, 1972; Levine & Elliott, 1970; Mahoney, Van Wagenen, & Meyerson, 1971; Van Wagenen, Meyerson, Kerr, & Mahoney, 1969). Some programs have also been published in training manuals for use by parents, teachers, or residential staff (Baker, Brightman, Heifetz, & Murphy, 1977; Baldwin, Fredericks, & Brodsky, 1973; Bensberg, 1965; Bettison, 1982a; Foxx & Azrin, 1973; Kaines, 1979; Watson, 1973a,b). However, few authors have identified every element in the toileting sequence shown in Fig. 1. In addition, only two programs contained procedures directed specifically at ensuring correct sequencing (Bettison, 1982a,b; Mahoney *et al.*, 1971). In both cases, chaining procedures (either forward or backward) were used to attach each element to the chain in correct order. Other programs either taught the identified skills at the same time or added them one at a time in an order unrelated to the natural sequence.

Experimental controls were incorporated into the trials of three complex programs in an attempt to evaluate their effectiveness (Azrin, Bugle, & O'Brien, 1971; Azrin & Foxx, 1971; Passman, 1975; Sadler & Merkert, 1977; Tierney, 1973). Passman trained three profoundly retarded adults using the shaping and fading procedures described by Watson (1973a). Trainees were toileted every 2 hours and trained in turn to sit on the toilet, void in the toilet, remove clothing, replace clothing, and approach the toilet from increasing distances. A tone and candy were delivered automatically, following the onset of toilet voiding, by an apparatus next to the toilet which was triggered when urine or feces touched moisture-detecting plates lining a bowl inserted in the toilet. Praise was also given when staff heard the tone. Once trainees began toileting themselves, only completely independent toilet use was rewarded, and praise was delayed until trainees returned to the ward. After 34 days of independent toileting, the tone, candy, and delayed praise were withdrawn for 10 days and then reinstated for a further week.

While this reversal did not test the effects of the complex program itself, it did show quite clearly that rewards maintained independent toileting once it had been established. Self-initiated toileting increased, returned to baseline level during extinction, and recovered with the reinstatement of reward. Accident rate was similarly reduced, became more frequent, and reduced again under the same conditions.

Tierney (1973) used a group design to test training effects, in which a control group remained in standard care and a matched experimental group received training. Trainees were taken to the toilet and rewarded for voiding. Once toilet voiding occurred regularly with no accidents, the assistance given for sitting, removal of clothing, and toilet approach as well as the rewards were gradually faded. Voiding accidents were ignored and removal of wet or soiled clothing was delayed for a set period. Although this program did not include procedures to teach all components of the toileting skills, more than three-quarters of the trainees improved. However, it is not surprising that four made no progress, less than half became accident free, and none became self toileting. Unfortunately, it is not possible to accurately assess the contribution of training, as no common measure of toileting for the two groups was reported.

The third program which was evaluated was that devised by Azrin and his colleagues. Two studies reported experimental trials and procedural refinements which were eventually described in full in a training manual (Foxx & Azrin, 1973). The procedure involved the use of rewards to strengthen toilet approach, handling clothing, sitting, toilet voiding, flushing the toilet, and remaining dry. Responses were elicited by prompts and graduated manual guidance rather than by a strict shaping procedure, and these were gradually faded while rewards were made increasingly intermittent as behavior was established. Incompatible stimuli and behavior were reduced to a minimum, and increased fluid intake with toileting every half-hour ensured frequent practice. This last procedure was first reported by Van Wagenen et al. (1969). Accidents were punished with reprimands, an overcorrection procedure, and time out from reinforcement. Pants and toilet alarms ensured immediate delivery of consequences. After the first self-initiated toileting occurred, toileting by the trainer ceased, reinforcement was transferred to self-initiated toilet use, and reinforcement schedules were thinned. Trainees were gradually moved back into their usual environment once they were self-initiating most of the time. A less intensive program of rewards for remaining dry and punishment for accidents was continued until there were no accidents for several weeks.

Azrin et al. (1971) presented evidence from an accidental reversal with one profoundly retarded child during early trials of the procedure. Voiding accidents decreased in frequency during training, increased when training was withdrawn, and were reduced to zero with the reinstatement of training. However, as with Passman's (1975) study, it was reward for independent toileting which was tested during reversal, rather than the full training program. The second evaluation compared the performance during training of two groups of institutionalized men below IQ 50 and matched for frequency of pretraining voiding accidents (Azrin & Foxx, 1971). One group received training while the other remained in standard care. There was a marked decrease in voiding accidents for the experimental group, with no corresponding decrease for the control group. However, subsequent training for the control group resulted in a similar decrease.

Sadler and Merkert (1977) published an independent evaluation of the Azrin and Foxx program in which it was compared with a strict toileting schedule and standard care. The study was carried out in a day center for severely and profoundly retarded children. Frequency of voiding accidents was again the dependent measure, recorded for 2 weeks before the procedures were introduced, for 1 week after 3 months of training, and for a further week at the end of 4 months of training. Then half of the standard care and scheduled toileting groups began training with the Azrin and Foxx program, while the remaining children continued as before. After a further 2 months, all intervention was withdrawn and voiding accidents were again recorded.

At the 3- and 4-month assessments, mean number of accidents had reduced significantly more for the training group than for either the scheduled or standard care groups, and this difference was even greater at the final assessment. Furthermore, the same order of reduction in voiding accidents occurred for the children transferred from scheduled toileting and standard care to the Azrin and Foxx program. Evidence was also provided for generalization to home, where no training had been provided.

This last study provided the first real evidence that the effects of training with the Azrin and Foxx procedures can be maintained when intervention is withdrawn and can be generalized to other environments. However, it is a pity that none of these five evaluations showed how toileting skills, other than the inhibition of voiding accidents, were affected. Without such evidence, there is no certainty that some or all of the independent toileting skills, which were reported as resulting from training, were not already possessed by trainees and were in fact acquired during training.

Several recent reports have presented nonexperimental evidence for the acquisition of toileting skills during training with the Azrin and Foxx program or modifications of it (Bettison, Davison, Taylor, & Fox, 1976; Butler, 1976; Dixon & Smith, 1976; Singh, 1976; P. S. Smith, Britton, Johnson, & Thomas, 1975), and one recent study not only presented quantitative evidence, but also employed a multiple baseline across subjects to test for training effects (Lancioni, 1980).

Trainees in Lancioni's study were profoundly retarded deaf–blind children. Modifications to the Azrin and Foxx program were therefore designed to accommodate the sensory handicaps. Training occurred for 4 hours every morning, but records were kept for 11 hours a day, thus providing additional data concerning generalization. However, the baseline and generalization periods were not intervention free. The alarm devices were operating and toilet voiding was rewarded. This procedure was similar to that employed in training directed at toileting as a single unit.

This study, besides showing the gradual acquisition of independent toileting skills, also demonstrated that reinforcement alone became effective only after the entire toileting sequence was established as a unit. Continuous graphs showed quite clearly that neither independent toileting nor accident rate were initially affected by simple reinforcement. However, once the full training program was introduced, independent toileting was gradually established and voiding accidents decreased to zero. The afternoon data showed little or no generalization until training had reached the stage where the children were fully independent during the morning training sessions. At this point most of the training procedures, other than reward for independent toileting and the alarms, had been withdrawn, so that the training and nontraining environments were much the same.

D. Factors Influencing Acquisition during Training

The research reviewed so far has examined how effective toilet-training programs are in establishing one or more of the skills involved in toileting. The evidence gives some support to the view that the entire toileting sequence is more likely to be acquired when training is directed at a number of the component skills rather than at only one or two. However, such programs involve a complex mix of procedures, some of which have no basis in prior research or theory.

Several studies have attempted to tease out the specific contribution of individual procedures as they are incorporated in one or other of the complex programs. In addition, there has been some interest in the influence of nontraining factors on success during toilet training, although it has not been the primary focus of research. The evidence concerning nontraining factors will therefore be dealt with first, followed by a more detailed review of the evidence relating to individual training procedures and their contribution.

1. THE INFLUENCE OF NONTRAINING FACTORS

With few exceptions, research into the acquisition of toileting skills by retarded persons has been with those in institutions. The likelihood that such persons will acquire toileting skills under conditions of standard care is low (Eyman *et al.*, 1970, 1975). Those with lower general intelligence and lower initial toileting ability have the poorest prognosis (Eyman *et al.*, 1970, 1975; Lohmann *et al.*, 1967; R. E. Smith & Sanderson, 1966). In addition, there is some evidence that toileting skills are less likely to be acquired by older persons who remain incontinent (Lohmann *et al.*, 1967). Furthermore, if toileting skills have not been acquired within the first year or so of admission, they are unlikely to be acquired later (Eyman *et al.*, 1970). There have been few attempts to discover whether these or any other nontraining variables also affect the likelihood that toilet skills will be acquired when training is provided, although information of this kind could be of practical use in both identifying those most likely to benefit from training and selecting the most appropriate training procedures for particular individuals.

Three published studies (Kimbrell *et al.*, 1967; P. S. Smith & Smith, 1977; Spencer, Temerlin, & Trousdale, 1968) and two unpublished studies (Bettison, 1982b) provided data on the relationship of nontraining factors with improvement during training. The factors considered were age, general level of functioning, whether care was provided at home or in an institution, length of institutionalization, and pretraining toileting skill. The Kimbrell study compared behavior-shaping techniques with standard care, as described earlier. The measure of toileting was the score on the toileting section of the VSMS. Smith and Smith replicated the Azrin and Foxx (1971) program and looked at the reduction in voiding accidents and the training time required to achieve these reductions. Spencer *et al.* were only concerned with bowel control. They rewarded toilet sitting and defecation in the toilet and measured changes in the proportion of defecations which occurred in the toilet.

The two studies by Bettison which are relevant here were part of a series of studies concerned with incontinence and toilet-training strategies for the retarded. Study One compared three major training strategies employed in the Azrin and Foxx program with each other and with three corresponding control conditions. The main measurement of improvement consisted of the toileting scale of the Balthazar Adaptive Behavior Scales (Balthazar, 1982), which provided a composite score based on a number of the skills involved in self-toileting. Several other measures were also extracted from the training records, including time in training and the number of voiding accidents, toilet voidings, and self-initiated toiletings, each as a percentage of total daily voidings. Study Two compared the effects of two training strategies and corresponding control conditions when they were incorporated into a program employing backward chaining procedures. The toileting measures considered in this study included those used in Study One, together with a measure of time taken to void in the toilet and ratings of accident size and the five nonvoiding tasks (see Fig. 1).

a. Age. The range of ages in the three studies which examined this factor were as follows: 5–18 years (Kimbrell *et al.*, 1967), 4–20 years (Bettison, 1982b), and 6–56 years (P. S. Smith & Smith, 1977). The first two studies found no significant relationship between age and progress during training, although, in the Kimbrell *et al.* study, the younger trainees tended to make greater gains than the older trainees. In contrast, Smith and Smith found that those under 18 years of age showed a significantly greater reduction in voiding accidents during training than those over 18 years, and they achieved this reduction more rapidly. It is possible that the data from the other two studies may also have reached significance with trainees from a wider age group.

b. General Level of Functioning. Both Bettison (1982b) and P. S. Smith and Smith (1977) examined the relationship between general level of functioning as assessed by the VSMS and progress during training. Social Age ranged from 1.8 to 3.5 in Bettison's Study One ($n=32$) and from 2.6 to 3.0 in Study Two ($n=18$). In both studies age was controlled during the analysis of this relationship. The range in the Smith and Smith study was 1.5 to 2.5 ($n=8$). The relationship was not significant in either of the Bettison studies. Smith and Smith did find a significant relationship, but it was based on a very small group with no control for age, a factor which they had already found was related to improvement during training.

c. Institutionalization. Bettison (1982b) also considered length of institutionalization and home versus institutional care. All 32 trainees in Study One had been resident in an institution for varying lengths of time. This factor proved to be unrelated to progress during training. In Study Two, half the children lived with their parents and half lived in an institution. There was no significant difference in the progress made by these two groups during training, although, at follow-up 7–14 months later, the home group were found to have maintained their skills significantly better than the institution group. This finding adds further support to other evidence for the importance of consistent, individualized attention in relation to toileting skills as displayed in nontraining environments (Eyman *et al.,* 1975; Gray & Kasteler, 1969).

d. Pretraining Toileting Skill. It is by no means clear from these few studies that the factors discussed above have any influence on progress during training. However, a factor which would seem to be directly related to at least the speed of acquisition is the amount of skill already possessed by the trainee. Bettison (1982b) examined this factor in the two studies already described. In Study One using the Azrin and Foxx program, training time was significantly less for trainees who had more toileting skills to start with than for those with few skills. In addition, the more skilled trainees were toileting themselves more often by the end of training.

Study Two, on the other hand, used a chaining program designed to overcome some of the problems experienced with the Azrin and Foxx program. In this study, no significant relationship was found between prior skill and any of the eleven measures of toileting skill during training. Differences in initial toileting skill were, in fact, largely equalized by the end of the maximum training period of 28 days. All but one of the 18 trainees were performing most of the toileting sequence independently, and 15 were self toileting and accident free. In contrast, the level of skill reached at the end of 28 days in Study One was much more variable. Only 17 of the 32 trainees were consistently toileting themselves, 6 others were performing some parts of the sequence independently, while 9 had made almost no progress. One additional study examined this factor but only considered bowel control as it was affected by a simple reinforcement program (Spencer *et al.,* 1968). They actually found that trainees with a higher proportion of initial defecations in the toilet showed the smallest increase in the proportion during training and concluded that such trainees were therefore less able to benefit from training. However, it is more likely that these trainees had less room for improvement, as they were already close to the physiological limit of defecations which can occur.

e. Summary. On the basis of these results, Bettison (1982b) concluded that, as procedural refinements in toilet training are developed which allow the entire toileting sequence to be established, nontraining factors such as those discussed here may become increasingly irrelevant to the amount and speed of progress which individual trainees can make. Nevertheless, there may be other nontraining factors which are important. One, which is highly related to continuing incontinence under conditions of standard care and which has usually been the basis for exclusion from toilet training, is the existence of a number of pathological conditions (Bettison, 1983). It is important that such factors be identified, not only to prevent individuals from being subjected to unnecessary failure, but also to encourage further research into alternative procedures specifically directed at accommodating these factors (Bettison, 1978, 1981a).

2. COMPONENTS OF TRAINING PROGRAMS AND THEIR EFFECTS

The evaluation of specific training procedures has been directed at groups of procedures derived from particular theoretical or methodological strategies developed in the laboratory. Three major training strategies, commonly employed in the more complex toilet-training programs for retarded persons, have been investigated in four separate studies. Each of these studies illustrates the difficulties faced when attempting to isolate the contribution of specific training components when a number of procedures are applied in combination to a sequence of related and predetermined responses.

One strategy consisted of contingent consequences for voiding. This has usually involved positive reinforcement for toilet voiding and, in some programs, punishment for voiding accidents and additional rewards for remaining dry. A second strategy has involved some form of behavior shaping for the nonvoiding skills, employing procedures such as prompting, guidance, positive reinforcement, and fading. A third strategy has employed alarm devices to detect and signal the onset of voiding. Mahoney and his colleagues (Mahoney *et al.*, 1971; Van Wagenen *et al.*, 1969) used a pants alarm which could be activated either by voiding or by a trainer via a hand-held FM radio transmitter. The sounding of the alarm was used as a prompt for toileting. This use of the alarm was incorporated into a forward chaining procedure which was tested with three 18- to 21-month-old children and five older retarded children, although no experimental studies of the program have been reported. Azrin and his colleagues employed alarm devices somewhat differently (Azrin *et al.*, 1971; Azrin & Foxx, 1971). A pants alarm signaled the onset of a voiding accident and was followed by a mild punishment. A separate toilet alarm signaled the onset of toilet voiding which was then followed by a positive reinforcement.

One study looked at the contribution of pants alarms and shaping procedures for the nonvoiding skills, using an analysis of variance design (Wright, 1975). Four experimental groups, each containing four children, received positive reinforcement for toilet voiding. Children in two of the four groups wore pants alarms which signaled when toileting was to occur (Mahoney *et al.*, 1971; Van Wagenen *et al.*, 1969), and children in two groups did not wear alarms but were toileted at the most likely voiding times, as indicated by baseline records. In one group in each condition children also received a faded prompting and physical guidance procedure for the nonvoiding skills (Azrin & Foxx, 1971; Foxx & Azrin, 1973), while in the other group children had these tasks done for them if they did not carry them out voluntarily. Two further groups received no training and acted as control groups. Training continued for 60 days, and continuous records were kept of accident rate, toilet voidings, self-initiated toiletings (including those where help was needed with clothing or other tasks), and fully toileting.

All experimental groups improved on all measures, while the two control groups showed no improvement. In addition, the shaping-plus-pants-alarm group self-initiated significantly more than the other groups. Shaping, irrespective of whether the pants alarm was used, led to more fully independent toileting. The pants alarm appeared to increase the efficiency of training during acquisition, since by the end of training children in the shaping-plus-pants-alarm group who had not reached full independence were self-initiating more, but the pants alarm did not affect whether or not children finally achieved full independence.

Although the actual function of the pants alarm cannot be determined from Wright's data, this study indicated that there may be some small advantage gained from using pants alarms to signal the onset of voiding so that the trainee can be rushed to the toilet.

P. S. Smith (1979) compared the two uses of alarm devices with two groups of five retarded children. The basic Azrin and Foxx program was modified so that it could be used with both alarm procedures. Both groups sat close to the toilet, received extra fluids and were prompted to the toilet every half-hour, were rewarded for voiding in the toilet, and were additionally rewarded every 5 minutes if they were dry. The prompts were gradually faded and, when self-initiated toileting was established, the children were gradually moved further from the toilet and the alarms were removed. However, one group was toileted when the pants alarm sounded in addition to being prompted to the toilet every half-hour by the trainer-activated alarm. The other group received mild punishment when the pants alarm sounded, and the half-hour toiletings occurred without the alarm as a prompt.

All five children trained with the Azrin and Foxx method achieved independent toileting in the 12 weeks allotted, compared with four of five trained with the Mahoney method. However, the difference in improvement for the two methods was not significant. Furthermore, the one child who did not reach independence was more resistant to training in general than the other children. Trainers found the Mahoney method more difficult than the Azrin and Foxx method, and the Mahoney alarm devices were more expensive and bulkier. For these reasons, Smith favored the Azrin and Foxx method, although there was little to choose between the two systems in terms of success rate. Evidence was also provided for the benefit of extra fluid intake during training (P. S. Smith & Wong, 1981).

As in the Wright (1975) study, the operation of the pants alarm was not the sole focus of the Smith experiment. Several other major differences in procedure accompanied the different uses of the alarm. Hence, one can only speculate on the actual role of the pants alarm in the two training methods. However, while Mahoney et al. (1971) recognized the function of the alarm as a discriminative stimulus for the learner, Smith was the first to discuss its possible complex effects on the acquisition of bladder control and questioned its value when used as a cue for toileting. He suggested that when toileting is established in response to the onset of voiding, as signalled by the pants alarm, it is tied to the stimulus of a full bladder. This may maintain a reliance on reflex voiding rather than inducing the voluntary control necessary to void before the bladder reaches its maximum capacity, a skill which ensures the preplanned voiding necessary for total accident-free functioning during everyday activities. Thus, a device which was first introduced as a partially automated method to assist the experimenter with response detection may in fact have quite complex effects on trainee performance. Its function when paired with punishment for voiding accidents is also unclear (Wright, 1975).

Bettison (1982b), as mentioned earlier, investigated the role of all three training strategies as they were combined in the Azrin and Foxx program (Azrin & Foxx, 1971; Foxx & Azrin 1973). This study, referred to as Study One for convenience, used a three-way factorial design with two levels on each factor. The first level consisted of one of the three training strategies and the second was a corresponding control condition. These were as follows. In the control condition for contingent consequences, consequences were delivered noncontingently at random times during the training day so as not to coincide with the targeted behavior. The number of each type of noncontingent consequence delivered each day was determined by the number of occurrences in the previous day of the behavior associated with it. This condition was intended to approximately equalize the amount of systematic attention received by the experimental and control groups. The shaping procedures used to train the nonvoiding skills were tested against a control condition in which the tasks were done for trainees if they did not perform them independently or in response to a single instruction. The alarms in the third control condition were set off manually by the trainer, and the number and timing of their occurrence was determined in the same way as for noncontingent consequences.

Trainees were randomly allocated to eight groups of four and each group received a different combination of training and control procedures. Age, sex, length of institutionalization, general level of functioning, and pretraining toileting skill were controlled by both matching groups on these variables and including them as covariates in the data analysis. The dependent variable was improvement on the day- and nighttime toileting scales of the Balthazar Adaptive Behavior Scales (Balthazar, 1982) described earlier. The assessment was of performance in the everyday environment rather than in the training environment.

No significant effects of training strategies were found, either in relation to each other or when compared with the control conditions. Nevertheless, there was significant improvement in daytime toileting irrespective of training strategy, with 23 of the 32 trainees showing at least some improvement and 13 completing training to criterion. Nighttime toileting was no different after training than it had been before training.

These results support earlier evidence that the Azrin and Foxx program does lead to improvement in toileting skills, although the three major strategies used in the program did not appear to be crucial and the success rate was not as high as in other studies (Azrin & Foxx, 1971; Sadler & Merkert, 1977; P. S. Smith, 1979). Smith suggested that it is the structured framework provided by intensive toilet training programs which may be the crucial factor, rather than the exact nature of the training procedures themselves. The Bettison study appeared to support this view. However, uncontrolled influences in the everyday environment where toileting was assessed in this study may also have cancelled any training strategy effects. For this reason, Bettison extracted several toileting measures from the training records.

Although these measures were not entirely satisfactory, they did tentatively indicate some training strategy effects. To summarize, shaping appeared to enhance acquisition of the nonvoiding skills, as indicated by Wright (1975), and contingent consequences increased the speed with which toilet approach, pants down, sitting, and toilet voiding together were performed. Shaping and contingent alarms also contributed to this increase in performance speed, but the way in which they contributed was not clear because several skills were incorporated in the measure which displayed this effect, and each skill may have been affected differently by the two strategies. The primary skills of bladder and bowel control were not acquired well enough to reveal any training strategy effects. Even when the full program incorporating the three training strategies was used, both in this study and in an earlier pilot study (Bettison et al., 1976), some skills did not improve and some trainees made little or no progress.

A possible explanation for the lower success rate in the Bettison studies lies in the greater improvement among trainees who had more toileting skills before training. Azrin and Foxx (1971) did not assess pretraining toileting ability. However, they recorded an average accident rate before training of approximately two per day. In the Bettison studies, most trainees were having five or more accidents a day before training, and some never voided in the toilet. This suggests that Azrin and Foxx's trainees had more ability to hold back voiding than many of the trainees in these studies, and they may also have had more toileting ability generally. They were therefore more likely to succeed during training than many of the trainees in these studies, a number of whom either failed to acquire all the components of toileting or failed to join them together as a smooth and correctly sequenced performance. Bettison concluded that the Azrin and Foxx procedures were directed at only some parts of the toileting sequence and were therefore ineffective for trainees who had not already acquired those aspects which were not taught adequately.

An examination of individual training records from the Bettison studies, together with other reports of toilet training with the Azrin and Foxx procedures (A. Pfadt, personal communication, October, 1982; Singh, 1976; P. S. Smith, 1979; Smith *et al.*, 1975), identified a number of program inadequacies which can only be summarized here. The punishment and overcorrection procedure was generally ineffective and sometimes positively rewarding. The transition from bladder training to self-initiation training after the first independent toileting did not allow the new skills to stabilize, and trainees often stopped toileting themselves and began having more voiding accidents. Many trainees had difficulty acquiring the pants-up-and-down and the toilet-flushing responses and were still requiring considerable prompting and guidance at the end of training. In addition, several trainees learned to void only enough in the toilet to set off the toilet alarm and receive the reward and hence continued to have frequent voiding accidents.

Not all the elements of self-toileting were included in the sequence of training. On every trial during the first bladder-training phase, the learner went through the entire toileting sequence, as defined in the program. This occurred every half-hour during training. Although the extra fluids increased the chance that some urine had accumulated in the bladder by the end of each half-hour, there still remained a considerable element of chance. In fact, many toiletings during training in the Bettison study did not result in voiding, since toileting often occurred shortly after an accident, leaving no time for the accumulation of sufficient waste in the bladder. This may explain the failure of many trainees to acquire the skills involved in voluntarily bringing about voiding in the toilet. Moreover, tightening the perineal muscles in the presence of bladder or bowel tension, which is an essential element in the toileting sequence, was not taught as part of that sequence, although the regular pants checks and punishment-plus-overcorrection procedures attempted to teach it outside the toileting sequence. The pants-check procedure in particular, as represented in Figure 2A, clearly strengthened feeling the pants rather than tightening the perineal muscles, especially since the bladder or bowel tension, as the signal for this response, was not usually one of the stimuli present during the pants checks.

A number of individuals in the Bettison study also confused the order of responses when carrying out the toileting sequence. This may have been because the responses were not added to the sequence one at a time. It may also have been because some of the linking stimuli were not established as discriminative stimuli within the chain. For instance, several trainees tried to pull their pants up or down when the opposite response was required, began to sit again after pulling their pants up, or began standing part way through seating themselves on the toilet. These responses had not come under stimulus control. The two responses, pants up and pants down, shown in Figure 2B illustrate this.

In these two situations the position of the trainee by the toilet and the position of the pants on the body are the naturally occurring stimuli which should come to

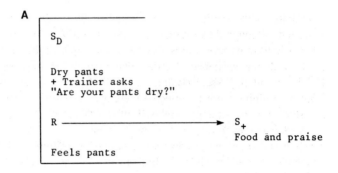

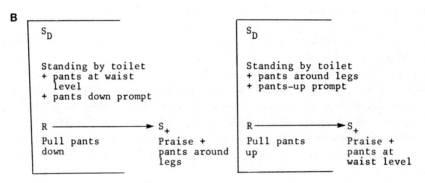

FIG. 2. Analysis of the pants-check procedure and the procedures to teach pants down and pants up in the Azrin and Foxx toilet training program.

control the two responses. However, the position at the toilet was the same in both cases, leaving the position of the pants as the only indication of which response was required. The two different prompts were designed to aid this discrimination during acquisition, but, unless the person actually learned to pay attention to the position of the pants, environmental control could not be achieved reliably. Moreover, in normal self-toileting, the presence of bladder or bowel tension is an additional, naturally occurring discriminative stimulus for pants down, and its absence then comes to signal pants up after voiding has occurred. Since toileting trials in the Azrin and Foxx program often occurred in the absence of bladder or bowel tension, especially when they followed close on an accident, these stimuli were unable to function as cues in this way.

Despite these problems, some quite specific training-strategy effects were indicated, although the evidence for these effects was complicated by both inadequacies in training procedures and the lack of separate measures of each response in the toileting sequence. Neither one overall toileting measure such as the Balthazar toileting scale (Balthazar, 1982) nor the partial measures extracted from the training records reflected the entire acquisition process or the specific nature of training-strategy effects. Bettison therefore devised a number of measures to enable each response in the toileting chain to be monitored throughout baseline and training. In addition, a new toilet-training program was designed which incorporated many of the existing procedures but arranged them according to a more detailed functional analysis of toileting as an operant chain. Particular attention was given to the training and overlearning of each component skill, sequencing, stimulus control, further expansion of the more difficult skills into a more detailed sequence, and minimizing the possibility of errors during acquisition. This program and the response measures have been described in full in a manual (Bettison, 1982a). Briefly, the self-toileting sequence was presented to the learner as a chain to be acquired, starting with those elements at the end of the sequence and progressing back through the chain in reverse order to that in which the elements would eventually be carried out (see Fig. 3). The main toileting sequence incorporating the naturally occurring linking stimuli is represented down the center line of the figure, with the programmed discriminative stimuli branching to either side. During the strengthening of each response element, a predetermined response rate was required before the next element was added for strengthening. Trials for pants up and standing from the toilet, as the first two responses to be learned, occurred three times every half-hour during training. However, once the third response, voiding in the toilet, and the following responses were added for strengthening, bladder or bowel tension became an essential discriminative cue, and trials only occurred when these stimuli were present.

The sounding of the pants alarm indicated the onset of voiding in the pants. Since bladder or bowel tension was always present at the time of an uncontrolled voiding, all trials during acquisition followed the sounding of the pants alarm. The trainer shouted "NO" as the alarm sounded, and the learner was then quickly moved through the toileting sequence by the trainer but was not required to initiate any response until the one to be strengthened was reached. The toileting trial began at this point, using prompts and physical guidance to shape each response.

Most of the response elements of this chain already occur frequently in the repertoire of any retarded person who may be trained using this program. For instance, all trainees frequently walked, seated themselves, remained sitting for long periods, got up from a sitting position, and voided. Incorporating these responses into the self-toileting sequence generally required only that they be

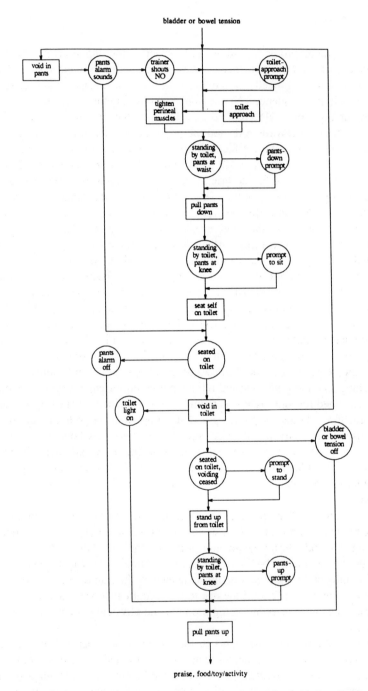

FIG. 3. Representation of the chaining program. Circles denote discriminative stimuli and rectangles denote the appropriate response.

brought, as units, under the discriminative control of the natural linking stimuli in the chain. However, the pants-down and pants-up responses were often incomplete or did not exist at all before training. When this was the case, the subloops shown in Fig. 4 were added to the chaining procedures, using the usual backward chaining methods.

The theoretical advantage of these procedures over the Azrin and Foxx (1971) procedures resided in their placement in the sequence. The aversive consequence and the positive reinforcement were both attached to the discriminative stimulus of bladder or bowel tension. Eventually bladder or bowel tension should have come to signal that tightening the perineal muscles before any voiding occurred would allow the learner to avoid the aversive stimulus, while performance of the toileting sequence would lead to the reward.

The arrangement of discriminative cues attempted to overcome the confusion which some children in Bettison's Study One experienced during the Azrin and Foxx program. The pants alarm continued to sound during the performance of the first four responses which normally occurred in the presence of bladder or bowel tension during toileting. It was intended that the pairing of that tension with the alarm would bring it into awareness so that it would eventually come to exert control on its own. The onset of voiding in the toilet switched on a toilet light which remained on until the child left the toilet cubicle after pulling the pants up correctly. Thus, the light was on during the last three responses in the toileting sequence. These responses normally occurred during the relief from and absence of bladder or bowel tension. Consequently, as a result of the chaining process, the light became a conditioned reinforcer to strengthen perineal relaxation and voiding. It also became a discriminative stimulus which signaled that standing and pulling up pants were appropriate. It was hoped that the pairing of relief from bladder or bowel tension with the light would allow that state to exert control over these responses.

Once a near-continuous rate of accurate toileting in response to bladder or bowel tension alone was reached, the chain was regarded as established. No further strengthening of elements in the chain occurred and the remaining programmed stimuli were gradually faded. As each response in the chain was acquired, the prompts and physical guidance were also faded. Similarly, at the end of training, the trainees were gradually moved further away from the toilet until they were moving freely about the unit. Once accident-free, self-initiated toileting was again occurring reliably, the pants and toilet alarms, then the extra fluids were removed, and the trainees were ready to resume their usual activities with the addition of a simple maintenance program to help them transfer their new skills.

This program was used to again examine training-strategy effects in a second investigation referred to as Study Two (Bettison, 1982b). However, because of the complicated nature of the effects found in Study One, only the application of

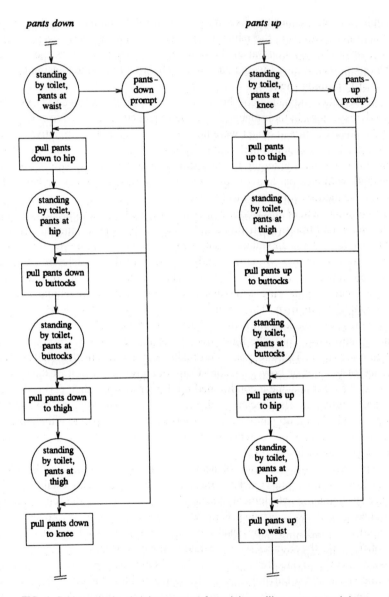

FIG. 4. Subloops in the chaining program for training pulling pants up and down.

positive reinforcement was considered. The most puzzling result during investi-gation of the Azrin and Foxx program was the failure to find clear and consistent effects of contingent consequences. Not only is the effect of consequences cen-tral to many learning theories which deal with the acquisition of new behavior (Hilgard & Bower, 1975), but toileting has generally been regarded as an instru-mental response which is particularly amenable to the effects of consequences (Ellis, 1963; Gardner, 1971; Watson, 1967). If toileting is an instrumental re-sponse, then manipulation of consequences in an environment which provides sufficient behavioral control should lead to clear effects on acquisition. In Study One, the consequences consisted of both the delivery of reward to strengthen self-toileting and remaining dry and the application of punishment to suppress voiding outside the toilet. The manipulation of this combination of procedures may have complicated the results, especially as the effects of punishment are less certain than the effects of positive reinforcement. Therefore, only the effects of manipulating positive reinforcement were considered in Study Two.

Two aspects of reinforcement were compared with each other and with a control condition. Three matched groups of six trainees each, as described ear-lier, received training. One group also received positive reinforcement, consist-ing of an individually preferred reward, praise, and physical affection, con-tingent on correct completion of the task. The second received noncontingent positive reinforcement, delivered 10 to 60 minutes after each successful re-sponse, providing that toileting was not occurring. This provided roughly equal amounts of reinforcement in each condition. The third group received no system-atic positive reinforcement. Training-strategy effects were analyzed using the t test. Planned comparisons were also made comparing the contingent with the noncontingent group and the two reinforcement groups together with the no-reinforcement group.

Improvement in the pants-up, standing, and sitting skills was not analyzed, since all children achieved mastery in all groups, indicating that reinforcement was clearly not essential for the learning of these components. In addition, neither the provision of reinforcement nor its contingency made any significant difference to training time or the number of training phases completed during training. The remaining measures consisted of ratings of the pants-down and toilet-approach responses and accident size, the recorded time taken to void in the toilet, and the number of voiding accidents, toilet voidings, and self-initiated toiletings, each as a percentage of total daily voidings. No significant effects on improvement of either reinforcement or contingency were found except in rela-tion to the measure of voiding accidents. The proportion of voidings which were accidents decreased considerably more with noncontingent than with contingent reinforcement.

This last finding may have resulted from the way accidents were treated in the chaining program. The loud "NO" which followed immediately when an accident began did, in fact, induce the muscle action required to inhibit involuntary voiding, as shown by a significant decrease in accident size during training. In doing so, it probably acted as a negative reinforcer, with the muscle action, thereby operating as an avoidance response. This procedure was immediately followed by toileting, with a reward delivered at the end of the chain whenever toilet voiding occurred in the contingent reinforcement condition. According to operant theory, the discriminative stimuli preceding each response in the chain should have acquired reinforcing properties as a result of this process. The loud "NO" may also have come to function as a discriminative stimulus for the next element in the toileting chain which followed it. Therefore, it may also have acquired positive reinforcing characteristics, thus reducing its effectiveness as a negative reinforcer. However, if this did occur, it was not a strong enough effect to prevent considerable reduction in voiding accidents for most trainees.

While reinforcement and contingency did not affect acquisition during training, the training program itself resulted in significant improvement in all measures except the time taken to void in the toilet. The lack of significance in this case was probably caused by the large number of trainees with baseline scores at or just below the best possible score, thus leaving little room for improvement. Similarly, scores on the Balthazar daytime toileting scale 7–14 months after training had ceased were significantly better than before training, but again displayed no significant training-strategy effects.

Conclusions about the relative merits of the Azrin and Foxx and chaining programs on the basis of these results can only be tentative, since there were many differences in the conditions for the two studies. Moreover, the importance of monitoring each component skill when investigating the acquisition of complex behavioral sequences only emerged gradually during the project of which these two studies were part. Nevertheless, three toileting measures were available from both studies which provided some evidence that the chaining program was more effective than the Azrin and Foxx program.

The measures consisted of improvement in toilet voiding, self-initiated toilet voiding, and voiding accidents as shown by the difference between scores in the first 3 and the last 3 days of training. The contingent and noncontingent groups in both studies, who otherwise received the full training program, were compared on these measures using two-way analysis of covariance to control for both the original matching variables and the beginning of training scores. These last were controlled because higher voiding rates were induced by the extra fluids from the first training day in the Azrin and Foxx program, whereas extra fluids were introduced later in the chaining program. The contingency effect was predictably nonsignificant. However, toilet voiding and self-initiated toileting improved significantly more with the chaining than with the Azrin and Foxx program. The reduction in accident rate was also greater with the chaining program, although this last finding was not significant. This was also the least improved of the skills taught in both programs. In addition, no trainees in Study Two confused the order of responses, and every toileting resulted in voiding after the first day or two of bladder training.

IV. CONCLUSIONS AND NEW DIRECTIONS
FOR RESEARCH

What can be concluded from the research reviewed here? The evidence clearly shows that, for trainees who have few toileting skills, independent toileting and bladder and bowel control are more likely to be acquired when training involves a number of procedures and treats toileting as a complex behavioral sequence. However, the common assumption that systematically applied contingent reinforcement is the major or most effective training procedure under these circumstances has not been borne out by Bettison's (1982b) studies. Nevertheless, reinforcement becomes important once the entire sequence is established and ready for the final strengthening and generalization to take place (Azrin *et al.*, 1971; Passman, 1975). What then are the effective components of the more complex programs?

Both Wright (1975) and Bettison (1982a) provided some evidence that various shaping procedures are important in both establishing the nonvoiding skills and enabling trainees to take control of their own toileting. In addition, alarms which signal the onset of voiding added to the efficiency of training, although the way in which the alarms are used does not appear to be important (P. S. Smith, 1979). This last conclusion, however, should be treated with caution, since the value of the Van Wagenen *et al.* (1969) method may be that it enables chaining methods to be used rather than that it ties toileting to a full bladder as Smith suggests. There is also some evidence that increased fluid intake during training increases bladder capacity and the likelihood that voiding will occur in the toilet (P. S. Smith & Wong, 1981). The beneficial influence of increased fluids on bladder capacity is also supported by a number of studies with nonhandicapped children (Doleys, 1977; Fielding, 1980; Hagglund, 1965; Harris & Purohit, 1977; Mahoney, 1973; Yeates, 1973).

The more complex programs also involve a number of nonoperant procedures whose effectiveness has not been examined. The acquisition of new, complex skills appears to involve quite different principles from those involved in the strengthening and maintenance of behavior which already exists as a unit. A number of authors interested in skill mastery by retarded children in educational settings have similarly differentiated between the acquisition of new skills and the later strengthening and maintaining of already acquired skills (Haring, Liberty, & White, 1980; Rosenshine, 1980). Task breakdown, cues, prompts, and various forms of guidance were seen by these authors as the important factors during acquisition, while reinforcement contingencies became important in the latter stage. The former procedures force or mold the behavior to be learned rather than allowing trial-and-error learning to take place. In Bettison's (1982a,b) chaining program, each response in the toileting sequence was also practiced many times, both during acquisition and after mastery had been achieved. These procedures together both ensured that the behavior to be learned occurred and provided continuous feedback about the nature of the required responses. The operation of response–feedback loops during acquisition has been seen as important by a number of theoreticians (Atkinson & Wickens, 1971; Bloomfield, 1972; Estes, 1971) and may have made reinforcement redundant in Bettison's chaining program.

Some important aspects of research methodology in the evaluation of training programs for complex skills were also highlighted. Much toilet-training research has been limited both by a lack of adequate baselines and by the response measures used. A baseline which provides only a simple measure of voiding accident rate in the natural environment may only indicate the rate of accidents maintained by that environment rather than the level of toileting skill possessed by an individual. In Bettison's Study Two, the baseline was taken in a controlled environment which removed the natural contingencies and constraints in order to determine the operant level of each component skill. Under these conditions several potential trainees with high accident rates in the natural environment became self toileting and accident free without training. The differentiation between operant level and the environmentally maintained level is important for both research and practice. In training research, the concern is usually to discover procedures which will lead to the acquisition of new behavior or the strengthening of partially learned behavior, rather than merely facilitate the performance of behavior which is already an established part of the person's repertoire. Furthermore, training procedures which do not lead to real acquisition are of no practical assistance to intellectually handicapped persons whose lack of self-toileting is due to the absence of required skills.

Bettison (1982b) also demonstrated that the component skills involved in toileting may respond in different ways to different aspects of training. It is therefore important that each component is monitored adequately both before and during training. Separate measures of each skill also enabled Bettison to isolate a number of acquisition problems which were not catered for in the two programs which were examined. The inhibition of involuntary voiding was not completely mastered by many trainees, and several failed to bring defecation under control. Experience since these studies has confirmed that new procedures may be needed to induce both these skills in at least some incontinent retarded persons.

Finally, a few studies have been concerned with procedures to enhance generalization of toileting skills to real-life settings. An indication of one direction for future research in this regard was given by the superior skill maintenance of children living at home compared with institution children in Bettison's Study Two (1982b). Stokes and Baer (1977) have also summarized other procedures which may prove useful.

REFERENCES

Ando, H. (1977). Training autistic children to urinate in the toilet using operant conditioning techniques. *Journal of Autism and Childhood Schizophrenia, 7,* 151–163.

Atkinson, R. C., & Wickens, T. D. (1971). Human memory and the concept of reinforcement. In R. Glaser (Ed.), *The nature of reinforcement.* New York: Academic Press.

Azrin, N. H., Bugle, C., & O'Brien, F. (1971). Behavioral engineering: Two apparatuses for use in toilet training retarded children. *Journal of Applied Behavior Analysis, 4,* 249–253.

Azrin, N. H., & Foxx, R. M. (1971). A rapid method of toilet training the institutionalized retarded. *Journal of Applied Behavior Analysis, 4,* 89–99.

Baker, B. L., Brightman, A. J., Heifetz, L. J., & Murphy, D. M. (1977). *Toilet training: Steps to independence: A skills training series for children with special needs.* Champaign, IL: Research Press.

Baldwin, V. L., Fredericks, H. D. B., & Brodsky, G. (1973). *Isn't it time he outgrew this? Or a training program for parents of retarded children.* Springfield, IL: Charles C. Thomas, 1973.

Balthazar, E. E. (1982). *Balthazar scales of adaptive behaviour for the profoundly and severely mentally retarded. A system for program evaluation and development: Sec. 1. The scales of functional independence.* Palo Alto, CA: Consulting Psychologists.

Bensberg, G. J. (Ed.). (1965). *Teaching the mentally retarded: A handbook for ward personnel.* Atlanta, GA: Southern Regional Education Board.

Bensberg, G. J., Colwell, C. N., & Cassell, R. H. (1965). Teaching the profoundly retarded self-help activities by behavior shaping techniques. *American Journal of Mental Deficiency, 69,* 674–679.

Bettison, S. (1978). Toilet training the retarded. Analysis of the stages of development and procedures for designing programmes. *Australian Journal of Mental Retardation, 5,* 95–100.

Bettison, S. (1980). Daytime wetting and soiling. In A. M. Hudson & M. W. Griffin (Eds.), *Behavior analysis and the problems of childhood.* Collingwood, Victoria, BC: PIT.

Bettison, S. (1981a). The problem of toilet training and the retarded. *Division of Clinical Psychologists Bulletin, Australian Psychological Society, 13,* 30–33.

Bettison, S. (1981b, October). *Self control of bladder and bowel functions: Behavior analysis and a new toilet training programme for intellectually handicaped persons.* Paper presented at the conference of the Australian Group for the Scientific Study of Mental Deficiency, Perth.

Bettison, S. (1982a). *Toilet training to independence for the handicapped. A manual for trainers.* Springfield, IL: Charles C. Thomas.

Bettison, S. (1982b). *A comparison of toilet training strategies for the retarded.* Unpublished doctoral dissertation, University of Adelaide.

Bettison, S. (1983). *A study of incontinence in a State residential institution for the retarded.* Manuscript submitted for publication.

Bettison, S., Davison, D., Taylor, P., & Fox, B. (1976). The long term effects of a toilet training programme for the retarded. A pilot study. *Australian Journal of Mental Retardation, 4,* 28–35.

Bijou, S. W., & Baer, D. M. (1961). *Child development I: A systematic and empirical theory.* New York: Appleton-Century-Crofts.

Bijou, S. W., & Baer, D. M. (1965). *Child development II: Universal stages of infancy.* New York: Appleton-Century-Crofts.

Blackwood, R. O. (1963). Operant conditioning as a method of training the mentally retarded. *Dissertation Abstracts International, 23,* 2974A.

Bloomfield, T. M. (1972). Reinforcement schedules: Contingency or contiguity? In R. M. Gilbert & J. R. Millenson (Eds.), *Reinforcement Behavioral Analysis.* New York: Academic Press.

Butler, J. F. (1976). Toilet training a child with spina bifida. *Journal of Behavior Therapy and Experimental Psychiatry, 7,* 63–65.

Caldwell, K. P. S. (Ed.). (1975). *Urinary incontinence.* London: Sector.

Clarke, A. M., & Clarke, A. D. B. (Eds.). (1974). *Mental deficiency: The changing outlook* (3rd ed.). London: Methuen.

Dayan, M. (1964). Toilet training retarded children in a state residential institution. *Mental Retardation, 2,* 116–117.

Dixon, J., & Smith, P. S. (1976). The use of a pants alarm in daytime toilet training. *British Journal of Mental Subnormality, 22,* 20–25.

Doleys, D. M. (1977). Behavioral treatments for nocturnal enuresis in children. A review of the recent literature. *Psychological Bulletin, 84,* 30–54.

Ellis, N. R. (1963). Toilet training the severely defective patient: An S-R reinforcement analysis. *American Journal of Mental Deficiency, 68,* 98–103.

Estes, W. K. (1980). Reward in human learning: Theoretical issues and strategic choice points. In R. Glasser (Ed.), *The nature of reinforcement.* New York: Academic Press.

Eyman, R. K., Silverstein, A. B., & McLain, R. (1975). Effects of treatment programs on the acquisition of basic skills. *American Journal of Mental Deficiency, 79,* 573–582.

Eyman, R. K., Tarjan, G., & Cassady, M. (1970). Natural history of acquisition of basic skills by hospitalized retarded patients. *American Journal of Mental Deficiency, 75,* 120–129.

Fielding, L. (1972). Initial ward-wide behavior modification programs for retarded children. In T. Thompson & J. Grabowski (Eds.), *Behavior modification of the mentally retarded.* New York: Oxford University Press.

Fielding, D. (1980). The response of day and night wetting children and children who wet only at night to retention control training and the enuresis alarm. *Behavior Research and Therapy, 18,* 305–317.

Foxx, R. M., & Azrin, N. H. (1973). *Toilet training the retarded: A rapid program for day and night time independent toileting.* Champaign, IL: Research Press.

Gardner, W. I. (1971). *Behavior modification in mental retardation.* Chicago: Aldine.

Giles, D. K., & Wolf, M. M. (1966). Toilet training in institutionalized severe retardates: An application of operant behavior modification techniques. *American Journal of Mental Deficiency, 70,* 766–780.

Grabowski, J., & Thompson, T. (1972). A behavior modification program for behaviorally retarded institutionalized males. In T. Thompson & J. Grabowski (Eds.), *Behavior modification of the mentally retarded.* New York: Oxford University Press.

Gray, R. M., & Kasteler, J. M. (1969). The effects of social reinforcement and training on institutionalized mentally retarded children. *American Journal of Mental Deficiency, 74,* 50–56.

Hagglund, T. B. (1965). Enuretic children treated with fluid restriction or forced drinking. A clinical and systematic study. *Annales Paediatriae Fenniae, 11,* 84–90.

Hamilton, J. (1971). Environmental control and retardate behavior. In H. C. Rickard (Ed.), *Behavioral intervention in human problems.* New York: Pergamon.

Haring, N. G., Liberty, K. A., & White, O. R. (1980). Rules for data based strategy decisions in instructional programs: Current research and instructional implications. In W. Sailor, B. Wilcox, & L. Brown (Eds.), *Methods of instruction for severely handicapped students.* Baltimore: Brookes.

Harris, L. S., & Purohit, A. P. (1977). Bladder training and enuresis: A controlled trial. *Behavior Research and Therapy,* **15,** 485–490.

Hilgard, E. R., & Bower, G. H. (1975). *Theories of learning* (4th ed.). Englewood Cliffs, NJ: Prentice-Hall.

Hjalmos, K. (1976). Micturition in infants and children with normal lower urinary tract. *Scandinavian Journal of Urology and Nephrology Supplement,* No. 37.

Hundziak, M., Maurer, R. A., & Watson, L. S. (1971). Operant conditioning in toilet training of severely retarded boys. In A. M. Graziano (Ed.), *Behavior therapy with children.* Chicago: Aldine.

Kaines, I. (1979). *A manual for toilet training using electronic alarms.* Adelaide: South Australian Institute for Developmental Disabilities.

Kimbrell, D. L., Luckey, R. E., Barbuto, P. F. P., & Love, J. G. (1967). Operation dry pants: An intensive habit-training program for severely and profoundly retarded. *Mental Retardation,* **5,** 32–36.

Kolvin, I., MacKeith, R. C., & Meadow, S. R. (Eds.). (1973). *Bladder control and enuresis.* London: Heinemann.

Kugel, R. B., & Wolfensberger, W. P. (Eds.). (1969). *Changing patterns in residential services for the mentally retarded.* Washington, DC: President's Committee on Mental Retardation.

Lancioni, G. E. (1980). Teaching independent toileting to profoundly retarded deaf–blind children. *Behavior Therapy,* **11,** 234–244.

Leath, J. R., & Flournoy, R. L. (1970). Three-year follow up of intensive habit-training program. *Mental Retardation,* **8,** 32–34.

Levine, M. N., & Elliott, C. B. (1970). Toilet training for profoundly retarded with a limited staff. *Mental Retardation,* **8,** 48–50.

Lohmann, W., Eyman, R. K., & Lask, E. (1967). Toilet training. *American Journal of Mental Deficiency,* **71,** 551–557.

MacKeith, R., Meadow, R., & Turner, R. K. (1973). How children become dry. In I. Kolvin, R. C. MacKeith, & S. R. Meadow (Eds.), *Bladder control and enuresis.* London: Heinemann.

Mahoney, K. (1973). Frequency and quantity of nocturnal urinary emissions after diurnal toilet training and after training to restrain reflex voiding in children. *Dissertation Abstracts International,* **34,** 1705A.

Mahoney, K., Van Wagenen, R. K., & Meyerson, L. (1971). Toilet training of normal and retarded children. *Journal of Applied Behavior Analysis,* **4,** 173–181.

Muellner, S. R. (1958). The voluntary control of micturition in man. *Journal of Urology,* **80,** 473–478.

Muellner, S. R. (1960a). Development of urinary control in children. *Journal of the American Medical Association,* **172,** 1256–1261.

Muellner, S. R. (1960b). Development of urinary control in children: A new concept in cause, prevention and treatment of primary enuresis. *Journal of Urology,* **84,** 714–716.

Muellner, S. R. (1965). Primary enuresis in children: A new concept of its cause and treatment. *Journal of the Kentucky Medical Association,* **63,** 253–255.

O'Connor, G., Crawford, L., & Gunn, R. (1964). Data collection systems in an institution for the mentally retarded. In J. Levy & R. M. Hunter (Eds.), *Data collection and utilization in institutions for the mentally retarded.* Boulder, CO: Western Interstate Commission for Higher Education.

Passman, R. H. (1975). An automatic device for toilet training. *Behaviour Research and Therapy,* **13,** 215–220.

Roos, P., & Oliver, M. (1969). Evaluation of operant conditioning with institutionalized retarded children. *American Journal of Mental Deficiency,* **74,** 325–330.

Rosenshine, B. V. (1980). *Direct instruction for skill mastery.* Paper presented to the School of Education, University of Milwaukee, Milwaukee.

Sadler, O. W., & Merkert, F. (1977). Evaluating the Foxx and Azrin toilet training procedure for retarded children in a day training centre. *Behavior Therapy*, **8**, 499–500.

Schaefer, C. E. (1979). *Childhood encopresis and enuresis. Causes and therapy*. New York: Van Nostrand-Reinhold.

Schuster, M. M. (1968). Motor action of rectum and anal sphincters in continence and defecation. In C. F. Code (Ed.), *Handbook of physiology: Sec. 6. Alimentary canal: Vol. 4. Motility*. Washington, DC: American Physiological Society.

Singh, N. N. (1976). Toilet training a severely retarded non-verbal child. *Australian Journal of Mental Retardation*, **4**, 15–18.

Smith, P. S. (1979). A comparison of different methods of toilet training the mentally handicapped. *Behaviour Research and Therapy*, **17**, 33–43.

Smith, P. S., Britton, P. G., Johnson, M., & Thomas, D. A. (1975). Problems involved in toilet training profoundly mentally handicapped adults. *Behaviour Research and Therapy*, **13**, 301–307.

Smith, P. S., & Smith, L. J. (1977). Chronological age and social age as factors in intensive daytime toilet training of institutionalized mentally retarded individuals. *Journal of Behavior Therapy and Experimental Psychiatry*, **8**, 1–5.

Smith, P. S., & Wong, H. (1981). Changes in bladder function during toilet training of mentally handicapped children. *Behavior Research of Severe Developmental Disabilities*, **2**, 137–155.

Smith, R. E., & Sanderson, R. E. (1966). Relationship of habit training to measured intelligence in severely retarded patients. *California Mental Health Research Digest*, **4**, 154–155.

Spencer, R. L., Temerlin, M. K., & Trousdale, W. W. (1968). Some correlates of bowel control in the profoundly retarded. *American Journal of Mental Deficiency*, **72**, 879–882.

Stokes, T. F., & Baer, D. M. (1977). Implicit technology of generalisation. *Journal of Applied Behavior Analysis*, **10**, 349–367.

Tierney, A. J. (1973). Toilet training. *Nursing Times*, **27**, 1740–1745.

Tizard, J. (1974). Services and the evaluation of services. In A. M. Clarke & A. D. B. Clarke (Eds.), *Mental deficiency: The changing outlook* (3rd ed.). London: Methuen.

Tredgold, R. F., & Soddy, K. (1956). *A textbook of mental deficiency* (9th ed.). London: Baillière.

Van Wagenen, R. K., Meyerson, L., Kerr, N. J., & Mahoney, K. (1969). Field trials of a new procedure for toilet training. *Journal of Experimental Child Psychology*, **8**, 147–159.

Watson, L. S. (1967). Application of operant conditioning techniques to institutionalized severely and profoundly retarded children. *Mental Retardation Abstracts*, **4**, 1–18.

Watson, L. S. (1973a). *Child behavior modification. A manual for teachers, nurses and parents*. New York: Pergamon.

Watson, L. S. (1973b). *How to use behavior modification with mentally retarded and autistic children: Programs for administrators, parents, teachers and nurses*. New York: Pergamon.

Wolf, M. M., Risley, T., Johnston, J., Harris, F., & Allen, E. (1967). Application of operant conditioning procedures to the behavior problems of an autistic child: A follow-up and extension. *Behaviour Research and Therapy*, **5**, 103–111.

Wright, J. M. C. (1975). *Comparison of toilet training techniques with institutionalized retarded children*. Unpublished master's dissertation, University of Queensland.

Yates, A. J. (1970). *Behavior therapy*. New York: Wiley.

Yeates, W. K. (1973). Bladder function in normal micturition. In I. Kolvin, R. C. MacKeith, & S. R. Meadow (Eds.), *Bladder control and enuresis*. Philadelphia: Lippincott.

Young, G. C. (1973). The treatment of childhood encopresis by conditioned gastroileal reflex training. *Behaviour Research and Therapy*, **11**, 499–503.

Index

A

Action decrement, molar variability and, 81
Adaptation, home environments and, 279, 281
Aggression, social competence, employment and, 243
Anxiety, sexual deviance and, 305
Apology training, sexual deviance and, 302, 309
Aptitude X Treatment Interactions, computer-assisted instruction and, 127
Arousal, molar variability and, 75
  action decrement, 81
  optimal stimulation, 78
Attribution theory, intrinsic motivation and, 6, 7
Autism, errorless discrimination training and, 136, 144, 145, 158
Aversive imagery, sexual deviance and, 295, 306
  fetishism, 293, 296, 297
Avoidance
  molar variability and, 75
  toilet training and, 344

B

Backward chaining procedures, toilet training and, 331, 341
Balthazar Adaptive Behavior Scales, toilet training and, 331, 335
Balthazar toileting scale, 339, 344
Biobehavioral differences, home environments and, 279
Bladder control, toilet training and, 319–322, 326, 335–337, 345
Boredom, molar variability and, 74, 76, 77
Bowel control, toilet training and, 319–322, 326
  nontraining factors, 330, 332
  program components, 336

C

Categorizing, rehearsal deficit hypothesis and, 49
Catholicism, families, mentally retarded children and, 205, 206
Cerebral palsy, families, mentally retarded children and, 207
Chaining, toilet training and, 327, 332, 337, 340, 342, 344, *see also* Backward chaining procedures
Choice Motivator Scale, intrinsic motivation and, 12, 15, 17–22, 27
Choice-sequence preference, molar variability and, 84
Chunking, rehearsal deficit hypothesis and, 55, 57
Classical conditioning
  sexual deviance and, 306
  toilet training and, 322
Cloze tests, reading and, 181, 182, 184, 190
Cognitive environmental sets, 261
Complexity
  computer-assisted instruction and, 107
  molar variability and, 78, 79
Comprehension, reading and, 170, 180–184, 189, 190
Computer-assisted instruction, 105, 106
  active learning and, 108, 109
  effectiveness, 106, 107
  individualized instruction, 109–112
  mentally retarded and, 115, 116
    literature, 125, 126
    programming, 116–119
    research, 119–125
    research suggestions, 126–128
  motivation and, 107, 108
  reading and, 179, 180
  tutoring and, 112–115
Conditioned response, molar variability and, 85, 90, 92

Conditioned stimulus, molar variability and,
    85, 90
Consistency, home environments and, 268,
    269, 280
Construct validity, intrinsic motivation and, 17
Contextual analysis, reading and, 169
Contextual cues, reading and, 186, 190
Contingency
    sexual deviance, treatment of, 306, 308
        exhibitionism, 292
        pedophilia, 294
    toilet training and, 333, 335, 336, 344–346
Contingent reinforcement, intrinsic motivation
    and, 27
Cortical satiation, molar variability and, 81,
    86, 87
Counterconditioning, sexual deviance and,
    306, 313
Cues
    reading and, 171
    toilet training and, 335, 339, 341
Cultural-familial retardation, intrinsic motiva-
    tion and, 3
Cumulative rehearsal, rehearsal deficit hypoth-
    esis and, 52, 65
Curiosity
    computer-assisted instruction and, 108
    molar variability and, 74–78

                            D

Delay, reading and
    stimulus fading and, 172
    toilet training and, 327
    trial-and-error methods, 173
Delayed cue, errorless discrimination training
    and, 136, 137, 145–147, 156, 159
    error criteria, 153, 154
    stimulus manipulations, 152, 157
Demographics
    families, mentally retarded children and,
        208, 209
    social competence, employment and, 248
Dependency, home environments and, 282
Deprivation, *see also* Social deprivation
    intrinsic motivation and, 8
    molar variability and, 74–76
Deviance, families, mentally retarded children
    and, 210

    family organization, 219
    labeling process, 211
Deviance, sexual, *see* Sexual deviance
Dictionary skills, reading and, 169
Differential reinforcement of other behavior,
    sexual deviance and, 293, 294, 306,
    308
    exhibitionism, 296
    public masturbation, 301–303
Differentiation, molar variability and, 82, 84
Discovery learning, computer-assisted instruc-
    tion and, 108, 109, 112
Discrimination
    computer-assisted instruction and, 123, 124,
        127
    molar variability and, 84, 91, 96
    reading and, 167
        stimulus fading, 171, 172
        word recognition, 168
    sexual deviance, behavioral treatment of,
        310
    toilet training and, 338
Discrimination reversal, 142
Discrimination training, errorless, *see* Errorless
    discrimination training
Discriminative stimuli, toilet training and, 320,
    334, 335, 337–341, 344
Disinhibition, molar variability and, 74, 88,
    90–93, 98
    orienting reflex, 93–97
Distar Reading Program, 177, 178
Distractibility, computer-assisted training and,
    115
Distraction, molar variability and, 74, 84, 88,
    90, 93, 96–98
Down's syndrome
    molar variability and, 85
    reading and, 174, 181
    sexual deviance, treatment of, 301
Drive reduction, molar variability and, 74, 75
    curiosity, 75
    optimal stimulation, 77
Duration-lengthening process, rehearsal deficit
    hypothesis and, 49

                            E

Ecology, home environments and, 261, 279,
    286

Effectance motivation, 217, 235, 237, 239
Elaborative rehearsal, 49
Electric shock, sexual deviance and, 293, 308
Elicited verbalization, rehearsal deficit hypothesis and, 53, 54
Elimination phase, families, mentally retarded children and, 220
Emotional behavior, social competence, employment and, 231, 232
Employment, social competence and, 225–229, 249–253
  job termination, 229–235
  observational research, 241
    social behavior at work, 241–47
    social interactions, context of, 247, 248
  studies, 235–241
Ergonomics, computer-assisted instruction and, 117–119
Errorless discrimination training, 135–137, 147, 158–160
  delayed cue, 145–147
  error criteria, 153–155
  reading and
    stimulus fading, 171
    trial-and-error methods, 173
  steps, number of, 156, 157
  stimulus fading, 138–141
  stimulus manipulations, 147–153, 157, 158
  stimulus shaping, 141–143
  superimposition
    fading and, 142–145
    shaping and, 145
  task, nature of, 155, 156
Exhibitionism, behavioral treatment of, 291–293, 296, 297, 309–311, 313
Extinction
  errorless discrimination training and, 136
  molar variability and, 84, 85, 91–93
  sexual deviance and, 306, 308
    exhibitionism, 293, 296
    public masturbation, 303
  toilet training and, 327
Extrinsic motivation, 8, 37–40
  computer-assisted instruction and, 112
  effectance motivation and, 7
  individual difference measurement, 11, 13, 17
  interactive relationships, 25, 26
  research, 9, 10, 26, 27, 29

self-regulation, 31–34
trait, correlates of, 17–24

F

Facial screening, sexual deviance and, 303, 306, 307
Fading, *see also* Stimulus fading
  errorless discrimination training and, 136, 137, 139–141
    stimulus manipulation, 148, 158
    superimposition, 142–145, 152, 154, 157, 159
  reading and, 172, 173
  sexual deviance, treatment of 302, 311
  toilet training and, 327, 328, 333, 334, 341
Failure-avoiding, intrinsic motivation and, 5, 6, 15
Families, mentally retarded children and, 201, 202, 220
  clinical model, 202, 203
    parents, effects on, 203–206
    siblings, effects on, 206, 207
    treatment services, 207–210
  family organization model, 213–216
    family types, 216, 217
    successive minimal adaptations, 217–220
  labeling-dramaturgical model, 210, 211
    labeling process, 211
    methodological difficulties, 212, 213
    normalization, 212
Fantasy, computer-assisted instruction and, 108, 126, 128
Faradic aversion therapy, sexual deviance and, 298
Faradic shock, sexual deviance and, 292, 293, 306
Fatigue
  molar variability and, 80
  sexual deviance, treatment of, 297
Feeblemindedness, intrinsic motivation and, 2, 3
Feedback
  computer-assisted instruction and, 108, 127, 128
    tutoring, 113, 114
  intrinsic motivation and, 24,37
  molar variability and, 81

sexual deviance, treatment of
maintenance, 312
promiscuity, 304
public masturbation, 301, 303
social competence, employment and, 234
toilet training and, 346
Fetishism, behavioral treatment of, 291, 293,
296–298, 306, 313
Feuerstein's Learning Potential Assessment
Device, 21
Fisher Exact Probabilities Test, computer-assisted instruction and, 122
Foster care
home environments and
classification, 264, 265, 267, 285
grouping, 283
set delineation, 275
toilet training and, 323
Free recall
intrinsic motivation and, 20, 21
rehearsal deficit hypothesis and, 63
Frustration, molar variability and, 85
Frustration-aggression hypothesis, intrinsic
motivation and, 2, 4, 5
Frustration tolerance, molar variability and, 85

G

Galvanic skin response, molar variability and,
85, 94
Generalization
molar variability and, 93, 97
reading and, 192
comprehension, 181
phonics, 177, 178
word recognition, 168, 174, 175
rehearsal deficit hypothesis and, 51, 67
sexual deviance, treatment of, 291, 293,
294, 306, 309
toilet training and, 329, 345

H

Habilitation
home environments and, 270, 271, 281,
282, 284
sexual deviance and, 315
toilet training and, 323
Habituation, molar variability and, 94–96, 98

Heterogeneity, home environments and, 278
Hierarchy, home environments and, 273
Home environment, taxonomy of, 259, 275,
286, 287
classification
reasons, 262–269
schemes, 269–272, 283–286
definitions, 260–262
grouping, 279–283
principles, 273, 274
set delineation, 274–279
Homeless, home environments and, 275, 277

I

Imagery, rehearsal deficit hypothesis and, 47
Impression management, families, mentally retarded children and, 210
Impulsivity, computer-assisted instruction and,
127
Incentive
intrinsic motivation and, 36
research, 12, 18, 25, 27, 29
self-regulation, 30, 35
social learning theory, 7
molar variability and, 76, 77
Incontinence, toilet training and, 319, 322
nontraining factors, 330
systematic training programs, 322
Independence
home environments and, 284
toilet training and, 334, 345
Individual Education Plans, computer-assisted
instruction and, 120
Individual pacing, computer-assisted instruction and, 117
Individual System of Instruction, computer-assisted instruction and, 110
Individualization, computer-assisted instruction
and, 106, 109–112, 125, 126
programming, 116–118
tutoring, 112, 113
Individualized attention, toilet training and
institutionalization, 331, 332
systematic training programs, 323, 324
Inhibition, *see also* Reactive inhibition; Stimulus inhibition
molar variability and, 74, 84, 85, 88, 91–
93, 95, 98
boredom, 76

curiosity, 75
distraction, 96
toilet training and, 326, 329, 346
Initial Teaching Alphabet, reading and, 178,
    179
Insecurity, molar variability and, 83
Institutionalization
    families, mentally retarded children and
        clinical model 202, 203, 205, 207–209
        labeling-dramaturgical model, 213
    home environments and, 265, 276
    intrinsic motivation and, 35, 36
        research, 11
        rigidity hypothesis, 3
        traits, correlates of, 18
    molar variability and, 83, 86–89, 95, 97
    sexual deviance, treatment of, 307, 310, 315
        exhibitionism, 292
        maintenance, 311, 312
        pedophilia, 299
        promiscuity, 305
        trichophobia, 295, 305
    toilet training and, 319, 325, 328, 335, 347
        nontraining factors, 330–332
        systematic training programs, 322–324
Instrumental Enrichment, intrinsic motivation
    and, 27, 28
Interactive relationships, intrinsic motivation
    and, 24–26
Intermediate Care Facilities for the Mentally
    Retarded, 266
Intrinsic motivation
    behavior effectiveness and, 1, 2, 8, 35–40
        development of, 13–17
        frustration-aggression hypothesis, 4, 5
        interactive relationships, 24–26
        mental age deficit, 29, 30
        research, 8–13, 26–28
        rigidity hypothesis, 2–4
        self-concept, 4
        self-regulation, 30–35
        social learning theory, 5–7
        trait, correlates of, 17–24
    computer-assisted instruction and, 107–109
IQ
    computer-assisted instruction and, 120
    families, mentally retarded children and,
        204
    intrinsic motivation and, 10, 15, 16, 19, 22–
        24, 39, 40

molar variability and, 87–90, 95
reading and, 166, 167
    phonics, 177
    remediation, 191
    sexual deviance, treatment of, 295, 301, 304
    social competence, employment and, 230,
        248
    toilet training and, 323, 325, 328

J

Job responsibility, vocational competence and,
    226, 231

L

Labeling, rehearsal deficit hypothesis and, 55,
    59, 60, 65
Labeling-dramaturgical model, families, re-
    tarded children and, 202, 210, 211, 220
    labeling process, 211
    methodological difficulties, 212, 213
    normalization, 212
Labeling theory, families, mentally retarded
    children and, 201
    clinical model, 203, 204, 208
    family organization model, 219
Learning theory, molar variability and, 83, 84
Likert-type scale
    intrinsic motivation and, 12
    social competence, employment and, 237,
        239
Lipreading, intrinsic motivation and, 53, 54
Locus of control, intrinsic motivation and, 5,
    6
Long-term memory, rehearsal deficit hypoth-
    esis and, 49

M

Mainstreaming
    families and, 205
    reading and, 190
Maintenance
    reading and, 174, 175, 192
    sexual deviance and, 291, 294, 295, 306
        311, 312, 314
        pedophilia, 300
        public masturbation, 301–303
    toilet training and, 326, 327, 341, 345, 346

Maintenance rehearsal, rehearsal deficit hypothesis and, 49, 51, 64
Manifest Anxiety Scale, intrinsic motivation and, 8
Manifest content analysis, intrinsic motivation and, 12
Masturbation, public, sexual deviance and, 291, 294, 295, 308, 309, 312, 313
  exhibitionism, 292
  maintenance, 312
Meaningfulness, molar variability and
  distraction, 97
  optimal stimulation, 77
Memorization, reading and, 183
Memory
  computer-assisted instruction and, 25, 27
  rehearsal deficit hypothesis and, 47, 48, 67
    historical background, 48, 50, 51
    primacy effects, 60
    retention intervals, 63
Mental age
  computer-assisted instruction and, 125
  intrinsic motivation and, 35, 39
    deficit, 29, 30, 37
    development of, 13, 15
    interactive relationships, 24
    research, 10, 13
    rigidity hypothesis, 3
    self-regulation, 34
    social learning theory, 6
  molar variability and, 84–86, 97
    cortical satiation, 86, 87
    orienting reflex, 95
  reading and, 165, 182, 190
Metropolitan Achievement Tests, intrinsic motivation and, 22, 23
Minnesota Adaptive Instructional System, computer-assisted instruction and, 111
Minnesota Multiphasic Personality Inventory, families, mentally retarded children and, 204
Miscue analysis, reading remediation and, 184
Mnemonic strategies, rehearsal deficit hypothesis and, 47
Mobilization phase, families, mentally retarded children and, 219
Modeling
  intrinsic motivation and, 29, 30
  sexual deviance, treatment of, 312

Modified alphabet approaches, reading and, 178, 179
Molar variability, 73–75
  action decrement, 81
  boredom, 76, 77
  cortical satiation, 81, 86, 87
  curiosity, 75, 76
  disinhibition, 90–97
  inhibition-related theories, 84, 85
  learning theory, 83, 84
  optimal stimulation, 77–79
  personality theory, 77–79
  reactive inhibition, 80, 81, 87–90
  response variability, 79, 80
  stimulus inhibition, 86
Motivation, *see also* Extrinsic motivation; Intrinsic motivation
  computer-assisted instruction and, 106–108, 112, 116, 128
  home environments and, 281
  molar variability and, 74
    action decrement, 81
    optimal stimulation, 77, 78
    personality theory, 82, 83
    reactive inhibition, 89
  reading and, 184
  social competence, employment and, 232–234

N

Normalization, families, mentally retarded children and
  family organization model, 219
Novelty
  computer-assisted instruction and, 107
  molar variability and, 77–79

O

Operant conditioning
  sexual deviance and, 306, 307, 313
  toilet training and, 322
Optimal stimulation, molar variability and, 77–79
Orienting reflex, molar variability and, 74, 93–97
Overcorrection
  reading and, 185, 186
  sexual deviance and, 294, 306

maintenance, 311
public masturbation, 301–303
toilet training and, 328, 337
Overgeneralization, families, mentally retarded
children and, 212, 213

P

Paired associates
computer-assisted instruction and, 124
reading and, 168, 171
rehearsal deficit hypothesis and, 59
Partial reinforcement extinction, intrinsic
motivation and, 5
Pedophilia, sexual deviance and, 291, 293,
294, 298–300, 307, 309, 313
Perceived Competence Scale for Children,
38
Perseveration, molar variability and, 82, 84
Personal System of Instruction, computer-assisted instruction and, 110
Phonics, reading and, 177, 178
remediation, 188, 191
word recognition, 168, 169, 175, 180
Phonological pairing, reading and, 176
Picture cues, reading and, 169, 170, 175
Picture Motivation Scale, intrinsic motivation
and, 13, 14, 25, 28, 31, 33
Polarization phase, families, mentally retarded
children and, 220
Popularity, intrinsic motivation and, 38
Position probe task, rehearsal deficit hypothesis and, 58, 59, 61
Position response bias, intrinsic motivation
and, 13
Presentation rate, rehearsal deficit hypothesis
and, 61, 62, 64
Primacy, rehearsal deficit hypothesis and, 54,
56–62, 64
Production deficiency, rehearsal deficit hypothesis and, 51, 64
Promiscuity, sexual deviance and, 291, 295,
303–305, 308
Prompting
errorless discrimination training and, 159
stimulus fading, 140
stimulus manipulation, 148
superimposition, 144
reading and, 171
toilet training and, 333, 334, 337, 341

Psycholinguistic models, reading and, 186
Psychotherapy, sexual deviance and, 291, 297
Punishment
sexual deviance and, 302, 303, 307, 309,
313
toilet training and, 326, 327, 333–335, 337,
343

R

Race, intrinsic motivation and, 15, 29
Raven's Progressive Matrices, intrinsic motivation and, 21
Reactive inhibition, molar variability and, 80,
81, 87–90
Reading acquisition, 165–167, 189–192
comprehension, 170, 180–184
word recognition, 167–171, 180
behavioral approaches, 173–175
modified alphabet approaches, 178, 179
phonics, 177, 178
phonological pairing, 176
programmed instruction, 179, 180
stimulus fading, 171, 172
symbol accentuation, 175
tactile-kinesthetic procedures, 176
trial-and-error methods, 172, 173
Reading comprehension, computer-assisted instruction and, 124
Reading remediation, 184, 185, 191
antecedent control procedures, 186, 187
errors, attention to, 187
overcorrection, 185, 186
repeated reading, 185
word supply, 187, 188
Recall, see also Free recall
intrinsic motivation and, 21
molar variability and, 96
reading and, 183
rehearsal deficit hypothesis and, 47, 52, 64,
66
presentation rate, 61, 62
primacy effects, 57, 58, 60
repetition, 55
retention intervals, 62, 63
self-pacing, 55–57
Recency effect, rehearsal deficit hypothesis
and, 59, 61, 62
Reciprocal inhibition, sexual deviance and,
304

Rehearsal, computer-assisted instruction and, 128

Rehearsal deficit hypothesis, 47, 48
  historical background, 48–53
  presentation rate, 61, 62
  primacy effects, 57–61
  repetition, 53–55
  retention intervals, 62–64
  self-pacing, 55–57

Reinforcement
  computer-assisted instruction and, 116, 127
  errorless discrimination training and, 146
  intrinsic motivation and, 16, 24, 25, 30–32, 35–37
  molar variability and, 74, 75
    action decrement, 81
    boredom, 76
    curiosity, 75
    disinhibition, 91
    inhibition, 85
    learning theory, 84
    optimal stimulation, 77, 78
    personality theory, 83
    reactive inhibition, 80
  reading and
    behavioral approaches, 173, 175
    comprehension, 183
    overcorrection, 186
    stimulus fading, 172
  sexual deviance, treatment of, 293
    exhibitionism, 296
    fetishism, 297, 298
    maintenance, 311, 312
    public masturbation, 301, 303
    toilet training and, 324–326, 328, 329, 345, 346
    nontraining factors, 332
    program components, 333, 341, 343, 344
    systematic training program, 324
  tutoring and, 113

Relaxation training, sexual deviance and, 293, 295, 306
  fetishism, 297, 298
  pedophilia, 298
  promiscuity, 304
  trichophobia, 305

Remedial branching, computer-assisted instruction and, 117

Remediation, families, mentally retarded children and, 202, 210

Repetition, rehearsal deficit hypothesis and, 52–55, 57, 58, 63–65

Response chain, sexual deviance and, 307

Response latency, sexual deviance and, 307
  fetishism, 298
  pedophilia, 298, 299

Response preference, molar variability and, 84

Retention, computer-assisted training and, 109, 120–122

Retention intervals, rehearsal deficit hypothesis and, 62–64

Revisionist phase, families, mentally retarded children and, 219, 220

Rigidity
  intrinsic motivation and, 24
  molar variability and, 73, 74, 80, 97
  personality theory, 82, 83

Rosenzweig Picture Frustration Study, intrinsic motivation and, 5

Rubin Vase-Profile Reversible Figure, molar variability and, 87

S

Scale of Intrinsic Versus Extrinsic Orientation in the Classroom, 37, 38

Schizophrenics, intrinsic motivation and, 9

Selective remembering, rehearsal deficit hypothesis and, 57, 66

Self-concept theory, intrinsic motivation and, 2, 4

Self-cueing, errorless discrimination training and, 149, 152, 180

Self-monitoring
  intrinsic motivation and, 25
  sexual deviance and, 312

Self-pacing, rehearsal deficit hypothesis and, 52, 53, 55–57, 59

Self-regulation, intrinsic motivation and, 11, 25, 27, 29, 30

Self-report
  intrinsic motivation and, 27, 37, 38
  sexual deviance and, 293, 314

Sensory deprivation, home environments and, 276

Sequential memory taks, rehearsal deficit hypothesis and, 56, 57, 59, 65, 67

Service-path analysis, families, mentally retarded children and, 209, 210
Sex, intrinsic motivation and, 15, 22, 24, 31,40
Sexual deviance, behavioral treatment of, 291,
293–295, 313–315
evaluation, 305, 306
dependent measures, 307, 308
experimental design, 308–310
generalization, 312, 313
independent variables, 306, 307
maintenance, 311, 312
subject description, 310, 311
exhibitionism, 292, 296
fetishism, 296–298
pedophilia, 298–300
promiscuity, 303–305
public masturbation, 300–303
trichophobia, 305
Shaping, see also Stimulus shaping
errorless discrimination training and, 136,
137
stimulus manipulation, 159
superimposition, 145,157
toilet training and, 327, 345
nontraining factors, 330
program components, 333–336
systematic training, 324
Sheltered workshops, social-vocational competence and, 229, 232, 235, 237, 249
Shock, sexual deviance, treatment and, 298,
299
Short-term recall, rehearsal deficit hypothesis
and, 49
Short-term storage, rehearsal deficit hypothesis
and, 50, 63
Siblings, families, mentally retarded children
and, 201
clinical model, 202, 203, 206, 207
family organization model, 213, 214, 219,
220
Sign language
reading and, 186
social competence, employment and, 243
Simplified Spelling Society's system, reading
and, 178
Simulation, computer-assisted instruction and,
109, 112
Social Adjustment Training, sexual deviance
and, 295, 304

Social class, intrinsic motivation and, 15, 29,
39
Social competence, employment and, see Employment, social competence and
Social context, social-vocational competence
and, 227, 247
Social deprivation
intrinsic motivation and, 3, 39
molar variability and, 83
Social learning
intrinsic motivation and, 2, 5–7, 15
vocational competence and, 251
Social reinforcement, intrinsic motivation and,
3, 27, 36
Social skills training, sexual deviance and,
304, 311, 312, 314, 315
Social structure, home environments and, 280,
281
Social validity, sexual deviance and, 308
Social-vocational competence, 226–229, 241,
244, 250, 252, 253
Socioeconomic status
families, mentally retarded children and,
203, 206–208
intrinsic motivation and, 14, 15, 24
Spontaneous alteration, molar variability and,
80, 81
S-R Inventory of Anxiousness, intrinsic
motivation and, 17
Stereotypy, molar variability and, 73, 82
Stigma, families, mentally retarded children
and, 203, 210, 214, 219
Stimulus conditions, social competence, employment and, 245
Stimulus control
errorless discrimination training and, 148,
158
toilet training and, 337, 339
Stimulus fading
errorless discrimination training and, 136–
141, 147
delayed cue, 146
manipulation, 157
reading and, 190, 192
word recognition and, 171, 172
Stimulus generalization, molar variability and,
75
optimal stimulation, 79
stimulus satiation, 81

Stimulus inhibition, molar variability and, 86
Stimulus preference, molar variability and, 83
Stimulus satiatian, molar variability and, 86
  boredom, 76
  reactive inhibition, 80, 81
Stimulus shaping, errorless discrimination training and, 136, 141–143, 147, 157
Strategy adoption, rehearsal deficit hypothesis and, 65–67
  self-pacing and, 55
Strategy use, computer-assisted instruction and, 128
Structural analysis, word recognition and, 169
Structural social arrangement, home environment and, 278
Success-striving, intrinsic motivation and, 5, 6, 15
Superimposition, errorless discrimination training and, 136, 137
  fading, 142–145, 147, 152, 154, 159
  shaping, 145, 147
  stimulus fading, 139, 157
  stimulus manipulation, 148
Surprisingness, molar variability and, 78, 79
Symbol accentuation, word recognition and, 175
Systematic desensitization, sexual deviance and, 295, 305
Systematic training program, toilet training and, 322–324

T

Tactile-kinesthetic procedures, reading and, 176
Taffel-type task, intrinsic motivation and, 127
Task-production competence, 226, 231, 232
Taxonomy of home environments, *see* Home environments, taxonomy of
Therapy Group, sexual deviance and, 295, 304
Time out
  sexual deviance and, 303
  toilet training and, 328
Toilet training, 319
  acquisition, 322, 329, 330
  as complex skill, 326–329
  nontraining factors, 330–332
  program components, 333–345

  as single unit, 324–326
  systematic training program, 322–324
  control, 320–322
Trait X Treatment Interactions, computer-assisted instruction and, 127
Transfer
  computer-assisted instruction and, 120–122, 128
  errorless discrimination training and, 148
  phonics and, 178
Trichophobia, behavioral treatment of, 291, 295, 305
Tutoring, computer-assisted instruction and, 105, 110, 112–115
Typological classification schemes, home environments and, 269, 270

U

Unconditioned response, molar variability and, 74
Unconditioned stimulus, molar variability and, 74
UNIFON, reading and, 178

V

Vineland Social Maturity Scale, toilet training and, 324, 330, 331
Visual Figural After-Effect Test, molar variability and, 87
Vocational rehabilitation, social competence and, 226, 227, 238

W

Whole-word approaches, reading and, 171
  behavioral approaches, 173–175
  phonics versus, 178
  phonological pairing, 176
  stimulus fading, 171, 172
  symbol accentuation, 175
  tactile-kinesthetic procedures, 176
  trial-and-error methods, 172, 173
Word recognition, 167–170, 180, 189, 190
  behavioral approaches, 173–175
  computer-assisted instruction and, 123, 124
  modified alphabet approaches, 178, 179
  oral reading errors, 184

phonics, 177, 178
phonological pairing, 176
programmed instruction, 179, 180
repeated reading, 185
stimulus fading, 171, 172

symbol accentuation, 175
tactile-kinesthetic procedure, 176
trial-and-error methods, 172, 173
Working memory, rehearsal deficit hypothesis
    and, 49